WARTIME DORSET
The Complete History

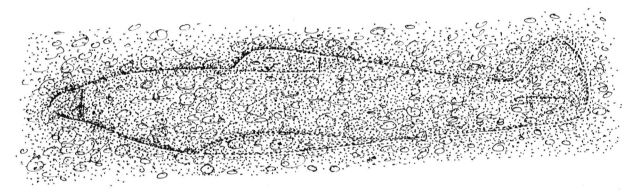

WARMWELL SPITFIRE: CONTEMPORARY DRAWING, IN WET CEMENT BESIDE THE BRIDGE AT SOUTHBROOK, BERE REGIS, BY VILLAGE BOY FRED PITFIELD

RODNEY LEGG

Dorset Publishing Company
National School North Street Wincanton Somerset BA9 9AT

For **Debbie Callaghan**, formerly Lachter,
to prove that this politically incorrect subject is full of humanity

Printing credits
Typesetting and layout by Julie Green. Set in Verona 10 on $12^{1/2}$ point. Printed by F W B Printing at Bennetts Mead, Southgate Road, Wincanton, Somerset BA9 9EB. Telephone 01-963-33755.

Digital imaging of photographs by Richard Gilson at Radstock Reproductions (Yeovil) Limited, Stoke-sub-Hamdon, Somerset TA14 6QR.

Publishing details
Published by Dorset Publishing Company at Wincanton Press, National School, North Street, Wincanton, Somerset BA9 9AT. Telephone 01-963-32583.

Distribution
Trade distribution and library sales by Halsgrove from Lower Moor Way, Tiverton, Devon EX16 6SS. Telephone 01-884-243-242.

Updatings
Information for further editions will be welcomed by the author, Rodney Legg, at Wincanton Press, National School, North Street, Wincanton, Somerset BA9 9AT.

International standard book number
ISBN 0 948699 75 2

Foreword

My aim is to produce a grand narrative of the war as seen from one county. I write as a prose historian who has become the applied specialist in things Dorset and military. The two interests began to coincide at an early stage in what has now been a career of 33 years editing and publishing Dorset's county magazines. For the past two decades I have either been sent or come across in research the material for Dorset's pivotal part in the Second World War that was initially accumulated at the rate of one disclosure a week. They still had an immediacy that could only be encapsulated by the vibrancy of diary entries. It was a sustained flow for many years but the supply was seriously disrupted, being almost totally disconnected, at the approach of the millennium. Then anno domini accelerated its toll and wartime obituaries appeared daily in the broadsheets.

What was no longer coming through in quantity tended to be compensated for by the quality of latter-day revelations. For the first time, in this fifth expansion of the material, there is an index entry for "Friendly fire". As we now realise, it accompanies all wars but will always be understated at the time, in cover-ups to mitigate embarrassment and grief. So were debacles such as the Slapton Sands disaster – which actually took place in Lyme Bay and was seen from Portland – and the loss of the troopship *Leopoldville* at Christmas 1944, taking with her more than 800 American GIs from Piddlehinton Camp.

Likewise, for obvious reasons, the secret war. In a way everything to do with the war was deception wrapped in misinformation, with contemporary accounts being deliberately distorted or misplaced. Or just plain censored. What we are now aware of is a level of decisive intrigue that almost all of those involved would take to the grave. Fortunately, a few who were both exceptions and exceptional did talk towards the end of their day, and reams of intercepted and decoded German radio traffic has since found its way into the public domain.

More will emerge but publication of this comprehensive re-telling of Dorset's war story could not be delayed indefinitely. It seemed sensible to draw a line under the accumulated material at the end of the century. A total of more than a thousand submissions of detailed information were reviewed and have been condensed into 850 separate entries. Many of these are new or expanded, with correction or corroboration from other informants, but as before I shall remain open to business for additional material and remain in hope of another return to the subject.

As for my interest in conflict studies, I was a post-war baby-boom "mistake", born in 1947 to a 45-year-old wartime A.R.P. warden and his 43-year-old wife. Theirs was the generation of two world wars. Two uncles had done their bit in the trenches of the Great War; Frank Watts being gassed at Ypres and Bill Bennett at least being on the safe side of a bayonet in the mud at Passchendaele. He demonstrated with a souvenir Lee-Enfield rifle to show me the knack of removing steel from ribs. Theirs was the horror and squalor of trench warfare. They also told of Christmas truces in No Man's Land. I would be the first eager recipient of the bottled stories that were never told to the aunts.

On the other hand, "Dirty Uncle Arthur" – as he was known for his colourful language – had a wonderful war off-roading on two wheels through the second half of the re-play, from 1942 to 1945, across the Western Desert and then up through Italy. Arthur Legg was a motor-cycle despatch rider, ferrying messages between the generals and the front-line, which meant that the rest of his life would be an anti-climax. Neighbours in Easter Road and around the Bournemouth suburb of Moordown had not shared anything like that degree of fun. Infantrymen from the Dorsetshire Regiment returned from a much less enjoyable world tour for their first home leave in six years. The closer they had come to meeting the Japanese the emptier their faces tended to be.

Signs and relics of war were all around us. I played in a gas-mask and crawled into the air-raid shelter below our garden shed. It and the chicken-run were constructed with timbers removed from the centre section of Bournemouth Pier which was blown-up by the Royal Engineers in 1940. We used a stirrup pump to water the lettuces. Windows with oiled glass were forensic proof of bomb-blasts towards Charminster. Ration coupons were still in use.

Going into town on the bus was a tour of bomb-sites. Alma Road Schools, on both sides of the road, were gaping gashes of exposed brickwork and cellars. We looked down into a similar hole in the ground at what was Beales. The Lansdowne had its grim incision at the former Metropole Hotel where Dominion airmen were among the hundred-plus dead in Bournemouth's infamous Sunday lunchtime blitz on 23 May 1943. The Square had its holes at Woolworths from 1941 and across to the Central Hotel and the Punshon Memorial Church from the 1943 attack, and scenes of devastation extended along Exeter Road to within sight of the beach. Inevitably such events also left damaged minds.

Miss Thomas, my teacher in the junior school beside East Way, was distressed that I chose the Second World War as my subject for a Boy's Own style thesis. She was doubly upset as the secondary offence was to write it with my left hand. The nib would scratch into the paper and blot. The problem was compounded as the wrist dragged across the page and wet words smudged. The pen would be pulled from my left fingers and rammed into those of a listless right hand which remains resolutely non-literary to this day. An additional trauma was that my brain and feet were incapable of co-ordination for country dancing. Such were the rigours of education in the mid-Fifties. History, as she was taught, was also kept in her place which started with Tudor females and ended with the Industrial Revolution. We were not allowed within a century of Edward and Mrs Simpson.

I always learnt more from those around me and the Daily Express, which a reluctant family was coerced into replacing by the Daily Telegraph, before I gained independence with The Guardian and then The Times. Children used to be able to talk to adult males before the modern age of feminism and paranoia. Not that every question received an answer.

What I was never told by the wartime worker who returned each summer to holiday with Aunt Effie and Uncle Frank, with whom he had been billeted through the second half of the war, was just what he had been doing in the Max Factor factory at West Howe. Before cosmetics they were making the H2S ground-mapping radar sets that would enable the Lancasters of Bomber Command to flatten German cities. The ethics of that campaign were hardly an issue for those involved.

The Bournemouth-Poole conurbation had been on the front-line for the Battle of Britain and suffered a thousand dead, at home and abroad, during the conflict. Civilian losses would have been doubled or worse but for the Major Strategic Night Decoy on Brownsea Island which attracted a thousand tons of German bombs that would otherwise have fallen across our cosy suburbia between Hamworthy flying-boat base and the Airspeed works at Christchurch Aerodrome.

May the people's war endure into this millennium as the last momentous event of our national history.

Format

A glossary follows, to familiarise readers with wartime words and abbreviations, after which the story unfolds chronologically, as a sequence of diary entries. General entries for the month, where applicable, appear at the end of the month concerned. The index at the back is to dates rather than page numbers. It applies to the main text but does not include the captions to photographs. Where possible these are also in chronological order.

Glossary

(including abbreviations, though these have been avoided wherever possible)

A.A. = Anti-Aircraft [British].

A.A.A. = Anti-Aircraft Artillery [American].

A.A.F. = Auxiliary Air Force.

Ack-Ack = Anti-Aircraft.

A.D.G.B. = Air Defence of Great Britain.

A.D.R.E. = Air Defence Research and Development Establishment, at Somerford, Christchurch.

A.E.F. = Allied Expeditionary Force.

A.F.P.U. = Army Film and Photographic Unit.

A.F.S. = Auxiliary Fire Service.

A.I. = Air Interception [Radar].

A.L.G. = Advance Landing Ground.

A.M.G. = Allied Military Government.

A.P.M. = Auxiliary Paddle Minesweeper.

A.R.P. = Air Raid Precautions [later known as Civil Defence].

A.S.D.I.C. = Anti-Submarine Detection and Investigation Committee.

A.T.S. = Auxiliary Territorial Service.

Aufklärungsgruppe = Luftwaffe reconnaissance unit [A.G.].

B.B.C. = British Broadcasting Corporation.

Blitzkrieg = Lightning War [first used by the Germans when they invaded Poland, but later used as "Blitz" for any significant bombing raids].

B.O.A.C. = British Overseas Airways Corporation, operating flying-boats from Poole Harbour and later "land" airliners from Hurn Aerodrome.

Bordfunker = German radio operator.

Comops = Combined Operations.

CP = Command Post.

DD = Duplex-Drive [in amphibious Allied vehicles].

DUKW = DUCK = Amphibious landing craft.

E-boat = Eil-Boot = Fast boat. The generic term for German high-speed coastal craft. The plural is Eil-Boote.

Enigma = German electric typewriter with three encoding wheels for mechanical cryptographic conversion, deciphered by a second keyboard.

E.N.S.A. = Entertainments National Service Association.

Erprobungsgruppe = Luftwaffe experimental unit, making proving flights in combat.

Flak = German anti-aircraft artillery [Fliegerabwehrkanonen].

Fliegerkorps = sub-division of a German Luftflotte, though it could also act independently of the area command concerned.

Flight = non-combative R.A.F. unit of specialist aircraft.

Freya = the earliest German early-warning radar, on the 2.5 metres wavelength.

Geschwader = German formation of 90 aircraft, with 30 in each of three Gruppen, plus a Staff Flight with four aircraft. Exceptionally 120 aircraft with 30 in each of four Gruppen with IV Gruppe being a training unit.

G.C. = George Cross, being the military award instigated by King George VI in 1940, for Home Front heroism.

GI = General Infantryman, of the United States Army.

G.M. = George Medal, being the "civilian V.C." [later translated into the George Cross].

Group = R.A.F. command sub-division, controlling sectors and aerodromes.

Gruppe = 27 German aircraft in three Staffeln, plus a Staff Flight with three aircraft.

H2S = ground-mapping airborne radar of Bomber Command, developed at Langton Matravers and manufactured in Bournemouth.

H.D.P. = Hochdruckpumpe [High Pressure Pump] = V3.

H.G. = Home Guard [Horse Guards being the earlier military abbreviation].

H.M.A.S. = His Majesty's Australian Ship, seconded to Admiralty control.

H.M.C.S. = His Majesty's Canadian Ship, seconded to Admiralty control.

H.M.N.Z.S = His Majesty's New Zealand Ship, seconded to Admiralty control.

H.M.S. = His Majesty's Ship or Submarine, belonging to the Royal Navy.

H.M.T. = His Majesty's Trawler, being an armed support vessel of the Royal Navy.

Ibsen = Incendiary Bomb Separating Explosive Nose.

Jagdgeschwader = Luftwaffe fighter formation [J.G.].

Kampfgeschwader = Luftwaffe aerial bombing formation [K.G.].

LCA = Landing Craft Assault.

LCH = Landing Craft Headquarters.

LCR = Landing Craft Rockets.

LCT = Landing Craft Tanks.

LCVP = Landing Craft Vehicles and Personnel.

L.D.V. = Local Defence Volunteers [renamed the Home Guard by Prime Minister Churchill].

LSI = Landing Ship Infantry.

LST = Landing Ship Tanks.

Luftflotte = German divisional flying area, covering all Luftwaffe units in its geographical zone. Luftflotten is the plural.

Luftwaffe = the German "offensive air arm", breaching the Treaty of Versailles, the existence of which confirmed by Hermann Göring on 8 March 1935.

M = Minensuchboot = German minesweeper. The plural is Minensuchboote.

M.T.B. = Motor Torpedo Boat.

M.V. = Motor Vessel.

N.A.A.F.I. = Naval, Army, and Air Force Institutes.

Nachtjagdgeschwader = Luftwaffe night-fighter formation [N.J.G.].

N.F.S. = National Fire Service.

Pluto = Pipe Line Under The Ocean.

PoW = Prisoner of War.

R = Raumboot = German armed minesweeper. Raumboote is the plural.

R.A.= Royal Artillery.

Radar = Radio Direction and Ranging [also see R.D.F.].

R.A.F. = Royal Air Force.

R.A.F.V.R. = Royal Air Force Volunteer Reserve.

R.C.A.F. = Royal Canadian Air Force, operating in Europe under R.A.F. command.

R.D.F. = Radio Direction Finding [this English term was soon supplanted by the American mnemonic, Radar].

R.E. = Royal Engineers.

R.E.M.E. = Royal Electrical and Mechanical Engineers.

R.M. = Royal Marines.

R.M.A. = Royal Military Academy, at Sandhurst.

R.N. = Royal Navy.

R.N.R. = Royal Naval Reserve.

R.N.V.R. = Royal Naval Volunteer Reserve.

R/T = Radio Telephony.

S.A.S. = Special Air Service Regiment.

Schlactgeschwader = Luftwaffe ground-attack aerial formation.

S = Schnellboot = German motor torpedo boat. Schnellboote is the plural.

S.G.B. = Special Gun-Boat.

S.H.A.E.F. = Supreme Headquaters, Allied Expeditionary Force.

S.O.E. = Special Operations Executive.

Squadron - standard R.A.F. and U.S.A.A.F. combat formation, comprising about 12 operational aircraft.

S.S. = Steamship or Schutzstaffel [for the German miltary organisation orginally founded as Hitler's protection squad in 1925].

Staffel = nine aircraft in the German equivalent of a squadron. Staffeln is the plural.

Stukageschwader = Luftwaffe dive-bombing formation [S.G.], equipped with Junkers Ju.87s.

T = Torpedoshulboot = German submarine tender, adapted for a combat role. Torpedoshulboote is the plural.

T.A. = Territorial Army.

T.A.F. = Tactical Air Force.

T.R.E. = Telecommunications Research Establishment, at Worth Matravers and Langton Matravers.

Trots = water runways for flying-boats, in Poole Harbour.

U-boat = U-boot = Unterséeboot = Undersea boat. Unterséeboote is the plural.

U.S. = United States.

U.S.A.A.F. = United States Army Air Force.

U.S.S. = United States Ship.

V1 = German Vergeltungswaffen [Reprisal Weapon] 1, being the "Doodlebug" flying-bomb.

V2 = German Vergeltungswaffen [Reprisal Weapon] 2, being the long-range ballistic missile.

V3 = see H.D.P.

V.C. = Victoria Cross, being the nation's highest military honour for valour in the face of the enemy.

W.D. = War Department.

Wehrmacht = German Armed Forces.

Window = aluminium foil strips, dropped in packets to simulate the radar echoes of aircraft.

Wing = R.A.F. and U.S.A.A.F. formation comprising three combat squadrons.

Würzburg = German paraboliod gun-laying radar, on a wavelength of 53 centimetres.

W.V.S. = Women's Voluntary Service.

X-Gerät = German receiver for the Wotan I system of radio beams for blind-bombing navigation.

Y-Gerät = German receiver for the Wotan II system of radio beams for bomber navigation and targeting.

Zerstörergeschwader = German heavy fighter or fighter-bomber formation [Z.G.].

1939

During January
Hawks and doves.

The politicians have split into the hawks and the doves. Viscount Cranborne, South Dorset's MP, cautions Wyke Regis Women's Institute about the threat posed by Hitler and Mussolini: "These dictators have tasted blood and have applied a policy of force and had considerable effect with it. We must make England an impregnable fortress."

Clement Attlee, the leader of the Labour opposition, was a little less specific when he addressed farm workers in the Corn Exchange, Dorchester: "People may ask what I would have done at Munich. Suppose you had a man who was driving a heavy lorry. He drove it mile after mile on the wrong side of the road, and after narrowly missing other vehicles, came to a position where a collision seemed inevitable, swerved and ran over a child. You might ask me what I would have done had I been driving. I would not have driven on the wrong side of the road. The trouble is that the Government has been driving on the wrong side. I would remind you that the right side for an Englishman to drive is on the left,"

It is not, however, a time when Europe is keeping to the left.

Saturday 18 February
Khaki, not hosepipes, for Bournemouth's young men.

Speaking tonight at a Territorial Army dinner in the Christchurch Drill Hall, Lieutenant-Colonel Arthur Malim, second in command of the 5th and 7th Battalions, the Hampshire Regiment, was unequivocal that "the duty of every young man who is patriotic is to be in the Territorial Army".

He was particularly scathing at a suggestion that the Auxiliary Fire Brigade had no shortage of recruits because of the attractions of the blue and scarlet uniform:

"We can supply the uniform, not blue with scarlet facings, but His Majesty's khaki. That is where the young men of Bournemouth ought to be — not running around with hosepipes.

"It will be a bad day for Bournemouth and other towns if they cannot get men to take an active part in a battalion of His Majesty's Army, as part of the field force that will defend the lives and liberties of the people when the time comes. Fit young men of the right age ought to be in the Territorial Army — not in those civilian organisations which are all very well for old men who are not fit."

Fire tenders: trailer pumps gathered at the Central Fire Station, Holdenhurst Road, Bournemouth, in 1939

ON MANOEUVRES: 76TH HEAVY REGIMENT OF THE ROYAL ARTILLERY AT BERE REGIS IN 1939

SOUGHT PEACE: PRIME MINISTER NEVILLE CHAMBERLAIN

Saturday 18 March

Dorchester Evacuation Committee prepares for 4,612.

A survey of parishes in the Dorchester Rural District, in which Abbotsbury and Maiden Newton are the only significant places that have failed to respond, show that a total of 4,612 evacuees could be accommodated in the area. Dorchester Evacuation Committee has reservations, however, and will tell the Ministry of Health that water supplies and sanitary facilities are inadequate.

Friday 2 June

Reception Areas prepare for evacuees.

Billeting Officers met with local government officials for a conference at Dorchester today to discuss how the Reception Areas would handle their expected influx of children evacuated from London. The local reception centre is Maud Road School in Dorchester, which will provide light refreshments and disperse the youngsters with a bag of food each that is sufficient for 48 hours. Quite where to house them aroused deeper discussion.

It was agreed to send 1,600 children into the borough of Dorchester, 1,900 to the surrounding rural district, and 1,300 into the Beaminster area.

Friday 2 June

Portland destroyers sail to aid of trapped submariners.

The Portland-based 6th Destroyer Flotilla of Tribal-class vessels, led by H.M.S. *Mohawk*, has been ordered to sail immediately for Liverpool Bay where a new submarine has failed to surface during sea trials. They are to render assistance to the 1,095-ton H.M.S. *Thetis* which has 90 men trapped aboard.

GAS MASKS: NEWLY ISSUED TO WEYMOUTH GRAMMAR SCHOOL LADS, WALKING BESIDE THE RADIPOLE LAKE. THE TALLEST IS COLIN DOWELL AND TO HIS RIGHT ARE JOHN LING AND FRANK BONIFACE. THEY WERE BORN IN 1928

DORSET BOUND: EVACUEES WERE ARRIVING OFF EVERY TRAIN

GLASSES RAISED: BY TANK CREWS DINING AT BOVINGTON CAMP IN 1939

Footnote: Nothing could be done to save them. It was to be the worst peacetime submarine tragedy, with the agony also being extended for days for those on the surface ships as well, knowing they had no means of helping their comrades who were trapped on the seabed.

Thetis would later be raised. Restored, refitted, and renamed, she became H.M.S. *Thunderbolt* and joined the British Mediterranean Fleet in the autumn of 1940. She would be reported missing on 21 April 1943.

During June
Anti-Aircraft guns issued at Poole.

The 310th Anti-Aircraft Battery, which has 130 recruits training at the Mount Street Drill Hall in Poole, has been issued with the new 3.7-inch Ack-Ack guns.

During June
Territorial gunners reorganised.

The 375th and 376th Queen's Own Dorset Yeomanry Batteries, with recruits from Shaftesbury, Blandford, and Sherborne, have been amalgamated. The new Territorial Army unit will retain the historic name, as the 141st (Queen's Own Dorset Yeomanry) Field Regiment, Royal Artillery.

Likewise the 218th Field Battery, based in the Drill Hall at the Lansdowne, Bournemouth, has merged with the Dorchester and Bridport 224th (Dorset) Field Battery to form the 94th (Dorset and Hants) Field Regiment, Royal Artillery.

GAS MASKS: EVERYONE IN BRITAIN HAD ONE

During June
1st Dorsets garrison Malta.

The 1st Battalion of the Dorsetshire Regiment have arrived in the Grand Harbour, Valetta, aboard the troopship *Neuralia* from Bombay. They had been serving in India since 1936. These Regular Army soldiers are to man the south-eastern sector of the Mediterranean island's defences.

Malta has been occupied by Britain since 1800, with its naval dry dock having been opened in 1871. In Italy, Sir Percy Loraine was received as British Ambassador in Rome on 27 May, to be lambasted by Mussolini for "the manifest British policy of encirclement" which was blamed for compromising any remaining value in the Anglo-Italian Agreement.

Sunday 9 July
Dorset tests the Black-out.

04.00 hours. The lights have gone out all across Dorset and 14 other southern counties of England. Aeroplanes are overhead to monitor the results. Air Raid Precautions directives state that even a light of one candle-power can be seen from a height of two miles on a clear night.

Urban kerbs, posts, and poles are to be pained white to lessen the need for street lighting. The weather has co-operated with this Sunday morning's experiment.

During July
Huge tented camp sprouts across Blandford's downland.

Race Down, to the east of Blandford, is smothered with more than a hundred marquees and 500 smaller tents, concentrated across the former hutted lines around Cuckoo Clump that were used in the Great War to train

BLACK-OUTS: CURTAINS AS REQUIRED BY LAW, CREATING A NEW BREED OF DOOR TO DOOR SALESMEN

the Royal Naval Division which would land at Gallipoli in the Dardanelles.

It was here, it is said, that Sub-Lieutenant Rupert Brooke wrote those immortal lines: "If I should die, think only this of me: That there's some corner of a foreign field that is for ever England."

The mobilisation this time is for a Militia Camp to provide volunteers with basic physical and weapons training in a gentler introduction to military life.

Tuesday 1 August
5th Dorsets reformed.

The 5th Battalion of the Dorsetshire Regiment, a Territorial unit many of whose volunteers are from Poole,

has been reformed under the command of Colonel Sir John Lees of Post Green, Lytchett Minster. It is part of the 43rd (Wessex) Division. Sir John was wounded twice in the Great War.

Footnote: He would serve as an honorary bodyguard to King George VI.

Thursday 3 August
'War today ... is unlikely' — Defence Minister.

"War today is not only not inevitable but is unlikely. The Government have good reason for saying that." — Sir Thomas Inskip, the Minister for the Co-Ordination of Defence.

Wednesday 9 August
The King at Weymouth — 'It's raining everywhere.'

Thousands of visitors pack Weymouth to see King George VI visit the town for a review of the Reserve Fleet which is being mobilised in Portland Harbour. A total of 120 ships have gathered.

For most in the Royal Navy Volunteer Reserve the last summer of the Thirties has already ended, but on shore the holidaymakers are having their last fling. An estimated 45,000 converged on the station and the situation was worsened by the delay to trains that the royal visit caused. Many fainted in the crush and the St John Ambulance Brigade commandeered the waiting room and parcels office as a field hospital for casualties.

As for the King, he failed to see the ships off Bincleaves because of mist and drizzle. The Mayor expressed regrets about the rain. "Don't worry, Mr Mayor," the King replied, "it's raining everywhere."

FOURTH DORSETS: MEN OF THE 4TH BATTALION, DORSETSHIRE REGIMENT, QUEUE TO ENTER THE UNDERGROUND COOKHOUSE AT CHICKERELL CAMP IN 1939. SOME ARE WEARING THE FORAGE CAPS WHICH WERE IN THE PROCESS OF REPLACING STIFF ARMY HATS. BERETS WOULD THEN SUCCEED THE FORAGE CAPS. THE MEN WERE AT CHICKERELL FOR BREN-GUN TRAINING

interception towards one hundred per cent which is our goal. I am satisfied with our progress, and I confidently believe that a serious attack on these islands would be brought to a standstill within a short space of time."

Footnote: Prophetic words. "Our technical equipment" now included secrets of the German "Enigma" military cipher machines, courtesy Polish cryptanalysts in July.

Friday 11 August
Bournemouth Auxiliary Fire Service in action.

04.00 hours. The second major test of the effectiveness of the Black-out has been postponed for 24 hours due to continuous rain. Bournemouth's eleven zones of the Auxiliary Fire Service, each with its own local emergency station, are going ahead as planned with their own mass turn-out.

Fifty-four mock incidents have been devised. Five hundred firemen are involved. The exercises are being watched by Home Office Assistant Secretary F. W. Smith and the Inspector of Fire Brigades, Tom Beakes, together with the Mayor of Bournemouth and council officers.

Saturday 12 August
Radar exercises: 'Eastland' intercepted.

Sustained exercises for the past four days, involving 1,300 aircraft of the Royal Air Force split between "Westland" defenders and "Eastland" attackers, have shown that the country's 25 Radio Direction Finding [radar] stations detected almost every attacking formation. This was despite the appalling weather, including rain, wind, and fog, which caused frequent suspension of both attacking and interception flights.

The taller aerials of the radar stations sent out radio waves from 350 feet, which were then reflected back from the intruding aeroplanes and received on the station's lower set of 250-feet aerials. The fractional difference of time between the transmitted and returned signal was measured on a calibrated cathode-ray tube to indicate the altitude and direction of intruding aircraft whilst they were up to 150 miles offshore.

Air Chief Marshal Sir Hugh Dowding, Air Officer Commander-in-Chief at Fighter Command, today broadcast on the B.B.C. wireless to tell the nation that the exercise had been successful, though he stopped just short of directly mentioning the art of Radio Direction Finding:

"It only remains for us to see that our technical equipment keeps ahead of that of our potential enemy. What we have been doing is to work at increasing

Sunday 13 August
Black-out, sirens, and Portland mock battle.

Air-raid sirens have sounded across south Dorset at 00.15 hours this Sunday and a black-out is being enforced. The lights have gone out on the ships of the Reserve Fleet at anchor in Portland Harbour and there is the drone of aerial activity. Destroyers are being deployed as "enemy" vessels to test the defences at the entrance to the harbour.

In the villages the death-bells tolled and bewildered country people staggered out of bed to find what was happening. In Weymouth the news had already got around, or at least among those who had been out on the town, dancing and drinking, or laughing with Elsie and Doris Waters. There was a noticeable absence of sailors about last night.

Wednesday 30 August
Dorchester councillors consider 'War imminent'.

Dorchester Rural District Council has decided that "in view of the imminent outbreak of war, that the whole power of the council so far as allowed by law, be delegated to an Emergency Committee until further orders".

During August
Imperial Airways becomes B.O.A.C. and moves to Poole.

The amalgamated Imperial Airways and British Airlines are to be known from next year as the British Overseas Airways Corporation, which will operate under the chairmanship of Lord Reith, the founder of the B.B.C. Its fleet of Short C-class "Empire" flying-boats is being moved with their support facilities from Hythe, on Southampton Water, to Poole Harbour.

Here Salterns Pier and its club-rooms have been requisitioned from the Poole Harbour Yacht Club and water runways — "Trots" as they are called — are being marked out by lines of tyres in the Wareham Channel off Hamworthy and the Main Channel between Salterns and

UNDER CANVAS: EXERCISE IN THE RAIN AT BERE REGIS FOR A ROYAL ARTILLERY UNIT WITH 25-POUNDER GUN ON TURNTABLE, AND LIMBER BESIDE IT

Brownsea Island. The yacht club is now the Marine Terminal.

Footnote: Airways House was opened in a Poole shop, 4 High Street, and the showrooms at Poole Pottery became the reception area and customs clearance point for incoming passengers. Harbour Heights Hotel was to became the rest centre for those due to embark from nearby Salterns Pier on early morning flights.

During August
Ansons bomb Warmwell 'factory'.

217 Squadron, flying Avro Ansons that carry the identity letters "MW", is now operational for coast patrols at the aerodrome to the east of Dorchester near Warmwell, where the Royal Air Force set up its School of Air Firing in May 1937. Their last public display as the Warmwell Armament Training Squadron was a bombing exercise for a 10,000-strong crowd at the open day.

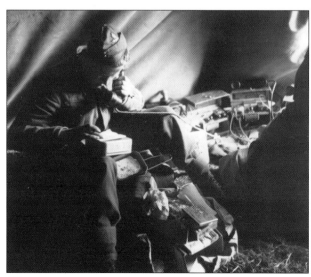

WIRELESS TENT: THIS WOULD BE THE FIRST ELECTRONIC WAR

Five Ansons came in and a bomb was dropped on a make-believe factory, a building on the other side of the grass airfield, as the attacking planes were buzzed by three Hurricanes. One of the Ansons was "disabled" and forced to land. Forty planes took part in the day, including a squadron of Singapore reconnaissance flying-boats from Southampton Water.

During August
Lyme Bay and Crichel Down Bombing Ranges.

There will be more practice bombs heard in Dorset as the Air Ministry has announced that 16 square miles of Lyme Bay, lying six miles off Lyme Regis, will be designated as a bombing range for daylight use. A limit of 120-lb has been placed on live bombs that can be dropped. It is to be known as the Lyme Bay Bombing Range.

An inland bombing range is being established on Crichel down, in the parish of Long Crichel, on the chalky foothills of Cranborne Chase.

Footnote: De-requisition of Crichel Down Bombing Range would turn into what can be called another story! Civil servants attempted selling the land to a third party — rather than first offering it back to former owner Commander Toby Marten of Crichel House — thereby precipitating the Crichel Down Scandal [1954]. This caused the resignation of Conservative Agriculture Minister Sir Thomas Dugdale and nearly ended the political career of his Parliamentary Secretary, Peter Carrington, almost before it had started.

During August
Christchurch 'death rays' excite the newspapers.

Sensational stories are appearing in the national newspapers that the Air Defence Research and Development Establishment at Somerford, Christchurch, has perfected the "death ray". This is an intensely strong electromagnetic wave which, it is said, can heat up anything in its path — including living tissue — to the point at which it explodes.

Footnote: This was no precursor of the laser or star-wars, or even the microwave oven. As long ago as 1935, Arnold Wilkins had demonstrated at the Radio Research Establishment, at Slough, that the energy needed for death rays was way beyond present technology. It was, on the other hand, a convenient cover for the development of radar systems.

TRAINING CAMP: 76TH HEAVY REGIMENT, ROYAL ARTILLERY, IN THE RAIN AT BERE REGIS

During August
Horse-drawn wagons bring out Blandford diggings.

Contractors with convoys of horse-drawn wagons are removing thousands of tons of earth and chalk from the site of the military encampment that is to be constructed across Race Down to the east of Blandford.

Friday 1 September
The lights go out.

A full "Black-out" will be enforced from today. All street lighting and illuminated advertisements are being turned off and curtaining must be made light-tight to prevent any seepage through windows. Regulation masks are to be fitted to car headlights. Sidelight lenses must also be dimmed with double sheets of paper.

Sunday 3 September
Britain mobilises as Bournemouth floods.

The mobilisation of the Armed Forces took place yesterday as the rains fell once more. In Bournemouth the 750 men and 26 women of the Auxiliary Fire Service were called-up to their places of duty and found themselves answering 15 flood calls between 21.45 hours last night and 01.35 today.

Bobby's department store in the Square had to be pumped out, with the loss of two tons of sugar, as did a flooded air-raid shelter. Electrical transformers exploded and the Pier Approach Baths found itself with an embarrassment of water in its basement this Sunday morning.

Ironically, it is now regarded as an emergency reservoir for fire-fighting purposes, with 150,000 gallons being held, so this was an exercise which may have to be repeated.

Sunday 3 September
War is declared at 11.15.

This morning, as sun follows the rain and the country goes to church, war hums through military communication lines from 10.00 hours as all units are informed that unless Germany pledges to remove her troops from Poland, war is to be declared by Great Britain. At 11.15 the Prime Minister, Neville Chamberlain, broadcasts to the nation from the Cabinet Room in Number Ten Downing Street:

"This morning the British Ambassador in Berlin handed the German Government a final note stating that unless we heard from them by eleven o'clock that they

ON PATROL: UNIDENTIFIED DESTROYER, OUT OF PORTLAND, CUTTING THROUGH THE WAVES AS "THE SENIOR SERVICE GUARDS THE SECURITY OF OUR COASTS"

were prepared at once to withdraw their troops from Poland a state of war would exist between us.

"I have to tell you now that no such undertaking has been received, and that consequently this country is at war with Germany.

"You can imagine what a bitter blow it is to me that all my long struggle to win peace has failed . . ."

Sunday 3 September
Portland's 'Kelly' finds she is at war.

Working-up on sea trials off Portland, having sailed from Chatham on 29 August, the newly commissioned flagship K-class destroyer H.M.S. *Kelly* — named for Admiral of the Fleet Sir John Kelly and commanded by the King's cousin Captain Louis Mountbatten — received a signal midway through the morning lecture.

Chief Petty Officer Primrose handed it to Captain Mountbatten. "Thank you," he said, before continuing.

"This is the stage in my lecture at which I usually point out how valuable the automatic station-keeper would be in wartime, when the captain and other officers on the bridge have so many things to do besides keeping the ship in station [position] on the other ships of the flotilla. I usually say, 'Now I have given you the basic principles of operating my gear. If war should at this moment break out, you know enough about it to work it.'

"Well, war has at this moment broken out."

He proceeded to read the signal: "FROM ADMIRALTY TO ALL CONCERNED — HOME AND ABROAD. MOST IMMEDIATE. COMMENCE HOSTILITIES AT ONCE WITH GERMANY."

Monday 4 September
Dorset's first 4,000 evacuees.

There are already 4,000 evacuees in Dorset, mainly children from London, and the number is increasing by every train. Billeting allowances are 8 shillings 6 pence a head to the host families. Many schools are so overcrowded that shift systems are being introduced, with the local children coming for the morning, and evacuees for the afternoon.

Tuesday 5 September
'Kelly' claims a U-boat in Lyme Bay.

In today's K Destroyer Flotilla News, the daily newspaper of the Royal Navy's 5th Destroyer Flotilla based at Portland, Bob Knight reports to the crew of H.M.S. *Kelly* on the fishy sequel resulting from anti-submarine depth charges that yesterday claimed a U-boat off Bridport.

"That's war — that was; but we must not lead ourselves to believe that some of the catch will always appear on the breakfast table.

"The presence of mind of Posty in producing a gaff to lift the whales inboard while the ship had stopped to obtain a sample of the oil on the sea is much to be admired.

"We all hope that *Kelly's* and the *Acheron's* efforts [another destroyer] did away with one of the pests that sank, without warning, the liner *Athenia* on Sunday night [3 September, off Ireland] — and, of course, we hope that the lucky messes in the *Kelly* enjoy their breakfast.

"There is plenty of corroborative evidence to show that there were two U-boats here yesterday — one in Weymouth Bay and one in West Bay.

"The periscope of the former was seen from the signal bridge of the *Resolution* [battleship] and the M.A.S.B. and the tracks of two torpedoes fired at the *Kelly*. They missed us by 30 or 40 yards, so certainly we were lucky. To be missed by one submarine and bag another [later, in Lyme Bay] all in the first day [at sea] is good going."

Tuesday 12 September
'Kelly' leaves Portland to pick up the ex-King.

11.00 hours. "One of Britain's fastest and newest destroyers is being sent to France to bring home the Duke and Duchess of Windsor." That's the buzz, following a story in the Daily Mirror on Saturday 9 September, and the crew of H.M.S. *Kelly*, at Portland, have put two and two together.

Their commander, Captain Louis Mountbatten, was called to the Admiralty last week. Now, they have just been ordered "to raise full steam and make for Le Havre".

The "Officer X" they are due to meet at the French port is Major Randolph Churchill, son of Winston, the First Lord of the Admiralty. With him are the Duke and Duchess of Windsor, the former King Edward VIII and his wife, Wallis Simpson,who are at this moment being driven half-way across France. They are to be brought back to Farewell Jetty at Portsmouth.

Wednesday 13 September
Dorchester girls deliver 14,000 gas-masks.

Volunteers at Dorchester are distributing 14,000 gas-masks and 24 men came to the council's depot in Poundbury Road and offered to fill sandbags. By the end of the day they had stacked 5,000.

The ladies are helping too — particularly the staff and pupils of the Dorset County School for Girls who are cycling the district delivering gas-masks. Many of these have been assembled by the inmates of Dorchester Prison.

Saturday 16 September
Belgian steamer blown up off Portland.

The 6,000 ton Belgian passenger liner *Alex van Opstal*, empty and homeward bound to Antwerp from New York, was blown up today by a German mine south of the Shambles, Portland. All 49 crew, plus eight passengers, were saved, though six have been detained in hospital in Weymouth. They were rescued by a Greek steamer.

The explosions, heard in Weymouth, are the first to be experienced in Dorset from the current hostilities.

Tuesday 19 September
'Kelly' joins 'Kingston' at Portland.

Having attended upon the tragic scene of the torpedoed aircraft-carrier H.M.S. *Courageous* in the South Western Approaches and on 17 September recovered pillows and a lavatory door from the sunken *Accrington Court*, brought up by depth charges, the destroyer H.M.S. *Kelly* has returned to Portland.

She is joining H.M.S. *Kingston*, the newly arrived second ship of the 5th Destroyer Flotilla, for the latter's working-up trials. Torpedo discharges will be the order of the day.

Saturday 23 September
2nd Dorsets on their way to France.

The 2nd Battalion of the Dorsetshire Regiment today left Aldershot on their way to join the British Expeditionary Force in France.

The 2nd Dorsets, the 1st Battalion of the Queen's Own Cameron Highlanders, and the 7th Battalion of the Worcestershire Regiment, comprise the 5th Infantry Brigade.

It and the 4th and the 6th Infantry Brigades make up the 2nd Division, commanded by Major-General M. G. H. Barker. Commander-in-Chief of the British Expeditionary Force is General Lord Gort V.C.

Sunday 24 September
Prayer is the best weapon.

It is three Sundays on from the declaration of war upon Germany. Adela Curtis, the mystic writer, has told her sisters of the Christian Contemplatives' Community at

LORD GORT: LEADING THE BRITISH EXPEDITIONARY FORCE IN FRANCE (SECOND FROM RIGHT)

St Bride's Farm, Burton Bradstock, that she abhors pacifism and regards "the most effective of all weapons in our warfare" as "faithful prayer".

During September

Training for A.A. duties (without a gun).

A Royal Artillery Anti-Aircraft Regiment is giving basic training to recruits at Blandford Camp. Very basic training, in fact, as it lacks any operational weapons with which to put them through their paces.

Sunday 1 October

Hitler's coffee beans impounded at Weymouth.

In the first four weeks of war 1,000 tons of contraband cargo that was intended for Germany has been confiscated, mainly from neutral vessels, and impounded at Weymouth. A total of 513,000 tons had been searched in 74 ships that were bound for European ports.

The prize must go to ten bags of fine coffee beans seized from a Danish vessel. They are labelled: "Adolf Hitler." The little dictator is teetotal and vegetarian.

Friday 6 October

Bournemouth fireman dies in exercise.

Auxiliary Leading Fireman Reg Cooper slipped from a moving Auxiliary Fire Service van and was killed by its wheels in an accident today outside a disused church in Nortoft Road, Bournemouth. The building is a fire station operated by number 7 Zone of the town's A.F.S. An exercise was being held.

Bournemouth has eleven such auxiliary fire stations. Eighty emergency fire pumps have now been delivered to the town.

Twenty-five pumps are required to turn-out for a major wartime incident.

Saturday 7 October

Dutch freighter sinks off Portland.

Another ship has been sunk by a German mine off the Shambles Lightship, south-east of Portland Bill. She was the Dutch steamship *Bynnendyk*, returning to Rotterdam from New York.

The 42 crew were able to abandon the blazing wreck and watched her gradually sink from the bows, from the rescue vessel that was taking them into Weymouth.

Thursday 12 October

More survivors brought into Weymouth.

The *Alex Andrea*, a Belgian oil tanker, has docked at Weymouth to bring home the crew of a Whitby steamer, the *Sneaton*, that was torpedoed by a German U-boat in the South Western Approaches. She was outward bound, carrying coal, to the Argentine. A stoker was killed.

The U-boat commander surfaced his vessel to watch the men abandoning ship and called to them in English: "So long, boys. Sorry I had to do it, but it was my duty."

Saturday 14 October

Dorset sailors die in the 'Royal Oak'.

The nation is in a state of shock after an audacious attack on the Royal Navy's main Fleet base in Home Waters. A German submarine slipped into the Royal Navy anchorage of Scapa Flow, in the Orkney Isles, between 01.30 and 01.45 hours this morning and torpedoed the 29,000-ton battleship H.M.S. *Royal Oak*. She turned over and went down into the cold, grey waters with 786 men still inside her.

The whole country is stunned and there is hardly a town in the country that doesn't have a wife or a mother who is not suffering personal grief.

In Weymouth, Petty Officer William Helmore left a widow in Hillcrest Road with three children, the youngest of whom he had never seen. Seventeen-year-old Billy Savage came from Holton Heath, near Wareham. Petty Officer Charles Beeling's parents live at Plush, near Piddletrenthide. Twenty-year-old John Hocking had been living with his grandfather at Martinstown, near Dorchester. Poole's losses include Dennis Brown of Broadstone and Vernon Fay of Branksome Park.

For others, however, the knock on the door tonight brought relief after a day of despair.

Sunday 15 October

Night calls bring better news.

Among those whose agonies have turned out to be unnecessary are two sets of Weymouth parents whose sons were aboard the torpedoed battleship H.M.S. *Royal Oak*. Able Seaman Victor Ayles and Stoker Cecil Lucking have survived. So too has Ronald Kenny of Ackerman Road, Dorchester, though the news was not brought to his mother until 02.00 hours this Sunday morning. Another call in the early hours was made to St Helen's Road, Broadwey, where Weymouth police were able to tell Mrs Barrett that she still has a husband, Petty Officer W. Barrett.

Footnote: Lieutenant-Commander Gunther Prien and his crew in *U47* were feted as heroes on their return to Berlin. Prien would write his memoirs before losing his life in the North Atlantic, on 7 March 1941.

During October

Swimming hero distributes Poole's gas-masks.

Harry Davis, who in his 66 years has saved numerous people who were drowning, is taking an active part in Poole's Air-Raid Precautions and has made himself responsible for the distribution of 7,500 gas-masks to local residents.

Saturday 11 November

The Armistice service takes on a new meaning.

This Armistice Day is different. Throughout the decade the November services marking the end of the Great War have included expressions of pacifism. They were often a communal revulsion at the memory of the carnage in the trenches of the Western Front and Gallipoli.

Now, however, they are reverting to a full military flavour as the country once more steps back into uniform.

"Once war seems inevitable again, a million martyrs will have died again," Labour Prime Minister Ramsay MacDonald said at the Cenotaph in 1934.

Few will have experienced similar thoughts during the silence at 11.00 hours today. The picture houses concentrate on newsreel coverage for civilian air-raid precautions. The public is being reintroduced to warfare. Joining the armed forces had also been out of fashion. Even with high unemployment the level of Army recruitment remained inadequate.

All that has now changed. These days the only partially acceptable pacifists are the "Chocolate Soldiers" of the Friends Ambulance Unit that has been re-formed by the Quaker Cadbury, Fry, and Rowntree families.

Saturday 18 November

Poole firm celebrates its silver jubilee.

Hamworthy Engineering's 300 employees are marking their firm's silver jubilee with a weekend dance at the Woodlands Hall, Parkstone. The Poole-based company was formed at the start of the last war, in 1914, so it does not seem inappropriate to be celebrating the occasion at the beginning of another one.

Wednesday 22 November

Portland mines claim another ship.

The German mines floating off the Shambles, to the south-east of Portland, have claimed yet another vessel, the Greek steamship *Elena R.*

Wednesday 22 November

Five dead but 'Kittiwake' limps into Portland.

The Royal Navy has also nearly lost a ship to the German minefield in the central English Channel. Five ratings were killed aboard the new K-class destroyer H.M.S. *Kittiwake*, but though listing she has been able to limp back into Portland Harbour.

Sunday 31 December

Churchill visits Weymouth, Portland, and Minterne Magna.

Yesterday, Saturday, the First Lord of the Admiralty, Mr Winston Churchill, visited the Contraband Control Centre at Weymouth and went on to Castletown Royal Naval Dockyard at Portland. He called it "my first day off for nearly four months" as he departed to spend the night with Lord and Lady Digby at Minterne House, Minterne Magna. One of their daughters, Pamela, recently married Mr Churchill's son, Randolph.

Today, Sunday, is New Year's Eve but Mr Churchill will be unable to enjoy it relaxing in the Dorset countryside. He has spent the morning working on despatches that have followed him from the Admiralty and after lunch he is leaving for London.

Sunday 31 December

Year in perspective (and Dorset girl weds a Churchill).

The song of the year on both sides of the Atlantic is *There'll Always Be An England* by Ross Parker and Hughie Charles: "There'll always be an England / While there's a country lane / Wherever there's a cottage small / Beside a field of grain."

In Germany the Luftwaffe test the world's first turbojet aircraft, Hans von Ohain's Heinkel He.178. German physicists split the uranium nucleus with neutron bombardment, causing Albert Einstein to write to President Roosevelt that a "nuclear chain reaction in a large mass of uranium" would "lead to the construction of bombs". Britain and Germany hoard food. The Germans have 8,500,000 tons of grain in store, with the promise of a further million tons from Russia in 1940.

Britain is the largest global buyer of food — taking 40 per cent of world trade. Rationing is planned and state intervention extends to the enrichment of bread and margarine with vitamins and trace elements; though only in that is Britain ahead of American food fads.

Across the Atlantic, the Birds Eye label of General Foods introduce pre-cooked frozen foods. Nylon, linking the names of New York and London, becomes a commercial product. In Connecticut the Warner Lingerie Company introduces cup-sizes for bras. Igor Sikorsky flies the first American helicopter. Al Capone leaves prison, now a vegetable from syphilis.

German physician F. H. Müller publishes *Tabakmissbrauch und Lungencarcinoma*; the world has been told that smoking causes lung cancer, not that many are taking the warning seriously. Another Müller, Paul, develops DDT for the Geigy Company and saves the Swiss potato crop from Colorado beetles.

Batman and Robin join the comic strips.

"This is London," Ed Murrow says nightly to most of the 27,500,000 United States families who listen to the radio. His closing line is always the same: "Goodnight and good luck."

Ten per cent of Britons own 88 per cent of the nation's wealth.

The wedding of the year for Dorset's social set came after Mr Churchill had stepped back into Whitehall as

SOCIETY WEDDING: PAMELA DIGBY FROM MINTERNE MAGNA MARRIES RANDOLPH CHURCHILL — SON OF WINSTON — AT ST. JOHN'S, SMITH SQUARE. THE MARRIAGE DID NOT LAST BUT SHE DID NOT DISCARD THE FAMOUS NAME, EVENTUALLY BECOMING MRS PAMELA DIGBY CHURCHILL HAYWARD HARRIMAN AND THE UNITED STATES AMBASSADOR TO PARIS.

First Lord of the Admiralty. His son, Randolph, married the Honourable Pamela Digby, daughter of Lord and Lady Digby of Minterne Magna.

AVRO ANSONS: COASTAL PATROLS USE WARMWELL AERODROME

1940

Wednesday 7 February
Bournemouth A.R.P. has 11 Fire Stations.

Bournemouth's Air Raid Precautions organisation now has its headquarters in the basement of the Town Hall, telephone number 7220. All reports of damage of whatever character are to be made to there. The town has been split into eleven zones, each with its own fire station. Some such as the Central Fire Station and Pokesdown Fire Station are regular fire service establishments but most are auxiliary depots set-up in buildings such as the San Remo Towers at Boscombe and Lee Motor Works in Wimborne Road, Winton.

Wednesday 28 February
Young scientists arrive in Purbeck.

Several young radio research scientists are being posted to the Isle of Purbeck. Boffins Alan Hodgkin and Bernard Lovell have arrived at Worth Matravers with the advance party from the Air Ministry's Telecommunications Research Establishment at Dundee, which is to set up a new base between Worth Matravers village and Renscombe Farm. They will be joined by Dr Robert Cockburn. The group's sole lecturer is Leonard Huxley who is endeavouring to train R.A.F. personnel to understand and use the complex equipment that is being devised.

Footnote: All four would go on to be knighted in their eminent post-war careers. By 5 May 1940 the whole of the Telecommunications Research Establishment had been evacuated from Scotland to Worth.

Saturday 2 March
Luftwaffe attack Channel shipping.

Long-range enemy aircraft from Kampfgeschwader 26 today attacked shipping in the English Channel east of St Alban's Head. The steamship *Domala* was set on fire.

Wednesday 20 March
Steamship 'Barnhill' sunk off Purbeck.

Shipping in the Channel has again been attacked by bombers from Kampfgeschwader 26. The 5,439-ton freighter S.S. *Barnhill* sank off the Isle of Purbeck. The crew escaped by lifeboat.

Sunday 31 March
Paper made into shells at Holton Heath.

Paper is being consumed in great quantities by the Royal Naval Cordite Factory at Holton Heath and made into nitro-cellulose. This guncotton pulp is mixed with nitro-glycerine; the basis of cordite SC which is the propellant for the Navy's shells.

The factory has used 4,279,141 pounds of paper in the past year. That is 1,910 tons.

WAR BOY: PETER FRANKLIN WITH HIS FATHER'S RIFLE AT BOVINGTON CAMP

During March
Enemy bombers fly along a radio beam.

A Heinkel He.111 bomber (1H+AC) of Kampfgeschwader 26 — the celebrated Löwen-Geschwader [Lion Wing] — which was shot down during the month contained a navigation note confirming the existence of a radio directed beam-bombing system. "Radio Beacon Knickebein from 06.00 hours on 315 degrees," it revealed, on being translated and sent to the boffins of the Telecommunications Research Establishment who are moving to Worth Matravers.

Friday 12 April
Narvik wreath at Hardy Monument.

A laurel wreath hangs on the door of the Hardy Monument, the memorial tower to Nelson's flag captain on the hills above Portesham — the village known to Thomas Hardy as "Possum" — in memory of the men of the Royal Navy who lost their lives two days ago in Narvik fjord, Norway.

A card reads: "To the unfading memory of Captain Warburton-Lee, R.N., H.M.S. *Hardy*, and the gallant men who died at Narvik. Nelson's Hardy and Hardy's Possum salute you."

H.M.S. *Hardy* was named for Vice-Admiral Thomas Masterman Hardy. His commemorative tower is now owned by the National Trust.

Tommy gunner: the weapon being a Thompson sub-machine gun, in an Allen-Williams steel turret with no back door

Footnote: Bernard Warburton-Lee caught the enemy by surprise in the early hours of 10 April when he penetrated Ofotfjord with the Royal Navy's 2nd Destroyer Flotilla. He then took *Hardy, Havock,* and *Hunter* into Narvik harbour, while *Hotspur* and *Hostile* stood guard outside, but joined the action later.

There was a short but intense exchange at close quarters, in which two German destroyers were sunk, for the loss of *Hardy* and *Hunter.* Warburton-Lee was mortally wounded. He would be posthumously awarded the Victoria Cross.

Havock and *Hotspur* were damaged, but continued the action as they escaped into the open sea, setting fire to the German transport *Rauenfels.* The ship was carrying ammunition. The British destroyers "were peppered with ironmongery as she went up".

Wednesday 24 April
Holton Heath munitions factory hit.

An oil incendiary bomb exploded at 22.10 hours tonight beside the wash-water settling house of the nitro-glycerine complex at the Royal Naval Cordite Factory, Holton Heath. The wooden settling house began burning but Walt Dominey and his fire-fighting team brought the fire under control and averted what could have been a major disaster.

Saturday 4 May
Two Poole flying-boats destroyed in Norway.

Two Short "Empire" flying-boats, *Cabot* and *Caribou,* which had been seconded to 119 Squadron at Invergordon, have been attacked at anchor by a Heinkel He.115 floatplane in Bodø fjord. They had arrived today

to bring radar equipment to the beleaguered British troops at Harstadt in northern Norway.

Footnote: The equipment was lost in the attack though the injured crews were rescued and brought home by a British destroyer. A further raid, the following morning, sank the flying-boats. They had been scheduled to operate B.O.A.C.'s planned peacetime Atlantic service in 1940.

Sunday 5 May
Telecommunications Research Establishment moves to Purbeck.

The Air Ministry's Telecommunications Research Establishment, which has pioneered the development of early warning radio-direction finding equipment known as radar, has been evacuated from Dundee to Dorset.

It is being housed in a hutted encampment on a plateau — known locally as The Plain — beside Renscombe Farm, a short distance inland from Chapman's Pool, at Worth Matravers in the Isle of Purbeck.

The Telecommunications Research Establishment was previously known as the Air Ministry Research Establishment and used to be based at Bawdsey in pre-war days. It is headed by scientists A. P. Rowe and Robert Watson-Watt.

Footnote: R.D.F., originally the initials for Radio Direction Finding, came to be regarded as Range and Direction Finding, but both would be replaced by the American description Radio Direction and Ranging, thanks to its catchy palindrome mnemonic — radar.

Wednesday 8 May
Special Duty Flight arrives at Christchurch.

The Air Ministry's Special Duty Flight is arriving at Christchurch Aerodrome from St Athan, near Barry, in Glamorgan. It at present comprises six Ansons, four Blenheims, two Harrows, two Fairey Battles, and three adapted "Special Aircraft". These are a Hurricane, an Anson, and a High Altitude Machine.

The aeroplanes, which are to be augmented by other arrivals of a variety of types, carry experimental radar aerials and other items of secret equipment. They will be at the disposal of the Christchurch-based Air Defence and Research Development Establishment and scientists of the Telecommunications Research Establishment at Worth Matravers.

Friday 10 May
Attlee recalled from Bournemouth as the Chamberlain Government falls.

Labour leaders Clement Attlee and Arthur Greenwood were recalled to London, from their party conference in Bournemouth, as the Chamberlain Government recoiled in crisis following the German invasion of the Low Countries. Neville Chamberlain had offered them positions in a proposed new National Government.

They accepted the posts (Attlee as Lord Privy Seal; Greenwood as Minister Without Portfolio) but rejected Chamberlain's continued leadership. This exemplifies Parliament's present mood, characterised by the intervention in full uniform of Sir Roger Keyes, and Leo Amory's reusing to devastating effect of a 17th-century Parliamentary jibe that had originally been targeted at Oliver Cromwell: "In the name of God go!"

Speeches of the Opposition, of Duff Cooper from Chamberlain's own benches, and a vehement attack by Lloyd George, were followed by a Pyrrhic victory. In this he carried the vote but lost the confidence of his party; 33 Conservative rebels had voted against and at least a further 60 abstained.

Chamberlain went at once to Buckingham Palace to tender his resignation to the King. He then broadcast tonight to the nation: "You and I must rally behind our new leader, and with our united strength, and with unshakeable courage, fight and work until this wild beast, that has sprung out of his lair upon us, has been finally disarmed and overthrown."

The King has been advised to send for Winston Churchill to form the new three-party coalition Government.

Saturday 11 May
Churchill's Dorset's ancestry.

With the fall last night of Neville Chamberlain's Government and Mr Churchill's appointment as Premier it is being noted with approval in Dorset this weekend that his most distinguished ancestor, John Churchill, the first Duke of Marlborough, was the son of Winston Churchill of Round Chimneys Farm, Glanvilles Wootton, "of a good Dorset family".

Winston Spencer Churchill is the grandson of the seventh Duke of Marlborough. Last year his son, Randolph, married the Hon. Pamela Digby of Minterne Magna.

Tuesday 14 May
Dutch refugees to camp on Brownsea Island.

Following the sudden Nazi invasion into the Low Countries, which also delivered the coup de grâce to the Chamberlain Government, an armada of dozens of overloaded Dutch vessels is being shepherded by the Royal Navy into Poole Harbour. The refugees will be temporarily camped on Brownsea Island where they can be properly screened by doctors, police, and the security service before being admitted into the country.

An estimated 3,000 are on their way.

Thursday 16 May
2nd Dorsets withdraw towards France.

"Où est la route pour France?" a Dorsetman heard as Algerian troops were beaten back by the German advance through Belgium. The 2nd Battalion of the Dorsetshire Regiment also found itself under further orders to withdraw in the face of the same overwhelming odds.

Sunday 19 May
2nd Dorsets see civilians bombed and strafed.

For the first time the Dorset soldiers serving in Belgium, now pulled back to Tournai near the French border, have seen the bodies of civilians who were bombed and strafed by German aircraft. The town is on fire.

Friday 24 May
2nd Dorsets invited to surrender.

With German radio announcing that the ring around the French, Belgian, and British Armies has "definitely closed" the 2nd Battalion of the Dorsetshire Regiment — now withdrawn to La Bassée, south-west of Lille — has been showered from the air with leaflets. These invite them to desert: "You are surrounded — why fight on? We treat our prisoners well."

MID AIR: ANOTHER TOMMY GUNNER LEAPS INTO ACTION, IN A CLIFF EXERCISE AT BOURNEMOUTH

SLIT TRENCHES: THESE, AT BOURNEMOUTH, WITH THEIR SHEEP HURDLES AND PROTECTED ACCESS FOR THE INFANTRY, CREATE A SCENE REMINISCENT OF THE WESTERN FRONT, AS WAS THE SIMULATED USE OF POISON GAS

WAR RELIC: SURVIVING STEEL TURRET GUN-NEST, SET IN NATIONAL TRUST DOWNLAND ABOVE SEACOMBE BOTTOM, WITH ITS LINE OF SIGHT FACING THE OTHER WAY, TOWARDS THE ENGLISH CHANNEL, FROM THE STONE CLIFFS OF THE ISLE OF PURBECK

Wednesday 29 May
Observers told not to fraternise with Local Defence Volunteers.

Too much fraternisation is taking place with other civilian units, Dorset's local commander of the Observer Corps, Wing Commander Stewart, has told his men: "Head observers must consult their officers before making any commitments with the Local Defence Volunteers. No instruction has been received with regard to co-operation and any tendency to mingle at posts should be discouraged."

WAREHAM ACTUALLY: CAMOUFLAGING A PILLBOX "SOMEWHERE IN ENGLAND"

Friday 31 May
Churchill flies from Warmwell to Paris.

Prime Minister Winston Churchill has flown in a twin-engined de Havilland Flamingo transport aircraft from Hendon, via Warmwell Aerodrome on the Dorset coast, to Paris for secret discussions on the deteriorating military situation. Nine Hurricane fighters from 601 (County of London) Squadron were deployed to escort the Premier's aeroplane. They waited overnight to bring it safely home.

Churchill met the French Premier and talked with Major-General Edward Spears, the British Prime Minister's personal representative with the French Government and armed forces. The clutch of young pilots, even after their night on the town, reminded him of "the angels of my childhood".

Among those escort pilots was Flying Officer William Rhodes-Moorhouse, whose father was the first airman to win the Victoria Cross, in 1915, and is buried on a Dorset hillside at Parnham, which was the family home near Beaminster.

Footnote: As is son Willie, interred next to his father. He was awarded the Distinguished Flying Cross during the Battle of Britain and would be

NATURAL CONCEALMENT: A PILLBOX BEHIND THE CHESIL BEACH, AT LANGTON HERRING, WITH THE ENTRANCE SET IN AN OLD STONE WALL (ON THE SOUTH SIDE), ALSO SEEN FROM THE NORTH-WEST (SHOWING NORTH AND WEST SLITS) AND FROM THE INSIDE (WEST SLIT). IT IS AT ORDNANCE SURVEY MAP REFERENCE SY 608 825

killed in Hurricane P8818 during a complex dog-fight with Messerschmitt Bf.109s above Tonbridge, Kent, on 6 September 1940. 601 Squadron grieved, and lost its aggressive spirit, according to Squadron Leader Max Aitken, who was the eldest son of Lord Beaverbrook and would be his successor at the head of Express Newspapers.

War artist Captain Cuthbert Orde wrote that all were affected from the commanding officer to the humblest aircraftman: "They couldn't believe it — it just couldn't have happened. His extraordinary combination of gaiety, joie de vivre, personal attraction, and fighting qualities was something that just didn't disappear suddenly."

Friday 31 May
2nd Dorsets evacuated from Dunkirk.

After five days and nights of marching and fighting as they made their way north towards the Channel coast, the main contingent of the 2nd Battalion of the Dorsetshire Regiment last night completed an orderly withdrawal,

TRAINING FLAMES: AIR RAID PRECAUTIONS VOLUNTEERS AND FIREMEN TORCH A DERELICT THATCHED COTTAGE OFF CASTLE LANE, BOURNEMOUTH, ON 17 MARCH 1940

Battalion, and a Motor Transport Company was also formed as part of the Hants and Dorset Transport Column.

Saturday 1 June
Fleeing French troops arrive in Weymouth.

The first train carrying Free French soldiers into Weymouth arrived at 05.00 hours. They are being taken to the former Christ Church, opposite the station, which has been converted into a refugee Welcome Club. They are being issued with their first rations — half a loaf and a tin of bully-beef — and dispersed to various schools, halls, and private accommodation.

Sunday 2 June
Hardy and love of England.

Thomas Hardy was a patriot, speakers emphasised at the ceremony in Dorchester to mark the centenary of the author's birth. It was held beside his memorial statue in Colliton Walks today, Sunday, although the precise anniversary is Tuesday 4 June.

Earl Baldwin of Bewdley, the former Conservative Prime Minister [Stanley Baldwin], laid a wreath and commented that he himself felt reservations during the week, that the celebration should be postponed due to the dismal news from France.

On further consideration, however, he thought there was nothing unseemly even at a moment like the present for the English people to gather together in the part of England made famous by a very great Englishman, to express their sense of what they owed to him: "He has for many increased their knowledge and love of England — for which her sons today are laying down their lives."

under fire, to the Mole at Dunkirk, where they boarded a Thames dredger.

They were appalled to see that she seemed to be half-full of water but heard that dredgers are always like that.

Footnote: The miracle of Dunkirk was that the number of evacuated troops totalled 338,228.

During May
Local Defence Volunteers have six Dorset units.

Major-General Harry Marriot-Smith is organising the Local Defence Volunteers under instructions from the War Office. Dorset is being covered by six battalions.

Footnote: Churchill would soon have them renamed — as the Home Guard. The 3rd Dorset Battalion was later split to create another, the 7th (Wareham)

Tuesday 4 June
Poole and Weymouth craft help evacuate Dunkirk.

Pleasure craft from Poole and Weymouth are in the armada of Operation Dynamo that today completed the evacuation of the British Expeditionary Force from the beaches at Dunkirk.

COAST DEFENCE: A NEWLY-EMPLACED 9.2 INCH ANTI-SHIP GUN BEING LOADED AND FIRED AT EAST WEARES, PORTLAND, BY 102 COAST DEFENCE BATTERY OF THE 552ND (DORSET) COAST REGIMENT, ROYAL ARTILLERY. "EVER READY," THE ORIGINAL CAPTION RAN. "MEN ON DUTY KEEP WATCH AS A SEARCHLIGHT SWEEPS THE SEA." THE GUN THEN OPENED FIRE INTO THE NIGHT, ACROSS WEYMOUTH BAY

Among the flotilla of craft taken to Dover from Poole were Harvey's *Ferry Nymph* and *Southern Queen*; Davis's *Felicity* and *Island Queen*; and Bolson's *Skylark VI*, *Skylark VIII*, and *Skylark IX*; and *Thomas Kirk-Wright*, which is the harbour's inshore lifeboat. These eight vessels were commandeered by the Royal Navy.

The lifeboat, with its shallow draught, had the distinction of going into the beaches. She survived shore-fire from Germans positioned less than 40 yards away.

The pleasure craft stood offshore and proved ideal for taking aboard soldiers by the dozen.

As for Poole's fishing fleet, which had also loyally turned up in response to the Admiralty's appeal, they were summarily rejected by the Navy. The Poole fishermen, who consider they are something of an élite, as the port's only true seamen, felt humiliated to find themselves being sent home from Kent by train as their vessels were impounded for possible reserve use. They had been deemed unsuitable for the present kind of mass transit.

GUNNERS' BADGE: THAT OF THE COAST DEFENCE BATTERIES OF THE ROYAL ARTILLERY, FEATURING A MUZZLE-LOADING GUN AND ITS CANNON BALLS — NO LONGER ENTIRELY APPROPRIATE, AS MOST CLIFFTOP FORTIFICATIONS ARE NOW RECEIVING THEIR FIRST MODERN GUNS

The retreat from the jaws of defeat has turned into a miracle of defiance in a successful evacuation of unprecedented proportions. A total of 330,000 soldiers have been brought out to fight again another day. Of these a third are French and 6,000 of these, from Flanders, have been sent to Weymouth.

There, at least, the seaside has hotels and facilities, but concern is being expressed in Dorchester that in the wake of the military there will be a further civilian influx for which the county town is totally unprepared. A further 2,300 evacuees are earmarked for Dorchester Rural District. Only now are air-raid shelters being constructed in the town.

Footnote: Of the local boats, the *Island Queen* and *Southern Queen* were sunk off Dunkirk. *Skylark VI* was abandoned with bomb damage but would later be salvaged and towed back to Bolson's Shipyard in Poole where she was refitted with a larger engine and became an Air-Sea Rescue craft. The disgruntled fishermen returned by train for their rejected vessels a few days later.

Saturday 8 June
Evershot officer lost in 'Glorious' sinking.

Lieutenant-Commander Charles John Thompson Stephens was among those lost this afternoon in the sinking of the aircraft-carrier H.M.S. *Glorious*, off Narvik, by gunfire from the German battlecruisers *Scharnhorst* and *Gneisenau*. He was aged 35.

Commander Stephens was the son of Major John August Stephens of Evershot, who served in the Royal Field Artillery and died in 1925, after a prolonged illness that resulted from injuries suffered in the Great War.

Sunday 9 June
Germans mine the channel into Poole Harbour.

Last night the Germans mined the Swash Channel that leads into the entrance of Poole Harbour, in anticipation of its use in some military relief operation to bring out beleaguered units of the British Army struggling in Normandy.

ISLAND GUNNERS: 347 COAST BATTERY OF THE ROYAL ARTILLERY, EMPLACED IN THE TREES BEHIND BRANKSEA CASTLE, ON BROWNSEA ISLAND

Wednesday 12 June

Poole boats rescue troops from St Valery.

Overall, Operation Cycle failed to live up to the Admiralty's expectations of a second mini-Dunkirk, but for some of the Poole boats taking part it was a triumph. They last night played a key role in bringing 3,321 soldiers, a third of them British, from the salient at St Valery-en-Caux.

This time the Germans were ready for a maritime rescue mission, though it was the fog that disrupted the efforts of the early hours on Tuesday, the 11th, and sent 6,000 Scottish troops into prisoner-of-war camps. As part of their counter-measures the Germans mined the Swash Channel into Poole Harbour. It has been rendered partially clear by Navy divers from Portland.

Not completely, however, as the *Princess Juliana* found. She was sailing out of Poole last night, when she hit a mine off the Training Bank, and was lifted clear of the water. George Brown, the pilot, was rescued, as were three of the Dutch crewmen.

An urgent call!

RECRUITS WANTED FOR THE AUXILIARY FIRE SERVICE

APPLY WITHIN OR AT ANY FIRE STATION

RECRUITS WANTED: BY THE AUXILIARY FIRE SERVICE, AS THE "PHONEY WAR" ENDS AND THE LUFTWAFFE TAKES OVER FRENCH AIRFIELDS

Footnote: The appropriately-named Ivor Holland, instrumental in the rescue of *Princess Juliana's* survivors, was to be awarded the Order of the Red Lion by the Netherlands Government-in-exile.

Thursday 13 June

Two more Warmwell escorts for Churchill.

Nine Spitfires of 609 (West Riding) Squadron from R.A.F. Middle Wallop have been deployed to Warmwell Aerodrome for the past 72 hours in order to act as fighter escorts for Prime Minister Winston Churchill's Flamingo.

He has flown to France twice, on the first occasion with Secretary of State for War Anthony Eden and Generals Dill and Ismay from the Imperial General Staff, to try and persuade Prime Minister Paul Reynaud to continue fighting the Germans.

On the second occasion the London party comprised Churchill and Ismay with Lords Halifax and Beaverbrook.

The first flight was to Briare, near Orleans, and the second to Tours. These journeys reflected the state of the nation. "Eight thousand feet below us on our right was Havre, burning," Churchill writes. "Presently I noticed

DUNKIRK EVACUATED: THE BRITISH EXPEDITIONARY FORCE, INCLUDING THE 2ND BATTALION OF THE DORSETSHIRE REGIMENT, IS BROUGHT HOME BY OPERATION DYNAMO IN MAY-JUNE 1940. THE ARMADA OF 800 VESSELS RANGED IN SIZE FROM PLEASURE BOATS, FROM AS FAR AWAY AS POOLE, TO 39 BRITISH DESTROYERS AND TEN OTHER WARSHIPS. CIVILIAN VESSELS BROUGHT HOME A TOTAL OF 135,054 MEN AND ROYAL NAVY AND FRENCH NAVY VESSELS CARRIED A TOTAL OF 197,139; OF THESE 98,671 WERE TAKEN OFF THE BEACHES, AND 239,555 EMBARKED FROM DUNKIRK HARBOUR. THE FACE IN THE CROWD, WEARING A DUFFEL COAT AND LOOKING STRAIGHT AT THE CAMERA, IS TED ROBERTS

ENGLAND ALONE: THE DORSET BEACHES BECAME THE FRONT-LINE IN JUNE 1940

some consultations going on with the captain, and immediately after we dived to a hundred feet or so. They had seen two German aircraft firing at fishing boats. We were lucky that their pilots did not look upwards. Arrived over Tours, we found the airport had been heavily bombed the night before, but we and our escort landed smoothly in spite of the craters." Moving about on the ground was equally fraught, with the Prime Minister's car hardly moving, in a stream of refugees.

A total of twelve pilots took part in the two flights: Michael John Appleby, A. R. D. Barratt, Stephen Gerald Beaumont, John Bisdee, Adolf Jarvis Blayney, James Richebourg Buchanan, Peter Drummond-Hay, John Charles Dundas, Alexander Rothwell "Paul" Edge, F. J. "Frankie" Howell, Gordon Mitchell, and Charles Nevil Overton.

based minesweepers, H.M.S. *Kindred Star* and H.M.S. *Thrifty*.

Thursday 13 June

Eleven killed as 'Abel Tasman' is blown-up off Poole.

Three of the flotilla of 15 craft returning from St Valery-en-Caux with remnants of the British and French Armies successfully ran the gauntlet of the Swash Channel into Poole Harbour today. The fourth and unlucky craft was the *Abel Tasman*, fortunately returning empty.

She hit a mine and was blown to pieces, killing all eleven of her complement from the Royal Navy Volunteer Reserve. An order was then flashed to the remaining ships for them to turn around and sail to Southampton instead.

Thursday 13 June

'British Inventor' mined off St Alban's Head.

The steam tanker *British Inventor* has struck a mine off St Alban's Head. Although she stayed afloat long enough to be put under tow the line had to be released as the stricken vessel began to go under.

Channels into the ports of Weymouth and Poole are being kept open through the efforts of two Portland-

Saturday 15 June

Swash Channel has first magnetic mines.

The mines that have claimed two ships in recent days in the Swash Channel at the outer entrance to Poole Harbour include some, at least, of a new magnetic type that explode when they come close to a steel ship. The C-type mines have not yet been retrieved intact for examination and today the first attempt to do so burst into a spectacular failure on Studland beach.

Harold Cartridge with the Poole fishing boat *Smiling Through*, operating under Navy orders, managed to tow one on a 700-feet line from the Bar Buoy to the sandy shallows off Studland — where, for some unknown reason, it decided to explode, though without delivering more than a shock and a shake to Cartridge and his craft.

Footnote: The Germans were slow in deploying this potentially devastating weapon. The first to be dismantled by the British would be recovered from Shoeburyness, Essex, on 22 November 1940; the Germans had been lax in not incorporating an anti-handling device.

Dragon's teeth: anti-tank defences from 1940, across the Chesil Beach beside the West Fleet at Abbotsbury (photographed after some subsidence by Colin Graham in 1983). Cubes of concrete are 3.5 feet high and four feet apart, in a double row, with nine feet between the parallel lines set on a continuous cement base

Monday 17 June
Coal-barge soldiers dock at Poole Quay.

A London coal-barge, the motor-vessel *Alnwick* from Fulham Dock, chugged into Poole Quay at midday, having successfully dodged both the Luftwaffe and the mines of the Swash Channel. She carried a cargo of fully-armed British soldiers withdrawn from Cherbourg. They were greeted by a crowd of cheering civilians who tossed the men packets of cigarettes and bottles of beer.

An infantryman of the 51st Highland Division played the bagpipes as remnants of Ark Force, the 154th Infantry Brigade who had been tasked to protect the evacuation, stepped ashore.

Footnote: They were then treated to a wash in municipal swimming baths and accommodation at St Walburga's Catholic School, Malvern Road, Bournemouth.

Wednesday 19 June
Highcliffe sighting of French refugees.

Two boats, apparently carrying French troops fleeing from Cherbourg, have been spotted by the Local Defence Volunteers from their Highcliffe look-out, the Cliff Top Cafe. The craft are heading for Steamer Point, Christchurch.

Thursday 20 June
First air-raid warning.

Condition Red: this is the first air-raid warning at Christchurch, though there have been earlier alerts for Condition Yellow, the precautionary message from Fighter Command that enemy air activity is to be expected.

With Condition Red the activity has been monitored and appears to be coming our way — it is an instruction to take to the shelters, given as a two-minute warbling blast on the sirens.

Enemy aircraft were sighted at 8,000 feet, and a burst of gunfire heard, but no bombs were dropped.

Later there was a continuous two-minute wail from the sirens to declare that it was now All Clear.

Footnote: Christchurch would experience 956 air-raid warnings, the vast majority of them also being of little consequence. The last would be on 15 July 1944.

Thursday 20 June
Weymouth tears as the Frenchmen leave.

Tearful farewells marked Weymouth's parting with the French soldiers, the last of whom have now left to resume the war with fighting units. They were taken to heart, in a way that perhaps the Londoners and others weren't — but the town has experienced an influx unprecedented for anywhere in England.

In one sad incident a Catholic priest tried to say something kind to an unhappy Belgian woman but utterly failed.

"Are they all yours?" joked Father Jules Ketele when he saw she had three children with her. A good Catholic should have known better!

She burst into tears and sobbed that she had seven children when she left home eight days ago; these are all she has left.

The total number of arrivals for the past week has been 27,400 refugees, of which the bulk — 23,743 of them — have come from the Channel Islands, which face impending German invasion.

Footnote: The Germans took over the Channel Islands at the end of the month, on 30 June and 1 July, and would occupy them for the rest of the war.

Friday 21 June
Christchurch Ansons fly in search of the 'Beam'.

The Telecommunications Research Establishment, at Worth Matravers, has organised a special mission tonight for three Anson aeroplanes from the Special Duty Flight at Christchurch Aerodrome.

They will try, in poor weather, to use American radar receivers, to track the course of a German radio direction signal, intended to aid the navigation of bombers, that appears to lead inland from the North Sea in the vicinity of Spalding, Lincolnshire, intersecting with another similar "beam" from the south, above the Rolls-Royce aero-engine factory at Derby. The Anson tracking this second signal is being flown by Flight-Lieutenant H. E. Bufton, with Corporal Mackie as radio operator.

Footnote: The Flight spawned a Special Counter Measures Unit which would function as part of 109 Squadron.

Sunday 23 June
Wooden glider makes blips on Worth's radar.

A British Avro 504N biplane today took off from Christchurch Aerodrome to tow a German Minimoa glider into the middle of the English Channel and released the wooden craft at 10,000 feet for it to glide back towards the Isle of Purbeck. The pilot, Philip Wills, returned below cliff level at St Alban's Head and prepared for a potentially fatal impact but was saved by the phenomenon of currents rising on sunny days beside south-facing vertical surfaces.

The object of the exercise was for the Telecommunications Research Establishment at Renscombe, Worth Matravers, to establish with its radio direction finding aerials [R.D.F., now known as radar] whether short-wave radiation that bounced off metal bombers would also reflect from wooden gliders. Worth houses the country's principal radio research unit.

The answer was affirmative; to the relief of the scientists and the War Cabinet as the country is in fear of a mass invasion of German gliders. As for the Avro 504, it has a remarkable pedigree dating back to the beginning of the Great War, having been used in the first organised bombing raid — that on the Zeppelin sheds at Friedrichshafen, Lake Constance, on 21 November 1914.

Tuesday 25 June
69th Infantry Brigade takes over at Poole.

The 69th Infantry Brigade, late of France and the Dunkirk beaches, is now back in the front line — at Poole and east Dorset where it has taken over the anti-invasion defences from the Queen's Bays. The Officer Commanding, Brigadier Barstow, is based at Bovington Camp.

The Brigade comprises the 7th Battalion of the Green Howards; the 5th Battalion of the East Yorkshire Regiment; and the 6th Battalion of the Green Howards, who are being dispersed into the countryside.

The Adjutant of the Green Howards has found that the unit no longer possesses a duplicator — and is to ask Poole Corporation if he may borrow theirs.

During June
Anti-ship guns emplaced around Poole Bay.

The 554th Coast Regiment of the Royal Artillery, with its headquarters at the Conningtower, West Road, Canford Cliffs, has sited former naval guns, taken from warships and armed merchantmen at the end of the Great War and put into store, as the teeth of the anti-ship defences around Poole Bay.

They are being emplaced as follows, in fortifications built by the Royal Engineers:

Two 6-inch guns at Battery Hill, Brownsea Island, manned by 347 Coast Battery. Two 5.5-inch guns on Hengistbury Head manned by 172 Coast Battery. Two 6-inch guns at Mudeford manned by 175 Coast Battery. Two 4-inch guns at Swanage manned by 386 Coast Battery.

Each set of emplacements has a complement of about a hundred men.

During June
Ship and boom defences for Poole Harbour entrance.

An Examination Ship is positioned in the Swash Channel at the entrance to Poole Harbour. The duty is being undertaken by the ex-Belgian trawler *Rose Arthur*, now His Majesty's Trawler *XVI*, with her sister craft H.M.T. *XVII* (*Roger Robert*) and H.M.T. *XVIII* (*Marguerita Marie Louisa*). The alert code for the sighting of enemy forces is "Blackbird". That for a landing of troops is "Gallipoli". For a landing of tanks it is "Caterpillar".

Once a warning of invasion has been radioed and received on the mainland the craft's duty is to suspend the watching brief with a final signal — "Finish" — and head to sea to intercept and engage enemy vessels.

As for the harbour entrance, between Sandbanks and Shell Bay, it has a steel boom with suspended torpedo heads that have been provided by the Royal Naval Cordite Factory at Holton Heath. There is a passage open at the centre in daytime, but in the evening this is closed, by boatman George Mitchell.

Inside the harbour, six pleasure craft have been requisitioned by the Royal Navy, and armed with machine guns. They are *H1* to *H6*; the boats of the Poole Harbour Patrol.

In the Main Channel of Poole Harbour an old steamship, the *Empire Sentinel*, has been packed with explosives and in the event of invasion the Harbour Patrol will sink her, to block the approaches to the port. Their prime duty is to ensure the closure of this channel.

Footnote: Only one of the pleasure boats, *Etrillita* in peacetime, was retained as a patrol craft. The others were phased out and replaced.

During June
British mines laid in Poole Harbour.

The Naval Officer-in-Command, Poole, is completing the laying of a minefield between Sandbanks and Brownsea Island to prevent the intrusion of German submarines or surface vessels.

During June
Urban anti-tank "Islands" at Poole and Christchurch.

Anti-tank "Islands" of urban coastal areas,

ARISH MELL: THE GAP IN THE CHALK CLIFFS OF WORBARROW BAY, A MILE FROM EAST LULWORTH, BLOCKED BY DRAGON'S TEETH AND HOOPS OF BARBED WIRE, PLUS A SEMI-OBSOLETE MEDIUM TANK FROM LULWORTH CAMP

impregnable to tank attack, have been established behind concrete obstacles, minefields, and flame traps, at the Old Town in Poole and between the railway and the rivers at Christchurch. The Garrison Headquarters is also strongly defended in the centre of Bournemouth.

The whole of the conurbation, from Upton to Mudeford, is under the control of the Garrison Commander in Bournemouth.

During June

Royal Naval Air Station Sandbanks.

Seaplane training for Fleet Air Arm pilots is now based at Poole, from the middle of the month, with the removal from Calshot on Southampton Water to Sandbanks of 765 Naval Air Squadron and the Royal Navy Seaplane School. At Calshot they had been heavily bombed.

The school and its squadron trains pilots on the Walrus biplane, the Fleet and Air-Sea Rescue workhorse, which is one of the most distinctive maritime aeroplanes. It has a characteristic chugging sound and a high profile with a stabiliser on the tail and floats at the tips of the wings. Sailors know it as the "Shagbat".

On Sandbanks slipway the machines are stored with their wheels down and wings folded back. The unit also has the veteran Swordfish torpedo-reconnaissance biplane, known as the "Stringbag", and Kingfisher and Seafox floatplanes.

The base is known as Royal Naval Air Station Sandbanks.

Footnote: To Poole people, however, it was the more prosaic H.M.S. Tadpole — because it handled beginners with seaplanes that were dwarfed by the flying-boats operating from Poole Harbour with B.O.A.C. and R.A.F. Coastal Command. The name H.M.S. *Tadpole* was later adopted by the Royal Navy for real, in 1943, for a pre-invasion Landing Craft Training Establishment.

LUFTWAFFE PHOTOGRAPHS: SHOWING (above) BRITISH VESSELS MOORED IN THE NORTHERN PART OF PORTLAND HARBOUR, FROM THE CHESIL BEACH (LEFT) TO THE NOTHE PROMONTORY AND WEYMOUTH HARBOUR (TOP RIGHT). SHIPS ARE IDENTIFIED BY NUMBERS AND ANTI-AIRCRAFT BATTERIES BY LETTERS. ON THE NORTH SIDE OF SMALL MOUTH, BETWEEN THE FERRYBRIDGE ROAD AND THE RAILWAY (BETWEEN THE BRIDGES) IS A MUNITIONS FACTORY, WHITEHEAD TORPEDO WORKS. ITS JETTY EXTENDS 1,000 YARDS SOUTH-EASTWARDS INTO THE HARBOUR. BINCLEAVES GROYNE IS THE NORTHERN ARM OF THE BREAKWATERS, WITH THIS AND THE JETTY OF THE ADMIRALTY TORPEDO RANGES BEING PINPOINTED BY THE INNER 'A'

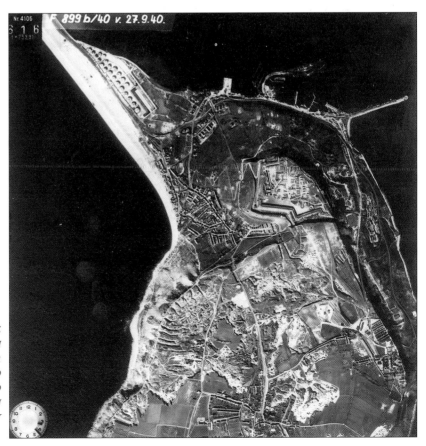

PORTLAND DOCKYARD: EXTENDING FROM THE LINES OF OIL TANKS BEHIND THE CHESIL BEACH (TOP LEFT) TO CASTLETOWN AND THE INNER BREAKWATER (TOP RIGHT). ON THE ISLAND HEIGHTS ARE VERNE CITADEL, NOW PORTLAND PRISON, AND EXTENSIVE QUARRIES, SEEN IN ANOTHER OF THE LUFTWAFFE SPY PHOTOGRAPHS

(Left) TORPEDO RANGES: LOOKING SOUTH-EASTWARDS FROM THE MAINLAND AT WEYMOUTH, ALONG BINCLEAVES GROYNE, WITH THE LONG RANGE IN THE FOREGROUND AND THE SHORT RANGE STRETCHING OUT TO THE RIGHT

(Below) SUBMARINE NETS: OFF THE NORTH EAST BREAKWATER OF PORTLAND HARBOUR, SEEN IN A GERMAN RECONNAISSANCE PHOTOGRAPH, WITH THOSE OF THE EAST SHIP CHANNEL (BOTTOM RIGHT) BEING CLOSED, AND THOSE OF THE NORTH SHIP CHANNEL OPEN (TOP LEFT)

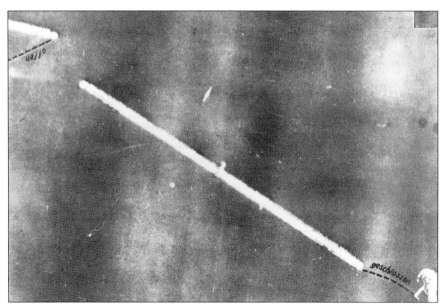

Canon Burrows is currently arranging their accommodation at hotels and with his congregation. There is growing competition for space as thousands more pass through the town like refugees. It is said that at the moment there is only one fully-equipped operational division in the whole of the British Isles, and that is Canadian.

During June

Bridport drops Belgian for a British hero.

Sometimes pub names must move with the times. Such was the case with Bridport's King of Prussia, at 52 East Street, which became the King of Belgium when he was the nation's darling for standing up to the Kaiser in 1914. After a disastrous retreat he bravely regrouped his forces to hold the Ypres salient for the duration of the Great War and led his men on the final Allied offensive back into Belgium.

Sadly, King Albert the hero was killed in a climbing accident on 17 February 1934, and his successors have been noticeably lacking in that quality of defiance in defeat. They were quick to capitulate to the next wave of invading Germans.

This time, however, Palmer's Brewery is choosing a hero who cannot be deposed — they have decided that Lord Nelson has stood the test of time.

During June

Bovington's tank collection scrapped or used as pillboxes.

The unique collection of the world's first tanks at the Armoured Fighting Vehicles School, Bovington Camp, has been dispersed to help the war effort. Many have been taken away for scrap and others are now in strategic positions as stationary pillboxes.

The vehicles had been put in a shed after Rudyard Kipling visited Bovington in 1923 and expressed disappointment that nothing was then being done to preserve them.

During June

Four hundred French soldiers rest in Bournemouth.

As the exhausted evacuated armies are dispersed from their reception ports a detachment of 400 French soldiers have been told to report to Bournemouth for a short recuperation while billets are located. A vicar, Canon Hedley Burrows, found they had been told to report to St Peter's Hall in the centre of the town.

He telephoned the Town Clerk at the Town Hall to ask who was in charged of these men.

"You are!" he was told.

Monday 1 July

Ration Books and Identity Cards.

Ration Books for food come into force this morning, with green coupons for meat, yellow for butter and margarine, and orange for cooking fat.

Identity Cards are being issued to all those living in the Military Control Areas, which in Dorset now include the entire coast and its town and extend 20 miles inland.

The Commissioner responsible for the control of civilians in the South-West Region is Sir Geoffrey Kelsall Peto. The 62-year-old, old Etonian and ex-Royal Wilts Yeomanry, has been a director of Morgan Crucible Limited since 1903. Between the wars he was an M.P. and Parliamentary Private Secretary, first at the India Office, and then the Board of Trade. He accompanied Walter Runciman on the 1938 mission to Czecho-Slovakia.

The process of issuing the National Registration Identity Cards is being delegated to local officials who can check the identities of the persons making applications. Those issued at Sandbanks, for instance, will be signed by the Officer Commanding Troops, Poole Defence Area.

Persons without cards who have business or private reasons for entering Military Control Areas will be required to give their names and addresses, and those of the people they are visiting, at police or military vehicle check-points. Passengers and pedestrians are also asked to co-operate. Police will be carrying out spot-checks inside these zones, such as on buses, and at random in public places.

Tuesday 2 July
All Bournemouth and Poole beach-huts must go.

All beach chalets and huts are to be removed from the vicinity of beaches at Poole, Bournemouth, and Christchurch, having been subjected to a blanket requisition order by the military. Their clearance is necessary to ensure a proper field of fire from the cliffs and across the sands.

Tuesday 2 July
Green Howards wiring-up Bournemouth beach.

The low-tide line for the ten-mile entirety of Bournemouth beach, from Sandbanks to Hengistbury Head, is a priority for wiring-up with barriers. The sands will then be mined.

These defences will be erected by the Green Howards who are also to build emplacements at intervals, and to guard weak-points such as the Chines.

They are beginning at the western end by sealing-off Sandbanks where particular strong-points will be the Haven Hotel and Sandbanks Pavilion.

Wednesday 3 July
Bournemouth gets its first bomb.

Southampton received its first enemy bombers on 19 June and today, at 00.12 hours, came Bournemouth's turn. A single high-explosive bomb fell at Cellars Farm Road, Southbourne. It set a house on fire and damaged 18 other properties.

The explosion and blaze caused considerable consternation. Rumours as the suburbs awoke were that at 02.45, on the other side of the River Stour,

GERMAN BOMBS: THE LUFTWAFFE GUN-BAY VIEW OF ITS EXPLOSIVES RAINING DOWN ON THE FORT GUARDING THE NORTH END OF THE OUTER BREAKWATER OF PORTLAND HARBOUR, TO THE LEFT OF WHICH IS THE EAST SHIP CHANNEL. NORTH IS TO THE LEFT IN THIS PHOTOGRAPH, WITH THE HARBOUR BEING AT THE BOTTOM AND THE OPEN SEA AT THE TOP. THE FLOATS OF ANTI-SUBMARINE NETS SHOW AS A DOUBLE LINE OF DOTS EXTENDING INTO THE LOWER LEFT-HAND CORNER OF THE PICTURE, TOWARDS THE NORTH EASTERN BREAKWATER, AND ARE GESCHLOSSEN (CLOSED)

Christchurch police had issued a warning that German parachutists had landed.

Thursday 4 July
Control points surround Sandbanks.

Effectively, from today, the Sandbanks peninsula at Poole is sealed off, with military control points in operation at Shore Road and the former Haven Hotel ferry point, as well as the Studland road where it now ends at Shell Bay.

On Saturday the position will be regularised by the issue of permits to the 544 inhabitants who have been told to gather at the Haven Hotel to have their photographs taken. They will also have to undergo an interview before they are accredited with official clearance documents.

Thursday 4 July

Dozens killed and Portland hero keeps firing as he dies.

Ninety Junkers Ju.87 "Stukas" today attacked Convoy OA 178 between Portland and Hengistbury Head, sinking the steamship *Elmcrest* and three other vessels. A further nine ships were damaged.

The dive-bombers then turned to the west and attacked Portland Harbour at 08.50 hours, sinking two ships, including the anti-aircraft auxiliary H.M.S. *Foylebank*, moored beside the Admiral's Buoy. The vessel was built by Harland and Wolff at Belfast in 1930.

A dozen "Stuka" dive-bombers came at her and one of the first casualties was 23-year-old Leading Seaman Jack Mantle who went to school at Affpuddle but was recently living in Southampton.

Despite having his legs shattered as bombs tore the ship apart, causing loss of electrical power, he stayed at his

FIRST BOMB: FOR BOURNEMOUTH, SETTING FIRE TO A HOUSE IN CELLARS FARM ROAD, SOUTHBOURNE, ON 3 JULY 1940, ALSO CAUSING RUMOURS THAT GERMAN PARACHUTISTS HAD LANDED

pom-pom and continued firing, even as he suffered further wounds and must have known he was mortally injured. Anti-aircraft fire accounted for one of the "Stukas" which was sent crashing into the harbour. It belonged to Stukageschwader 51 and took with it Leutnant Schwarze and his crewman.

Fifty-nine of Jack Mantle's comrades were also killed and a total of 60 were injured. Somehow one in three, the further lucky 60, came out of it unscathed as the burning vessel turned over and sank.

Perhaps the unluckiest people on Portland today were nine contractors from McAlpine's, who had been digging a tunnel. They sheltered inside it during the raid and came out of it when it was thought to be over; to be killed by the last bomb from a single German aeroplane that turned back from the sea. Four of these workers were boys.

The Luftwaffe has moved its squadrons forward to occupied airfields on the Cherbourg peninsula from where it is little more than 70 miles from the Dorset coast.

Footnote: There were repercussions. The Admiralty closed the English Channel to ocean-going merchant vessels, though coastal convoys would continue.

Jack Mantle would be gazetted on 3 September — the war's first anniversary — with the first Victoria Cross that the Royal Navy had won inside territorial waters. He is buried in Portland Naval Cemetery, on the Verne Common hillside, with the following epitaph: "Because we did not choose to shame the land from which we sprang."

Open-air gatherings were henceforth restricted. Only family mourners were allowed to attend the funerals that resulted from the day's events.

At one of the services the Methodist minister of Fortuneswell, Rev F. Jowett, said: "We owe a tribute of gratitude and affection to the one who has departed. He has given his life for his King and country, and those things for which we Englishmen stand."

They will become common words.

Friday 5 July
E-boats maul remnants of Convoy OA 178.

The survivors of Convoy OA 178, which suffered considerably yesterday from an onslaught of Junkers Ju.87 "Stuka" dive-bombers, were harassed last night by E-boats. The flotilla of German Schnellboote attacked off Poole Bay.

One Allied ship has sunk and two more are damaged.

Footnote: E-boat was the generic term for these craft, being the Anglicised shorthand for the German "Eil-Boot" meaning "Fast Boat". Specifically they were Schnellboote (plural), or Schnellboot (singular), being the German motor torpedo-boat (or S-boat in alternative Anglicised shorthand).

HARBOUR GUNSHIP: FOYLEBANK BEFORE CONVERSION, FOR THE ROYAL NAVY, AS AN ANTI-AIRCRAFT AUXILIARY TO GUARD PORTLAND NAVAL DOCKYARD

Smoking hulk: H.M.S. Foylebank in her death throes left ablaze and sinking by German Ju.87 'Stukas', in Portland Harbour, on 4 July 1940. They had killed 60 of her crew; including Leading Seaman Jack Mantle, for a posthumous Victoria Cross. This would be the first won by the Royal Navy in British territorial waters

Footnote: The bow section was later pulled clear and removed for scrap. The stern and mast, however, remained clearly visible from Weymouth beach until the winter of 1941. The wreck was then blown-up by Navy divers.

Friday 5 July
Bournemouth's piers are blown-up.

In view of their potential use to the enemy, not only for German airborne landings, but also as supply points for any conventional invasion force, the precautionary measure has been taken of "blowing" the seaside piers at Bournemouth and Boscombe. The Royal Engineers today carried out a series of explosions to demolish the central sections of both structures.

The seaward ends — the scene of the famous end-of-the-pier shows — are being left as islands. It is a sad epitaph to those years of joy and a reminder, not that one is needed, of the state of siege that has descended upon southern England. It is going to shock anyone who cherishes memories of those Victorian bathchairs.

Saturday 6 July
Warmwell taken over by Fighter Command.

Fighter aircraft are to be based beside the central Dorset coast in order to counter the Luftwaffe's increasing threat to Channel shipping and in direct response to this week's audacious attack on the Royal Navy base at Portland.

The Deputy Chief of the Air Staff, Air-Vice Marshal W. Sholto Douglas, issued the redeployment order and today R.A.F. Warmwell became a front-line defensive aerodrome with the arrival from R.A.F. Northolt of the Spitfires of 609 (West Riding) Squadron commanded by Squadron Leader Horace Stanley "George" Darley. The aircraft carry the squadron code letters "PR" and their motto is "Tally ho!". They were formed on 10 February 1936.

Control of the grass airfield at Warmwell has been transferred to No. 10 Group of Fighter Command, the headquarters of which are at Rudloe Manor, Box, near Bath.

Warmwell's sector base and home aerodrome is Middle Wallop, near Andover, Hampshire. The pilots return there in the evening and come back to Dorset the following morning.

Friday 5 July — 'Hartlepool' sinks beside Weymouth Harbour entrance.

S.S. *Hartlepool*, a British freighter, has sunk on the north-east side of the entrance to Weymouth Harbour. The vessel had been crippled by German "Stuka" dive-bombers that attacked a convoy in the southern sector of Weymouth Bay.

She was put in tow with the intention of beaching her on Weymouth sands, but shipped too much water and went down in four fathoms, little more than half-a-mile offshore. She lies to the north of the ship-channel into Weymouth Harbour, though less of a navigation hazard than might have been, as her superstructure and mast remain visible at high tide.

SHORT WAR: H.M.S. BRAZEN, IN PORTLAND HARBOUR, WOULD BE AN EARLY CASUALTY. THE GERMANS SANK HER IN THE CHANNEL IN JULY 1940

Scramble time is 15 minutes and the accommodation is tented.

The advent of the eight-gun fighter is revolutionising aerial warfare. There were 187 Spitfires in squadron service on the Sunday when war was declared — by the end of September 4,000 were on order. Their production has the highest priority.

Footnote: There was an inflexible meals timetable at Warmwell that often caused friction and Darley would damn Dorset for its treatment of his men. Once he started the day with a row with the cooks, and had to prepare his own breakfast, breaking off to take to the sky to fight off some "Stukas".

Back on the ground, he rang the Station Commander to say he wished to be spared any thanks "for saving the hangars, personnel, and planes, not to mention the officers' mess and kitchens".

Lance Corporal Tony Hollister, from Bovington, witnessed a gratuitous insult from an ex-Indian Army major to a couple of Warmwell pilots.

"Take your bloody hands out of your pockets and salute a senior officer," he bellowed. They proceeded to deflate him with unprintable public school drawl. There used to be a simple phrase for causing apoplexy amongst such persons: "I always regarded the terrorists as the cream of Bengal."

Sunday 7 July
Top-brass visit to Christchurch Aerodrome.

The Special Duty Flight, based at Christchurch Aerodrome and fulfilling the aviation needs of the Air Ministry's Telecommunications Research Establishment scientists, today received a top-brass visit.

Air Marshal Arthur William Tedder, the Director-General of Research and Development, was accompanied by Air Vice-Marshal Roderic Maxwell Hill who is Director of Technical Development for the Air Ministry and Ministry of Aircraft Production.

Footnote: Hill would be promoted into Tedder's job, on the latter's posting to the Middle East, later in the year.

Tuesday 9 July
Warmwell pilot and 'Stuka' leader killed off Portland.

Dive-bombers attacked Channel shipping off Portland this evening and 609 Squadron was scrambled from R.A.F. Warmwell. Three of its Spitfires closed in on two

Junkers Ju.87 "Stukas" but then at least nine Messerschmitt Bf.110s pounced on the British fighters from above and behind them.

These attacking aircraft were spotted by Pilot Officer David Moore Crook in Spitfire P9322, "PR" L for London. He yelled a radio warning to his two companions.

Pilot officer Michael Appleby had just switched his set from transmit, in time to hear the word "Messerschmitts", and pulled his Spitfire clear.

The third Spitfire, flown by Pilot Officer Peter Drummond-Hay, must still have had its radio on transmission mode and was lost in the action, over the sea south of Portland Bill. The pilot is missing, presumed dead.

Then, David Crook writes, in his combat report: "I found myself very near to a Ju.87 so stalked it through cloud and when it emerged into clear sky I fired all the rest of my ammunition at very close range. He turned over a dived in flames into the sea."

The dive-bomber was piloted by Hauptmann Friedrich-Karl Freiherr von Dalwigk zu Lichtenfels, the 33-year-old Staffelkapitän of I Gruppe, Stukageschwader 77. Their code markings are S2.

Footnote: Writing his memoirs, published as *Spitfire Pilot* in 1942, David Moore Crook recalled the interception and his thoughts on achieving his first kill: "I saw dimly a machine moving in the cloud to my left and flying parallel to me. I stalked him through the cloud, and when he emerged into a patch of clear sky I saw that it was a Ju.87. I was in an ideal position to attack and opened fire and put the remainder of my ammunition — about 2,000 rounds — into him at very close range. Even in the heat of the moment I well remember my amazement at the shattering effect of my fire. Pieces flew off his fuselage and the cockpit covering, a stream of smoke appeared from the engine cowling and he dived down vertically. The flames enveloped the whole machine and he went straight down, apparently quite slowly, for about 5,000 feet, till he was just a shapeless burning mass of wreckage.

"Absolutely fascinated by the sight, I followed him down, and saw him hit the sea with a great burst of white foam. He disappeared immediately, and apart from a green patch in the water there was no sign that anything had happened. The crew made no attempt to get out, and they were obviously killed by my first burst of fire.

"I had often wondered what would be my feelings when killing somebody like this, and especially when seeing

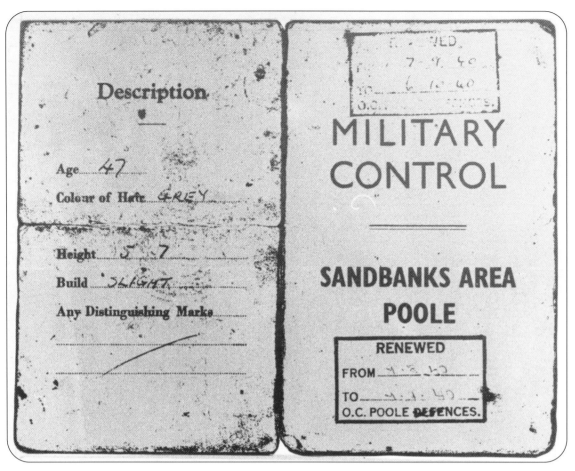

POOLE PASSPORT: ISSUED TO GARAGE PROPRIETRESS MRS LOUISA DINGWALL ON 6 JULY 1940 WHEN SHORE ROAD, SANDBANKS, WAS BLOCKED BY A CONTROL POINT

First casualty: the initial German loss of the Battle of Britain which was brought down to land on 11 July 1940, at Povington Heath, to the north of the Purbeck Hills at Tyneham. The Messerschmitt Bf.110 belonged to the III Gruppe, Zerstörergeschwader 76

them go down in flames. I was rather surprised to reflect afterwards that my only feeling had been one of considerable elation — and a sort of bewildering surprise because it had been so easy."

Von Dalwigk had joined the Luftwaffe in 1933. He would be posthumously awarded the Knight's Cross on 21 July 1940.

David Crook made "a perfectly bloody landing" at Warmwell and returned to R.A.F. Middle Wallop shortly before dusk: "We got back and I went to my room in the mess. Everything was just the same as Peter and I had left it only 18 hours before; his novel was still in the window where he had thrown it during our hurried dressing. But he was dead now. I simply could not get used to such sudden and unexpected death, and there flashed across my mind the arrangements we had made to go up to London the following day. It all seemed so ironical, so tragic, so futile.

"I felt that I could not sleep in that room again, and so I took my things and went into Gordon's bed next door and slept there." It was unoccupied; Gordon Mitchell had been grounded with a damaged Spitfire and was spending the night in a tent at Warmwell. "But I could not get out of my head the thought of Peter, with whom we had been talking and laughing that day, now lying in the cockpit of his wrecked Spitfire at the bottom of the English Channel."

There would be more grief. "It was the last time I ever saw him," he writes of Gordon. Another friend, "Pip"

Barran, answered the telephone to find it was Peter's wife: "The telegram had not yet reached here, and so Pip had to tell her the news. It all seemed so awful; I was seeing for the first time at very close quarters all the distress and unhappiness that casualties cause. I walked out of the mess and drove to the station, very thankful to be doing something that took my mind on to other subjects. And I never saw Pip again, either."

Gordon Mitchell and Pip Barran would have their tragedies on 11 July 1940.

Tuesday 9 July
Poole now a sealed-off town.

Poole is now part of the Defence Area, with access restricted to those who have an acceptable reason for entering the town, under a regulation signed by Regional Controller Harold Butler.

Wednesday 10 July
Poole flying-boat arrives in Sydney.

The British Empire's air link resumed today with the arrival in Sydney of a B.O.A.C. flying-boat from Poole. Another has reached Durban. They both flew a horseshoe-shaped route to Lisbon and then across the southern Sahara.

From here the Australian plane turned northwards, via Khartoum and Cairo, to join the usual peacetime flight-path across Palestine, the Persian Gulf, India, and Malaya.

FIRST PRISONER: OBERLEUTNANT GERHARD KADOW, WHO CRASHED ON POVINGTON HEATH, TYNEHAM, ON 11 JULY 1940

The other route, to South Africa, is via Lagos and Leopoldville.

Thursday 11 July

Anti-glider precautions erected at Poole.

Among the various anti-landing traps being laid to discourage enemy glider forces are rows of telegraph poles which are being cut into sections and dug into the fairways of Parkstone golf links and across Branksome playing fields. The poles are ten feet apart and form parallel rows every hundred yards.

Thursday 11 July

Two more Warmwell losses.

Two more Spitfires from R.A.F. Warmwell's 609 Squadron have been lost in action over the English Channel while fighting off a "Stuka" bombardment of a convoy of British merchant ships.

The attacks took place in Lyme Bay, involving 50 enemy aircraft, and 609 Squadron went to the aid of the hard-pressed Hurricanes from R.A.F. Exeter which had battled alone against an attack earlier in the day by 20 bombers and 40 fighters. The steam-yacht *Warrior II* was sunk in this first attack and another ship was damaged in the second raid.

The two Spitfire pilots who have failed to return to Warmwell are Flying Officer Philip Henry "Pip" Barran in L1096 and Pilot Officer Gordon Thomas Manners Mitchell in L1095. Barran was picked up from the sea, five miles off Portland Bill, but was badly wounded and burnt, dying before he could be brought ashore. He was aged 31.

Mitchell, a 29-year-old Cambridge hockey blue and Scots international, is missing, presumed dead. He was last seen diving into the attack but nobody saw him again. They bring the squadron's Dorset losses to three, in the past 36 hours, in flights in which the Spitfires found themselves hopelessly outnumbered.

Pilot Officer David Moore Crook, returning from leave in Hampstead to the Operations Room at R.A.F. Middle Wallop, heard that the rest of the squadron was in the air and fighting over the South Coast. He put the day's events into perspective in notes which will become a book: "When one thinks of the losses sustained in war, particularly by the Army, to lose three people seems very trifling. But in a squadron there are so few pilots, and it really seems more like a large family than anything else, and therefore three deaths at once seems very heavy indeed. If Gordon's death was a greater blow to me personally, Pip's death was a terrible blow for the squadron. He was more than a mere member of the squadron; you might almost say that he was the foundation stone upon which it was first formed and built."

Footnote: Pip Barran is buried at Leeds Cemetery, where his family owned a colliery and brickworks, and Gordon Mitchell's body would be washed ashore near Newport, Isle of Wight. He was buried at All Saints' Church, Letchworth, Hertfordshire, on 25 July 1940.

Thursday 11 July

Hurricane shot down off Portland Bill.

Sergeant-Pilot Frederick John Powell Dixon, in Hurricane N2485 of 501 Squadron from R.A.F. Middle Wallop, was shot down at 08.00 hours today while trying

to defend shipping ten miles south-east of Portland Bill. He baled out but is presumed to have drowned. The Weymouth lifeboat spent hours searching for him in vain.

Footnote: The kill was claimed by Oberleutnant Franziket of III Gruppe, Zerstörergeschwader 76. Frederick Dixon had drowned; his body was recovered off France and is buried in the extension to Abbeville Communal Cemetery. He was 21.

Thursday 11 July
Tyneham Germans are first flyers taken prisoner.

Hurricanes of 238 Squadron from Middle Wallop have claimed the double distinction of being the first R.A.F. unit to bring down a German aircraft on Dorset soil, thereby delivering the first Germans to be taken prisoner in the current conflict [which became known as the Battle of Britain].

The two enemy flyers were in Messerschmitt Bf.110C (2N+EP) which came down at 12.05 hours on Povington Heath, in the parish of Tyneham between East Lulworth and East Holme, who survived a crash-landing. They are Oberleutnant Gerhard Kadow, pilot, and Gefreiter Helmut Scholz, gunner, of III Gruppe, Zerstörergeschwader 76.

They flew from Laval, with a refuelling stop at Dinard, and were among the fighters escorting Junkers Ju.87 "Stuka" dive-bombers that attacked Channel shipping off Portland.

Premier's visit: Winston Churchill (above and opposite) inspects coast defences at Sandbanks on 17 July 1940. It was the day after Hitler issued his directive ordering preparations for landings in England. These photographs sum up the national spirit of resistance, as expressed by Churchill to Parliament on 4 June 1940 with the best war speech this side of Shakespeare: "We shall defend our island, whatever the cost may be, we shall fight on the beaches, we shall fight on the landing grounds, we shall fight in the fields and in the streets, we shall fight in the hills; we shall never surrender . . ."

Their twin-engine aeroplane has twisted propellers and a dented underside but is otherwise undamaged. The pilot failed in an attempt to set it ablaze.

Thursday 11 July
Göring's nephew among three other German losses.

Luftwaffe losses off Portland include a Junkers Ju.87B of 11/LG 1 shot down at 11.30 hours by Flight-Lieutenant Sir Archibald Hope, in a Hurricane of 601 Squadron from R.A.F. Tangmere. His colleagues claimed a Messerchmitt Bf.110C of III Gruppe, Zerstörergeschwader 76, killing Oberleutnant H. D. Göring — nephew of the Commander-in-Chief of the Luftwaffe — and crewman Unterofficer Zimmerman.

They completed the hat-trick when Flight Lieutenant Hugh Joseph Riddle claimed a third of the credit in destroying another Messerchmitt Bf.110C, with pilot Leutnant Schroder and his crewman. This was a multi-squadron kill for a pack of Hurricanes, with Wing Commander John Scatliff "Johnny" Dewar, of 87 Squadron from R.A.F. Exeter, plus the Green Section of 238 Squadron from R.A.F. Middle Wallop contributing their gunfire.

Footnote: A fourth bomber, a Junkers Ju.87B of 11/LG 1, was damaged by Sergeant-Pilot Leonard Northwood Guy, in a Hurricane of 601 Squadron from Tangmere. It managed to limp back across the Channel and force-landed at St Inglevert.

Friday 12 July
More Spitfires sent to Warmwell.

An unblooded support squadron, 152 (Hyderabad) Squadron, has flown into Warmwell Aerodrome, led by Squadron Leader Peter Devitt who learnt to fly at the age of 19 in 1930. Their markings are "UM" and motto "Faithful ally". The squadron is equipped with Spitfires and had its practice flights in the north of England.

It was originally formed on 1 October 1918 and has been operating from Acklington Aerodrome, Northumberland, since 2 October 1939.

Friday 12 July
Northumberland Fusiliers prepare Bournemouth's defences.

Veterans of Dunkirk, the 4th Battalion of the Royal Northumberland Fusiliers have arrived in Bournemouth, after a short stay at Yeovil followed by a few days in tents at Piddlehinton.

On the seaside they will be taking over coastal defences from the Royal Artillery and will lay mines and erect wood, steel, and concrete anti-invasion obstacles.

Saturday 13 July — '**Stay put if the Germans invade**' — **mayors order.**

Learning from the chaos brought to Belgium and France by refugees blocking the roads in the hours that preceded the arrival of German troops, the three mayors of the Bournemouth conurbation have emphasised that there is to be no civilian evacuation if the enemy invades.

All major roads would be sealed-off for the use of the Army and if the enemy comes he will in the Bournemouth area take on the burden of an army of occupation with a quarter of a million population to control and support. Resistance will continue from the "Fighting Boxes" garrisoned by upwards of 50 armed men, and in some cases 200 or more.

These, it is said, are "fortified, supplied, and organised to withstand siege without outside assistance".

Saturday 13 July
German aircraft suffer in dog-fights off Portland.

Spitfires from 609 Squadron, whilst flying a convoy protection patrol over the English Channel, today encountered German aircraft at 15,000 feet, off Portland. Flying Officer John Charles Dundas, in R6634, came out of the sun at a Messerschmitt Bf.110 which he claimed to have destroyed, and had a dog-fight with other German fighter-bombers. He then landed back at R.A.F. Warmwell.

Meanwhile, Radipole-born Pilot Officer Rogers Freeman Garland "Mick" Miller, in Spitfire L1065 of 609 Squadron, took on and damaged a Bf.110, and then found a Dornier Do.17P, a photo-reconnaissance aircraft, of 2(F)/123. The coup de grâce for the latter was executed by the Hurricanes of 238 Squadron from Middle Wallop on the Hampshire Downs. Leutnant Weinbauer and Oberleutnant Graf von Kesselstadt attempted to land it on the Chesil Beach, close to the oil-tanks on Portland, but the aircraft slid into the sea.

Footnote: Dundas's claimed Bf.110 kill was not in fact destroyed but managed to struggle back to France.

As for the Dornier, Harry Buckley of Buckland House, Buckland Ripers, recalled that wreckage was recovered from the water at the time, and would find some himself more than half a century later: "Strangely enough, in the spring of 1997, I picked-up a radial engine piston and a condensing rod at the spot of the crash. They had been washed ashore."

Saturday 13 July
Australian Hurricane pilot killed at Preston.

Australian volunteer, 23-year-old Flying Officer John Connelly Kennedy, from Sydney, was killed today at South Down, above Chalbury Lodge, at Preston, near Weymouth. Hurricane P2950 of 238 Squadron, from R.A.F. Middle Wallop, was watched by an observer by telescope, who reported: "It was flying slowly north at about 1,500 feet and the cockpit cover was slid back. Suddenly as I watched it nosed down and crashed into the ground almost vertically. The crash was at the top of South Down Hill."

It is thought that Kennedy may have been wounded by return fire during the afternoon encounter over the Chesil Beach in which a damaged Dornier Do.17 (4U+DK) was intercepted and finished off by 238 Squadron. He is presumed to have been heading from the scene of that encounter towards Warmwell Aerodrome.

If this was the case, it raises the question of why he was flying north, rather than north-east. Had he been looking for somewhere to put down, the obvious place would have been the wide marsh at Lodmoor, over which he had just flown.

As for the German aircraft, the identification markings on the Dornier indicate that it belonged to a reconnaissance unit; the 2nd Staffel of Aufklärungsgruppe 123.

Footnote: Flying Officer Kennedy is buried in the R.A.F. plot at Warmwell churchyard. His crash site has been wrongly recorded in historical accounts, which have moved it to Little Mayne Farm, West Knighton, where he is said to have flown into power cables.

Tuesday 16 July
'I have decided to prepare a landing against England.'

Luftwaffe "Enigma" machine-coded radio messages are today carrying a directive from Hitler. The translation of the deciphered intercept, passed to Prime Minister Churchill by the Government's Code and Cipher School, reads: "I have decided to prepare a landing operation against England and if necessary to carry it out."

The cryptographic headquarters, at Bletchley Park, Buckinghamshire, is headed by Commander Alexander Dennison and forms a department of M.I.6, the Secret Intelligence Service.

Wednesday 17 July
Churchill lays bricks on the Dorset invasion coast.

Winston Churchill today saw the invasion precautions along the most vulnerable beaches of the South Coast when he inspected units at Branksome Chine and Sandbanks. He showed his skill as a bricklayer at Branksome with a practical contribution to the defences that are taking shape.

While driving to Dorset from Gosport, the Prime Minister recalled to General Alan Brooke, the chief of Southern Command, that it was from the rustic bridge at Alum Chine that he had fallen 20 feet in 1892, at the age of 17, and very nearly plunged to his death. He was unconscious for many days.

They dined at the Armoured Fighting Vehicles School, at Bovington Camp, and were taken to Wool Station for 20.00 hours and Churchill's train back to London.

Brooke is less than confident with what he has seen, as he confides tonight to his diary: "What has been going on in this country since the war started? The ghastly part is that I feel certain that we can only have a few more weeks before the Boche attacks." For all that, he admitted, it was imperative to "maintain a confident exterior".

Footnote: Brooke was unimpressed by his men's equipment and means but Churchill realised he had a considerable asset in Brooke — two days later he was promoted Commander-in-Chief Home Forces. On Christmas Day in 1941 he became Chief of the Imperial General Staff.

Thursday 18 July
Warmwell celebrates revenge.

Warmwell's Spitfire pilots have returned with their first undisputed kills. Two German aircraft have been shot down, with the honours shared by 152 Squadron and 609 Squadron, thereby restoring the latter's morale after their own recent losses. The engagement over Lyme Bay was the first action for newly-arrived 152 Squadron.

Flight-Lieutenant Edward Sidney Hogg claimed the destruction of a Dornier Do.17M bomber of the Staff Flight of Kampfgeschwader 77 which had been attacking Channel shipping. Oberleutnant Strecker and his three crewmen were killed.

On the debit side, 609 Squadron has lost another Spitfire, and has a second machine awash on a beach, but this time both pilots are safe. Flight-Lieutenant Frank Jonathan Howell parachuted into the sea from Spitfire R6634 during a mid-afternoon dog-fight five miles from Swanage. He had been shot down by a Junkers Ju.88. A Royal Navy launch picked him up.

The Navy then found Flying Officer Alexander Rothwell Edge on Studland beach. He had brought Spitfire R6636 down on the sands after Junkers' machine-gun fire had smashed his engine cooling system. As the tide came in the fighter was covered by the sea.

Footnote: R6636 was salvaged and would fly again.

Saturday 20 July
Three R.A.F. fighters shot down off Swanage.

Pilot Officer Frederick Hyam Posener, a 23-year-old South African volunteer, has been shot down in an engagement with enemy aircraft off Swanage. He is the fourth Spitfire pilot from R.A.F. Warmwell to be killed this month.

He was flying K9880 with 152 Squadron, which only yesterday flew its first operational sortie from Warmwell Aerodrome.

The same action, over the English Channel 15 miles south of Durlston Head, has critically injured 25-year-old Sergeant Pilot Cecil Parkinson. He was flying Hurricane P3766 of 238 Squadron, from R.A.F. Middle Wallop, which was shot down in flames. Though Parkinson baled out, and was picked-up by the destroyer H.M.S. *Acheron*, he is suffering extensive burns.

A third R.A.F. fighter was also lost over the sea between Purbeck and the Cherbourg peninsula. Pilot Officer Edmund John Hilary Sylvester, in a Hurricane of 501 Squadron which has recently returned from France, has been claimed by Leutnant Zirkenbach of I Gruppe, Jagdgeschwader 27. He was aged 26.

Issued by the Ministry of Information in co-operation with the War Office
and the Ministry of Home Security

Beating the INVADER

A MESSAGE FROM THE PRIME MINISTER

IF invasion comes, everyone—young or old, men and women—will be eager to play their part worthily. By far the greater part of the country will not be immediately involved. Even along our coasts, the greater part will remain unaffected. But where the enemy lands, or tries to land, there will be most violent fighting. Not only will there be the battles when the enemy tries to come ashore, but afterwards there will fall upon his lodgments very heavy British counter-attacks, and all the time the lodgments will be under the heaviest attack by British bombers. The fewer civilians or non-combatants in these areas, the better—apart from essential workers who must remain. So if you are advised by the authorities to leave the place where you live, it is your duty to go elsewhere when you are told to leave. When the attack begins, it will be too late to go ; and, unless you receive definite instructions to move, your duty then will be to stay where you are. You will have to get into the safest place you can find, and stay there until the battle is over. For all of you then the order and the duty will be : " STAND FIRM ".

This also applies to people inland if any considerable number of parachutists or air-borne troops are landed in their neighbourhood. **Above all, they must not cumber the roads.** Like their fellow-countrymen on the coasts, they must " STAND FIRM " The Home Guard, supported by strong mobile columns wherever the enemy's numbers require it, will immediately come to grips with the invaders, and there is little doubt will soon destroy them.

Throughout the rest of the country where there is no fighting going on and no close cannon fire or rifle fire can be heard, everyone will govern his conduct by the second great order and **duty,** namely, " CARRY ON ". It may easily be some weeks before the invader has been totally destroyed, that is to say, killed or captured to the last man who has landed on our shores. Meanwhile, all work must be continued to the utmost, and no time lost.

The following notes have been prepared to tell everyone in rather more detail what to do, and they should be carefully studied. Each man and woman should think out a clear plan of personal action in accordance with the general scheme.

Winston S. Churchill

STAND FIRM

I. What do I do if fighting breaks out in my neighbourhood ?

Keep indoors or in your shelter until the battle is over. If you can have a trench ready in your garden or field, so much the better. You may want to use it for protection if your house is damaged. But if you are at work, or if you have special orders, carry on as long as possible and only take cover when danger approaches. If you are on your way to work, finish your journey if you can.

If you see an enemy tank, or a few enemy soldiers, do not assume that the enemy are in control of the area. What you have seen may be a party sent on in advance, or stragglers from the main body who can easily be rounded up.

CARRY ON

2. What do I do in areas which are some way from the fighting?

Stay in your district and carry on. Go to work whether in shop, field, factory or office. Do your shopping, send your children to school until you are told not to. Do not try to go and live somewhere else. Do not use the roads for any unnecessary journey; they must be left free for troop movements even a long way from the district where actual fighting is taking place.

3. Will certain roads and railways be reserved for the use of the Military, even in areas far from the scene of action?

Yes, certain roads will have to be reserved for important troop movements; but such reservations should be only temporary. As far as possible, bus companies and railways will try to maintain essential public services, though it may be necessary to cut these down. Bicyclists and pedestrians may use the roads for journeys to work, unless instructed not to do so.

ADVICE AND ORDERS

4. Whom shall I ask for advice?

The police and A.R.P. wardens.

5. From whom shall I take orders?

In most cases from the police and A.R.P. wardens. But there may be times when you will have to take orders from the military and the Home Guard in uniform.

6. Is there any means by which I can tell that an order is a true order and not faked?

You will generally know your policeman and your A.R.P. wardens by sight, and can trust them. With a bit of common sense you can tell if a soldier is really British or only pretending to be so. If in doubt ask a policeman, or ask a soldier whom you know personally.

INSTRUCTIONS

7. What does it mean when the church bells are rung?

It is a warning to the local garrison that troops have been seen landing from the air in the neighbourhood of the church in question. Church bells will *not* be rung all over the country as a general warning that invasion has taken place. The ringing of church bells in one place will not be taken up in neighbouring churches.

8. Will instructions be given over the wireless?

Yes; so far as possible. But remember that the enemy can overhear any wireless message, so that the wireless cannot be used for instructions which might give him valuable information.

9. In what other ways will instructions be given?

Through the Press; by loudspeaker vans; and perhaps by leaflets and posters. But remember that genuine Government leaflets will be given to you only by the policeman, your A.R.P. warden or your postman; while genuine posters and instructions will be put up only on Ministry of Information notice boards and official sites, such as police stations, post offices, A.R.P. posts, town halls and schools.

FOOD

10. Should I try to lay in extra food?

No. If you have already laid in a stock of food, keep it for a real emergency; but do not add to it. The Government has made arrangements for food supplies.

NEWS

11. Will normal news services continue?

Yes. Careful plans have been made to enable newspapers and wireless broadcasts to carry on, and in case of need there are emergency measures which will bring you the news. But if there should be some temporary breakdown in news supply, it is very important that you should not listen to rumours nor pass them on, but should wait till real news comes through again. Do not use the telephones or send telegrams if you can possibly avoid it.

MOTOR-CARS

12. Should I put my car, lorry or motor-bicycle out of action?

Yes, when you are told to do so by the police, A.R.P. wardens or military; or when it is obvious that there is an immediate risk of its being seized by the enemy—then disable and hide your bicycle and destroy your maps.

13. How should it be put out of action?

Remove distributor head and leads and either empty the tank or remove the carburettor. If you don't know how to do this, find out now from your nearest garage. In the case of diesel engines remove the injection pump and connection. The parts removed must be hidden well away from the vehicle.

THE ENEMY

14. Should I defend myself against the enemy?

The enemy is not likely to turn aside to attack separate houses. If small parties are going about threatening persons and property in an area not under enemy control and come your way, you have the right of every man and woman to do what you can to protect yourself, your family and your home.

GIVE ALL THE HELP YOU CAN TO OUR TROOPS

Do not tell the enemy anything

Do not give him anything

Do not help him in any way

(55001) Wt. 46381/P1009 14,050,800 (2 kds.) 5/41 Hw. G.51

INVASION 1940: LONE SOLDIER AND BARBED WIRE AT SEATOWN, NEAR BRIDPORT, WITH GOLDEN CAP — THE HIGHEST CLIFF ON THE SOUTH COAST — IN THE BACKGROUND. THIS PICTURE WAS CAPTIONED "THE SCOTTISH COAST" WHEN RELEASED TO THE PRESS; NOT JUST TO CONCEAL THE LOCATION BUT BECAUSE THE PREPARATIONS WERE LESS THAN ADEQUATE FOR WHAT MIGHT BE NEEDED IN CENTRAL SOUTHERN ENGLAND

Footnote: Cecil Parkinson died from his injuries the following day. He is buried in St Michael's churchyard, Stoke, which is now a suburb of Coventry.

Sunday 21 July
Hurricanes shoot down Dornier at Blandford.

The Hurricanes of 238 Squadron, from R.A.F. Middle Wallop, have claimed the Dornier Do.17P (5F+OM) which was shot down at 15.00 hours over Nutford Farm, Pimperne, a mile north of Blandford. Its three crew were wounded in the crash and taken into the farmhouse before being driven to hospital.

The "5F" identification markings on the fuselage of the enemy aircraft indicate that it belonged to reconnaissance unit Aufklärungsgruppe 14. The normal crew for a Dornier bomber is four. In a reconnaissance role, however, it carries three — as they leave out the bomb aimer.

Sunday 21 July
Norwegian tanker ablaze off Swanage.

Swanage Coastguard reported a vessel on fire, about ten miles out in the English Channel directly south of

Durlston Head, at 18.15 hours this evening. The lifeboat *Thomas Markby* was launched at 18.27 from the slipway at Peveril Point and made good speed in a light sea.

She headed towards the distant smoke and found the Norwegian tanker *Kollskegg* burning towards the bow after being dive-bombed by the Luftwaffe. Her crew had already been taken off by a British destroyer. The lifeboat waited until a dockyard tug arrived on the scene to take the tanker in tow, and then sent a party aboard, to assist in fastening the lines.

Monday 22 July
No. 4 Commando formed at Weymouth.

No. 4 Commando, which was formed in Weymouth earlier this month, today held its first parade, followed by the commanding officer's opening address, which was given in the Pavilion on the Esplanade.

Footnote: Though it would spend only a few weeks training in south Dorset in the summer of 1940, the battalion returned to the Weymouth area in August 1942, to prepare for the Dieppe Raid.

Wednesday 24 July

400 killed in liner torpedoed off Portland.

The Vichy French liner *Meknes* has sunk after being torpedoed by German submarine *U572* off Portland. She was carrying 1,100 neutral French sailors, of whom 400 are estimated to have perished.

Thursday 25 July

Two German planes and Spitfire shot down.

Squadron Leader Peter Devitt today led the Spitfires of 152 Squadron from Warmwell in their second successful interception. Calling "Tally ho!" — the hunting motto of their sister squadron — and hearing an "Achtung, Spitfire" response, his fighters attacked a Dornier Do.17 of Staff Flight of

UNARMED COMBAT: LOOKING PAINFULLY REAL IN MILITARY TRAINING TAKING PLACE IN THE TENNIS COURT OF THE SANDBANKS HOTEL, BANKS ROAD, POOLE. ITS NAME HAS BEEN REMOVED IN ACCORDANCE WITH DEFENCE REGULATIONS

Kampfgeschwader 1 which was accompanied by a group of Junkers Ju.87 "Stuka" dive-bombers, passing over Portland.

The Dornier crashed at 11.23 hours at East Fleet Farm, Fleet, near Weymouth, killing one of the crew. A second man broke a leg and was taken to Weymouth Hospital. The pilot, who only suffered bruises, recovered in John Nobbs's farmhouse. He passed Players cigarettes to his captors; they had been looted in France. He was eventually sent to Warmwell.

As that drama was being acted out on the ground one of the "Stukas" was seen to be streaming smoke and dropping towards the sea.

Both kills were claimed by Sergeant-Pilot Ralph "Bob" Wolton, flying "UM" F for Freddie, with the coup de

grâce to the Dornier being delivered by Flying Officer Edward Christopher "Jumbo" Deanesly. He then went after the stricken "Stuka" at 11.30 hours but received some return fire and ended up baling out wounded, as Spitfire K9901 crashed into the sea, five miles south of Portland Bill.

Deanesly was picked-up by the S.S. *Empire Henchman* and dropped off at Lyme Regis. He was taken to hospital for treatment to a minor injury.

Friday 26 July

E-boats sink three ships off Dorset.

An E-boat Flotilla, comprising three German motor torpedo boats — Schnellboote *S19, S20,* and *S27* — have sunk three merchant vessels in attacks in the Channel between Portland and the Isle of Wight.

Saturday 27 July

609 Squadron loses fourth pilot, off Weymouth.

Losses resumed for 609 Squadron today when 25-year-old Pilot Officer James Richebourg "Buck" Buchanan, leading Green Section in Spitfire N3023 from R.A.F. Warmwell, lost his life in combat over Weymouth Bay. His fighter, on a convoy protection sweep, was attacked by a group of Messerschmitt Bf.109s after he apparently spotted a Junkers Ju.87 and dived down through broken clouds to attack it. Two other Spitfires, guarding his tail, lost sight of him and could do nothing to help.

Footnote: The kill was claimed by Oberleutnant Framm of I Gruppe, Jagdgeschwader 27. Buchanan's body was not recovered.

BAYONET PRACTICE: INTO DUMMIES IN THE DUNES AT THE REAR OF SANDBANKS HOTEL (SINCE BUILT UPON)

Saturday 27 July
Admiralty bans Channel convoys.

Reviewing the unacceptable rate of losses amongst merchant shipping in the waters between Dorset and the Cherbourg peninsula, the Admiralty today suspended coastal convoys in the English Channel.

Thirty-six merchant ships have been sunk this month, five of them when Convoy CW8 was mauled by Junkers Ju.87 "Stuka" dive-bombers. Three Royal Navy destroyers have now been lost in the English Channel and the North Sea.

Monday 29 July
Destroyer loss shock — Germans have radar.

H.M.S. *Delight*, a 1,375-ton destroyer of the "Defender" class was today dive-bombed by Junkers Ju.87 "Stukas" and set on fire 20 miles south of Portland Bill. She has been left a floating wreck but is to be put in tow and brought into Portland Harbour.

Footnote: Shortly after she was attacked an intercepted German radio message in the "Enigma" code was deciphered by the British Code and Cipher School at Bletchley Park, Buckinghamshire. It stated that the warship "had been sunk with the aid of Freya reports".

"Freya" was clearly the codename for some device. Her name was plucked from Norse mythology and Dr Reginald Jones, head of scientific intelligence at the Air Ministry, had already heard of "Freya Gerät" (Freya apparatus).

Jones writes in his memoirs that seeing a mention of "Freya-Meldung" (Freya reporting) on 5 July he had bought a book on myths from Foyle's and found that "Freya was the Nordic Venus who had not merely sacrificed but massacred her honour to gain possession of a magic necklace, Brisingamen, This necklace was guarded by Heimdall, the watchman of the Gods, who could see a hundred miles by day or night."

CLIFF EXERCISES: THE 12TH BATTALION OF THE HAMPSHIRE REGIMENT SCALING THE SANDY SLOPES OF HENGISTBURY HEAD, BOURNEMOUTH, WITH THEIR OBJECTIVE BEING ITS COAST DEFENCE BATTERY (above) OF THE ROYAL ARTILLERY

The last phrase is the crucial one — making Heimdall a wholly appropriate code for radar, though rather too obvious. Freya was chosen, by association, in its place. Either way, the German obsession with things Nordic would compromise their security.

Twelve days before the loss of *Delight*, on 17 July, Jones had used this reasoning to predict the existence "of a coastal chain and detecting system with a range of a hundred miles". The sinking of the destroyer removed any possibility that Freya was detecting associated objects in the sky — for *Delight* had neither balloon protection nor a fighter escort.

"The apparatus must have been able to detect her directly," Jones concluded. It appeared to be sited

FIRING PROCEDURES: TO A PAINTED BACKDROP OF PINES AND TELEGRAPH POLES, IN A REALISTIC REPRESENTATION OF THE ROAD ACROSS THE HEATH FROM WAREHAM, FOR A SIMULATED DEMONSTRATION AT THE GUNNERY WING OF THE ARMOURED FIGHTING VEHICLES SCHOOL AT LULWORTH CAMP

near the village of Auderville on the Hague peninsula north-west of Cherbourg, but it had to be very different from our own coastal chain stations, since it was completely undetectable on the best air photographs that we possessed of the area.

"This confirmed the idea that Freya was a fairly small apparatus which had already been suggested by the fact that it had been set up so quickly after the Germans had occupied the Channel coast."

The story would resume in February 1941 with the picking up of a German radar signal on St Alban's Head by a scientist from the nearby Telecommunications Research Establishment, at Worth Matravers.

Monday 29 July
Admiralty bars Channel to daytime destroyers.

The English Channel has been placed off-limits to destroyers in daytime as a result of the loss earlier today of H.M.S. *Delight*, 20 miles south of Portland Bill. It brings to four the losses of Royal Navy destroyers in the English Channel and southern North Sea so far this month — the others being H.M.S. *Brazen* (in the Straits of Dover), H.M.S. *Codrington* (Port of Dover) and H.M.S. *Wren* (Aldeburgh).

Tuesday 30 July
Burnt-out destroyer sinks in Portland Harbour.

In the early hours today the burnt-out hulk of the destroyer H.M.S. *Delight*, crippled in yesterday's air attack, sank in Portland Harbour. She had been put in tow and brought in by a dockyard tug. The vessel was so badly damaged, had she remained afloat, that she would have been scrapped.

Tuesday 30 July
Fighter Command chief visits Christchurch.

Air Chief Marshal Sir Hugh Dowding, Air Officer Commander-in-Chief at Fighter Command, today visited the Special Duty Flight at Christchurch Aerodrome for a briefing on their top-secret work for the Telecommunications Research Establishment.

During July
Warmwell is R.A.F. station 'XW'.

R.A.F. Warmwell in the centre of south Dorset, at 207-feet above sea level on a featureless gravel plain four miles east-south-east of Dorchester, has been issued with the pundit code "XW". This is being displayed in huge white

letters, ten-feet high, and will also be flashed in Morse code at night, in red light, from a mobile beacon.

During July
3,500 mines laid in Ringstead Bay.

As an example of the extent of the efforts being made to deny the enemy landing space on vulnerable South Coast beaches, a total of 3,500 mines have now been laid along just one mile of beach and low cliffs at Ringstead Bay. Similar quantities are being buried in the shingle and sands of Kimmeridge, Worbarrow, Swanage, Studland, Bournemouth, and Barton-on-Sea.

During July
Home Guard cover-up the Cerne Giant.

Members of the Home Guard have dragged scrub and branches across the hillside north of Cerne Abbas to conceal the famous 180-feet high chalk-cut figure of a naked man that is etched into the turf of the Dorset Downs. It was considered that this ancient curiosity, known as the Cerne Giant, might be of practical use as a navigation marker for German aircraft, particularly any making northward across the Dorset coast from Portland towards Bristol.

Likewise the prominent Cornish marble obelisk on Ballard Down, above Swanage, has been toppled. It was originally a lamp standard in central London.

Local authority workmen are busily digging up milestones and taking down road signs so that Germans invaders will not find their routes spelt out on the ground. At Hazelbury Bryan the village name has been erased from a charity-bequest panel hanging in the church porch.

It will still, however, be relatively easy to identify the major conurbation as it would be impractical to remove all clues, such as the hundreds of cast-iron drain covers that proclaim "COUNTY BOROUGH OF BOURNEMOUTH".

During July
Poole camouflage requests rejected.

The Air Ministry has turned down requests from Dorset County Council for the camouflaging of prominent buildings in Poole, saying that this would make attacks more likely: "Low flying aircraft would easily see these buildings even if they were camouflaged, and, if they were seen to be camouflaged they would be taken to be more important targets than they really were. Thus camouflaging them would attract attack rather than avoid it."

During July
'British Resistance' guerrilla hideouts in Dorset.

Thirty-two underground hideouts have been secretly established by the Royal Engineers in woods and commons scattered through the Dorset countryside to conceal the weapons, explosives, and food necessary for Auxiliary Units of British Resistance to operate behind German lines in the event of an invasion.

This is considered most likely to take place on the sandy beaches between Studland Bay and Hurst Castle, with secondary landings to the west, in Lyme Bay.

The plan for guerrilla resistance is that elite units of the Home Guard should have the local knowledge and connections to sustain a campaign of harassment against the occupying forces. Each unit is under the control of regular Army officers to ensure the necessary level of expertise and professionalism.

Footnote: Schoolboys from North Perrott would discover the bunker secreted just above the spring-line in a dense coppice west of Higher Meerhay Farm, below Mintern's Hill, north of Beaminster.

During July
Boulogne award for Dorset hero.

Major "Billy" Fox-Pitt, who was awarded the Military Cross for gallantry whilst commanding a Welsh Guards company at Ginchy on the Somme in 1916, has been gazetted for the Distinguished Service Order in recognition of his leadership and example in holding out against strong German armoured attacks for two days in the attempt to defend Boulogne. The two battalions of the 20th Guards Brigade had been sent to France at short notice.

Footnote: Fox-Pitt would be appointed Aide-de-camp to King George VI, 1945-47, and in retirement in Dorset — at Marsh Court, Caundle Marsh — he hunted with the Blackmore Vale until the age of 79. He would die in 1988 at the age of 92.

During July
Fascist Dorset landowner interned.

A major Dorset landowner has been arrested and imprisoned with the round-up of pre-war members and supporters of Sir Oswald Mosley's British Union of Fascists. He is Captain George Henry Lane Fox Pitt-Rivers of Hinton St Mary, who was last in the news when he opposed the billeting of city children in rural Dorset. Pitt-Rivers is being held under Defence Regulation 18b.

Footnote: By next month there were 1,600 detained in prison without trial; three out of four of them were Mosley's members. All but 400 would be released during the winter of 1940-41. Pitt-Rivers would remain among those who were still interned.

Sunday 4 August
Poole flying-boat crosses the Atlantic.

The Short "Empire" flying-boat *Clare*, which took off early yesterday from the "Trots" in Poole Harbour — as the water runways are known — today landed on the east coast of the United States and thereby resumed the Trans-Atlantic service. She carried three American government VIPs and will return with ferry pilots.

The flying-boat's pilots are Captain J. C. Kelly Rogers and G. R. B. Wilcockson, with crewmen Burgess, Rotherham, and White.

Footnote: See 14 August 1940 for *Clare's* second crossing.

Monday 5 August
French General leaves Poole to arrange a coup.

Colonel René de Larminat, the High Commissioner of Free French Africa, has flown from Poole in the "Empire" flying-boat *Clyde* to arrange a coup d'état in the Vichy-controlled French colonies in the Congo basin. They are flying via Lagos, Nigeria, to Leopoldville in the Belgian Congo from where the general and his staff officers will begin their programme for the repossession of French Equatorial Africa.

Footnote: The Free French Army, led by General Carretier, walked back to power after taking Brazzaville by complete surprise.

Thursday 8 August
More mines laid off Dorset.

The Channel shipping lanes have been subject to further German minelaying in the past 36 hours. The Raumboote — armed motor minesweepers — of the enemy's 3rd Mine Laying Flotilla have been active off Dorset. They have been protected by Schnellboote of the 5th E-boat Flotilla.

Thursday 8 August
German and Warmwell losses around Convoy CW9.

Convoy CW9 has broken through the enemy's blockade of the English Channel, heading westwards from the Thames, but with severe losses. Three ships were sunk and one damaged by E-boat attacks off the Isle of Wight. Two Royal Navy destroyers were called out from Portsmouth to give help.

An air attack by 60 planes was intercepted and driven off but the convoy then fell victim to a second wave of more than 130 aircraft off Bournemouth. Here three more ships were lost and 13 damaged. The Germans lost 14 aircraft.

Spitfire K9894 of 152 Squadron from R.A.F. Warmwell was damaged in the dog-fight and headed for home. "UM" N for Nuts force-landed at Bestwall, on the east side of Wareham, where Sergeant Pilot Denis Norman Robinson made a dramatic escape. After bouncing across a meadow he struck a ditch, where the propeller ploughed into the soft ground, and the fuselage ended up standing vertically. Robinson was able to jump down on to the grass.

Another Spitfire of 152 Squadron was successfully brought down by Pilot Officer Walter Beaumont in a field at Spyway Farm, on top of the Purbeck cliffs at Langton Matravers.

VERTICAL SPITFIRE: FROM WHICH SERGEANT DENIS ROBINSON CLAMBERED DOWN TO THE GRASS AT BESTWALL, HALF A MILE EAST OF WAREHAM, ON 8 AUGUST 1940. THE "UM" MARKINGS ARE THOSE OF 152 SQUADRON FROM R.A.F. WARMWELL

Saturday 10 August
Bournemouth cyclist killed in air-raid.

Bombs fell last night on Bournemouth. At 47 Alyth Road, which was demolished at 23.24 hours, the disrobed lady of the house fell back into the safety of her bath as the roof and ceiling collapsed around her.

Less fortunate was a cyclist in Meon Road where five high-explosive bombs dropped at about 06.30 this morning. He was killed. Thirty-eight houses suffered damage.

Sunday 11 August
Big air-raid on Weymouth and Portland.

A massed formation of Luftwaffe bombers and fighters, estimated to consist of more than 150 aircraft, was plotted by Ventnor radar as it gathered over the Cherbourg peninsula at 09.45 hours. Two other Chain Home radar stations confirmed a strength of "100 plus".

By 10.07 they were in mid-Channel, with some 90 Messerschmitt Bf.109s and Bf.110s sweeping towards Portland from the south-east, to clear the way for following formations of 50 Junkers Ju.88 and 20 Heinkel He.111 bombers.

The Junkers — of I Gruppe and 2 Gruppe of Kampfgeschwader 54 — attacked from 10,000 feet at around 10.30, dropping 32 bombs inside Admiralty property at Portland and three bombs on the Royal Naval Torpedo Depot at Bincleaves, Weymouth. A total of 58 bombs fell on the borough. Quite a number also fell harmlessly, in the open sea, as well as Balaclava Bay and Portland Harbour.

Almost everywhere it was the same story of near misses and lucky escapes. Though appearing to be more serious, a fire beside No. 3 oil-tank at Portland was contained, and the adjoining blaze that made the beach road impassable was due to burning grass.

The main pipeline was fractured in three places with the loss of about 200-tons of oil. About the only serious damage was to the shipwright's shop at Bincleaves which received a direct hit.

Sunday 11 August
Five Bf.110s claimed by Warmwell's Spitfires.

Five twin-engined Messerschmitt Bf.110s were accounted for this morning by the Spitfires of 609 Squadron from R.A.F. Warmwell, in a fast-moving action that swirled high above Portland from 10.10 to 10.35.

Pilot Officer David Moore Crook, flying R6986 ("PR" S for Sugar), records in his log: "We took off at 09.45 and after patrolling round Warmwell saw some smoke trails out to sea. Investigated and found a large force of Bf.110s flying round in circles at 25,000 feet, Hurricanes already engaging them. We all attacked separately. I climbed well above the scrum and then saw a Bf.110 some distance from the others. I dived on him and fired a burst from the rear quarter which missed as I could not get sufficient deflection. I then came into very close range and fired. I hit him and he did a climbing turn to the right, stalled, and started to turn over. I narrowly missed colliding with him and did not see him again. Found myself with Messerschmitts all around so dived away as hard as I could and returned to Warmwell."

Most of the kills fell into the sea, including one shot down by Pilot Officer Noel le Chevalier Agazarian of 609 Squadron, but one crashed on land near Swanage. It has been credited to Flying Officer John Dundas, whose Spitfire, R6769 of 609 Squadron, took shots through the starboard wing and rudder from the gunner of the stricken Bf.110.

DEFENCE BADGE: ADOPTED BY SOUTHERN COMMAND AFTER THE DUNKIRK EVACUATION, BEING BASED UPON A REPRESENTATION OF THE SOUTHERN CROSS. A RECTANGULAR VERSION APPEARED ON DORSET'S MILITARY VEHICLES

Top secret: the Telecommunications Research Establishment at Worth Matravers. It clustered around Renscombe Farm (left of centre). Seen from the south-west, from a reconnaissance aircraft above the Purbeck cliffs, at Emmetts Hill. Four radio aerials can be seen and a variety of radar apparatus. Four separate compounds can be distinguished. Site A is in the near distance on the left. Site E is in the dark patch of the middle distance behind Renscombe Farm. Site B is the large rectangular complex extending from the farmyard to beyond the right-hand edge of the picture. Site C is the small circular-fenced installation crossed by the track, to St Alban's Head, in the near distance on the right

Sunday 11 August
152 Squadron loses pilot off Lulworth.

Pilot Officer John Sinclair Bucknall Jones, flying Spitfire R6614 of 152 Squadron from R.A.F. Warmwell, was shot down at 10.50 hours by Messerschmitt Bf.109s, over the sea several miles off Lulworth Cove. Aged 21, from Marlborough, he was seen to bale out but is believed to have drowned.

He is the second flyer from 152 Squadron to be lost in combat since they arrived at Warmwell and the station's sixth Spitfire pilot to be killed in the past month.

Footnote: John Jones's body would be washed ashore in France. He lies in Sainte Marie Cemetery at Le Havre.

Sunday 11 August
Junkers lands on Portland.

Flying Officer James Murray Strickland, in a Hurricane of 213 Squadron from R.A.F. Exeter, bagged a twin-engined Junkers Ju.88 (B3+DC) in style this afternoon. The German pilot almost succeeded in bringing his crippled bomber down upon "The Castles" as Portlanders call the flat top of the 275-feet cliffs at Blacknor Fort, Portland. This spot overlooks Lyme Bay from the centre of the western side of the stony island.

The sheer cliffs and the rocks were outmanoeuvred but not the fort's line of telephone wires.

These retracted the undercarriage. The pilot was seriously hurt as the aircraft bounced to a halt but his three comrades had only superficial injuries. The markings "B3" indicate that the Junkers belonged to Kampfgeschwader 54, a bomber wing whose death's head emblem — Totenkopf, as a tribute to the 2nd S.S. Division — appeared on the fuselage just aft of the transparent nose.

Sunday 11 August
Tangmere Hurricanes lose four pilots off Portland.

The Hurricanes of 601 Squadron from R.A.F. Tangmere, Sussex, lost four pilots in the intensive aerial combat off Portland Bill. The first to fall into the sea was Pilot

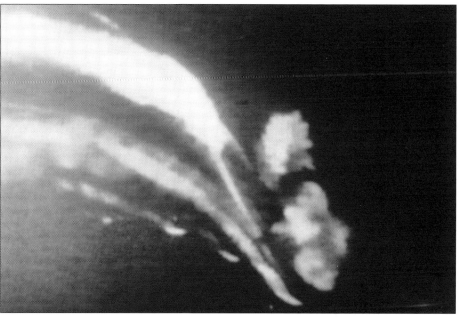

Destroyer attacked: Luftwaffe combat camera coverage of bombs disabling H.M.S. Delight, on 29 July 1940, in an attack that would reveal the existence of German radar

Officer Julian Langley Smithers in P3885, at 10.23 hours. He was a 24-year-old stockbroker from Knockholt, Kent.

Next was Pilot Officer Richard Stephen Demetriadi, in R4092, at 10.24. He was the 21-year-old son of commercial diplomat Sir Stephen Demetriadi and the brother-in-law of Pilot Officer William Rhodes-Moorhouse, the son of the first flying V.C., who was born at Parnham House, Beaminster.

Just a minute later, the Messerschmitt Bf.109s claimed Pilot Officer James Gillan in P3783. He was a 26-year-old pre-war pilot who had served in Iraq, with the R.A.F.'s Persian Gulf Command, in 1936.

The fourth victim, at 10.30, was Pilot Officer William Gordon Dickie in L2057. He came from Dundee and was aged 24.

Footnote: The winds and tides would carry some of the bodies to the French coast. Julian Smithers is buried in Sainte Marie Cemetery at Le Havre. Richard Demetriadi lies in Cayeux-sur-Mer Communal Cemetery and at home his father bequeathed five acres of Ditchling Beacon, above Brighton, to the National Trust. The others went down with their aircraft.

Sunday 11 August
Exeter Hurricanes lose three pilots off Dorset.

There have been serious losses for the Hurricanes from R.A.F. Exeter in today's conflict over Portland. Three have been lost, with their pilots, into the English Channel.

Flight-Lieutenant Ronald Derek Gordon Wight, in N2650 of 213 Squadron, was shot down by Bf.109s at 10.23 hours. He was aged 22.

Sergeant Pilot Samuel Leslie Butterfield, also with 213 Squadron, was killed in the same engagement. He was aged 27.

Flying Officer Robert Voase Jeff D.F.C., aged 27, was last seen taking V7231 of 87 Squadron into a dive towards Messerschmitt Bf.109s, ten miles south of Portland Bill, at 11.00 hours.

At the same time, Pilot Officer John Reynolds Cock, a 22-year-old Australian in 87 Squadron, baled out of V7233 as he was shot down off Portland Bill. Though wounded he was able to swim ashore.

Minutes later, at 11.10, another 22-year-old, Pilot Officer Andrew Crawford Rankin McLure of 87 Squadron, limped from his gun-damaged Hurricane after it finished upside down in a crash-landing at R.A.F. Warmwell. He is nursing a relatively minor leg wound.

Footnote: The bodies of two of the pilots would be washed up in France. Samuel Butterfield is buried in the Eastern Cemetery at Boulogne and Ronald Wight at Cayeux-sur-Mer Communal Cemetery.

Robert Jeff had the distinction of having destroyed the first enemy aircraft to fall on French soil — a Heinkel He.111 bomber on 2 November 1939 — for which he was awarded the Croix de Guerre and the Distinguished Flying Cross.

John Cock would also survive a mid-air collision, on 24 October 1940, and left the R.A.F. as Squadron Leader, in 1948. From retirement in Renmark, South Australia, he returned to Britain for the occasion

MUNITIONS FACTORY: THE ROYAL NAVAL CORDITE FACTORY AT HOLTON HEATH, BESIDE THE MAIN BACKWATER OF POOLE HARBOUR, IN A LUFTWAFFE RECONNAISSANCE PHOTOGRAPH OF 12 AUGUST 1940. LYTCHETT MINSTER VILLAGE (TOP RIGHT) AND THE WAREHAM CHANNEL (BOTTOM) ARE MARKED, AS IS THE BOUNDARY OF THE MILITARY ESTABLISHMENT. IMMEDIATELY SOUTH OF IT IS THE WAREHAM TO POOLE RAILWAY LINE, WITH A DIRECT SIDING TO THE MUNITIONS PLANT, CROSSING OVER THE MAIN LINE, TO ROCKLEA JETTY (RIGHT, JUTTING OUT IMMEDIATELY NORTH OF THE MAIN PENINSULA)

CONTROL BUNKER: INSIDE OP1, WHICH WAS THE HEADQUARTERS FOR AIR RAID PRECAUTIONS AT THE ROYAL NAVAL CORDITE FACTORY ON HOLTON HEATH

of the recovery of the wreckage of V7233, by Portland divers, on 30 August 1983.

Sunday 11 August
Middle Wallop Hurricanes lose three pilots off Lulworth.

Hurricanes from R.A.F. Middle Wallop, on the Hampshire Downs, have also suffered severe losses in the dog-fights over Portland and the English Channel.

At 10.45 hours, three members of 238 Squadron were shot down and killed, by Messerschmitt Bf.109s off White Nothe and Lulworth Cove. The flyers were Sergeant Pilot Geoffrey Gledhill, aged 19, in P2978; Flying Officer Michal Jan Steborowski, aged 31, of the Polish Air Force, in P3819; and Flight-Lieutenant Stuart Crosby Walch, a 23-year-old Tasmanian, in R4097.

Footnote: Geoffrey Gledhill's body was washed ashore in France and is buried in the churchyard at Criquebeuf-en-Caux. He had only been with the squadron a week.

Monday 12 August
Heinkel shot down at Sturminster Marshall.

A Heinkel He.111 bomber (1G+AC), heading homeward via Dorset's Stour valley from a raid on Bristol docks, was intercepted at 02.00 hours this morning by a British night-fighter. The bomber was raked with cannon fire and the pilot, who has been identified as a "Gruppenkommandeur", parachuted to captivity along with his four crewmen.

Their aircraft crashed in flames at Sturminster Marshall. Its "1G" markings indicate it belonged to Kampfgeschwader 27, a bomber wing.

Monday 12 August
Warmwell's losses climb to eight.

Two more Warmwell Spitfire pilots from 152 Squadron have been killed in action today, over the English Channel off St Catherine's Point, bringing the squadron's losses to four and those for Dorset's front-line R.A.F. station to eight.

Australian Flight-Lieutenant Latham Carr Withall, in P9456, was shot down and killed by the gunners of Junkers Ju.88 bombers, within sight of the Isle of Wight. He was aged 29. Almost simultaneously, return gunfire accounted for 22-year-old Pilot Officer Douglas Clayton Shepley in K9999.

The same action, ten miles south of Bognor Regis, also destroyed two more Hurricanes and killed their pilots, from 213 Squadron, who had flown across Dorset from R.A.F. Exeter to operate at long-range against massed enemy formations. Sergeant Pilot Sidney George Stuckey, in P2802, and Sergeant Pilot Geoffrey Wilkes, in P2854, were both shot down into the sea at about 12.35 hours.

Surviving pilots are being shocked into arguing about faulty tactics. Replacements are inevitably going to be inexperienced but one of the flaws is sending them to sea to meet the enemy. Those who have now had weeks of combat urge that the Luftwaffe should be left to come to us. The other essential element for survival is to get as high as possible before going into action. "This is the whole secret of success in air fighting," Pilot Officer David Moore Crook of 609 Squadron writes in his manuscript *Spitfire Pilot.*

Footnote: The death of Douglas Shepley would be avenged by his mother, who raised £5,700 in south Yorkshire to buy Mark Vb Spitfire W3649, for 602 Squadron in 1941. Famously, it was the machine being flown by Wing Commander Victor Beamish when he spotted the German warships *Scharnhorst* and *Gneisenau*, as they made their Channel Dash on 12 February 1942. The memorial to both aircraft is the Shepley Spitfire public house at Totley, Yorkshire.

Tuesday 13 August
Warmwell Spitfires have five Dorset kills.

This has been Eagle Day. The Luftwaffe's Adlertag attack of nearly 300 aircraft against military targets in southern England has been routed. None of the enemy planes reached its target.

At noon, Messerschmitt Bf.110 (L1+FZ) crashed in flames at Swalland Farm, Kimmeridge. "L1" shows that it

TRANSATLANTIC CROSSING: FLYING-BOAT CLARE ON HER RETURN TO POOLE FROM THE FIRST WARTIME FLIGHT TO AND FROM THE UNITED STATES, ON 14 AUGUST 1940

belonged to Lehrgeschwader 1, a specialist unit formed to test new and adapted aircraft of all types, and innovative tactics, under operational conditions. The two crew baled out and were taken prisoner.

The two Spitfire squadrons at R.A.F. Warmwell were scrambled at 15.30 hours. "Achtung, achtung, Spit und Hurri," Pilot Officer David Moore Crook of 609 Squadron, flying R6699 ("PR-L"), heard repeatedly as he approached the German formations.

One of the 27 Junkers Ju.87 "Stuka" diver-bombers of II Gruppe Stukageschwader 2 that had been targeted on Middle Wallop Aerodrome, Hampshire, was shot down between Portesham and Rodden at 16.00 hours. Its two crewmen, Feldwebel Linderschmid and Gefreiter Eisold, died in the crash. The kill has been claimed by Flight Lieutenant Derek Boitel-Gill of 152 Squadron from Warmwell.

At the same time, Pilot Officer Crook sent a Messerschmitt Bf.109 smoking into the cloud and descended to see the debris of a crash which he thought was near the Hardy Monument. This, however, was that of another enemy aircraft, which came down "just outside a small village" according to Crook's description. This crash-site lay 200 yards from the railway station at the hamlet of Grimstone, near Stratton. Both crew were killed; Feldwebel Erich Haach of Krossen, and Gefreiter Heinrich Myer, or Meir, from Oberhausen. The two crew and the discovery of an unexploded 250-kilogram bomb in the wreckage confirm that it was a "Stuka" or a Bf.110 fighter-bomber.

As for the Messerschmitt Bf.109 E1 escort fighters that were being chased by 609 Squadron, as they turned for the coast short of fuel, Crook's crippled claim ended up in

Poole Harbour. The pilot, Unteroffizier Wilhelm Hohenseldt, was rescued and made prisoner of war.

Another Bf.109 was shot down off Weymouth. Its pilot, Leutnant Heinz Pfannschmidt, was also saved and taken prisoner. This kill was claimed by Pilot Officer Tadeusz Nowierski, who is avenging the rape of Poland. His compatriot, Flying Officer Piotr Ostaszewski-Ostoja, returned to Warmwell with two Junkers Ju.87s as "probably destroyed".

There were few lucky Germans, but the day's most fortunate Briton was Flying Officer John Dundas of 609 Squadron. His Spitfire, N3113, narrowly pulled clear from a collision with a "Stuka" and in the process he found his oil system ruptured by a bullet from its gunner. His propeller stopped. Dundas skilfully used his height, from over the sea off Portland, to glide down to a successful forced-landing at Warmwell Aerodrome.

Footnote: Eyewitness E. G. Read of Stratton recalled the Grimstone crash for me in 1981: "My neighbours and I had been watching an aerial battle and machine-gun ammunition clips had fluttered down around us. Suddenly there was a blood-curdling banshee wail. It was heart-stopping as it approached us.

"Right over our heads came the stricken plane [from the north-east]. There was dense black smoke pouring from its starboard engine [the "Stuka" was single-engined, so if remembered correctly, this indicates a Bf.110] and the two young airmen were clearly visible. They had just seconds to live. Later came the news that a German plane had crashed behind Grimstone Viaduct. We went there immediately on our bikes, but a sentry was there on guard with fixed bayonet. Beneath two

HOME GUARDS: POINTING LEE-ENFIELDS SEAWARDS ALONG THE NOTHE PROMONTORY, ABOVE WEYMOUTH HARBOUR, WITH THE FUNNEL OF A PADDLE-STEAMER GLIMPSED BEHIND THE BARRELS. THEIR ONE AND ONLY EXCURSION THIS SUMMER HAS BEEN THE EVACUATION OF DUNKIRK

PORTLAND GARRISON: THE ISLAND'S HOME GUARD COMPANY, OUTSIDE THEIR DRILL-HALL, AT EASTON

white parachutes were the crumpled bodies of the airmen.

"The next day the sentry had gone and we went souvenir hunting. I pulled off a small electrical bakelite plug that was stamped 'Made in England'. The two young flyers were interred in a green unploughed curve at the side of the field. Later two ornately carved and inscribed wooden crosses appeared at the spot. The bodies remained there from that sunny afternoon in 1940 until the late 1960s when they were reburied at Brookwood Military Cemetery, Surrey.

"I found their crosses in a dilapidated shed at Frampton churchyard in 1964. The galvanised roof was holed and they were covered in wet lichen. Since then both shed and crosses have disappeared. So, too, has my souvenir component, which I inadvertently threw out with an unwanted box of oddments before moving house in 1978."

WEYMOUTH BOMBED: NEWSTEAD ROAD, WITH THREE HOUSES DESTROYED AND MANY OTHERS DAMAGED, IN AUGUST 1940

Tuesday 13 August
Another Exeter Hurricane shot down off Portland.

Hard-pressed 213 Squadron, flying Hurricanes from R.A.F. Exeter, has lost another pilot off the Dorset coast. Contact ceased with P3348, being flown by 22-year-old Sergeant Pilot Philip Purchall Norris, over the sea near Portland, at 15.42 hours. He was shot down during combat and is presumed to have been killed.

The Hurricanes of 238 Squadron from R.A.F. Middle Wallop also took part in the dog-fights. One of the flyers, 22-year-old Sergeant Pilot Ronald Little, was driven away unhurt after P3805 had crash-landed at Bredy Farm, a mile east of Burton Bradstock.

Footnote: Philip Norris's body would be washed ashore in France. He is buried in Etaples Military Cemetery. Ronald Little's luck would run out near the Isle of Wight, on 28 September 1940, when Hurricane N2400 was shot down into the sea. His body was not recovered.

Tuesday 13 August
An entry in the Dorchester Observer Corps log.

Time: 16.35 hours. Location: Poundbury Camp, Dorchester [north-west of the county town].

Area of activity: South of sector R4, Dorchester. Report: "Confirmed hostile and friendly pilots approaching the post. Much machine-gun and cannon fire. Fierce contest going on. Plane shot down believed Bf.110, another plane down, much confused sound-plotting and heavy firing for a considerable period. One plane believed friendly, flying low east. Believed forced-landing this side of Maiden Castle House and in neighbourhood of the Fever Hospital."

Wednesday 14 August
Second Trans-Atlantic crossing from Poole.

The Air Ministry Under-Secretary, Harold Balfour M.P., is flying today from Poole to the United States on the second wartime Trans-Atlantic flying-boat crossing by *Clare*.

Footnote: The flying-boat was back in Poole on Sunday, 18 August 1940. Balfour had bought three Boeing 314s — "Clipper" flying-boats — from the Americans. These long-range boats will be delivered to British Overseas Airways at Poole early next year.

Wednesday 14 August

Heinkel shot down into Lyme Bay.

The destruction of a Heinkel He.111 bomber, shot down over Lyme Bay, has been claimed by Pilot Officer Harold Derrick Atkinson, flying Hurricane R4099 of 213 Squadron from R.A.F. Exeter. Atkinson, who is aged 21, was slightly hurt by return fire and is receiving medical attention for shell splinters in the arm.

Thursday 15 August

Kills for 152 Squadron and Spitfire pilot swims home.

Nine Spitfires of 152 Squadron from R.A.F. Warmwell were at 15,000 feet above Portland at 17.15 hours when they heard over the radio: "Many enemy aircraft approaching Portland from the south."

Two minutes later a cloud of black specs became visible in mid-Channel, at about the same height as the British fighters. There were an estimated 100 or more German aircraft, with Junkers Ju.87 in tight V-formations each comprising three "Stukas" surrounded by Messerschmitt Bf.110 fighter-bomber escorts.

The Spitfires climbed to 18,000 feet in a wide circle across Lyme Bay that brought them out of the south-western sun to descend through the German ranks about five miles south of Portland Bill. The resulting melee, which was joined by Hurricanes from R.A.F. Exeter, had a mixed outcome.

Ralph "Bob" Wolton of 152 Squadron was shot down in the engagement with the "Stukas" and fell out of his Spitfire seconds before it crashed into the sea. He managed to swim to one of the offshore marker buoys of the Chesil Beach Bombing Range, from which he was rescued by an R.A.F. launch from Lyme Regis.

Pilot Officer Harold John Akroyd, also of 152 Squadron, limped home to Warmwell with a jammed rudder, following an engagement off Portland in which he accounted for a Junkers Ju.87. Sergeant Pilot Denis Robinson shot down a Bf.110.

Flight-Lieutenant Frank Howell of 609 Squadron returned to Warmwell Aerodrome with the claim of a Junkers Ju.88 bomber kill. "How many Huns shall we get tomorrow?" is the sort of confident remark one now hears, though it may be premature to go as far as to say that the tide may have turned.

Thursday 15 August

New Zealand pilot dies a hero at Abbotsbury.

Twenty-seven-year-old Squadron Leader Terence Lovell-Gregg of 87 Squadron, from R.A.F. Exeter, failed in a desperate attempt to make a crash-landing in The Fleet lagoon late this afternoon. The Hurricane came in blazing from over the sea but was brought into a controlled

NEW ZEALANDERS: BOTH FLYERS BEING KILLED BY THE LUFTWAFFE OVER THE DORSET COAST ON THE SAME DAY, 15 AUGUST 1940, WITH SQUADRON LEADER TERENCE LOVELL-GREGG BEING LOST AT ABBOTSBURY AND PILOT OFFICER CECIL HIGHT (right) CRASHING IN BOURNEMOUTH

POOLE HEINKEL: DEMOLISHED UNDERWOOD AT BRANKSOME PARK, ON 25 SEPTEMBER 1940

descent for a forced landing. P3215 then clipped a tree beside Abbotsbury Swannery and its wounded pilot fell to his death at 18.00 hours.

Flying Officer Roland Prosper Beamont, one of the Exeter pilots, returned with the story of how Lovell-Gregg had led his squadron into the midst of a mass of German aircraft at 18,000 feet over the English Channel: "We saw the 'Beehive' almost straight ahead at the same height, and with his Hurricanes, Lovell-Gregg flew straight at the centre of the formation without hesitation or deviation in any way."

One hundred and twenty enemy aircraft were heading towards Portland. Lovell-Gregg was a quiet pre-war professional, from Marlborough in New Zealand, who had taught many of the emergent generations of flyers. His courage was never in any doubt, though he had led his squadron for only a month, since 12 July. The pilots knew him as "Shovel". There were only four of them with him when they scrambled at 16.00 hours today. Those five Hurricanes

were all the air-worthy machines that 87 Squadron could muster.

Undaunted by the adverse odds of 15-to-one that loomed in front, Lovell-Gregg asked the impossible of himself and his men: "Come on chaps, let's surround them!"

Only one of the five returned to Exeter this evening on his own wings. The second fatality at 18.00 hours was 19-year-old Pilot Officer Peter Woodruff Comely in P2872 who was shot down into the sea off Portland. Moments before he had accounted for a Messerschmitt Bf.110.

Sergeant Pilot James Cowley is recovering in Bridport Hospital from minor injuries caused in a crash-landing at Symondsbury which has written-off P3465. Sergeant Pilot Dudley Trevor Jay, in R2687, managed his forced-landing on softer ground and stepped out of R2687 unhurt, at Field Barn Farm, beside the marshland of Radipole Lake at Weymouth.

Footnote: William Dunford, then an Abbotsbury schoolboy, described for me how he put out the flames on Squadron Leader Terence Lovell-Gregg's burning body.

STUDLAND HEINKEL: BOMBER G1+BH, WHICH CRASH-LANDED AT WESTFIELD FARM WHILE ATTEMPTING TO ESCAPE FROM A RAID ON THE BRISTOL AIRCRAFT COMPANY AT FILTON, AT NOON ON 25 SEPTEMBER 1940

"Lovell-Gregg's Hurricane was shot down in flames, at about six to 6.30 p.m., but he recovered control to put the plane into a perfect glide and attempted to land in The Fleet lagoon at Abbotsbury Swannery. He came low over a small wood but was not quite high enough. The underside of the Hurricane hit the top of an oak tree, and Lovell-Gregg was thrown out of the cockpit. The plane went on through the trees and crashed.

"With another schoolboy I ran to the spot where the pilot had fallen. He was badly shot about and burning. We put out the flames with two buckets of water. About two hours later a truck came from Warmwell and we were then told the flyer's identity. Though he had those wounds, I am sure, had he made it into the water, that he would have survived."

Lovell-Gregg is buried in the R.A.F. plot at Warmwell churchyard. Ironically, in St Nicholas's Church at Abbotsbury, there is a plaque recording with thanks that no one from the parish died on active service or from enemy action in the Second World War — without any mention of their heroic defender from the other side of the world.

Thursday 15 August
New Zealand pilot killed over Bournemouth.

The eastern side of the Middle Wallop Sector also saw action today with a formation of bombers approaching Bournemouth. The Spitfires of 234 Squadron were scrambled from R.A.F. Middle Wallop at 17.05 hours and intercepted the bombers, which were heading homeward, over the town. A sustained air battle took place at 4,000 feet, during which Spitfire R6988 was hit by return fire from one of the German rear gunners.

It spiralled into Leven Avenue, to the west of Meyrick Park golf links, leaving a crater and wreckage across a wide area. One of the wings fell on a hedge in Walsford Road.

The pilot fell from the aircraft but his parachute did not open.

Pilot Officer Cecil Henry Hight, aged 22 from Stratford, New Zealand, had been seriously wounded and apparently passed out before he could pull the rip-cord. His body was found in Mr and Mrs Hoare's garden; his stomach had been ripped open by machine-gun bullets.

Footnote: The town has named Pilot Hight Road in his memory. Cecil Hight would be the only Allied airman to die over Bournemouth during the Battle of Britain. He is buried in Boscombe Cemetery and a memorial tablet was unveiled at St Peter's Church in the town centre on 7 April 1943.

Mr and Mrs Hoare's house was again to be visited by the war. Ian McQueen records in *Bournemouth St Peter's* that it was hit by a German bomb. Canon Headley Burrows recalled that it was the house where Hight's Spitfire had crashed.

"The dear old man, Mr Hoare, died," Canon Burrows said, but then they heard Mrs Hoare.

FIRE TENDER: MANNED BY NO. 7 ZONE OF THE AUXILIARY FIRE SERVICE AT BOURNEMOUTH, BASED IN NORTOFT ROAD, CHARMINSTER

"Who is that?" she asked.

"I am Canon Burrows. Keep still — they are going to get you out."

"Canon Burrows," she replied, "how kind of you to come and see me today."

Thursday 15 August
Damaged Spitfire crash-lands at Bournemouth.

Another Spitfire of 234 Squadron from R.A.F. Middle Wallop, badly damaged in the dog-fights over Bournemouth, made a successful forced-landing in fields beside the town. Its pilot was unhurt and a guard was sent from the Special Duty Flight at Christchurch to attend to the aircraft.

Thursday 15 August
Crook bags a Blenheim with friendly fire.

A Blenheim fighter-bomber of 604 Squadron from R.A.F. Middle Wallop, doing some practice flying around the aerodrome, was claimed today by Pilot Officer David Moore Crook of 609 Squadron from R.A.F. Warmwell after the Luftwaffe had bombed the squadron's home base on the Hampshire Downs. "In a fit of rather misguided valour," the Blenheim had fastened itself to the German formation as it ran for the coast, and began engaging the rear machines.

"We were rapidly overhauling the German formation, and when I was in range I opened fire at the nearest machine, which happened to be the Blenheim," Crook writes in his memoirs. "Quite naturally it never occurred to me that it could be anything else but a Junkers Ju.88. I hit both engines and the fuselage, and he fled away to the right with one engine smoking furiously. I saw him gliding down and noticed a gun turret on the fuselage which rather shook me, as I knew the Ju.88 did not have this."

The pilot was saved by the armour plating behind him and managed to make a crash-landing on the aerodrome: "The Blenheim was full of bullet holes and looked rather like a kitchen sieve. The rear-gunner got a bullet through his bottom, which doubtless caused him considerable discomfort and annoyance, but was not serious."

Friday 16 August
152 Squadron's Beaumont has a double.

Pilot Officer Walter Beaumont, flying a Spitfire with 152 Squadron from R.A.F. Warmwell, has scored his squadron's first double kills with two Messerschmitt Bf.109s brought down over the Isle of Wight at lunchtime.

Friday 16 August
'Boy' Marrs has his first Heinkel disallowed.

In the evening, as 152 Squadron's second patrol of the day was about to head for home, two Heinkel He.111 bombers were spotted below, at 3,000 feet over the Solent. The rear one was attacked at 18.15 hours by Pilot Officer Eric Simcox Marrs. "Boy" is his nickname; he is aged 19 but looks much younger.

As the Heinkel came out of a bank of mist he shot it up: "I left it with smoke coming from both engines and my own machine covered in oil from it. I don't think it could have got home and I'm pretty sure it didn't."

His claim is not being accepted, because a radio transmission was misunderstood, and no one else in the squadron saw the action. Marrs, however, is in no doubt, and he is writing to his father from R.A.F. Warmwell: "I am counting it as my first."

Friday 16 August
Canadian pilot killed off Portland.

Pilot Officer Joseph Emile Paul Larichelière, a 27-year-old Canadian flying a Hurricane of 213 Squadron from R.A.F. Exeter, failed to return today from combat off Portland.

Saturday 17 August
Warmwell's Robinson claims a 'Stuka'.

Sergeant Pilot Denis Robinson, in a Spitfire of 152 Squadron, returned to R.A.F. Warmwell from today's sweep over the English Channel with the claim of a Junkers Ju.87 "Stuka" successfully shot down into the sea.

Sunday 18 August
Warmwell's 'Boy' Marrs has his first confirmed kill.

Formations of more than 100 "Stuka" dive-bombers, escorted by Messerschmitt Bf.109 fighters, crossed the Channel to attack the radar station at Poling, Sussex, and aerodromes at Ford, Thorney Island, and Gosport. Eleven Spitfires of 152 Squadron were scrambled from R.A.F. Warmwell.

The Spitfires dived from 4,000 feet on the Junkers Ju.87 "Stukas" as they swept back to sea after dropping their bombs. Pilot Officer Eric "Boy" Marrs claimed a kill — his first to be confirmed.

"We dived after them and they went down to about a hundred feet above the water. Then followed a running chase out to sea. The evasive action they took was to throttle back and do steep turns to right and left so that we would not be able to follow them and would overshoot. There were, however, so many of them that if one was shaken off the tail of one there was always another to sit on. I fired at about six and shot down one. It caught fire in the port wing petrol tank and then went into the sea about 300 yards further on."

The "Stukas" were from I and II Gruppen of Stukageschwader 77, the same unit as Von Dalwigk's dive-bomber, shot down on 9 July. They suffered 16 losses as 43 Squadron, 601 Squadron, and 602 Squadron joined 152 Squadron in the action.

The Bf.109 escort fighters were routed by the Spitfires of 234 Squadron from R.A.F. Middle Wallop. They arrived at the station on Wednesday.

Sunday 18 August
Near misses for the Special Duty Flight.

As defending Hurricanes tangled with Messerschmitt Bf.109s over Bournemouth and Christchurch, the Special Duty Flight from Christchurch Aerodrome found itself uncomfortably close to the action. Flight-Lieutenant Douglas L. Rayment was unhurt but he brought back his Blenheim flying test-bed with bullet-damage to the starboard mainframe.

Sunday 18 August
Marrs goes 'Tally-ho' again.

17.25 hours. On his second combat patrol of the day, Pilot Officer Eric "Boy" Marrs of 152 Squadron from Warmwell Aerodrome has led the three Spitfires of Blue Section in a "Tally-ho" after a German Dornier Do.17 which was flying towards Portland.

The interception took place from 16,000 feet and the bomber dropped into cloud at about 5,000 feet. Marrs had emptied his guns and the third Spitfire claimed a share in the kill.

Footnote: Apparently it was not that decisive and the bomber managed to return to France.

Monday 19 August
'Enigma' decrypt gives warning of Warmwell attack.

01.52 hours. "From a reliable source, information has been received of an impending attack on Warmwell Aerodrome this morning. Aircraft are to be ready to leave at 07.00 hours." [The source being a German "Enigma" radio signal decoded by the Government Code and Cipher School, at Bletchley Park, Buckinghamshire.]

Wednesday 21 August
Two killed by afternoon bombs in Poole.

Mrs Pauline Fairbrother of 38 Market Street and Frederick Landrey of 18 South Road were killed this afternoon when a single German raider, a Junkers Ju.88, came in low over the Old Town area of central Poole from the Sandbanks direction.

It dropped six bombs. The one that killed Mr Landrey destroyed the National School air-raid shelter, thankfully unoccupied, and the others hit shops and timber stores.

Friday 23 August
Two killed by Lulworth raider.

A lone German raider attacked Lulworth Camp today just minutes after the "All Clear" had sounded. Recruits had resumed their infantry training and were back in the open as the aircraft approached. Sergeant J. Thompson shouted to them: "Get down and stay still!"

Eight bombs dropped on the sports-field, the ranges, and at St Andrew's Farm, which is inside the camp complex. Two men were killed and seven injured. The latter include quick-thinking Sergeant Thomson who received severe leg wounds.

He had been in the stores when he heard the aircraft approaching and but for his instant and brave response, when he put himself into the line of fire to warn the men, there would have been a greater number of casualties.

Friday 23 August
Twenty-four killed by bombs at New Milton.

Twenty-four people were killed and many injured this evening when Junkers Ju.88 bombers devastated Station Road, New Milton. The main street of the New Forest seaside village has numerous flats above the shops and is surrounded by a residential area.

Air Raid Precautions units, ambulances, and fire engines are in attendance from Christchurch and Lymington. Train services into Dorset have been temporarily diverted from Brockenhurst to Poole, northwards via Ringwood and Wimborne branch lines, but it seems that the railway track is probably undamaged.

Sunday 25 August
Shops bombed at Parkstone.

Early this morning a single German bomber attacked the Ashley Road and Constitution Hill area of Upper Parkstone, Poole. Three shops and a house were destroyed. Two people are injured.

Sunday 25 August
Decoded signals rouse Warmwell to day of action.

07.40 hours. "It is reliably reported that air attacks are to be expected during the course of today 25th August at Warmwell, Little Rissington, and Abingdon aerodromes, and reconnaissances by a single aircraft in the area Southampton-Aldershot-Brighton." [The intelligence source being German "Enigma" machine-coded radio signals deciphered by the Government Code and Cipher School at Bletchley Park.]

For R.A.F. Warmwell, radar confirmation of approaching aircraft came at 16.45 hours and by 17.00 the twelve Spitfires of 152 Squadron were airborne. Half an hour later the station was rocked by 20 bombs, which destroyed the sick quarters and damaged hangars.

The Spitfires had met Luftflotte 3 over Portland but despite the advance warning it was a more or less even match.

Footnote: Delayed action bombs would go off over the next couple of days.

LONDON BURNING: WITH THE BLITZKRIEG AT MILLWALL DOCKS CAUSING BOURNEMOUTH FIREMEN TO BE BUSSED TO THE EAST END, AND 609 SQUADRON SECONDED FROM R.A.F. WARMWELL TO THE AIR DEFENCE OF THE CAPITAL, IN SEPTEMBER 1940

Sunday 25 August

Three Hurricane pilots killed over Dorset.

Hurricanes of 87 Squadron and 213 Squadron from R.A.F. Exeter joined in today's dog-fights over Portland. Sergeant Pilot Sidney Richard Ernest Wakeling of 87 Squadron was killed at 17.25 hours when his fighter, V7250, plunged in flames at New Barn, on the hillside south of Bradford Peverell, north-west of Dorchester. He was aged 21.

Then 213 Squadron lost two fighters at about 17.30 hours — to Messerschmitt Bf.109s — into Lyme Bay. The missing flyers are Pilot Officer Harold Derrick Atkinson, in P3200, and Pilot Officer Jacques Arthur Laurent Philippart. Atkinson, a Yorkshireman, celebrated his 22nd birthday on Monday. Philippart, aged 31, escaped in May from the invading Germans, by air and sea, and became the first Belgian ace of the war. He was shot down off Portland by Hauptmann Mayer of I Gruppe, Jagdgeschwader 53.

A third fighter, N2646, crash-landed at Burton Bradstock but is repairable. The flyer, Sergeant Pilot Ernest Snowden, is unhurt.

Footnote: Two bodies would be recovered from the sea. Harold Atkinson is buried at Market Weighton, Yorkshire. Jacques Philippart, who had baled out, was buried in Exeter Higher Cemetery. In 1949 his remains were exhumed and repatriated, being interred at Evere, Brussels, in the Pelouse d'Honneur Cemetery.

Sidney Wakeling, who was from Kensington, is buried in the R.A.F. plot at Warmwell churchyard.

Sunday 25 August

German crashes from Weymouth to Purbeck.

There are reports of German aircraft being shot down across Dorset. A Messerchmitt Bf.109 has crashed on the

Chesil Beach at Chickerell and its pilot, Hauptmann Maculan, apparently fell out and drowned. To the north, a Bf.110 exploded at Tatton House, between Langton Herring and Buckland Ripers, killing both crew.

A Bf.109 belly-landed in an adjoining field, beside woodland at Tatton Farm, and its pilot escaped with wounds as it was engulfed in flames. Gefreiter Josef Broker of Jagdgeschwader 53 was taken prisoner. He will survive his burns. Credit for this kill is being claimed by Pilot Officer Walter Beaumont of 152 Squadron who has driven across the hill from R.A.F. Warmwell to arrive "in shirtsleeves and sweat" at the scorched scene of his triumph.

Shortly after 18.00 hours, a Bf.110 was reported crashing at Creech Barrow, the conical-shaped summit of the Purbeck Hills south of Wareham, and another Bf.110 (3M+KH) came down at Priory Farm, East Holme. Both sets of crew parachuted into captivity.

A third Bf.110 (3M+CH) was taken on by two Spitfires of 609 Squadron from R.A.F. Warmwell. Squadron Leader H. S. "George" Darley and American volunteer Pilot Officer Eugene Quimby "Red" Tobin gunned it down at East Chaldon, to the west of Lulworth. It became a fireball and the crew died in the explosion. "3M" indicates that these aircraft belonged to the 1st Staffel of II Gruppe, Zerstörergeschwader 2.

Squadron Leader Darley also accounted for the first Messerschmitt to be brought down. In all, 609 Squadron claims eleven kills, and certainly several Bf.110 fighter-bombers from II Gruppe Zerstörergeschwader 2 and V Gruppe Zerstörergeschwader 1 were destroyed, and Bf.109 fighters from II Gruppe Jagdgeschwader 2 — a fighter wing named Richthofen — though these escorts had succeeded in keeping the Spitfires from the Junkers Ju.88 bombers.

Sunday 25 August

152 Squadron has now lost six pilots.

Two more Spitfire pilots from 152 Squadron at R.A.F. Warmwell were lost late this afternoon in the intense combat off Portland. Both crashed into the sea.

Pilot Officer Richard Malzard Hogg was shot down by Messerschmitt Bf.109s at 17.22 hours. Minutes later, at 17.50, Pilot Officer Timothy Seddon Wildblood joined him in being posted "Missing in Action". Their demise brings the squadron's losses to six pilots, and those for the station to ten, since the start of the aerial onslaught in July.

609 Squadron just about scraped through the day with their numbers intact. The closest call was for Flying Officer Piotr Ostaszewski-Ostoja in R6986. The Spitfire was riddled by cannon fire from a Messerschmitt Bf.110 he engaged over Swanage. Though his flaps were damaged, the 20-year-old Pole succeeded in bringing the fighter and himself back to Warmwell Aerodrome, though the machine was written-off when he overshot the runway and crashed through the perimeter hedge. Damage to the pilot was confined to a minor arm injury.

Footnote: Piotr Ostaszewski-Ostoja would continue to have a reasonably good war, leaving the R.A.F. in 1946 as Wing Commander, and changed his name to Peter Raymond on deciding to stay in England.

Tuesday 27 August
152's Beaumont bales out off Portland.

Pilot Officer Walter Beaumont was able to bale out of Spitfire R6831, belonging to 152 Squadron from R.A.F. Warmwell, as it was hit by return fire from a Junkers Ju.88 bomber. His fighter crashed into Lyme Bay, eight miles west of Portland.

Beaumont, who survives to fight another day, had just shared the honours in the destruction of a Heinkel He.111 bomber.

Thursday 29 August
Extensive bomb damage at Poole.

04.00 hours. Though no one has been injured, high explosive and incendiary bombs have caused considerable damage to buildings in the Longfleet, Oakdale, and Parkstone suburbs of Poole.

Thursday 29 August
Bombs miss Christchurch.

Early this morning incendiary bombs landed near the Priory, Millhams Street, and at Queens Avenue in Christchurch. One was on the roof of the air-compressing station. There were also the thuds of high explosive bombs but daylight revealed they had dropped on the northern side of the town into heathland and woods at St Catherine's Hill. Ten had gone off and one had failed to explode.

During August
Burton Bradstock call for Hitler prayers.

Writing in *The Two Edged Sword*, Adela Curtis, leader of the Christian Contemplatives' Community at St Bride's Farm, Burton Bradstock, advises on methods of furthering the war effort through positive prayer:

"We are to summon each enemy leader by name. For cumulative effect the message should be spoken three times — Adolf Hitler! Adolf Hitler! Adolf Hitler! Hear the Truth!"

During August
Cranborne Chase motor-cycle exercises.

The 4th Battalion of the Royal Northumberland Fusiliers have been reorganised as a motorcycle reconnaissance column and are based at Blandford Camp. Their sidecar patrols are seemingly everywhere in the chalkland villages of Cranborne Chase.

The 2nd and 8th Battalions of the Northumberlands are also in Dorset, dispersed on anti-invasion duties, occupying the dairying country of the Blackmore Vale.

Wednesday 4 September
Eleventh Warmwell pilot killed.

Sergeant Pilot John Keeth Barker, in a Spitfire of 152 Squadron from R.A.F. Warmwell, failed to return today from an operational sortie over the Isle of Wight. He was last seen in combat 25 miles south-south-east of Bognor Regis and is believed to have been hit by return fire from a Dornier Do.17 bomber. The loss of the 23-year-old brings the squadron's fatalities to seven, and takes those for the station into double figures, since the air attacks began.

Sergeant Pilot Denis Robinson returned to Warmwell with the claim of a Junkers Ju.88 destroyed.

Footnote: John Barker had baled out but was killed. His body was washed ashore in France and buried in Etaples Military Cemetery.

Thursday 5 September
Bomb hits Druitt's House at Christchurch.

Druitt's House, the Christchurch solicitor's offices and former residence of one of the town's leading families which produced Montague John Druitt who was a suspect for Jack the Ripper, the Whitechapel murderer — was destroyed by a German bomb at 01.30 hours this morning.

Just after midnight a bomb had dropped on Iford golf course but that one failed to explode.

Saturday 7 September
Spitfire crashes near Dorchester.

Ralph "Bob" Wolton, flying at the rear of a flight of Spitfires with 152 Squadron from R.A.F. Warmwell, today lost control of his fighter whilst attempting a sudden dive. He jumped from the falling plane at 13,000 feet though he estimates it was not until nearly a thousand feet from the ground when he managed to sort out the cords and activate the chute. The Spitfire crashed near Dorchester.

RECONNAISSANCE COLUMN: MOTOR-CYCLE AND SIDECAR COMBINATIONS, AND UNATTACHED NORTONS FROM BLANDFORD CAMP, OF THE 4TH BATTALION OF THE NORTHUMBERLAND FUSILIERS. VETERANS OF THE BRITISH EXPEDITIONARY FORCE, DUNKIRK, AND DEFENDING BOURNEMOUTH BEACH, THEY SPREAD OUT ACROSS CRANBORNE CHASE, FROM AUGUST TO OCTOBER 1940. THE COTTAGES BESIDE THE RAISED PAVEMENT ARE AT COOMBE BISSETT, TOWARDS SALISBURY

No enemy aircraft was involved. Others, however, did meet up with the Luftwaffe today. Flight-Lieutenant Frank Howell of 609 Squadron returned to Warmwell Aerodrome with the claim of a Messerchmitt Bf.110 that he had shot down.

Saturday 7 September
The great invasion scare.

The German invasion appears to have started. Reports have been received of a seven-mile convoy heading towards the Dorset coast and there is a general flap that Operation Sealion is taking place and Field-Marshal Fedor von Bock is on his way with the victors of Poland, the Wehrmacht's Army Group B. The fuel tanks are to be fired to set the beaches ablaze and an aircraft from Gosport is dropping incendiaries to start them off.

Troops at Bournemouth have manned the cliffs and keep emphasising that this is not an exercise.

The Home Guard at the Supermarine aircraft factory in Southampton has been alerted to enemy landings at Portsmouth.

Saturday 7 September
Invasion expected tonight.

20.07 hours. A national alert has been issued by the War Office: "Condition Cromwell." An invasion is regarded as imminent and probable within twelve hours.

Footnote: Nothing happened! One set of "Fougasse" tanks ignited a beach but the plane was recalled to Gosport before it set alight to any more. There was no landing in Dorset or anywhere else. Despite that, invasion fears reached fever-pitch, though not without reason, for aerial reconnaissances were showing concentrations of ships and barges in harbours from Brest to Calais.

Tuesday 10 September
Fourteen bombs at Christchurch.

Fourteen bombs landed in the Christchurch area last night, at about midnight, fracturing water mains and bringing down telephone wires. There was serious blast damage to Hoburne Farm.

Six of the bombs fortunately exploded harmlessly on Chewton Common.

Thursday 12 September
Wing Commander lost on Dorset flight.

Hurricane pilot Wing Commander John Scatliff "Johnny" Dewar has been reported missing en route in a coastal flight across Dorset and Hampshire from his home base at R.A.F. Exeter to R.A.F. Tangmere in Sussex.

Footnote: John Dewar's body would be washed up at Kingston Gorse on Selsey Bill, Sussex, on 30 September. He is buried in St John's churchyard, North Baddesley, near Southampton. Aged 33, he was born in Lahore

Province, India, and would be the highest ranking Royal Air Force officer to be killed in the Battle of Britain.

Friday 13 September
609's Howell has his fourth kill.

Flight-Lieutenant Frank Howell, in a Spitfire of 609 Squadron from R.A.F. Warmwell, has claimed his fourth enemy aircraft destroyed. The latest is a Junkers Ju.87 "Stuka" dive-bomber.

Saturday 14 September
Warmwell loses a further pilot.

Flying Officer C. O. Hinks has been killed in a flying accident at R.A.F. Warmwell. He is the station's twelfth fatal casualty in the current series of sorties and combat.

Sunday 15 September
Warmwell's Spitfires defend London.

The Spitfires of 609 Squadron from R.A.F. Warmwell were drawn into the air defence of London today as what is being called the Battle of Britain reached its climax so far. Today claims for the day were 186 enemy aircraft destroyed. Among them were a Dornier Do.17 bomber shot down by Flight-Lieutenant Frank Howell and a half-share in another Dornier, claimed by Pilot Officer Eugene Quimby "Red" Tobin, a lanky and laconic American volunteer whose neutral Embassy in Grosvenor Square had tried and failed to send back to States.

"I reckon these will be a one way ticket, pal," he said as he pointed to the wings on his tunic.

Footnote: The Air Ministry was warned by its own intelligence department that "kill" claims were being overstated and that no more than 76 planes could have been destroyed on 15 September. Post-war examination of German records showed that even this was exaggerated; the real figure was 62.

For all that it was a victory. Air Chief Marshal Sir Hugh Dowding had handled his forces with precision and economy. They had not been wasted on pointless patrols.

A combination of radar and decoded German radio traffic meant that the sectors that were going to have a quiet day — as with Middle Wallop and Warmwell on 15 September — could be partly redeployed sideways to provide additional aircraft for an area where the resident defenders were about to be outnumbered.

Dowding's achievement, amounting to a triumph, was to deny the Luftwaffe its one prerequisite for winning the Battle of Britain. This was a combination of caution and reaction. Firstly, he insisted that there were always planes grounded in reserve, but used this element of restraint creatively, to ensure that something could always be done to counter the following day's attack.

Goring was frustrated by this and had ordered his commanders: "You must bring the R.A.F. up to battle."

Sunday 15 September

Cattistock carillon destroyed by fire.

14.30 hours. The tall 1873-built tower of Cattistock parish church has been gutted by fire, destroying its famous carillon of 35 bells. The village will miss the tunes.

Officially, the cause is not known, but locally it has been blamed on a cigarette discarded by a member of the Home Guard. The irony is that he was in the tower for fire-watching duty.

Sunday 15 September

Heinkels turn back from Portland Bill.

Intercepted by "B" Flight of six Spitfires of 152 Squadron from R.A.F. Warmwell, led by Pilot Officer Eric "Boy" Marrs, 30 Heinkel He.111 bombers dropped their bombs from 16,000 feet over Portland Bill and turned back towards France.

The Spitfires harried them for ten miles, claiming to have shot down two and damaged several others. Marrs writes: "If we had had the whole squadron up we could have broken their formation and knocked down quite a number. The extraordinary part about this raid was that there was no fighter escort."

One Heinkel He.111, probably belonging to Kampfgeschwader 55 from Chartes, was definitely destroyed.

The three Spitfires of Green Section each had a turn with five-second bursts of cannon fire. Pilot Officer Peter O'Brien, in Green One, attacked the starboard engine from astern. Sergeant Pilot Kenneth Holland, in Green Three, followed from astern and above, reporting black smoke pouring from the starboard engine. Then Pilot Officer Weston, in Green Two, delivered the coup de grâce, at 15.55 hours.

Tuesday 17 September

Marrs gets a Junkers but loses his 'Old Faithful'.

Pilot Officer Eric "Boy" Marrs was leading Blue Section of 152 Squadron from R.A.F. Warmwell over Portland earlier this afternoon. He was then told to rise to 20,000 feet on a course of 350 degrees, which eight minutes later was revised to 280 degrees, with the other two Spitfires following.

This flight-path brought him in sight of a lone Junkers Ju.88 bomber (L1+XC) above Shepton Mallet, Somerset. It belonged to operational test unit Lehrgeschwader 1.

"Tally ho!" Marrs called over the radio from Blue One, as he led the three fighters in line astern. The first burst from his guns hit the radiator of the bomber's starboard engine and had it streaming white ethylene glycol coolant. The aircraft, which was heading east, descended into thick cloud, and would crash-land at Ladywell Barn, two miles west of Imber, on Salisbury Plain. The spot is only three miles from Dauntsey's which was Marrs's public school.

Pilot Officer Marrs then had to contend with his own emergency as "Old Faithful" suffered engine failure. The machine in which the Dover-born 19-year-old had flown 130 hours was coaxed down from 12,000 feet on to the concrete runways of a training aerodrome at Yatesbury that is partly obstructed to prevent German landings

A bullet had smashed the air cooler and caused the Merlin engine to lose its oil. A maintenance squad is removing the Spitfire by road but young Marrs will never fly it again; probably it will go back into service with an instructional unit.

Sergeant Pilot Kenneth Holland, in Blue Two, also sustained damage from the Junkers — to hydraulic, glycol, and oil pipes — and came down at Yatesbury as well. He punctured his starboard tyre. The fighter had been hit by machine-gun fire in three places; and had himself pumped 1,650 rounds in the general direction of the Junkers.

Only one Spitfire, Blue Three flown by Pilot Officer Peter O'Brien, was able to fly home to Dorset and land at Warmwell Aerodrome.

The Ju.88 was from the Luftwaffe base at Bricy, near Orleans, and its crew was headed by Major Cramer, the Gruppe Kommander of Lehrgeschwader 1. He and two others would survive the forced-landing. The fourth crewman was killed.

They had been on their way towards factories at Speke, near Liverpool. Each Spitfire pilot is personally claiming one-third of the kill.

Tuesday 17 September

Operation Sealion postponed indefinitely.

Hitler today postponed Operation Seelöwe [Sealion], the planned invasion of England, which should give the country's nerves a reprieve until next spring. Winston Churchill has read out a deciphered German Enigma machine-coded radio message to the Chiefs of Defence Staff. In intercept is a minor order of huge significance — for the dismantling of loading equipment on Dutch airfields.

Churchill refers to Sealion as Operation Smith, to lessen the risk of compromising the source of those crucial Enigma intercepts that revealed its name. This is good news that cannot be openly shared with the nation.

Thursday 19 September

Bournemouth Garrison stood down.

With the abandonment of Operation Sealion, any immediate prospect of a German invasion has receded, and accordingly the Bournemouth Garrison has been stood down. The Garrison Commander has been replaced by a new posting — that of Officer Commanding Troops, Bournemouth.

Routine invasion patrols and counter-measures will continue in order to avoid indicating to the enemy that we realise the situation has changed.

Thursday 19 September
Warmwell's Holland claims a Junkers.

Green Section of 152 Squadron scrambled this afternoon from R.A.F. Warmwell and were ordered to patrol the cloud base at 10,000 feet. They found that the radio telephone of Green One, the leading Spitfire, was unserviceable, so Green Two — flown by Sergeant Pilot Kenneth Holland — took over and became Green One instead.

Holland was told to climb to 15,000 feet above Warmwell Aerodrome and vectored across the Isle of Purbeck towards a Junkers Ju.88 bomber over the English Channel. His combat report begins at 16.20 hours:

"As there was cloud at 10,000 feet, Green Two went below the cloud and I went above the cloud at 11,500 feet. When cloud broke I went down to given height and sighted Ju.88 ahead on the right two miles away. Green Two was left behind below cloud.

"I gave 'Tally-ho' on the R/T [radio telephone] but Green Two could not find me.

"I made alternate quarter attacks from left and right — from 300 to 200 yards — firing one burst of four second and five each of two seconds, aiming first at the gunners' positions and then at each engine.

"E/A [enemy aircraft] took slight evasive action, heading for cloud on a southerly course. White return fire after my second attack.

"I continued to attack and eventually the E/A, now at 8,000 feet, dived vertically towards the sea, with both engines on fire. As my ammunition was finished I flew on a northerly course, and came to the Isle of Wight.

"My engine was missing slightly, so I made for Portsmouth Aerodrome, where I landed. After checking engine returned to base. Rounds fired — 2,800."

Friday 20 September
Steamship sinks in Lyme Bay.

SS *Trito*, a British steam freighter, has sunk after being bombed by German aircraft in Lyme Bay.

Sunday 22 September
Seven bombs at Holdenhurst and Throop.

Bombs fell at 00.55 hours last night in a line across the hamlets of Holdenhurst and Throop, in gardens and meadows beside the River Stour, to the north of Bournemouth. Seven bombs damaged 24 buildings including Holdenhurst School and the nearby Vicarage. Here the eight occupants were unhurt but in one of the cottages a man was killed by a fragment of bomb casing.

Monday 23 September
Warmwell loses its 13th pilot.

Pilot Officer Walter Beaumont, flying Spitfire R7016 of 152 Squadron from R.A.F. Warmwell, is believed to have been shot down over the sea. He has been reported as "Missing in Action" and is the station's 13th airman to be lost during the present battle.

A 26-year-old Yorkshire science graduate, from Dewesbury, Beaumont was a pre-war member of the Royal Air Force Volunteer Reserve, who was called-up for full-time service in December 1939. He would claim 152 Squadron's first double set of kills, over the Isle of Wight, on 16 August. It was regarded as tempting fate when he drove from the base to visit the wreckage of another of his successes on 25 August.

Tuesday 24 September
Six killed as Navy trawler hits mine.

His Majesty's Trawler *Loch Monteith*, on an anti-invasion patrol in Lyme Bay, hit what is presumed to have been a mine at 02.45 hours this morning. The bows are severely damaged. Below deck six men were killed as they slept.

Her location is ten miles west of Portland Bill. She is being towed back to Portland by the dockyard tug *Pilot*.

Wednesday 25 September
Heinkels shot down at Poole and Studland.

A German mass bombing force of 220 attacking planes and their escorts passed northwards over Portland this morning and flew across west Dorset and the Somerset Levels to the Bristol Channel coast. They then turned north-eastwards, between the islands Steep Holm and Flat Holm, to make an approach across the water towards the Bristol Aeroplane Company's works at Filton. This was devastated by 350 bombs from 15,000 feet. The aerodrome rippled with flashes.

On the way home, however, the raiders were harried by the Royal Air Force. Five aircraft were brought down and a further three had to crash-land in France.

The two that were shot down in Dorset were both claimed by Hurricanes of 238 Squadron from R.A.F. Middle Wallop. One Heinkel He.111 (G1+LR) ploughed into Underwood, a house in Westminster Road at Branksome Park, Poole. All but one of its five crewmen were killed.

The survivor, who had baled out, landed unhurt in the sea off Branksome Chine: "A short, ugly, broad-chested Nazi airman was hoisted by the military into a truck to be taken away."

The second Heinkel He.111 (G1+BH) force-landed at Westfield Farm, Studland. Josef Attrichter, the flight mechanic, was taken from the wreckage but died half an hour later. The other four crewmen staggered out with little worse than aching backs.

Off-duty wine waiter Theo Janku took them prisoner with the aid of an unloaded Home Guard rifle and relieved them of their Lugers. On seeing there were casualties, the Studland villagers then tried to help the Germans, and provided cigarettes and tea.

The "G1" markings identify the Heinkels as belonging to II Gruppe of Kampfgeschwader 55. Their emblem is the coat of arms of Giessen.

Footnote: Later the second Heinkel was salvaged and reassembled for Cardiff's War Weapons Week. Before it was removed from Studland it had been guarded by a detachment of the Suffolk Regiment.

"This is war, not a bloody peepshow," one of the sentries snapped at onlookers.

It seems to have been from this bomber that a document was found forbidding the use of explosive ammunition against troop concentrations and other human targets.

The burial of the Branksome Park Germans in Parkstone Cemetery, next to the graves of British seamen, enraged the Poole Herald into protesting that "Nazi murderers and British heroes" had been placed side by side. A week later the newspaper felt utterly let down by one of his readers: "Someone has put flowers on the grave!"

Underwood would be blitzed again, by a bomb on 12 August 1943, and a block of flats — called Chatsworth — stands on the site.

Wednesday 25 September
Warmwell's Holland killed in Somerset.

Another of today's Heinkel kills, that of Hauptmann Helmut Brandt's He.111 (G1+EP) belonging to II Gruppe of Kampfgeschwader 55, is being credited to a Spitfire of 152 Squadron from R.A.F. Warmwell.

The wreckage of both aeroplanes lies strewn across fields at Church Farm, Woolverton, a village four miles north of Frome, Somerset. The crash sites are less than 500 yards apart and occurred within two minutes of each other.

Sergeant Pilot Kenneth Christopher Holland hit the ground first, in N3173, at noon precisely.

He died almost immediately from the effects of the crash and a severe bullet wound in his skull which caused him to lose control of the fighter. The 20-year-old had spotted the pilot baling out and apparently approached the stricken Heinkel to watch it come down. He was then hit at close range by return fire from its gunner who was about to die. The fatal shot penetrated the seal between the rounded port-side top of his toughened windscreen — double sheeted glass, to a thickness of 25 mm — making an exit hole four inches across.

Then at 12.02 the German bomber came down in flames. The pilot survived but the other four crew were killed, one in the fireball on impact, and the others from having jumped at a height too low for their parachutes to function.

Twenty-year-old Kenneth Holland also used the surname Ripley. He was an Australian orphan, from Manley in Sydney, who came to England to enlist in the Royal Air Force. He joined 152 Squadron at Warmwell on 1 August. His loss brings the squadron's death-toll to seven and that for the base to 14.

Squadron Leader Peter Devitt of 152 Squadron also had problems with a Heinkel He.111. The petrol tank of his Spitfire ruptured with a burst of return fire. He was able to make a successful forced-landing in the Avon valley between Bristol and Bath, at Skew Bridge, Newton St Loe.

BREATHING EXERCISE: BOURNEMOUTH FIREMEN BEING KITTED OUT WITH 'PROTO', TO PROVIDE A ONE-HOUR OXYGEN SUPPLY

Footnote: There is a memorial to Kenneth Holland/Ripley at Woolverton, beside the main road, at the junction opposite Woolverton House Hotel. He was cremated at Weymouth Crematorium.

The microphone of N3173's radio transmitter and the windscreen that let through the ill-fated shot are in Rodney Legg's Dorset collection. It is intact apart from the fatal hole. These poignant relics were preserved locally and sold at auction some years ago. They carried labels for "Lot 178".

Thursday 26 September
More Warmwell and German losses.

Flight-Lieutenant Derek Boitel-Gill led a section of 152 Squadron from R.A.F. Warmwell into combat against a formation of Junkers Ju.88 bombers and their Messerschmitt Bf.109 escort fighters over the sea to the west of the Isle of Wight.

One of the bombers was seen to fall into the water, resulting from an engagement by Sergeant Pilot Ralph "Bob" Wolton, but two of the attacking Spitfires were then gunned down in a dog-fight. Sergeant Pilot Jack McBean Christie, in K9882, is reported "Killed in Action". The 22-year-old brings the squadron's losses to eight and the Warmwell toll to 15.

Flying Officer "Jumbo" Deansley was able to bale out of K9982 and has been picked-up by an R.A.F. Air-Sea Rescue launch. It is landing him at Swanage. The vessel has also recovered Christie's body.

Some 60 Heinkel He.111s of Kampfgeschwader 55 have wrecked the Vickers Supermarine works at Woolston, Southampton — the main centre for Spitfire airframe assembly — with 70 tons of bombs. more than 30 people have been killed.

Footnote: Jack Christie is buried in Arkleston Cemetery, Renfrew. Boitel-Gill was no mean shot, having been credited with five kills in a week in August. He would be promoted Squadron Leader on 1 December 1940, and became Commanding Officer of 152 Squadron, and Wing Commander in June 1941. The following month he lost his life in a flying accident.

Friday 27 September
Marrs puts his Junkers down in the Bristol Channel.

Pilot Officer Eric "Boy" Marrs from 152 Squadron, flying a Warmwell Spitfire, started what was going to be an active day by finding a lone Junkers Ju.88 at 23,000 feet over Somerset. He followed it in a running fight across Exmoor, flying in places at only 50 feet above the heather and scattering the wild red deer, and had ethylene glycol coolant streaming from both engines of the bomber.

The German pilot headed for the coast, but towards a different channel from that over which the Dorset Spitfires usually patrol:

"As I expected both engines soon stopped. He made for the south coast of the Bristol Channel and landed about 20 feet from the beach in the water, running his machine up on the beach. I circled round and watched the crew get out. They waved to me and I waved back, and then hordes of civilians came rushing up. I watched the crew taken prisoner, beat up the beach, and then climbed away."

The tiny seaside resort treated to this excitement was Porlock, to the west of Minehead, where it is unusual for anything to happen. The town's single claim to fame is "a person on business from Porlock" who interrupted Samuel Taylor Coleridge as he was recalling and writing down his dream-poem *Kubla Khan* and remains unknown to this day.

Friday 27 September
Lulworth A.A. gunners get a Bf.110.

Anti-aircraft gunners at Lulworth Camp are jubilantly celebrating their first definite kill. The unlucky German aircraft was a Messerschmitt Bf.110 which had come low over the huts. There had been an air-raid warning and a red alert was in force. The stricken fighter crashed to the ground about 1,000 yards from the sea.

Friday 27 September
German planes crash all over Dorset.

German planes have crashed all over Dorset, plus Radipole-born Pilot Officer Roger Freeman Garland "Mick" Miller, in Spitfire X4107 of 609 Squadron from R.A.F. Warmwell. His death brings the squadron's losses to seven and those for the station to 16.

Otherwise it has been a one-sided debacle for the Luftwaffe. They attempted what became an abortive raid on Parnall Aircraft Limited — makers of gun turrets — at Yate, near Chipping Sodbury.

Ten fighter-bombers of Erprobungsgruppe 210, an experimental and proving unit from Cherbourg, led by Hauptmann Martin Lutz, had the support of 89 fighters. The Gruppe's aircraft have as their crest a red map of the British Isles superimposed with a yellow ring-type gun sight. Their objective today was to test bomb-carrying on Messerschmitt Bf.109s and Bf.110s.

The German attackers, coming in fast over north Bristol at 11,000 feet, were met head on by Flying Officer Edward Murray Frisby in a Hurricane of 504 Squadron from R.A.F. Filton. He scored a hit that damaged Lutz's leading plane and forced the others to turn sideways from their run towards the Parnall factory. The rest of 504 Squadron rounded on the scattering enemy and caused them to jettison their bombs. Escape was now the only German objective.

One of the Bf.110s was shot down over Fishponds, Bristol. Another came down at Haydon Hill near Radstock. That was at 11.45 hours.

At the same moment, over Bellamy's Farm, Piddletrenthide, there was a similar bang as one of the rearguard manoeuvres went wrong. Pilot Officer "Mick" Miller was leading the Spitfires of 609 Squadron which had been scrambled from Warmwell Aerodrome. His machine, X4107, had collided with Bf.110 (3U+FT) at 27,000 feet. Pilot Officer David Moore Crook witnessed the crash: "I was flying just behind Mick and he turned slightly left to attack a Bf.110 which was coming towards him. But the German was as determined as Mick, and refused to give way or alter course to avoid this head-on attack. Their aggregate speed of closing was at least 600 m.p.h. and an instant later they collided. There was a terrific explosion and a sheet of flame and black smoke seemed to hang in the air like a great ball of fire. Many little shattered fragments fluttered down, and that was all."

Miller and the Messerschmitt's wireless operator, Emil Lidtke, were killed instantly. Remarkably, however, the German pilot was blown sideways by the explosion and found himself parachuting (minus his boots) into a field. He was given some lemonade and taken off by police.

His dead comrade was treated with less respect, with farmer Ralph Wightman noting that after it had been removed from the wreckage it was left lying in full view for hours, before someone draped it with a sheet.

"All this happened in an instant," Crook continued, "and I turned right in order to get on to the tail of a Hun. My Spitfire immediately went into a very vicious right-hand spin — the atmosphere at these great altitudes is so rarefied that the machines are very much more difficult to manoeuvre — and when I recovered I had lost my German."

A fourth Bf.110 (3U+IM) was also exploding at 11.45, at 1,000 feet above Salter's Wood, Middlebere, in the Isle of Purbeck. It had been engaged by a Spitfire of 152 Squadron from R.A.F. Warmwell. In the crashed plane were Arthur Niebuhr and Klaus Deissen; both were killed.

Equally unfortunate, at 11.50, were the crew of another Messerschmitt, between Tyneham and Kimmeridge. This was almost certainly Bf.110 (3U+BD) manned by Hans Carschel and Unteroffizier Klose.

Luckier, just a mile away at 11.55, were the crew of Bf.110 (3U+DS). Fritz Schupp and Karl Nechwatal had been attacked by Spitfires and their port engine was hit and burning. Despite the damage, Schupp successfully brought the Messerschmitt down in a forced-landing, on a field beside Gaulter Gap and the Coastguard Cottages at Kimmeridge Bay. It boasts three kill-bars denoting R.A.F. aircraft destroyed.

These "3U" aircraft belonged to Zerstörergeschwader 26, the Geschwader named Horst Wessel, for the Nazi writer of a militant anti-Semitic song which has become the alternative national anthem.

At noon a second Bf.110 (S9+DU) made a belly landing. It had received engine damage over Iwerne Minster and came down at The Beeches, beside the main road from Blandford to Shaftesbury. The pilot, Friedrich Ebner, was unhurt. The gunner, Werner Zwick, is seriously injured and has been taken to Shaftesbury Hospital.

There was another noon crash, at Bussey Stool Farm, near Tarrant Gunville, where Bf.110 (S9+DH) finally bit the dust. This was the Messerschmitt of the operation's leader who had been thwarted by Murray Frisby over Bristol. Martin Lutz was still flying at speed but was losing height and then found the ground coming towards him on the top-lands of Cranborne Chase. In the final moments he hit trees before ploughing into the ground.

Martin Lutz and his radio operator, Anton Schon, were killed instantly. Lutz, aged 27, had flown with the Condor Legion in the Spanish Civil War.

As a finale, also within seconds of mid-day, two more Messerschmitts were put down into the sea off Dorset just as the safety of Cherbourg came into sight. They are Bf.110 (S9+JH), crewed by Gerhard Schmidt and Gerhard Richeter, and Bf.110 (S9+GK) with Wilhelm Rossiger and Hans Marx.

STATION GRAFFITO: FOR 152 SQUADRON OF R.A.F. WARMWELL AT DISPERSAL AMID THE BEECH TREES OF KNIGHTON HEATH WOOD

They were shot down about 25 miles south of Portland Bill, with one of the attacking Spitfires of 609 Squadron from R.A.F. Warmwell being flown by Pilot Officer Noel le Chevalier Agazarian. These "S9" aircraft belonged to Erprobungsgruppe 210.

Pilot Officer Crook joined the chase into mid-Channel: "I saw a Bf.110 about half a mile ahead and went after him on full throttle. He was also going flat out and diving to get extra speed, but my beloved Spitfire rose nobly to the occasion and worked up to over 400 m.p.h., and I caught him fairly easily, though we were about 20 miles out to sea by this time. The enemy rear-gunner, who obviously had wind up, opened fire at me at rather long range, though I could see his tracer bullets flicking past me. It is an odd thing when you are being fired at by a rear-gunner that the stream of bullets seem to leave the machine very slowly and in a great outward curve. You chuckle to yourself, 'Ha, the fool's missing me by miles!' Then, suddenly, the bullets accelerate madly and curl in towards you again and flick just past your head. You thereupon bend your head a little lower, mutter 'My God!' or some other suitable expression, and try to kill the rear-gunner before he makes any more nuisance of himself.

"I dived slightly to get underneath his tail, as he could not fire at me in that direction, and when in range I opened fire. I must have killed the gunner, because he never fired again, though I must have been visible to him at times and at very close range. I put all my ammunition into the fuselage and port engine and the latter started to smoke furiously. To my intense disgust my ammunition ran out before he went down, badly damaged though he was."

"O.K., O.K., help coming," Crook heard on the R.T. Another Spitfire arrived on the scene and delivered the coup de grâce to put the Messerchmitt into the sea.

Footnote: Ralph Wightman, a bucolic broadcaster in later life, recalled that the dead German airman at Piddletrenthide was shunned by the local clergy. He said it was eventually buried where it had been dragged, beside the hedgerow that forms the boundary of Bellamy's Farm, with Dole's Ash Farm.

The Spitfire came down to the east, towards Cheselbourne, and Roger Miller lies in Radford Semele churchyard, near Leamington Spa, Warwickshire.

The bodies of Gerhard Schmidt and Gerhard Richeter were recovered from the English Channel.

A whole book has been devoted to the events of this memorable day. *Luftwaffe Encore*, by Kenneth Wakefield, was published in 1979.

Friday 27 September
Agazarian's hat-trick for 609 Squadron.

R.A.F. Warmwell's Armenian-French Spitfire flyer, Pilot Officer Noel le Chevalier Agazarian of 609 Squadron, has scored a hat-trick of kills over the past three days. His previous claim was a month ago with a shared Messerschmitt Bf.110 on 25 August.

The current run of good fortune began with another shared kill, that of a Heinkel He.111 bomber, on 25 September. That was followed by an exclusive Messerschmitt Bf.109 fighter yesterday, and today the unshared and confirmed destruction of a Bf.110 fighter-bomber — put down in the sea — which has been identified as S9+GK of Erprobungsgruppe 210.

Footnote: Agazarian was killed later in the war but he left one of the most evocative of all memorials. His fighter from those Dorset days, R6915, survived the war and is now suspended over the main Battle of Britain display in the Imperial War Museum, Lambeth Road, London SE1. It dominates the exhibits, as does Dorset's Roman mosaic of Christ in the British Museum.

Saturday 28 September
Navy trawler sunk by mine off Portland.

An underwater explosion off Portland at 21.16 hours last night is believed to have sunk His Majesty's Trawler *Recoil*, which as the *Blankenburg* was captured from the Germans.

The explosion was heard from her sister vessel, H.M.T. *Angle*, which went to the spot to investigate. Though no wreckage was found there was a stench of diesel oil in the vicinity. This coincided with *Recoil's* last known position.

Sunday 29 September
Christchurch radar establishment hit.

Six high explosive bombs and a number of incendiaries dropped at 01.17 hours on the Ministry of Supply's Air Defence Experimental Establishment, which makes radar components, at Somerford, Christchurch. Damage, however, was slight. By 02.48 all the fires had been put out.

Monday 30 September
Morning and afternoon claims for Warmwell's Crook.

Scrambling at 11.00 hours from R.A.F. Warmwell, in Spitfire X4165, Pilot Officer David Moore Crook led Green Section of 609 Squadron as they swept in a line seawards across the Isle of Purbeck. Pilot Officer Mike Appleby quickly put a Messerschmitt Bf.109 into the sea, but Crook's action was protracted.

He records the record in his log: "We intercepted some Bf.109s at 23,000 feet over Swanage. The fools tried to escape by diving and we all went down after them. I got to about 600 m.p.h. and easily caught mine, gave it a burst, and he crashed into the sea I then chased another and put him into the sea about 25 miles from Cherbourg. It took me a long time to get back to the English coast . . . pleased to see the white cliffs."

Crook was airborne again in the afternoon, leading Green Section in combat, against six Bf.109s, ten miles north of Poole:

"I had a very enjoyable few minutes dog-fighting with one and though behind him all the time could not get sights properly on him. Finally he dived for cloud, but I chased him to Weymouth and then gave him a good burst. He turned over on his back and spun into cloud streaming glycol and smoke. I could not claim him as definite as I did not see him actually crash but he certainly never got back to France. This was my best day yet."

Footnote: David Crook would publish his story in *Spitfire Pilot*, in 1942, where he graphically expands on that combat dive after the Messerschmitts from 23,000 feet over Swanage: "The victim that I had selected for myself was about 500 yards ahead of me, and still diving hard at very high speed. God, what a dive that was! I came down on full throttle from 27,000 feet to 1,000 feet in a matter of a few seconds, and the speed rose with incredible swiftness — 400 m.p.h., 500, 550, 600 m.p.h. I never reached this speed before and probably never shall again. I have a sort of dim recollection of the sea coming up towards me at an incredible rate and also feeling an awful pain in my ears, though I was not really conscious of this in the heat of the moment. I pulled out of the dive as gently as I could, but the strain was terrific and there was a sort of black mist in front of my eyes, though I did not quite 'black out'.

"The Messerschmitt was now just ahead of me. I came up behind him, and gave him a terrific burst of fire at very close range. The effect of a Spitfire's eight guns has to be seen to be believed. Hundreds of bullets poured into him and he rocked violently, then turned over on his back, burst into flames and dived, straight down into the sea a few miles off Swanage. The pilot made no attempt to get out and was obviously dead.

"I watched him hit the water in a great cloud of white foam, and then turned round to see what was going on."

He then chased another Bf.109 towards France. Crook "put a good burst into him" and the cockpit covering broke off the machine as it then dived steeply: "I waited to see him hit the water, but he was only shamming, as he flattened out again just above the sea, and continued full speed for home, though his machine was now smoking and obviously badly hit. For the first time in this war, I felt a certain pity for this German pilot and was rather reluctant to finish him off. From the moment I saw him, he really had no chance of escape as my Spitfire was so much faster than his Messerschmitt, and the last few moments must have been absolute hell for him. I could almost feel his desperation as he made his last attempt to get away. But if I let him go, he would come back to England another day and possible shoot down some of our pilots. In the few seconds during which all this was happening, I did not consciously make these reflections; my blood was up anyway and I was very excited, but I distinctly remember feeling rather reluctant.

"However, I caught him up again and made no mistake this time. I fired almost all my remaining ammunition at very close range, and he crashed into the sea, going at terrific speed, and disappeared immediately. I circled round the spot, but there was no trace of anything.

"I now looked round and discovered that I could see the French coast clearly ahead and that I was only about 15 miles from Cherbourg. England was nowhere to be seen. In the excitement of the chase I had not realised how far we were going, and I turned round very hastily and started on my 60-mile trip back to the English coast. It seemed to take a long time, and I was very relieved when, still a long way out to sea, I saw the white cliffs begin in appear ahead. One never knows what an engine may do after running it so long on absolutely full throttle and the idea of drowning out in mid-Channel never did appeal to me."

He was now feeling elated: "I had always wanted to get two Huns in one fight. I approached the cliffs in Weymouth Bay, flying only a few feet over the water at nearly 300 m.p.h., and when I was almost hitting the cliff I pulled the stick back and rocketed over the top to the very considerable amazement of some soldiers who were on the other side. And so back home, flying very low the whole way, generally playing the fool and feeling happy and elated!

"Everybody was safely back and we had destroyed five Messerschmitts — quite a nice morning's work."

David Moore Crook was awarded the Distinguished Flying Cross on 17 October 1940.

His last operation with 609 Squadron, leading it in the Commanding Officer's absence, would be on 8 November 1940, also in Spitfire X4165. He became a flying instructor.

Norman Franks records Crook's fate in the book *Wings of Freedom*. On 18 December 1944, at the age of 30, he was lost over the North Sea, off Aberdeen, whilst flying Spitfire EN662 on a high-level photographic reconnaissance. He left a widow, Dorothy, and a four-year-old son, Nicholas.

Monday 30 September
Sherborne's 60 bombs in a few minutes.

Yeovil's barrage balloons were raised at 15.55 hours on a warm but cloudy afternoon. In Sherborne the air-raid sirens also wailed.

Thirty-seven Heinkel He.111 bombers were attempting to find the Westland Aircraft Company's factory in Yeovil but precision was impossible due to nine-tenths cloud cover at 20,000 feet.

Instead, flying in formation on a north-easterly line, they missed their target by five miles and began to bomb blind in the vicinity of Lenthay Common and then across the ancient yellow-stone town of Sherborne, raining

SHERBORNE BLITZED: PHILLIPS AND SON'S OUTFITTING DEPARTMENT (LEFT) AND THE PUBLIC BAR OF THE HALF MOON HOTEL, ON 1 OCTOBER 1940

SIDE VIEW: FROM THE BOTTOM END OF CHEAP STREET, SHOWING A SINGLE PROP PREVENTING THE REMAINDER OF PHILLIPS AND SON'S PREMISES FOLLOWING THE REMAINDER OF THE STORE, ON 1 OCTOBER 1940

SHERBORNE CRATER: IN THE JUNCTION OF CHEAP STREET AND HALF MOON STREET, SEEN FROM THE DEBRIS OUTSIDE PHILLIPS AND SON'S STORE, WITH THOSE OF BUTCHER CHARLES GREENHAM AND SHOE RETAILER JOSEPH FRISBY HAVING SUFFERED ONLY RELATIVELY SUPERFICIAL DAMAGE, ON 1 OCTOBER 1940

about 60 bombs down on its clustered terraces and between scholastic and ecclesiastical roofs.

Townspeople insist that the raid was over in a matter of minutes. Remarkably, the town's famous Abbey and other historic buildings are almost unscathed, and casualties are light considering the extensive overall damage to shops, homes, and roads. Fortunately the schools had just gone home.

Seventeen civilians are dead and there are 32 hospital cases, one of whom is critically injured.

Footnote: The badly injured person would die. Theirs was to be just about Sherborne's only direct sacrifice for the duration of hostilities. Only four others went to hospital as a result of the war for the whole period 1939-45.

Despite the devastation, in a line across the town from Lenthay to Coldharbour, it was of little architectural consequence. The buildings that carry the town's name — the Abbey, Sherborne School, the Almshouse, Sherborne Castle, and even the older ruined castle — survived with only flecks of superficial damage.

For all that it was by far the worse air attack of the war on one of Dorset's inland towns.

There was a heroine amongst the debris. Miss Maud Steele, the supervisor of the telephone exchange which was blown apart by a direct hit, stayed calm and ensured that the town's initial calamity reports were sent out by road.

She was to be awarded the George Cross for her pluck; it had been instituted by King George VI as the "Civilians V.C." only a few days previously. The town had 766 damaged buildings, some ten per cent of them virtually destroyed, out of a total of 1,700. The sewers as well as the phones were out of action. Blankets had to be brought in by the Red Cross and a council

appeal, competing with many others, raised £2,200 including contributions from Sherborne in Massachusetts.

For the 18 victims there is a brass plate behind the cross that commemorates the Great War in Half Moon Street, in front of the Abbey precinct:

THOSE WHO DIED IN THE AIR RAID ON
SHERBORNE
30 SEPTEMBER 1940

BUTLIN John
DAWE Leonard I.
GARTELL Albertina B.
GOULTER Percy H. D.
HUNT Douglas
IRELAND Henry
JEFFERY William C.
KNOBBS Edward D.
LEGG Horace G.
LE GALLAIS Albert I. E.
LINTERN Arthur J.
MARDEN Elizabeth A.
MORGAN William S.
REASON A. H.
TRASK Barry A.
WARREN Ronald K.
WARREN Robert G.
WARREN Patricia A.

In 1984, for the story of the disaster and the town's resilience and recovery, I interviewed the District Air Raid Precautions Controller, Edward J. Freeman M.B.E. who was also the Clerk to the Sherborne Urban District Council between 1936-74. The account was first published in Harold Osment's *Wartime Sherborne*.

In it Mr Osment poignantly recalls that one of the dead was a school-chum: "There came the cruel realisation, so cruel as to be almost beautiful, that we should never again see, let alone play with Bobby Warren."

This was how Mr Freeman recalled the day and its aftermath, from his bungalow beside the fields at Rimpton, to the north of the town:

"The Sherborne raid is being forgotten. Last year I heard a guide at Sherborne Castle say in answer to a question, about whether any bombs had fallen at Sherborne during the war, that he thought there had been one dropped in the town. I interrupted to say that I had been the town's A.R.P. Controller and there had been 300 bombs [60, actually] that fell in three minutes on 30 September 1940.

"At the time I was on the pavement in Yeovil standing in a queue to see a picture — it was one of the few days in the entire war when I was away from my desk. It was my birthday. The thud of the bombs in the east was followed by a pall of black smoke, which could only be from Sherborne, and I drove straight back. It took me 20 minutes to reach the council offices, picking my way through an unimaginable shambles.

"The theory is that the 50 German planes had been on their way to the Bristol Aeroplane Company works at Filton" [seriously damaged by an attack five days earlier, on 25 September, though in fact the attack was against Westlands at Yeovil] "and were intercepted by a squadron of Hurricanes, two of which were brought down each side of Yeovil. The local people thought one of the pilots was German as they saw his parachute open. The bombers came to us from the south-west, across Lenthay Common, and then they unloaded. We were underneath.

"There were no longer any services at all. No water, no telephones — the exchange had a direct hit — no gas, no electricity, and the sewers and all roads out of the town were blocked.

"One of the miracles was in Newland where Foster's Infants School received a direct hit and had to be pulled down afterwards. It was hit only a quarter of an hour after the children had left. One story I heard , though I cannot vouch for it, was that in The Avenue Miss Billinger climbed from her bath into the open air." [Miss Margaret Billinger lived at Stonegarth.]

"Perhaps the strangest damage was in Horsecastles where bombs landed on both sides of the terrace and then outhouses imploded away from the main buildings, which was caused by a bellows effect. Six or eight delayed action bombs went off twelve hours later. One caught us out as it was hidden under debris.

"The strangest debris came from the midnight bakery next to the Picture Palace in Newland. They had hoarded silver coins which were thrown on to the cinema roof and retrieved by my A.R.P. warden.

"As I plotted the bombs on to our A.R.P. area map and the number climbed into the hundreds I ran out of red pins. It was quite extraordinary that there hadn't been more casualties.

"The worst thing was a direct hit in the cemetery. The coffin of a friend whom we had buried a week earlier was blown out of the ground. My gravediggers disappeared and we did the best we could to clear up with a firm of undertakers from Yeovil.

WESTERN VIEW: LOOKING THE OTHER WAY ALONG HALF MOON STREET, ON 1 OCTOBER 1940

"Down Lenthay there was terrible damage and I sent the Billeting Officer down on his bike to see how many I had to re-house and find accommodation for. Ten of our council houses were completely destroyed, and there was damage to all the remaining 108 of them, mainly on a serious scale. To my astonishment when he came back he said, 'No need to worry — people have come forward and offered shelter. Everyone has been given a home somewhere.'

"It was quite extraordinary what happened there, and it happened all over the town. If ever I have admired the people of Sherborne as a whole it was after the raid. I had told the schools that they might have to put people up that night, but in the event it wasn't necessary. One little thing, after that raid there was no all-clear, as we had no electricity. From then on we had to use rattles and whistles for air-raid sirens.

"The ministry men thought I was exaggerating and panicking when they heard from me on the only emergency phone line we had left, but when they came down they apologised to me. They had never seen such devastation in a small country town.

"I took the Regional Commissioner around in my car. Twelve hours later all my tyres were flat, punctured by the glass.

CHEAP STREET: THE SCENE IN THE CENTRE OF SHERBORNE'S MAIN SHOPPING AREA, OUTSIDE T. E. GILLARD'S HAIRDRESSING SALON; WITH A SIGN ABOVE THE CLEARANCE TEAM PROCLAIMING "HAVE FAITH IN GOD", ON 1 OCTOBER 1940

THE AVENUE: SEDBER ON THE EAST SIDE (NOW KNOWN AS RATHGAR), ON 1 OCTOBER 1940

CENTRAL CHIMNEY: HOLDING UP STONEGARTH IN NEWLAND, AT THE SOUTH END OF THE AVENUE, WHERE MISS MARGARET BILLINGER SURVIVED THE BLAST IN HER BATH, ON 1 OCTOBER 1940

"Opposite Phillips and Son's store, outside the Westminster Bank [junction of Half Moon Street and South Street], an unexploded bomb had fallen, leaving a hole that the bomb disposal team had covered with sandbags. An officer calmly sat down beside these on a lump of stone and lit a cigarette. I showed some concern that we were sitting down beside a bomb. 'If it goes off, we won't know anything about it!' he said. 'It's a big one,' he said, 'but I can't touch it for a fortnight. In the meantime you'll have to evacuate everyone around.'

The police and Army sealed off the area and we got the stretcher cases out as best we could. I had to arrange temporary rationing arrangements because we couldn't get into the butcher's shop.

"A fortnight later that officer came back to me laughing, saying: 'You'll never believe this, Mr Freeman, but it was only a small one. The big hole was because it had gone down a disused well shaft!'

"I was flooded with visits from people in London, Bristol, Reading and the cities, and had to explain how we got out of difficulties. It is surprising how the help came that we needed — there was a wonderful spirit everywhere.

"The ministry admitted there were certain things we had to do that might be outside the law, but they said go ahead anyway as legislation was on its way.

"I still wonder how the devil we coped as well with it all. Twenty or thirty evacuees would come down the day after a London raid and we would have to find homes for them. The evacuation was worked out on paper and by the train timetables, but we would have cases where 600 would come down from one school, bound for Sherborne, and some of ours would get off at Sidmouth. We had to sort all that out, have the doctors inspect them, and give out 48-hour rations. You saw how people had been living in London. It was a trying time, particularly as my staff were being called up. We coped by making our minds up at a moment's notice.

"One night I had a red warning that there would be a raid, and suddenly the whole place was lit up by parachute flares, but then nothing happened. We had been told that if the flares dropped they would be followed by bombs. The lights ringed the town and someone phoned to say there was a landmine hanging over of his front door, but it was a flare that had caught in his chimney. He was so excited and frightened he said he couldn't get out of the house — I asked him what had happened to the back door!

Sherborne school: Foster's Infants School, on the east side of Tinney's Lane, on 1 October 1940

Semi-detached: Tanglin, on the east side of North Road, reduced to half a house (Green Bushes, to the left, would be rebuilt to match), on 1 October 1940

SHERBORNE HOUSE: HOMEMEAD, FRAMED BY A MONKEY PUZZLE, ON THE WEST SIDE OF ACREMAN STREET, ON 1 OCTOBER 1940

"I kept on good terms with most of the town. The only time I upset the school was when I requisitioned its tuck shop as a British Restaurant.

"Later in the war, because of our experiences, we were chosen for bomb instruction exercises, and a special invasion exercise in Newland in May 1943. For that one they had a particularly realistic casualty, with his eye hanging by a thread, provided by a butcher. I think they went too far. One old lady in the crowd fainted.

"My biggest regret is that I didn't keep a diary, but I never had the time. A little regret is that there was a relic that could have been preserved, three pieces of bomb-case that were embedded out of harm's way in a school wall [at Sherborne School]. I asked General Waller, the bursar, to leave them but he had them hooked out and the stone repaired."

Brigadier-General Richard Lancelot Waller [1875-1961], a veteran of the Boer War and the Great War, retired to Lindum House in Lenthay Road. He was the bursar of Sherborne School from 1931 to 1945. His last military post, in 1931, had been Chief Engineer at Southern Command; it was asking a bit much for him to appreciate the aesthetics of shrapnel.

Monday 30 September
The 'Boy' who just made it back to Warmwell.

The Heinkel He.111 bombers that jettisoned their bombs on Sherborne had been met by 152 Squadron as they flew at 21,000 feet over Portland. They had apparently been intending to raid the Westland Aircraft factory at Yeovil which makes the Whirlwind, though with only 100 produced this is set to

THE KNAPP: ANOTHER GASH IN ACREMAN STREET, BETWEEN COTTAGES AND TERRACED HOUSES, ON 1 OCTOBER 1940

RICHMOND ROAD: ASHBORNE (LEFT) WITH MUCH DEBRIS AND A FLAT-ROOFED EXTENSION (THE LATTER WAS NEVER REBUILT) AND NEXT-DOOR STONECROFT WITH COMPARATIVELY MINOR DAMAGE, ON 1 OCTOBER 1940

be dismissed as a failure. Anyway, the bombers were heading northwards from the coast.

Squadron Leader Peter Devitt could only muster eight Spitfires of 152 Squadron at R.A.F. Warmwell "and some of these should not have flown by peacetime standards". He was ordered by Sector Control to proceed as quickly as possible to Yeovil. Devitt found it covered with cloud and there was no sign of the enemy:

"Thinking that perhaps they had delivered their bombs and swung round through 180 degrees to starboard, as they had done on a previous Bristol raid, I turned the squadron eastwards in the hopes of picking them up. They had obviously turned this way so as not to be silhouetted against a background of white cloud for our fighters to pick up. It is always more difficult to pick up a camouflaged aircraft from above and with the earth below, but a fighter must have the advantage of height in order to deliver his full weight in the first attack.

"A few seconds after I had spotted them I saw their bombs falling away from beneath their bellies. On looking down to see what the target was, too my horror I saw the old school courts which I knew so well."

Devitt was at Sherborne School from 1924 to 1929.

"I was at that time just in a position to attack, which I did, but was molested by a pack of Bf.109s which I had not noticed sitting above the Heinkels, and above me as well. I could not see much of where the bombs fell as I was too intent on what was going on around me. I did,

however, see in one instant a great deal of smoke around the old buildings and so knew there must be some hits and damage and probably casualties."

After his engagement with the formation that was to cause havoc in the Abbey town of Sherborne, 19-year-old Pilot Officer Eric "Boy" Marrs (so called for his engagingly youthful looks) limped back to Warmwell in a crippled Spitfire and found only one of his wheels would come down. It would not then retract, and to attempt a landing on one wheel is much more hazardous than a belly-flop. He turned off the engine and glided in to land, touching down on the grass as gently as possible:

"I began to slew round and counteracted as much as possible with the brake on the wheel which was down. I ended up going sideways on one wheel, a tail wheel, and a wing tip. Luckily the good tyre held out and the only damage to the aeroplane, apart from that done by the bullets, is a wing tip which is easily replaceable.

"I hopped out and went to the Medical Officer to get a lot of splinters picked out of my leg and wrist. I felt jolly glad to be down on the ground without having caught fire."

Monday 30 September
Reddington is Warmwell's 17th loss.

R.A.F. Warmwell has had another loss today. Sergeant Pilot Leslie Arthur Edwin Reddington went down into

SHERBORNE ESTATE: THE URBAN DISTRICT COUNCIL'S HOUSING IN LENTHAY ROAD, ON 1 OCTOBER 1940. THE ESTATE RECEIVED THE FIRST OF SHERBORNE'S BOMBS AS THE LUFTWAFFE FORMATION APPROACHED THE TOWN FROM YEOVIL, ACROSS LENTHAY COMMON

SHERBORNE ROOFS: DETAIL OF DAMAGE TO SHERBORNE URBAN DISTRICT COUNCIL'S ESTATE IN LENTHAY ROAD (WHERE HOMES WOULD BE REBUILT TO THE SAME "DESIGN"), ON 1 OCTOBER 1940

the sea off Portland with Spitfire L1072 of 152 Squadron. He came from Coventry and was aged 26. His death brings the squadron's combat losses to eight and those for the station to 17.

Footnote: Reddington's wife was pregnant with their second daughter who would be named Lesley, in his memory, on her birth in February 1941.

Monday 30 September
56 Squadron crashes across Dorset.

56 Squadron from R.A.F. Boscombe Down, Wiltshire, has had half its Hurricanes put out of action over Dorset today, though without any losing any pilots. They initially got the worse of dog-fights with Messerschmitt Bf.109s and Bf.110s over Bournemouth.

Pilot Officer Kenneth John Marston managed to bring damaged Hurricane P2866 down at 11.30 hours at Longcutts Farm, East Knighton, near Winfrith Newburgh. He stepped clear of the crash-landing with shrapnel wounds and minor cuts. Sergeant Pilot Ronald Wilfred Ray also brought down P3655, on the same farm, though with a broken arm and other wounds.

Having returned to Dorset for the afternoon session, at 16.50, Sergeant Pilot Peter Hutton Fox was wounded in the right knee during combat over Portland. He baled out successfully but Hurricane N2434 came back to earth on the north side of the lane from Wootton Fitzpaine to Monkton Wyld.

Squadron Leader Herbert Moreton Pinfold also sustained damage in P2910 over Portland at 16.50 but was able to force-land, unhurt, at Warmwell Aerodrome. He was followed a few minutes later, equally uneventfully, by Pilot Officer Bryan John Wicks in P3870.

Next, at 17.00, Flight-Lieutenant Robert Sidney James Edwards was shot down in P3088, near Weymouth. He was caught by return fire from Dornier Do.17 bombers and Bf.110s but baled out unhurt.

Within minutes of this, Pilot Office Michael Hugh Constable-Maxwell had force-landed Hurricane L1764 on the pebbles of the Chesil Beach, across the water from Abbotsbury Swannery. The fighter has been written-off by the hostile terrain but the 23-year-old flyer walked away from the scene.

Monday 30 September
Hurricane of 87 Squadron crashes at Sherborne.

87 Squadron, from R.A.F. Exeter, lost a Hurricane — over Sherborne itself, at Burdon's Nurseries, Oborne Road — but Sergeant Pilot Herbert Walton baled out and was taken to the town's Yeatman Hospital with minor injuries.

Monday 30 September
504 Squadron also loses Hurricanes.

A series of losses for 504 Squadron from R.A.F. Filton began just before 17.00 hours when Sergeant Pilot Basil

Martin Bush was shot down and force-landed south of Yeovil with the pilot unhurt but P3021 written-off.

Hurricane P2987 was also damaged in the dog-fight. Pilot Officer Edward Murray Frisby found himself running out of fuel, only four miles from Warmwell Aerodrome, and made a successful forced-landing at 17.00 on the rolling chalk downland at Whitcombe.

Likewise Sergeant Pilot William Henry Banks was able to bring P3774 down into a Dorset field, in a repairable state, and with himself unhurt.

Their unfortunate comrade, at 17.15, was Flying Officer John Reginald Hardacre who was shot down and killed in P3414. He was seen falling into the sea off Weymouth.

Footnote: John Hardacre's body was washed ashore near Yarmouth, Isle of Wight, on 10 October. The 24-year-old, who was born in Birmingham, is buried in All Saints' churchyard at Fawley, Hampshire.

Monday 30 September
Messerschmitt downed at Sydling St Nicholas.

A Messerschmitt Bf.109 was shot down at 16.40 hours over Hundred Acres Field, Spriggs Farm, Sydling St Nicholas. It had been flown by Unteroffizier Alois Dollinger, of the 5th Staffel of fighter wing Jagdgeschwader 2 Richtofen from Octeville airfield at Le Havre. He had baled out three miles to the south, over Grimstone near Stratton, but the parachute failed to open and he fell to his death.

Footnote: The Sydling crash site would later be farmed by escaped British prisoner of war and author George Millar, who wrote *Maquis* [1945], *Horned Pigeon* [1946], and *Through the Unicorn Gates* [1950]. This was the longest range of all the Bf.109 crashes of 1940.

For the month as a whole, September 1940, Warmwell's 609 Squadron claimed 19 German aircraft for the loss of two Spitfires. Even allowing for over-claiming, the result was decisive.

The confusion over claims was inevitable in that often several fighters had a part in accounting for the same bomber and it was frequently impossible to follow victims down to the ground. Station morale would have been depressed by continual inquests over dubious claims. What dropped on to the fields showed the trend, but the sea could anonymously accommodate any amount of further hopes.

Monday 30 September
Hurricanes join the exhilarating coastal combat.

Perhaps the most exhilarating flying of the day was enjoyed by 238 Squadron, flying Hurricanes from R.A.F. Middle Wallop. Flight-Lieutenant Michael Lister Robinson, in R4099 ("VK" S for Sugar), led the nine fighters south over Poole Bay and turned at Swanage to head towards Portland.

They climbed into the cloud at 5,000 feet and rose to 15,000 above St Alban's Head, on a gyro-compass course westwards to get the advantage of the setting sun in Lyme Bay before wheeling into a dive on the German formations that were heading towards Portland.

They saw the enemy 3,000 feet below, to port, and swung into head-on attack. Robinson engaged a Messerschmitt Bf.110 from 300 yards, ripping it to pieces and sending an aerial oil-slick across his cockpit, which cleared sufficiently to give him a view of the Messerschmitt splashing down some ten miles south of Portland Bill.

Still with a smeared windscreen, he then saw another Bf.110, which was at 7,000 feet and heading back to France. Robinson gave chase and came to within 100 yards before opening up with three seconds of fire that pulled the port engine apart and moments later had the Messerschmitt explode. Its remains fell upside-down into the English Channel, 15 miles south of Portland Bill.

Robinson then flew north, towards Portland, and climbed to 25,000 feet to join a line of what he thought were Spitfires but turned out to be Messerschmitt Bf.109s. He still continued towards them and took on the closest, giving it a sustained six seconds of fire from 300 yards. Debris, smoke, and white glycol streamed out as it flipped over and dropped seawards.

Mike Robinson switched to his gravity tank: "Landed at Exeter, no petrol." It was 16.30 hours; he heard that others in 238 Squadron also had something to celebrate, including Pilot Officer Bob Doe who had shot down a Heinkel.

Robinson and Doe joined the squadron only two days ago.

During September
Blockship barrier to Weymouth Harbour.

The veteran cargo steamer *Kenfig Pool*, which has been moored beside Hope Quay in Weymouth Harbour since July, is being placed across the harbour entrance and prepared for scuttling. She is to act as a barrier in the event of German invasion.

During September
'Beams' scientist dispersed to Langton Matravers.

The Telecommunications Research Establishment at Worth Matravers has requisitioned Leeson House and Durnford School in the neighbouring village of Langton Matravers. Further expansion of its hutted encampment beside Renscombe Farm, on the western side of Worth, had been considered inadvisable. The tall aerials of the coastal radar research station are already attracting the attention of German bombers.

Scientists at Worth and Langton are deeply involved in what has become the "Battle of the Beams". The Luftwaffe is targeting inland English objectives by an intersection of radio pulses — one of synchronised dots and the other of dashes — transmitted from Kleve, in

Germany, near the Dutch border south-east of Arnhem, and from Stolberg near the Danish border.

Dr Robert Cockburn has developed a Radio Counter Measure which is codenamed "Aspirin". This duplicates the continuous Morse dashes, which are being transmitted on a frequency of 30 to 31.5 megacycles per second, which disorientates the German pilots by widening their direction beam.

A more ambitious plan was, in effect, to bend the beam by recording a sequence of synchronous German dots and re-transmitting the signal from a mast at Beacon Hill, near Salisbury. This scheme was thwarted, however, because the telephone land-line that Dr Cockburn was using, from Worth Matravers to Beacon Hill, was taken over by the military.

The signal was recorded in the Isle of Purbeck but without the telephone link it could not be re-radiated from Beacon Hill. Asynchronous signals are, however, having the desired effect without more sophisticated forms of interference being necessary.

Tuesday 1 October
Plane crashes off Hengistbury Head.

An unidentified aeroplane fell into the sea off Hengistbury Head, Bournemouth, at 10.55 hours. Machine-gun fire had been heard. No one baled out.

Tuesday 1 October
Two Hurricane pilots killed off Swanage.

Two Hurricanes of 607 Squadron from R.A.F. Tangmere were lost today at 11.20 hours in combat with Messerschmitt Bf.110s between Swanage and the Needles, Isle of Wight. Both fighters, and their pilots, fell into the sea.

The missing airmen are 24-year-old Flight-Lieutenant Charles Earle Bowen from Chelsea and Sergeant Pilot Norman Brumby, from Hull, who was 22.

Footnote: Norman Brumby's body would be recovered. He is buried in Hull Northern Cemetery.

Tuesday 1 October
Hurricane crashes near Sherborne.

Pilot Officer Aubrey Richard Covington is reported to have baled out of a Hurricane of 238 Squadron, from R.A.F. Chilbolton, into countryside near Sherborne. The pilot, who is unhurt, claims to have accounted for two Messerschmitt Bf.110s earlier in the day.

Wednesday 2 October
609 Squadron now exclusively at Warmwell.

The Mark-1 Spitfires of 609 Squadron are no longer flying their daily shuttle from R.A.F. Middle Wallop, on the Hampshire Downs, to Warmwell Aerodrome in south Dorset.

From today they cease to be day visitors and are to stay at R.A.F. Warmwell for the winter months. The change of base is a mixed blessing, as the time saved in flying backwards and forwards will have to be spent under canvas, in a dispersal area exposed to the elements. It has made the transition from summertime dust-bowl into winter swamp.

Friday 4 October
Robinson takes over 609 Squadron.

Hurricane pilot Squadron Leader Michael Lister Robinson has left 238 Squadron at R.A.F. Chilbolton, from which he has been defending the Dorset coast this busy past week, to take command of the Spitfires of 609 Squadron at R.A.F. Warmwell. His have been the first operational sorties from newly opened Chilbolton Aerodrome, on the Hampshire Downs between Stockbridge and Andover, to which the squadron had redeployed from Middle Wallop on 30 September.

R.A.F. Chilbolton has been assigned to 10 Group Fighter Command as a Relief Landing Ground to R.A.F. Middle Wallop.

Footnote: Michael Robinson would continue to have a hectic war, having arrived with several Messerschmitt claims, and went on to secure a rapid tally of kills in early summer 1941. He was awarded the Distinguished Flying Cross on 26 November 1940, followed by the Distinguished Service Order on 5 August 1941, and then posted to Biggin Hill.

It was as leader of Tangmere Wing, heading 340 Squadron, that he failed to return from a sweep along the English Channel on 10 April 1942.

Michael Robinson was the son of Sir Roy Robinson, chairman of the Forestry Commission, who would be created 1st Baron Robinson of Kielder Forest, in 1947.

Saturday 5 October
Hurricane pilot taken with burns to Shaftesbury Hospital.

Sergeant Pilot John William McLaughlin of 238 Squadron from R.A.F. Middle Wallop baled out of Hurricane P3611 on being shot down by Messerschmitt Bf.109s. He has been taken to Shaftesbury Hospital, critically injured, with multiple burns.

Four Hurricanes of 607 Squadron from R.A.F. Tangmere, damaged in dog-fights with Bf.109s, reportedly made forced-landings in the vicinity of Swanage at about 13.50 hours. None of the airmen was hurt.

Footnote: John McLaughlin would eventually receive pioneering skin-graft treatment at Queen Victoria Hospital, East Grinstead. He resumed R.A.F. service, in 1943-46, and later emigrated to Australia.

Monday 7 October
Four die as bomb blasts Weymouth bus depot.

Four died and many were injured when the Southern National bus depot at Weymouth received a direct hit by a German bomb. Fourteen buses and coaches were badly damaged.

Monday 7 October
More 609 Squadron kills but serious losses.

Both 609 Squadron and 152 Squadron from R.A.F. Warmwell clashed today with German aircraft on their doorstep, at times over the aerodrome itself, as an enemy force crossed the Channel at Portland to bomb the Westland Aircraft factory at Yeovil where a hundred civilian workers have been killed in a direct hit of an air-raid shelter.

Four kills were credited to 609 Squadron but for the loss of three Warmwell Spitfires with critical injuries to Pilot Officer Harold John Akroyd, the death of Sergeant Pilot Alan Norman Feary, and a serious leg injury to Pilot Officer Michael Staples.

Akroyd, who is aged 27, received crippling damage to his fighter over west Dorset. Spitfire N3039 burst into flames in a forced-landing at Shatcombe Farm, Wynford Eagle. Though pulled clear of the wreckage he is suffering extensive burns.

Feary was hit by Messerschmitt Bf.109s over Weymouth. He baled out from Spitfire N3238 as it crashed at Watercombe Farm, between Warmwell and Owermoigne, but it was too low for the parachute to open.

Staples and Spitfire N3231 were badly shot-up over the Blackmore Vale. Michael Staples baled out at 21,000 feet and proceeded to land without further injury as the fighter plunged into common land meadows at Netmead, on the east bank of the River Stour between Child Okeford and Bere Marsh, near Shillingstone.

A luckier combination were Flight-Lieutenant Frank Howell and Spitfire X4472, also of 609 Squadron. The airman made a successful forced-landing in fields at Vale Farm, Sutton Waldron, and the fighter is repairable.

Footnote: Harold Akroyd died of his burns the following day, in Dorset County Hospital, Dorchester. The two flyers are buried in the R.A.F. plot at Warmwell churchyard. "ONE OF THE FEW", Alan Feary's stone reads. He was aged 28. Staples would recover from what he described as "a big hole" in his leg but would not rejoin 609 Squadron.

The deaths of Akroyd and Feary brought the squadron's losses in the Battle of Britain to nine and those for R.A.F. Warmwell to 19.

Monday 7 October
Close call for Spitfire R6915 and John Dundas.

Engaging a defensive ring of 15 Messerschmitt Bf.110s, above Cheselbourne and Dewlish at 16.30 hours, Flight-

Lieutenant John Dundas, leading Blue Section of 609 Squadron from R.A.F. Warmwell, flew guns blazing over the top of the German aircraft. Then, as he climbed away from the circle of fighter-bombers, he came across a lone Bf.110 at 16,000 feet.

Approaching its tail he gave a sustained twelve seconds of fire from his eight guns. Both enemy engines belched smoke and white ethylene glycol coolant. John Dundas closed again on his crippled target but as he approached its gunner hit back with a shell that splintered his leg and sent Spitfire R6915 reeling into a spin.

Pilot and aircraft both recovered sufficiently to level out and glide back to Warmwell Aerodrome.

The burning Bf.110 was spotted crossing the coast at Weymouth, at 14,000 feet, and is presumed to have crashed in the English Channel, though Dundas will only have the credit for a probable kill. Flight-Lieutenant Frank Howell has also claimed the destruction of a Bf.110.

Footnote: Spitfire R6915 is the machine that now hangs from the ceiling of the Imperial War Museum as its centrepiece Battle of Britain exhibit. It has already been mentioned, on 30 September 1940, when its flyer was Noel le Chevalier Agazarian.

Despite this close call, John Dundas was back in the air the next day, and already had a decoration in the bag, being awarded the Distinguished Flying Cross on 10 October. He returns to our story on 27 and 28 November 1940.

Monday 7 October
152 Squadron has a good day.

As for R.A.F. Warmwell's other squadron, Pilot Officer Eric "Boy" Marrs, in Spitfire R6968, had led Blue Section of 152 Squadron at 20,000 feet over the eastern Frome valley. They descended upon 50 German Junkers Ju.88 bombers and Messerschmitt Bf.110 fighter-bombers with Bf.109 escorts.

These enemy fighters were weaving defensive circles behind the bombers. Marrs waited for the final Bf.109 to pull out of a ring, in order to catch-up with the bombers, and then struck at the last Bf.110 in the exposed line. It belonged to II or III Gruppen of Zerstörergeschwader 26 and had the nose section painted white.

As glycol coolant streamed from the Messerschmitt's starboard engine, Marrs switched his fire leftward across the fuselage: "Suddenly the back half of his cockpit flew off and out jumped two men. Their parachutes streamed and opened and they began drifting slowly earth-wards. Their aeroplane, left to itself, dived vertically into the sea, making a most wonderful sight and an enormous splash . . . everything seemed to have cleared off, so I circled round the two Huns. They took an awful long time to come down on land and I watched the Army rush up to capture them."

WARNING NOTICE: "TOO LOW FOR DOUBLE DECKERS" BEING CERTAINLY THE CASE ON 7 OCTOBER 1940, AFTER THE SOUTHERN NATIONAL BUS DEPOT IN WEYMOUTH TOOK A DIRECT HIT FROM A JUNKERS JU.88 BOMBER, KILLING FOUR

Monday 7 October
Bf.110 shot down at Lulworth.

15.45 hours: a formation of German aircraft, estimated in excess of 60, are approaching the Dorset coast at Lulworth.

15.50: the attackers are engaged from the ground by anti-aircraft gunners at Lulworth Camp and in the sky by Warmwell's Spitfires which are intercepting them as they enter the Frome valley.

15.55: meeting this heavy opposition the German aircraft have turned back towards the sea.

16.37: air-raid sirens give the All Clear at Lulworth Camp, from where a Messerschmitt Bf.110 was seen to fall into the sea, 2,000 yards off Arish Mell Gap.

Footnote: Shot down into Worbarrow Bay, by Pilot Officer John Urwin-Mann in a Hurricane of 218 Squadron from R.A.F. Chilbolton, this "Junkers Ju.88" which he claimed was in fact Messerschmitt Bf.110E (3U+DD) belonging to the Stabskette of III Gruppe of Zerstörergeschwader 26. It had been defending the bombers engaged in attacking the Westland Aircraft Company factory at Yeovil.

Leutnant Botho Sommer, the pilot, survived unhurt but his crewman, Unteroffizier Paul Preuler, was injured.

Monday 7 October
Bf.110 crashes into Ringstead Bay.

Messerschmitt Bf.110E (3U+FM), belonging to the 4th Staffel of Zerstörergeschwader 26 fell into Ringstead Bay, south of Owermoigne, whilst participating in the German raid on Yeovil. The crash occurred at 16.05 hours.

The two crew, Oberfeldwebel Erwin Genzzler and Unteroffizier Franz Heefner, both baled out unhurt.

Monday 7 October
Bf.110 makes a fireball at Stoborough.

Some of the Isle of Purbeck's most dramatic dog-fights of the Battle of Britain occurred this afternoon when the Luftwaffe attacked the Westland Aircraft Company at Yeovil.

Messerschmitt Bf.110 (3U+BT) belonging to the 9th Staffel of Zerstörergeschwader 26 came low across the Frome meadows and flew into the gorse-clad slope of Hyde Hill, south of Stoborough, at about 14.00 hours. The pilot, Leutnant Kurt Sidow, and his navigator, Gefreiter Josef Repik, died instantaneously in the fireball.

Monday 7 October
Bf.110 force-lands at Corfe Castle.

Messerschmitt Bf.110 (3U+JT) became another loss for the 9th Staffel of Zerstorergeschwader 26 when it force-landed near Corfe Castle this afternoon, after being engaged by the R.A.F. whilst taking part in the attack on the Westland Aircraft Company at Yeovil.

Gefreiter Bernhardt Demmig, the pilot, survived and has been taken prisoner of war, but his Bordfunker [radio operator], Obergefreiter Josef Bachmann, was killed.

They were shot down by Squadron Leader Michael Robinson, in a Spitfire of 609 Squadron from R.A.F. Warmwell, where he took command just three days ago. Flying Officer Richard Brooker joined in the kill, in a Hurricane of 56 Squadron from R.A.F. Boscombe Down.

Monday 7 October
Ju.88 crashes at Up Sydling.

A Junkers Ju.88 bomber (9K+SN), heading for the Westland Aircraft factory at Yeovil, was brought down at 16.20 hours on Tappers Hill, above the hamlet of Up Sydling, near Sydling St Nicholas. The kill has been claimed jointly by Sergeant Pilot Edmund Shepperd in a Spitfire of 152 Squadron from R.A.F. Warmwell and Flying Officer Bob Doe in a Hurricane of 238 Squadron from R.A.F. Chilbolton.

All four members of the German crew baled out successfully and were taken prisoner of war, after being rounded up by shotgun, following which the farm labourers performed a victory dance around the wreckage. The crewmen were Oberleutnant Sigurd Hey, Leutnant Friedrich Bein, Oberfeldwebel Christian Koenig, and Oberfeldwebel Josef Troll.

The bomber belonged to the 5th Staffel of II Gruppe, Kampfgeschwader 51.

Monday 7 October
Bf.110 crashes at Kingston Russell.

Messerschmitt Bf.110C (3U+JP) of the 6th Staffel of Zerstörergeschwader 26, which had been defending the bombers en route to the Westland Aircraft Company works at Yeovil, has crashed at Brickhills Field, near Kingston Russell House.

Crewmen Obergefreiter Herbert Schilling and Oberfeldwebel Karl Herzog were killed on impact.

Footnote: Further human remains were removed, together with wreckage and identification papers, during an excavation carried out by Andy Saunders in 1976. The flyers' graves are in the German War Cemetery at Cannock Chase. A propeller from the crash site, recovered by Pete Nash, is displayed in the offices of Dorset Publishing Company.

Monday 7 October
Hurricane crashes at Alton Pancras.

56 Squadron, flying Hurricanes from R.A.F. Boscombe Down, Wiltshire, joined in today's hectic air activity over Dorset and Somerset. A detachment were sent to Warmwell Aerodrome and scrambled at 16.00 hours.

They met an estimated 50 Messerschmitt Bf.110 fighter-bombers over Bulbarrow Hill in central Dorset.

Hurricane P3154 was shot down in flames from 25,000 feet above Austral Farm, Alton Pancras. Sergeant Pilot Dennis Hugh Nichols, aged 19 and on his first combat mission, was able to parachute clear of the stricken fighter but landed badly and has been taken to Dorset County Hospital, Dorchester, with a suspected fracture of the spine.

Footnote: Dennis Nichols would be in hospital for months and did not resume operational flying until 1942. He survived the war and enjoyed an active retirement, returning to Alton Pancras to see relics of P3154 being excavated from the crash-site in 1994.

Monday 7 October
Hurricane crashes at Winterborne Houghton.

Another Hurricane, V6777 of 238 Squadron from R.A.F. Chilbolton, has been shot down by Messerschmitt Bf.110s and crashed on the Dorset Downs at Great Hill, above Meriden Wood, Winterborne Houghton.

Pilot Officer Aubrey Richard Covington baled out over Dorset for the second time in a week — the first being near Sherborne, last Tuesday — though this time he is not quite unscathed, having been taken to Blandford Cottage Hospital for treatment of minor injuries.

Tuesday 8 October
Bomb wrecks Moreton church.

21.00 hours. Moreton's 18th-century parish church, an elegant Georgian structure, has been completely wrecked by a German bomb that fell beside the north wall. This collapsed and all glass has been blown out and destroyed. The building is a ruin.

Footnote: St Nicholas's Church would be restored and re-dedicated, in May 1950, and since 1955 has been enriched by the finest set of modern engraved glass windows in Britain — the creation of Laurence Whistler.

Thursday 10 October
Hurricane pilot killed at Wareham.

Czechoslovakian flyer Sergeant Pilot Jaroslav Hlavac of 56 Squadron, from R.A.F. Boscombe Down, was killed at 12.20 this afternoon when Hurricane P3421 was shot down at Manor Farm, Worgret, to the west of Wareham. He was aged 25, had been with the squadron just two days, and was in the process of intercepting a flight of Messerschmitt Bf.109s. The body is being taken to Warmwell churchyard for burial in the R.A.F. plot.

Hurricane P3984 of 238 Squadron, from the newly opened R.A.F. Chilbolton, Hampshire, crashed at 13.00 hours below Corfe Castle — missing the famous ruins by only 200 yards and plummeting into a roadside quarry just north of the Castle Hill. It came down close to the viaduct that carries the railway across the Studland road.

This time the pilot, though wounded, was able to bale out. Pilot Officer Bob Doe landed on Brownsea Island and has been taken to Cornelia Hospital in Poole. He is 20-years-old and was recently awarded the Distinguished Flying Cross.

The lunchtime problem for the Hurricanes seems to have been the dense cloud-base which extended up to 16,000 feet. As British fighters came up through it they were visible to the enemy formations in the clear sky above. For those potentially fatal final moments the sight of the R.A.F. pilots was still obscured by water droplets.

Friday 11 October
Poole boy killed by bomb.

Stanley Ricketts, an 11-year-old Poole boy, was fatally injured this evening by a German bomb as he walked home at Kingsbere Road. Incendiaries also landed in the Constitution Hill area and other parts of the town, included the Cornelia Hospital where Stanley died.

Bombed church: that of St Nicholas at Moreton, seen on 9 October 1940 in a snapshot by E. W. Pride that was confiscated by the military. (The Georgian building would be rebuilt and embellished with a remarkable series of windows engraved by Sir Laurence Whistler)

Monday 14 October
Lyme minefield claims another Navy trawler.

The British armed trawler H.M.T. *Lord Stamp* has sunk after striking a mine in Lyme Bay.

Tuesday 15 October
609 Squadron gets a Bf.110 over Bournemouth.

Leading Blue Flight of 609 Squadron from R.A.F. Warmwell, in Spitfire P9503, Flight-Lieutenant John Dundas flew through the gunfire of three Messerschmitt Bf.109 fighters at 14,000 feet above Christchurch. One Spitfire reported a bullet hole, but no apparent damage, though the squadron's flight pattern was thrown into disarray.

Dundas failed to regroup his flight and soared alone to 18,000 feet where he found some 15 Messerschmitt Bf.110 fighter-bombers. He made two runs at them, giving bursts of fire from only 100 yards, but then broke away as Bf.109s came towards the Spitfire from above.

A Bf.110 has reportedly crashed near Bournemouth as a result of the engagement. It will be the squadron's 99th accepted kill.

Wednesday 16 October
Bovington and Poole air-raids.

Cryptanalysts at Bletchley Park, deciphering the German "Enigma" radio traffic, gave warning of today's bombing raid on east Dorset, which hit Bovington and Poole. The intercepted signal was "Target No. 1 for Y".

Target No. 1 is known to be the Armoured Fighting Vehicles School, at Bovington Camp, and "Y" indicates that Y-beam radio direction signals were being used. The Y-Gerät target finding system is deployed by the pathfinding 3rd Gruppe of Kampfgeschwader 26 whose aircraft carry the identification marking "1H" to the left of the iron cross on their rear fuselage.

Thursday 17 October
Further Navy trawler goes down.

The Royal Navy's losses of armed trawlers to the German minefield off west Dorset continued today when H.M.T. *Kingston Cairngorm* blew up off Portland Bill.

Thursday 17 October
The 'False Invasion'.

An intended raid on the Dorset and Devon coast to cover the infiltration of fifth columnists, mostly Irish Republicans, has been thwarted by the Royal Navy. Submarine *L27*, an ex-Danish boat, has shadowed the attack on the German convoy and many of the enemy have drowned, including S.S. agents. It has been the day of the "False Invasion".

The German force included the 5th T-boat Flotilla — of 1,300-ton motor torpedo boats the size of a light destroyer — and the destroyers *Karl Galster*, *Frederich Ihrs*, *Hans Lody*, and *Erich Steinbrinck*. They are having a running fight to escape from a mixed Allied force of two British cruisers supported by two Free French destroyers, two Norwegian destroyers, and one each from the Dutch and Danish navies.

Friday 18 October
Warmwell pilot killed at Tadnoll Mill.

Sergeant Pilot Edmund Eric Shepperd, flying Spitfire R6607 of 152 Squadron from R.A.F. Warmwell, was killed today when his fighter plunged into the ground. No other aeroplane was involved and there was no obvious reason for the accident.

It happened at Tadnoll Mill, two miles south-east of Warmwell Aerodrome, in the northern extremity of Chaldon Herring parish.

Footnote: Edmund Shepperd was 23-years-old. He was born and would be buried at Binstead, Isle of Wight. His was the squadron's tenth fatality during the Battle of Britain and the 20th loss for the station.

Saturday 19 October
Bournemouth firemen go to London.

Bournemouth firemen, who were the first provincial reinforcements to arrive in the capital at the beginning of the Blitz in September, among the 50 pumps at Millwall Docks, have now instigated an exchange scheme with London firemen. Forty members of the Auxiliary Fire Service, from Bournemouth — divisional area 16C of No. 6 Region — will today swap duties for a week with some of the city's exhausted heroes.

Deputy Chief Officer Ken Devereux is leading the Bournemouth team and it is expected that they will gain valuable experience in tackling major bomb damage.

Footnote: Ted Hughes, who dealt with the administration at Bournemouth Fire Service headquarters, records in *Bournemouth Firemen at War* that 625 of his men attended city blazes in Southampton, Portsmouth, Exeter, and Plymouth — as well as London — and that on 83 occasions they drove their pumps to the action. Usually this was at night, with only much diminished cowled slit-lights, along roads without any direction signs.

Saturday 19 October
Two 12-inch guns en route to Dorset.

Two 12-inch Mark II railway-mounted howitzers, dating from the Great War, have been released to Southern Command from the Ordnance Depot at Chilwell, Nottingham. They have arrived at Ringwood where they will remain in a siding until they can be deployed in the Isle of Purbeck.

VILLAGE WARDENS: AIR RAID PRECAUTIONS VOLUNTEERS, IN THEIR LATER UNIFORMS OF THE WAREHAM AND PURBECK CIVIL DEFENCE CORPS, PHOTOGRAPHED BESIDE THE PAVILION ON THE RECREATION GROUND IN NORTH STREET, BERE REGIS. FRONT ROW — KEN WOOLFIES, CHARLES KELLAWAY, EVELYN LYS, JOCK STRANG, GERTRUDE MILLER, FRED LYS, AND EDWARD HEWITT. CENTRE — FRANK APLIN, HENRY HANN, CHARLES DAVIS, JACK LEGG, LOUIS JOYCE, NOBBY BARTLETT, AND HARRY PITFIELD. BACK — DENIS SKINNER, LESLIE BARNES, PERCIVAL PITFIELD, AND MICHAEL MILLER. CHARLES KELLAWAY GIVES THE AIR RAID WARNING ON HIS WHISTLE FROM A MORRIS MINOR. HE USES A HAND-BELL FOR THE ALL CLEAR.

Monday 21 October
Two share 609 Squadron's 100th kill.

Pilot Officer Sidney Jenkyn Hill and Flight-Lieutenant Frank "Frankie" Howell this afternoon shared the credit for the destruction of a Junkers Ju.88 bomber. The enemy aircraft was returning from strafing an airfield at Old Sarum, Wiltshire, and was approaching the coast, at 200 feet above the New Forest. The interception was brought about through radar, with the Flight-Lieutenant Fieldsend in the Operations Room calling the Spitfires on the R.T. and arranging the ambush: "He should be near you now, flying very low."

Both Spitfires dived to attack and Howell went in first, as the bomber dropped to tree height, then Hill opened fire, and almost immediately a terrific explosion left wreckage scattered across four fields. There was no survivor. The kill is 609 Squadron's 100th victory.

Aged 23, Sidney Hill is Dorset-born, from Ferndown, near Wimborne. He was flying Spitfire X4590. Frank Howell is a Londoner, from Golders Green. They were treated to a boozy party on their return at 18.30 hours from R.A.F. Warmwell to the squadron's home base at

R.A.F. Middle Wallop. This is the first Spitfire squadron to be credited with a hundred victories; No. 1 Squadron did it with Hurricanes in the Battle of France, four months ago. Champagne and brandy have been stacked to await the occasion. Pilot Officer David Moore Crook records it as "a very good party" in which everyone felt distinctly pleased with themselves and life in general: "We drank to the C.O., we drank to the Poles, we drank to the squadron, and in fact we toasted practically everything we could think of, in round after round of champagne cocktails."

Footnote: Sidney Hill would be killed by Messerschmitt Bf.109s, on 18 June 1941, and is buried in the New Cemetery at Folkestone, Kent. Hill's Spitfire survived the war and would be spotted by "Paul" Edge, on display at Grantham, in 1970.

Frank Howell, whose combat films were among the best to be taken during the Battle of Britain, was awarded the Distinguished Flying Cross on 25 October 1940. Posted to R.A.F. Filton, where he formed 118 Squadron on 20 February 1941, he later moved to the Far East where he was captured by the Japanese after the sinking of the battleship H.M.S. *Prince of Wales*, on 10 December 1941.

Post-war, Squadron Leader Howell lost his life in a bizarre aerodrome accident, being decapitated by the wing of a Vampire as he was filming his jets with a cine-camera, on 9 May 1948.

Tuesday 22 October
Portland minefield sinks the 'Hickory'.

The *Hickory*, a diesel-powered civilian vessel, is the latest victim of the German minefield off Portland.

Saturday 26 October
Bournemouth's Carlton Hotel becomes Rations Office.

The prestigious Carlton Hotel on the East Cliff at Bournemouth has been requisitioned by the Board of Trade for use as a ration-coupon issuing office for the documents that are now needed for the restricted allowances of petrol and clothes.

In recent months the new Rations Office has only had five residents, since visitors were banned from the Defence Area, and one of these, Mrs Myers, has been fined 10 shillings with £1-12s-6d costs for an infringement of the blackout. The hotel felt obliged to pay.

During October
Pilot Officer Pooch is Warmwell's mascot.

Pooch, the mascot of 152 Squadron at Warmwell Aerodrome, is reputed to have sired most of the bull terriers that are currently in R.A.F. service.

He carries the honorary rank of Pilot Officer and generally guards 152's dispersal hut. This is adorned with a growing collection of signs "lifted and borrowed" by M.G.-driving Spitfire pilots from the farms and countryside around Weymouth and Dorchester.

"JOE GUPPY'S CAMP" — the sign above the door, from Preston — is unlikely to be needed by Mr Guppy for the duration of the conflict. The losers of "SAFETY FIRST: BEWARE CATTLE" and similar miscellaneous instructions for highway usage can take solace from the fact that their messages of carefulness and courtesy are now being absorbed by impressionable young minds.

During October
31,000 acres of Dorset grasslands ploughed for corn.

Grain production for Dorset might well have been a record in any case, given the hot summer, but it is way beyond anything in living memory as a result of 31,000 acres of pasture being hastily turned over to arable food production. The familiar greens of downland sheep walks and the dairying vales gave way to golden expanses of wheat and barley.

More ephemeral, exotic even, were the dusky fields that suddenly turned into splashes of vivid cyan blue as the sky brightened. This crop is flax — the flowers of which open only for the sun.

T. R. Ferris, executive officer of the Dorset War Agricultural Committee, has announced next year's target: "The committee has been given a task of ploughing out of grass a further 22,000 acres of land for the 1941 harvest." Most of this land will be sown with grain but he is also appealing to gardeners and allotment holders "to do their utmost to increase food production by growing vegetables in all parts of the county".

During October
Dorset's African hero returns from the dead, to posthumous V.C.

Captain Eric Wilson of Long Crichel, who was seconded to the Somaliland Camel Corps, has been posthumously gazetted for the Victoria Cross as a result of his part in the heroic defence of the British colony in the Horn of Africa, during the Italian invasion of 4-19 August. He commanded a series of Bren gun positions that were blown to pieces in a sustained attack over four days and he held out until the end.

The award was cited in the London Gazette but the story does not end there as three days later news reached the British that Captain Wilson had survived and was prisoner of war.

Footnote: Neither would the story end there. As the war turned against the Italians he was liberated and then fought with the Long Range Desert Group. Lieutenant-Colonel Wilson retired from the Army in 1949 and became an administrator in Tanganyika, until 1961, before returning to a West Country cottage, at Stowell near Sherborne.

During October
Winterbourne Abbas loses last church band.

The last church band in England is now a memory as William Dunford, its sole surviving player, has taken his bass-viol home from Winterbourne Abbas parish church.

During October
Bournemouth's Home Guard totals 8,000.

Recruitment of civilian volunteers into the Hampshire Regiment (Home Guard) units under the control of the Officer Commanding Troops, Bournemouth — whose area includes the other two towns in the conurbation, namely Poole and Christchurch — is set to reach 8,000 men. The detachments and their approximate manpower on call, nominally at least, are:

3rd (Poole) Battalion — 2,500 men.

6th (Bournemouth) Battalion — 2,300 men.

7th (Boscombe) Battalion — 2,500 men.

22nd (Post Office) Battalion — 400 men.

B Company, Southern Railway Battalion — 300 men.

FIGHTER PILOTS: FLYING SPITFIRES WITH 152 SQUADRON AT R.A.F. WARMWELL, BEING FLIGHT-LIEUTENANT DEREK BOITEL-GILL (right), IN COMMAND OF 'A' FLIGHT; SERGEANT PILOT HOWARD MARSH (below, LEFT BESIDE THE DISPERSAL HUT) SITS NEXT TO SERGEANT PILOT JIMMY SHORT; AND SERGEANT PILOT "JOHNNY" JOHNSTON (bottom) STANDS BESIDE HIS MARK I MACHINE

BEST FRIENDS: SERGEANT PILOT EDMUND SHEPPERD WITH PILOT OFFICER POOCH, MASCOT OF 152 SQUADRON AT R.A.F. WARMWELL, IN SEPTEMBER 1940 (EDMUND SHEPPERD WOULD BE KILLED WHEN HIS SPITFIRE CRASHED AT TADNOLL MILL ON 18 OCTOBER 1940)

SQUADRON LEADERS: COMMANDERS OF THE WARMWELL SPITFIRES THROUGH THE BATTLE OF BRITAIN, BEING GEORGE DARLEY (above) OF 609 SQUADRON AND PETER DEVITT (top right) OF 152 SQUADRON

AIRFIELD TROPHIES: GEORGE WHITE WITH 152 SQUADRON'S COLLECTION OF ROADSIDE SIGNS, GATHERED FROM THE COUNTRYSIDE AROUND WARMWELL, DECORATING THEIR DISPERSAL HUT

SPITFIRE AUTHOR: PILOT OFFICER DAVID MOORE CROOK OF 609 SQUADRON WROTE HIS ACCOUNT OF THE BATTLE OF BRITAIN AT R.A.F WARMWELL. THE PENCIL SKETCH BY CAPTAIN CUTHBERT ORDE IS DATED 7 NOVEMBER 1940

During October

City pets evacuated to Shaftesbury.

The animal shelter opened by Nina, Duchess of Hamilton, on her estate at Ferne to the east of Shaftesbury has become a refuge for hundreds of city pets, made homeless by the bombings and the general upheavals of war. As far as possible they are being cared for as if they were still at home, with freedom and exercise, rather than being permanently impounded in cages. Larger animals, such as horses, ponies and goats, are also being given refuge.

In reply to criticism that it is a waste of resources to care for animals in wartime, the Duchess quotes a Regional Commissioner of the Ministry of Home Security: "Experience shows that effective arrangements for dealing with animal casualties and for caring for the domestic pets of homeless people plays an important part in the maintaining of public morale after air-raids."

Footnote: Nina was the widow of the 13th Duke of Hamilton who died on 16 March 1940. Three of their four sons — Lord Douglas Douglas-Hamilton, Lord C. N. Douglas-Hamilton, and Lord Malcolm Douglas-Hamilton — were serving with the R.A.F. at the outbreak of war. The first, now the 14th Duke of Hamilton, had been the chief pilot of the Mount Everest flight expedition in 1933. Ferne Animal Sanctuary survives, but has since moved to Wambrook, near Chard, in Somerset.

Friday 1 November

Rail-guns brought to Purbeck.

Two 12-inch Mark II railway-mounted howitzers have arrived in the Isle of Purbeck where the first gun-spur siding has been made ready near Furzebrook by the 14th Super Heavy Battery of 5th Corps of the Royal Artillery. The gunners came down from Catterick Camp, Yorkshire, on 15 October, and have now been introduced to their weapons.

The wagons incorporating the guns are being pulled by a Drummond K10 class mixed traffic locomotive, number 393.

Friday 1 November

Anti-Aircraft Co-Operation Unit at Christchurch.

H-Flight of the No. 1 Anti-Aircraft Co-Operation Unit has arrived at Christchurch Aerodrome from Gosport. Its varied assortment of the older types of aircraft include Avro Ansons, Tiger Moths, a Fairey Battle, Miles Magister, and a Bristol Blenheim. They will be available for use by research scientists, who are working on countermeasures against the German bombers, at the Air Defence Experimental Establishment, at Christchurch.

Footnote: The trials, which also involved Westland Lysanders, lasted until the end of July 1941.

OBSERVER POST: WARMWELL SPITFIRE (below) AND THEIR VAPOUR TRAILS (above), SEEN FROM POUNDBURY CAMP, OVERLOOKING DORCHESTER

HYDERABAD UNIT: SERGEANT PILOT GEORGE WHITE, IN A SPITFIRE OF 152 SQUADRON AT R.A.F. WARMWELL. HE WOULD BE KILLED OVER HOLLAND, NEAR EINDHOVEN, IN 1941

LEESON HOUSE: OUT-STATION OF THE TELECOMMUNICATIONS RESEARCH ESTABLISHMENT AT LANGTON MATRAVERS, REQUISITIONED FOR RADAR RESEARCH. GROUND MAPPING TECHNOLOGY, FOR R.A.F. BOMBERS, WOULD BE DEVELOPED IN A HUT IN THE GROUNDS

FATAL SHOT: CLOSE-RANGE CANNON FIRE FROM A STRICKEN HEINKEL BOMBER PUNCTURED THE ARMOURED GLASS WINDSCREEN OF KENNETH HOLLAND'S SPITFIRE, OF 152 SQUADRON FROM R.A.F. WARMWELL, WITH THE RESULT THAT THE AVERSARIES CRASHED TOGETHER IN A SOMERSET FIELD ON 25 SEPTEMBER 1940

Sunday 3 November
Motor-cycles leave Blandford.

The motor-cycle Reconnaissance Battalion at Blandford Camp, the 4th Battalion of the Royal Northumberland Fusiliers, are leaving Dorset today for Amesbury Abbey, Wiltshire.

Tuesday 5 November
Chilbolton Hurricane crashes at Shapwick.

Hurricane V6792, belonging to 238 Squadron from R.A.F. Chilbolton, Hampshire, was shot down over Bournemouth today in a dog-fight with a cluster of Messerschmitt Bf.109s. The crippled fighter glided inland, up the Stour valley, and Pilot Officer Brian Considine baled out wounded, over Sturminster Marshall. The fighter crashed near Shapwick.

Wednesday 6 November
Heinkel lands at Bridport — thinking it is France.

In the early morning a Heinkel He.111 of Kampfgruppe 100, the elite two per cent of German bombers operating from Vannes, Brittany, and acting as pathfinders for the attacking formations, suffered a compass failure. The crew were confused by the British masking of German radio direction beacons into thinking they were back in France. In fact they were over Dorset and running out of fuel.

The pilot force-landed on the shingle beach at West Bay, Bridport, and three of the four crew survived — though they soon had their locational illusions shattered and found themselves in captivity.

Soldiers guarded the aircraft, which carries the identification code "6N", and have had a difference of opinion with a naval detachment who came to drag the aircraft up the beach. The soldiers followed orders not to let anyone touch the bomber and as a result it was engulfed by the incoming tide.

The bomber has three vertical aerials and related radio equipment. This apparatus is to be salvaged for inspection by the Air Ministry boffins.

Friday 8 November
Both rail-guns now operational in Purbeck.

Another gun-spur has been completed at Furzebrook, amid heathland pines north-west of Corfe Castle, for the second railway-mounted 12-inch howitzer of the 14th Super Heavy Battery. It is positioned 300 yards from the gun that was emplaced on 1 November. Deployment of the second howitzer was only achieved with some difficulty as it had been brought down the branch line facing the wrong way — with the barrel pointing towards Sherborne. They could just reach Briantspuddle!

Last night the gun-carriage had to be re-attached to engine 393 and taken to the end of the line at Swanage, to go round the turntable, so that it now faces the coast. Both guns can fire 750-lb high explosive shells, at three minute intervals, and are controlled by clifftop observation posts on Ballard Down to the east, East Man to the south-east, and Tyneham Cap to the south-west.

They have a range of eight miles and are targeted on prospective invasion beaches. To protect them from the Luftwaffe they have been draped with 4,200 yards of Cullacort netting, suspended between the conifers, on 3,456-feet of scaffolding and 10,400-yards of wire.

Sunday 10 November
Christchurch Blenheim gives the enemy the slip.

Flight-Lieutenant Douglas L. Rayment of the Special Duty Flight at Christchurch Aerodrome has made another of his lucky escapes, this time evading some 20 enemy aircraft which he encountered at 30,000 feet. His specially adapted Blenheim bomber was carrying out a high-level scientific test-flight for the Telecommunications Research Establishment.

Thursday 14 November
Junkers explodes on Poole cobbler's shed.

This morning No. 10 Group Fighter Command, at its headquarters near Bath, plotted a single German reconnaissance aircraft crossing into the Middle Wallop sector from France. Pilot Officer Eric "Boy" Marrs, flying

1940 TROPHY: "SALVAGED" BY YEOVIL BOY E.R. CUFF WHO THE PREVIOUS YEAR HAD CYCLED TO WARMWELL AERODROME TO WATCH THE EMPIRE AIR DAY

Spitfire R6968 with 152 Squadron, and Sergeant Pilot Albert Wallace "Bill" Kearsey, in Spitfire P9427, were scrambled from R.A.F. Warmwell to investigate.

Kearsey spotted the intruder at 24,000 feet over the River Stour, between Blandford and Sturminster Newton, heading on a course for Yeovil or Bristol. Both Spitfires attacked and the Junkers Ju.88 turned southwards, trying to escape towards the English Channel.

Marrs engaged it first, coming up from underneath to a range of 150 yards, giving a burst that "started a fire under the port engine, an ominous red glow being clearly visible". Not that Marrs could take any further combative

BEAMED DOWN: THE STORY OF THE HEINKEL BOMBER AWASH AT WEST BAY, BRIDPORT, ON 6 NOVEMBER 1940 WOULD HAVE A NATIONAL SEQUEL ON 21 NOVEMBER 1940

We could lose the war by Fire! Be ready for FIREBOMB FRITZ!

We could lose the war by fire! *We could. But we WON'T.*
We of Britain's Fire Guard will see to that.

Fire Guard work is often dull. Sometimes its dangerous. But it's work that's *got* to be done. So we put into it every ounce of enthusiasm we've got. We watch unceasingly! We train till we're *really* good! We know all the awkward places, and how to get there. We won't be caught off guard as Firebomb Fritz will find.

FIRE GUARD TIPS

No. 3. *Don't be afraid of smoke. A lot of smoke doesn't necessarily mean a big fire. Nor does a lot of heat.*

No. 4. *Don't go into a smoke-filled building alone in case you should be overcome.*

BRITAIN SHALL NOT BURN!

ISSUED BY THE MINISTRY OF HOME SECURITY

FIREBOMB FRITZ: LEAFLET FROM THE MINISTRY OF HOME SECURITY WARNS OF INCENDIARY BOMBS. WEIGHING ONE KILOGRAM, THESE HAVE A CORE OF ALUMINIUM IRON OXIDE, ENCASED IN MAGNESIUM ALLOY

role in the action: "Unfortunately the rear gunner of the Junkers landed one plumb in the middle of my windscreen, splintering it in all directions and making it quite opaque."

Kearsey was still "going hard at it" and the Ju.88 dropped to 5,000 feet. The Warmwell pilots caught up with it again over Poole, with Marrs merely an observer because of his shattered windscreen, and Kearsey out of ammunition. Temporarily saved by the determination of the rear gunner, and the pilot's desperate struggle with the controls, the enemy aircraft was becoming a fireball. Out dropped one of the four crewmen but his parachute failed to open and his body fell through the roof of Kinson Potteries.

The pilot, Oberleutnant A. von Kugelgen, seemed to be making some last attempt to level the plane but it hit the ground near the end of Herbert Avenue, and exploded 50 feet from the cobbler's shed at Witcombe in Ringwood Road. Boot repairer Leonard Stainer and his family had narrow escapes, as did their neighbours. One night-time fire watcher was trapped in his bed by collapsing roof debris. Part of the fuselage ended up on top of Moore's Garage.

Friday 15 November
Coventry bombers pass over Christchurch.

Last night a massed formation of some 150 German aircraft flew across the Channel on a directional radio beam from the Cherbourg peninsula and crossed the coast at Christchurch and New Milton. They then headed up the Avon valley and passed two miles to the east of Salisbury.

Their code name for the operation was "Moonlight Sonata" and they were one of the three streams of German aeroplanes — totalling 449 aircraft — aiming for Target 53, which turned out to be Coventry.

The other streams crossed the English coast over Dover and the Wash.

The distinctive landmark of Coventry Cathedral would be targeted by the pathfinders of Kampfgruppe 100. The city was devastated by 1,500 bombs [503-tons], leaving 568 dead and many more injured. The cathedral and a third of the factories have been destroyed. The total number of damaged houses is estimated at 60,000.

Only one German bomber was lost, over Loughborough.

Friday 15 November
Escape flight from Belgium to Dorchester.

Two officers have escaped from Belgium in a light aeroplane which they took from an airfield near Dinant. They flew down the English Channel and landed in the Dorset countryside near Dorchester. One of the men is Belgian and the other French.

Saturday 16 November
Four killed in Poole blast.

Sidney Sherwood and his sons Fred, Henry, and Robert, were killed when a parachute mine landed on their home in Fancy Road, Poole, early this morning.

There were other blasts in Haskells Road, and Cynthia Road, causing serious injuries. Though she was able to shield her daughter, Molly, Mrs Lilian Kitkat was badly lacerated by flying debris and lost an eye.

Saturday 16 November
Fifty-three die in Bournemouth raid.

German bombers attacked Bournemouth last night and left major destruction in three suburbs. At about 03.30 hours today six parachute mines floated down on Westbourne, Malmesbury Park Road, St Leonard's Road, Turbary Common, and Alma Road Schools.

High explosive bombs and incendiaries have fallen at Gervis Road East, Meyrick Road, Knyveton Road, Groveley Manor, Terrace Road, Leven Avenue, Montague Road, and Southern Avenue.

Fifty-three people have been killed and 2,321 properties damaged.

Saturday 16 November
R. L. Stevenson's house is bombed.

Last night's Bournemouth air-raid badly damaged Skerryvore, which was Robert Louis Stevenson's house at Westbourne — near the head of Alum Chine — where he lived from 1885 until he left for the Pacific in 1887. Two poems about the house appeared that year in Underwood.

Footnote: Pleas for its restoration were ignored and the remains of the house were demolished in 1941. In 1954 the site became a municipal garden, with the footings of the building marked in concrete, and provided with a model of the Skerryvore Lighthouse for which it was named. Perhaps it could have been saved if he had produced *Treasure Island* there; probably not. *Kidnapped* and *The Strange Case of Dr Jekyll and Mr Hyde* were written while he was living in Bournemouth.

Sunday 17 November
Parachute mine devastates Chapelhay, Weymouth.

At 21.00 hours, when the Jack Buchanan programme had finished on the wireless, a German raider glided over Weymouth — he is said to have cut his engine — and dropped a parachute mine.

This caused the town's worst explosion of the war, destroying 77 of the tightly-packed terraced houses at Chapelhay, and damaging a further 879 properties. Twelve died, including a number of children who had gone upstairs to bed.

Footnote: The device had been intended for the harbour — investigation of its remnants showed it was a sea mine.

Monday 18 November
Poole houses evacuated.

Houses in Newtown, at Poole, were evacuated last night after an unexploded bomb had created a large crater in Gwynne Road. Not that it was anything like as large as the hole left by the bomb that did explode in Grove Road — you could put a house in that one!

Thursday 21 November
West Bay bomber could have foiled Coventry raid.

Scientists at the Royal Aircraft Establishment, Farnborough, have reassembled radio beam-flying equipment removed from the Heinkel He.111 bomber of the Luftwaffe's pathfinding Kampfgruppe 100 which crash-landed at West Bay on 6 November.

The aircraft had three vertical aerials and an intact X-Gerät radio receiver, also known as Wotan I, which is used for precision bombing by enabling the aircraft to follow a radio direction beam emanating from the Cherbourg peninsula.

What has surprised the Air Ministry boffins is that the apparatus is tuned to 2,000 cycles per second (approximating to the "C" which is two octaves above standard-pitch middle "C"), whereas British jamming countermeasures had assumed a note of 1,500 cycles (approximating to the "G" below this "C"). Therefore the pilot, receiving audio notes through his headphones, could filter out the British interference and continue to follow the correct beam.

The experts are less than pleased that this vital equipment was needlessly corroded, and full of sand, due to the crass folly of the Dorset soldiers who prevented sailors for pulling the aircraft up the beach. It became awash with the rising tide — causing avoidable damage to the delicate light-alloy electrical components.

Particular anger has been expressed that the secret could have been cracked in time to foil the devastating Coventry raid which took place a week ago: "Someone in Dorset should be shot!"

Footnote: The significance of the discovery, and the frustrations it unleashed, were outlined by Dr Reg Jones, who was head of scientific intelligence at the Air Ministry, in his memoirs *Most Secret War.* "So the filter could distinguish between the true beam," he wrote, "and our jamming, even though we had got the radio frequencies correct. It was one of those instances where enormous trouble is taken to get the difficult parts right and then a slip-up occurs because of the lack of attention to a seemingly trivial detail."

The revelation came too late to prevent the Coventry raid but it did ensure that radio countermeasures were perfected by the Telecommunications Research Establishment in time to save the vital Rolls-Royce aero-engine plant at Derby. On the night of 8 May 1941, in moonlit conditions similar to those of the Coventry raid, successful distortion of their signal caused Derby's bombs to fall on Nottingham — and those intended for Nottingham fell into open fields.

Wednesday 27 November
Spitfire follows a Junkers to France.

Though denied permission to intercept a Junkers Ju.88 that was heading south-west from Southampton, Flight-Lieutenant John Dundas was allowed to take up his section of 609 Squadron from R.A.F. Warmwell on a "practice flight" instead.

The two Spitfires climbed rapidly and found the bomber at 22,000 feet over Poole Bay, flying southwards into the sun. Throttling to 2,600 revolutions the Merlin engine of each fighter gave 280 miles per hour as the Spitfires closed on their target in its descent towards the Cherbourg peninsula.

Dundas put Spitfire X4586 into an attacking glide at 14,000 feet, firing with five-second bursts at 400, 300, and then 200 yards.

Flames shot out of the Ju.88's port engine and it lurched out of control as the three aircraft crossed the French coast. There being a German aerodrome visible below, the Spitfires did not follow their quarry any further towards the ground, and turned north-west for the 80-mile return flight to Dorset.

Thursday 28 November
609 Squadron loses two for a Luftwaffe ace.

"Whoopee! I've got a 109." Those were the last words received by radio transmission from Flight-Lieutenant John Dundas, flying Spitfire X4586 with 609 Squadron from R.A.F. Warmwell. "Good show, John," Flight-Lieutenant Michael Lister Robinson replied, after which nothing more was heard or seen of Dundas.

He had scrambled at 15.50 hours. Missing with him is Pilot Officer Paul Abbott Baillon, a solicitor, in Spitfire R6631, who only joined the squadron in October. Both have been lost over the sea off the Isle of Wight. They bring the losses for 609 Squadron to ten, but John Dundas has not died in vain.

Tonight it was announced by German radio that the Luftwaffe had lost one of its ace fighter pilots, Hauptmann Helmut Wick, who had 57 white kill-bars painted on the rudder of his Messerschmitt Bf.109E. He was leading Jagdgeschwader 2.

Thursday 28 November
Warmwell's 152 Squadron also loses two Spitfires.

Having congratulated itself on an "unusually quiet most of November" the month has also been marred for 152 Squadron at R.A.F. Warmwell by the loss of two pilots today. They bring the squadron's fatalities to eleven and those for the station to 24.

LULWORTH TANKS: ON MANOEUVRES FROM THE ARMOURED FIGHTING VEHICLES SCHOOL, THROUGH THE GROUNDS OF LULWORTH CASTLE. THESE VICKERS MARK VI LIGHT TANKS WERE KEY ELEMENTS OF THE THIN GREEN LINE WHICH GENERAL SIR ALAN BROOKE, COMMANDER-IN-CHIEF HOME FORCES, FIELDED AGAINST THE THREATENED GERMAN INVASION, BUT SOME WERE HANDED OVER, WITH THE 3RD HUSSARS, TO GENERAL ARCHIBALD WAVELL, COMMANDER-IN-CHIEF MIDDLE EAST, AND SHIPPED TO EGYPT

Polish Sergeant Pilot Zygmunt Klein's Spitfire, K9427, fell into the sea and Pilot Officer Arthur Roy Watson, flying Spitfire R6597, crashed near Wareham, as a result of dog-fights with Messerschmitt Bf.109s over Poole Bay and off the Needles, Isle of Wight.

The Polish flyer "just disappeared" but Watson "bungled his baling out and tore his parachute" which

SURVIVING SPITFIRE: MARK IA MACHINE R6915 OF 609 SQUADRON FROM R.A.F. WARMWELL, NOW IN HONOURABLE RETIREMENT AT THE IMPERIAL WAR MUSEUM, SAW BATTLE OF BRITAIN COMBAT OVER THE DORSET COAST, FLOWN BY PILOT OFFICER NOEL LE CHEVALIER AGAZARIAN

"streamed out behind him but owing to the tears did not open".

Watson's death was avenged almost immediately by Pilot Officer Eric "Boy" Marrs in Spitfire R6968. He crept up slowly on the culprit Bf.109, staying in his blindest spot, until he was within 100 yards. Then he fired for just one second, unleashing 55 rounds of .303 ammunition from each of his eight guns, to score "the easiest victory I've had".

The result was instantaneous: "Black smoke belched forth and oil splattered over my windscreen. He half rolled and dived away. I followed in a steep spiral to see what was going to happen but my speed became so great I pulled away and my wing hid him for a bit.

"When I looked again there was a large number of flaming fragments wafting down to the sea. One large black lump, which was not on fire, trailed a white plume which snapped open and became a parachute. This was the pilot, and must have baled out just before the petrol tank blew up. However, he landed in the sea and might just as well have blown up, for he was never found."

Friday 29 November
Spitfire plunges into Field Grove, near Durweston.

15.14 hours. A flight from 152 Squadron, including Spitfire R6907 flown by Pilot Officer John Woodward

Allen, was scrambled because of a suspected enemy fighter sweep. They were instructed to patrol a circuit of R.A.F. Warmwell at 25,000 feet.

Allen sent a radio message but it was unintelligible and nothing further was heard from him. His Spitfire was then seen to break away and dive shallowly, though under control. Suddenly it plummeted vertically towards the ground and completely disintegrated on impact at Field Grove, a wood half a mile west of Travellers' Rest, on the downs two miles south-west of Durweston.

The severity of the crash precludes any mechanical examination. It is thought that the pilot fainted because of loss of oxygen.

He had been flying Spitfires for three weeks and is the squadron's 13th fatality. Those for the station have now reached 25.

Footnote: The crash site was marked by a plaque, nailed on a dead tree trunk, but that was replaced in 1978 by a churchyard-style granite memorial.

Ernest Day of Okeford Fitzpaine recalled seeing the plane in difficulties: "It was late afternoon, the day that a sixpence fell from the sky, hit my right shoulder and fell in the main road at Thornicombe. The fighter was climbing. Then I saw, very high in the sky, three German bombers returning from Bristol. The fighter made one attack on

FRAMPTON ARMS: PROPRIETRESS MRS MABEL DRAPER, TELEPHONE WARMWELL 253, ACROSS THE ROAD FROM MORETON STATION, BEING THE CLOSEST PUBLIC HOUSE BOTH FOR R.A.F. WARMWELL AND ITS RAILWAY LINE (THE CONSERVATORY IS A POST-WAR ADDITION)

the bombers, then slowly descended towards me for a while, then it came straight down towards the ground with the throttle open.

"I stood thinking it was going straight into the ground, nose first, about 50 yards from me. Then what seemed like seconds before hitting the ground the throttle closed and the fighter turned out of the dive very sharply, just missing the ground. It proceeded on a course towards Blandford, very unsteadily, just missing the telegraph poles on Thornicombe Hill, but slowly gaining height.

"When it reached Gipsy's Corner it turned left [north-westwards], then it flew over Fairmile where it slowly descended and went out of my view. A few hours later a friend told me that the fighter crashed near Travellers' Rest."

Saturday 30 November
Bf.109 belly-lands on Purbeck spy mission.

Unteroffizier Paul Wacker of Jagdgeschwader 27, flying a Messerschmitt Bf.109 belonging to the 4th Staffel of Lehrgeschwader 2 — a specialist unit testing improvised aircraft under operational conditions — suffered engine failure whilst on a weather reconnaissance over Swanage this afternoon.

He was fortunate to belly-land on fields at Woodyhyde Farm, beside the railway between Swanage and Corfe Castle, having narrowly avoided heavily wooded countryside.

Footnote: The tail section of his fighter survives. It was used to repair another captured test-flown Bf.109 that is now displayed in the Royal Air Force Museum at Hendon.

SHATTERED STUMP: WHERE PILOT OFFICER JOHN WOODWARD ALLEN CRASHED, AT FIELD GROVE IN DURWESTON FOREST, ON 29 NOVEMBER 1940. CAPTAIN GERALD PORTMAN PLACED A MEMORIAL PLAQUE ON THE TREE (SINCE REPLACED BY A MUCH LESS EVOCATIVE GRANITE MEMORIAL)

During November
Bournemouth's death toll for month reaches 62.

It has been Bournemouth's worst month of the war so far. Five air-raids saw a total of six parachute mines, 24 high

"Boy" Marrs: youthful Spitfire pilot Eric Simcox Marrs of 152 Squadron at R.A.F. Warmwell, sketched by Captain Cuthbert Orde in December 1940, on being awarded the Distinguished Flying Cross. He had survived the dog-fights of the Battle of Britain but would be killed in the offensive war, by flak from the French coast, on 25 July 1941

RAILWAY HOWITZER: ONE OF THE 12-INCH GUNS WHICH ARRIVED AT FURZEBROOK, NORTH-WEST OF CORFE CASTLE, IN NOVEMBER 1940. IT FIRED SHELLS WEIGHING A THIRD OF A TON. THE FULL SEQUENCE OF LOADING A SHELL WAS CARRIED OUT BY 5TH CORPS ON 26 FEBRUARY 1941 FOR THE BENEFIT OF A VISITING PHOTOGRAPHER, MR MALINDINE, SENT BY SOUTHERN COMMAND. "ONE OF BRITAIN'S TEETH," THE CAPTION READS; OMITTING TO ADD THAT THE FILLINGS TENDED TO FALL OUT. FOR WHEN THEY WERE USED THE GUNS JAMMED.

ARMING

TROLLEYING

CRADLING

HOISTING

LOADING

LOCKING

ELEVATING

BURNING SEA: VIPs INCLUDING GENERAL HAROLD ALEXANDER (LEFT, TURNING TOWARDS THE CAMERA) WATCH OIL SLICKS EMERGING FROM UNDERWATER PIPES IN STUDLAND BAY, BETWEEN REDEND POINT (TOP LEFT) AND OLD HARRY ROCKS, TO BE IGNITED IN A DRAMATIC ANTI-INVASION MEASURE (below) ON 20 DECEMBER 1940

explosive bombs, and a number of incendiary devices dropped on the town. Sixty-two people were killed, 132 injured, and 2,829 properties damaged. By far the most damaging attack was that on the 16th.

During November

Shaftesbury Germans send their plane to Ipswich.

One of the more remarkable aeronautical feats of the war has solved a Dorset puzzle. Four German airmen baled out and walked into a village near Shaftesbury to give themselves up. "But where is their aeroplane?" everyone was asking. Meanwhile, 130 miles away, a Dornier bomber made a perfect belly-landing in mud flats at Ipswich. "Where are the crew?" people were asking in Suffolk.

The bomber, from the Cherbourg peninsula, was en route for Liverpool when it experienced an electrical storm near Shrewsbury during which its compass had flipped. They reached France but then feared, wrongly, that they were flying north into Britain, and turned back across the Channel for the third time, where they failed to find an airfield and decided to abandon the aircraft. It, however, continued on its automatic pilot and landed safely at Ipswich when the petrol ran out.

Sunday 1 December

Bournemouth A.A. gunners claim two planes.

Both last night and this evening there was bombing at Southampton. Enemy aircraft were harassed by

CHRISTMAS CHEER: THE TYPE 15 GROUND TO AIR MOBILE RADAR ANTENNA THAT WAS DEVISED AT WORTH MATRAVERS AND BUILT AT CHRISTCHURCH, INSTALLED IN A FIELD AT SOPLEY ON 25 DECEMBER 1940

Tuesday 3 December
Hurn Aerodrome bombed.

The new aerodrome being built at Hurn, north of Bournemouth, had its first air-raid today. Five high explosive bombs and a number of incendiaries fell at 18.50 hours.

Footnote: The site had previously been recommended by Sir Alan Cobham to Bournemouth Corporation for a municipal aerodrome, but in the event — a war — it was the Air Ministry that took the initiative, on behalf of the Royal Air Force.

Bournemouth's earlier airfield, Ensbury Park Aerodrome and Racecourse, had become a housing estate in 1932. Its first scheduled commercial flight, in a Handley Page bomber, was flown by William Sholto Douglas in 1919.

By 1940 he would be Deputy Chief of the Air Staff, and then Air Officer Commanding-in-Chief at Fighter Command in the midst of the conflicts of 1940-42. He finished the war as Marshal of the Royal Air Force and retired in 1948, being created 1st Baron Douglas Kirtleside.

Hurricanes and anti-aircraft fire as they flew over Poole Bay and Bournemouth, Six German planes are reported to have been shot down — with two of them being claimed by Bournemouth's anti-aircraft gunners.

One was seen to drop into the sea off Hengistbury Head.

Monday 2 December
Warmwell's Europeans claim double kill.

The flying partnership of 609 Squadron's two eastern Europeans, Pilot Officers Noel le Chevalier Agazarian and Tadeusz Nowierski, today achieved a double kill.

Scrambled from R A F Warmwell, they intercepted German aircraft off Thorney Island, Hampshire, and shared the destruction of a Messerschmitt Bf.110 fighter-bomber and a Dornier Do.17 bomber. The Spitfires broke up an attacking formation heading for Portsmouth.

Footnote: Noel Agazarian was then posted to the Middle East and lost his life when 274 Squadron was intercepted by Messerschmitt Bf.109s over the Western Desert on 16 May 1941. He is buried in Knightsbridge War Cemetery, at Acroma, Libya.

Tadeusz Nowierski became Polish Liaison Officer at the Headquarters of 11 Group Fighter Command, in 1942, and would be promoted to Group Captain, commanding R.A.F. Dunholme Lodge. He returned to Poland in 1947 and died in 1983.

Friday 13 December
Christchurch families evacuated just in time.

Families between Freda Road and Kings Avenue, Christchurch, were evacuated from their homes just in time this evening. A crater with an unexploded bomb, outside 1 Kings Avenue, had been reported at 09.25 hours but the decision to clear the area was delayed until 17.25.

A bomb disposal team had then taken a look and decided to leave the bomb for 96 hours.

Then, at 18.55, it went off — damaging three houses and rupturing gas and water pipes.

Friday 20 December
Alexander and Montgomery set Studland Bay on fire.

General Harold Alexander, General Officer Commanding-in-Chief of Southern Command, and Major-General Bernard Montgomery of 5th Corps, today stood on the clifftop between Redend Point and Old Harry Rocks, Studland, to watch the sea being set on fire.

Pipes have been laid from the beach in Project Fougasse to release oil in a series of slicks to form a continuous strip that is then ignited. It has been a calm day and the water was burning until the waves began to

SPITFIRE P9450: THE REASSURING PRESENCE IN DORSET'S SKY, FIELDED BY R.A.F. WARMWELL

disperse the slick. This is an anti-invasion measure that will only work in favourable weather — but the enemy will be trying to chose a day when landing conditions are ideal.

Footnote: The intention had been to repeat the exercise at night, because British intelligence suggested that the German troops feared a conflagration on the beaches, but the second attempt was a disappointment due to waves lashed up by a cold on-shore wind.

Tuesday 24 December
E-boats sink two ships off Dorset.

Convoy FN 366, sailing between Portland and the Isle of Wight, was last night attacked by the German 1st Schnellboot Flotilla. This comprises six large motor torpedo boats; *S26*, *S28*, *S29*, *S34*, *S56*, and *S59*.

The E-boats sank a Dutch ship, the *Maastricht*, and a Royal Navy armed trawler, H.M.T. *Pelton.*

Wednesday 25 December
Mobile radar goes into the field at Sopley.

A trailer-mounted ground-to-air radar antenna, developed by the Telecommunications Research Establishment at Worth Matravers and built at Somerford, Christchurch, by the Air Defence Experimental Establishment, is being tested for the first time today.

Known as Type 15, the mobile unit has been towed into the countryside, and placed on a flat part of Lord Manner's estate at Sopley, between the River Avon and the New Forest.

During December
Blandford's Battle Training Camp.

Blandford Camp is now designated a Battle Training Camp and provides a variety of intensive assault courses to simulate combat conditions.

SEASONAL TOUCH: THE 5TH BATTALION OF THE NORTHAMPTONSHIRE REGIMENT PUT A BREN GUN CARRIER AMONGST THE TURKEYS AT HOLDENHURST FARM, ON THE OUTSKIRTS OF BOURNEMOUTH, FOR A LITTLE MOCK WARFARE IN THE WINTER OF 1940

HOLDENHURST CAPTURED: BY THE 5TH BATTALION, THE NORTHAMPTONSHIRE REGIMENT, ON MANOEUVRES WITH THEIR BREN GUN CARRIERS THROUGH THE COUNTRYSIDE NORTH OF BOURNEMOUTH IN 1940

DEFENDING DORSET: SHOWING HOW TO DISGUISE WAR-WORKS, COURTESY THE CAMOUFLAGE SCHOOL OF SOUTHERN COMMAND, IN SHORE ROAD AT CANFORD CLIFFS

LAMBETH EXHIBIT: MARK I SPITFIRE R6915 OF 609 SQUADRON FROM R.A.F. WARMWELL, WHICH SAW REPEATED ACTION OVER DORSET IN THE BATTLE OF BRITAIN, NOW IN SUSPENDED ANIMATION AT THE IMPERIAL WAR MUSEUM

HENDON EXHIBIT: SPITFIRE X4590 AS "PR" F FOR FREDDIE OF 609 SQUADRON, IN WHICH PILOT OFFICER S. J. HILL CLAIMED A HALF SHARE OF A JUNKERS JU.88 SHOT DOWN ON 8 OCTOBER 1940, IS ANOTHER OF R.A.F. WARMWELL'S REMARKABLE SURVIVALS

THE VICTOR AND
THE VANQUISHED
—
NEAR HARDYS MONUMENT

FARM MEMORIAL: TO ADRIAN VAN DE WEYER OF THE RIFLE BRIGADE, KILLED AT CALAIS ON 26 MAY 1940, PLACED IN A FIELD ON THE FAMILY FARM AT SOUTH ADMISTON, NEAR TOLPUDDLE

SPITFIRE PILOT: DAVID MOORE CROOK OF 609 SQUADRON FROM R.A.F. WARMWELL WITH A "STUKA" HE SHOT DOWN EARLIER IN THE DAY, ON HILLS BESIDE THE HARDY MONUMENT, WITH "THE VICTOR AND THE VANQUISHED" BEING ITS CONTEMPORARY CAPTION

BLAST WALL: BEHIND THE SUSPENDED FIREMAN, TO PROTECT WINDOWS IN PELHAMS HOUSE, KINSON, WHICH BECAME THE BASE STATION FOR NO 8 ZONE OF BOURNEMOUTH'S AUXILIARY FIRE SERVICE IN 1940

1941

Saturday 4 January

Night-flying Hurricane ices-up over Portland and crash-lands.

Pilot Officer Bob Doe D.F.C., flying a Hurricane night-fighter of 238 Squadron from R.A.F. Chilbolton, Hampshire, found his engine cooling system icing-up last night as he flew over the sea off Portland Bill. His radio controller at Middle Wallop sector headquarters talked him inland towards Warmwell Aerodrome but the engine of V6758 was overheating badly and cut-out as he approached the snow-covered airstrip.

He avoided its hangars but found himself landing amongst a stack of oil-drums. These ripped the light-weight fighter apart but the pilot was brought out of the wreckage alive. He was given emergency treatment in the station sick-bay and then taken to Bovington Military Hospital where fragments of glass were removed from his eye.

Footnote: Leslie Dawson records, in the revised edition of *Wings over Dorset*, the comforting words that Doe remembered hearing from a nurse as he regained consciousness at Bovington. "Lawrence of Arabia died in this bed!" she said. The pilot would resume his wartime career and then flew post-war jet fighters, retiring from the R.A.F. as Wing Commander R. T. F. Doe D.S.O, D.F.C. and bar.

Saturday 4 January

Warmwell intruder shot-down off Portland.

Pilot Officer Eric "Boy" Marrs led Green Section of 152 Squadron, in Spitfire R6968, from R.A.F. Warmwell at 13.00 hours today in a sortie to find a single German aircraft that was reportedly entering the Middle Wallop sector.

Marrs became separated from his accompanying Spitfire in cloud and returned to Warmwell. As he prepared to land he was told to stay airborne as the intruder was now flying towards the aerodrome, from the sea, at about 5,000 feet. Marrs was just under the cloud layer at 4,000 feet.

He swept southwards over the chalk cliffs at White Nothe and across Weymouth Bay as a Dornier Do.17 lumbered above Ringstead Bay: "I approached from the sea and opened fire at about 400 yards from the port rear quarter. He then turned south and dived like stink for the clouds. I turned in behind him, and closing to about 250 yards, fired at the fuselage and two engines in turn. Black and white smoke came from the engines and all return fire from the gunners ceased. I was overshooting and just before he reached the clouds I had to break away."

The Dornier was spotted from the ground at Lulworth Cove, as it came out of the cloud, trailing smoke and losing height. Its attempted return to France ended in the English Channel, five miles south-east of Portland Bill. No one survived.

Friday 10 January

Two Poole men blown up as they leave shelter.

Leaving their garden air-raid shelter last night after an incendiary attack, Frank and Henry James of Canford Cliffs were blown up by the following wave of German bombers. The town was well alight for a time from numerous incendiaries and there was even a fire at the Fire Station. A total of 248 houses have been damaged though only one, a Lilliput bungalow, was completely gutted.

CLARE OVERHAULED: ADJUSTMENTS BEING MADE TO THE TRANS-ATLANTIC FLYING-BOAT'S FOUR GREAT PERSEUS ENGINES, IN JANUARY 1941, FOR HER RETURN TO POOLE HARBOUR AND THE NEW EMPIRE ROUTE TO AFRICA

UNEXPLODED BOMB: FELL BEHIND HEATHWOOD GARAGE AT HOLTON HEATH, HAVING MISSED THE ROYAL NAVAL CORDITE FACTORY IN AN AIR-RAID IN 1941

Henry James died yesterday and Frank, an auxiliary Coastguard, died today in Cornelia Hospital, Poole.

Monday 13 January
Observer Corps post machine-gunned at Dorchester.

00.38 hours: a Heinkel He.111 passed about 100 yards from the Poundbury Camp observation post, Dorchester, at an estimated 300 feet. 02.45: the post has been machine-gunned by an enemy aircraft. There are no casualties.

Saturday 25 January
More mines laid off Dorset.

Over the past three days the German destroyer *Richard Britzen*, operating with two T-boats, the *Iltis* [Polecat] and *Seeadler* [Sea Eagle] of about 1,300 tons displacement, have been laying mines off the Dorset coast.

Monday 27 January
Dorchester burglary ends in murder.

01.30 hours. Private David Jennings, aged 20, has been charged with the murder last night of Dorchester tailor Albert Farley of The Grove.

What started as a burglary had turned tragically wrong. Jennings was breaking into what he assumed was an empty licensed club and did so in the style of American gangster films. He shot the lock off the door. Unknown to Jennings, however, the premises were still occupied and

Farley was about to unlock the door from the other side. The tailor was shot dead.

Footnote: Jennings would hang at Dorchester Prison. Such homicides ceased to be murder under the Homicide Act 1957 and the Criminal Justice Act 1967, in that the jury could now decide whether the accused intended or should have foreseen the results of his action. Clearly he did not, in this case, as the object was theft from a building that was locked-up and apparently unoccupied.

The present definition would be manslaughter, though the original jurymen had little patience with such niceties. High East Street grocer Douglas Parsons told me: "We didn't think of things like that. We were at war."

During January
Airspeed moves to Christchurch Aerodrome.

Christchurch Aerodrome has been selected as a shadow-factory for an aviation company. Airspeed (1934) Limited will move to the grass pre-war club flying ground at Somerford, near Christchurch Harbour. The company is best known for the Envoy and the Oxford.

Footnote: A total of 550 of the twin-engined Oxfords would be made at Christchurch. Most went into service use as trainers.

During January
Worth scientist takes over Alexandra Palace T.V. transmitter.

In the last week of this month, Dr Robert Cockburn of the Telecommunications Research Establishment, from Worth Matravers, has commandeered the B.B.C.'s pre-war television transmitter at Alexandra Palace. It went off the air in mid-cartoon on the outbreak of war because of concern that the straight, horizontal, programme signal would be utilised by enemy bombers as a navigation aid to find the capital.

The powerful aerial, on Muswell Hill in north London, was brought back into action on the very night that the Luftwaffe refined its blind-flying system of following radio beams to English targets.

The bombers had changed to a frequency of 42.5 megacycles per second. This was successfully jammed by Cockburn in Countermeasure Domino. He re-radiated the German signal back to the attacking aircraft, from Alexandra Palace, at 46.9 megacycles per second.

Footnote: A second transmitting station, constructed on Beacon Hill, near Salisbury, extended Cockburn's jamming across the whole of southern England.

Saturday 1 February
First Catalina flying-boat lands on Poole Harbour.

The first of the long-range American-built Catalina flying-boats descended today on Dorset waters. Guba (G-AGBJ) was the graceful arrival, from Hythe on Southampton Water, and she is to use the "Trots" of

Poole Harbour — as the series of water-runways are known — for the home base of the B.O.A.C. service across the Bay of Biscay, to neutral Portugal.

She has brought a new sound. Hers are the Twin Wasp engines of Pratt and Whitney which are louder than the familiar Bristol Pegasus 9-cylinder radial engines of the Short "Empire" flying-boats.

Sunday 2 February
Fougasse breaks the black-out.

For a time last night there was no black-out over Bournemouth. You could read a newspaper in the Square. The cause was the ignition of the anti-invasion oil slicks of Project Fougasse on the beaches of Studland in the Isle of Purbeck.

It was a test; to remind the enemy that we are ready.

Wednesday 12 February
Coast battery fires on E-boats.

The two 6-inch guns at Hengistbury Head Coast Battery opened fire at 06.50 hours on E-boats out in the Channel.

Saturday 15 February
£1 million target for Bournemouth war effort.

Bournemouth War Savings Committee has organised the town's War Weapons Week, which was launched this morning by the Mayor, Alderman A. H. Little, at a thermometer-style target board mounted on the bus-shelter in the Square. Mayor Little will be riding around the town in military style, on top of a tank which will also display the progress being made, towards the required figure of £1 million.

He announced that £250,000 had been raised on the first day — including £100,000 from Bournemouth Corporation — and said that the money would be safe and secure in National Savings. It was not a gift to the Government, he emphasised, but a timely investment in the future that would yield 3 per cent interest per annum, free of tax.

The town's wartime savings rate has been running at nearly £100,000 per week but the campaign committee is seeking to increase this to an average of £150,000. It now has 525 savings groups, of which 262 are in places of employment, 155 are based on streets, and the remainder include clubs and schools.

Wednesday 19 February
Lysander drops leaflets on Bournemouth.

As Alderman Little addressed troops and townspeople from his vantage point beside the War Weapons Week Savings thermometer in the Square, a Westland Lysander flew low over Bournemouth and showered the town centre with leaflets: "A message to Bournemouth from the Royal Air Force. To the citizens of Bournemouth — the Royal Air Force is watching with great interest your War Weapons Week. Lend your money to the utmost as are lending our full support to you. We are banking on Bournemouth, too!"

Three Spitfires have just thrilled the crowd with a display of V-shaped formation flight and aerobatics.

Friday 21 February
Ibsley Hurricane crashes on Bournemouth.

One of three Hurricanes of 32 Squadron from R.A.F. Ibsley, giving a War Weapons Week flying display across the centre of Bournemouth in the late afternoon, failed to pull out of a victory roll. It crashed on the rear of houses at 36 and 38 St Clement's Road, killing the 22-year-old Czech pilot, but not injuring the only resident in the buildings, who was pulled from the rubble by firemen.

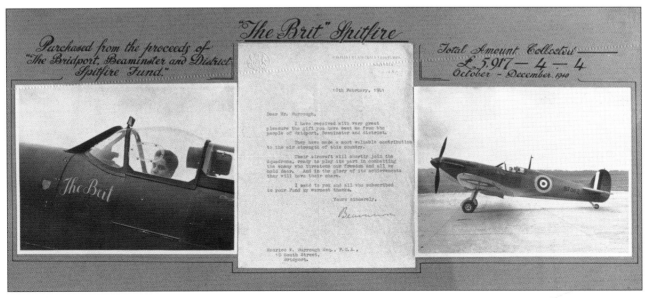

THE BRIT: *FIGHTER NAMED FOR BRIDPORT'S RIVER, PURCHASED WITH THE £5,917 PROCEEDS OF THE BRIDPORT, BEAMINSTER AND DISTRICT SPITFIRE FUND, IN FEBRUARY 1941. SHE WOULD BE HANDED OVER FOR SQUADRON SERVICE ON 10 MAY 1941*

*QUAD BESA: MARK II MODEL WITH
THE MACHINE-GUNS MOUNTED AS A
SELF PROPELLED ANTI-AIRCRAFT
BATTERY, DESIGNED AT LULWORTH
CAMP AND OPERATIONAL THERE IN
FEBRUARY 1941*

Monday 24 February
609 Squadron leaves R.A.F. Warmwell.

The Spitfires of 609 Squadron, Dorset's first home-fielded defenders of the Battle of Britain, have lifted off the turf of R.A.F. Warmwell for the last time. They are now stationed at Biggin Hill, Kent. With them went their two odd-job planes, a Puss Moth, and a Magister.

Monday 24 February
234 Squadron arrives at Warmwell.

Mark-I Spitfires of 234 (Madras Presidency) Squadron have arrived at Warmwell Aerodrome. Their markings are "AZ" and their motto "Ignem mortemque despuimu" ("We spit fire and death").

Monday 24 February
German radar signal picked up at Worth Matravers.

Derek Garrard, a scientist from the Air Ministry seconded to the Telecommunications Research Establishment at Worth Matravers, has succeeded in picking up transmissions on a V.H.F. receiver at the 2.5 metre wavelength. Having failed with the official equipment, he put an ordinary radio set in his car and drove off to St Alban's Head, to point it towards the Cherbourg peninsula; for which activity he was arrested as a suspected Fifth Columnist infiltrating a designated "Defended Area".

Having established his credentials, he returned to his office in London, with bearings that suggest a source in the area of Auderville, where coincidentally two square-meshed aerials in a field were photographed by Flight Officer W. K. Manifould two days ago. The 22-feet turntable apparatus is the "Freya" unit to which the Germans credited the sinking off Portland of H.M.S. *Delight* on 29 July 1940.

As a result, Air Marshal Sir Philip Joubert has called a meeting for this afternoon, with one item on the agenda: "To discuss the existence of German radar."

Footnote: More than 50 Freya units would be located by a combination of listening, intercepting messages, and reconnaissance flights, by the end of 1941.

Thursday 27 February
Lord Gort's son shot dead at Corfe Mullen.

Second-Lieutenant the Honourable C. S. Vereker, whose father, Lord Gort V.C., led the British Expeditionary Force in France, was shot dead today at Corfe Mullen. He was serving with the Grenadier Guards and is said to have failed to stop at a vehicle check-point manned by the Home Guard.

Footnote: Vereker is buried in the northern plot of the cemetery beside the Higher Blandford Road at Newtown, or Corfe Mullen South as it is now known.

During February

Worth Matravers veteran flyer to train paratroops.

Squadron Leader Louis Strange, the 50-year-old flyer from Worth Matravers, has been given responsibility for the training of British paratroops. He is the only pilot still flying on active service in this war who went to France with the first squadrons of the Flying Corps in August 1914.

Uniquely, he would not only be flying operationally with the Royal Air Force on Armistice Day in 1918, holding the M.C. and D.F.C., but came out of retirement to return to combat in Europe, leaving with a Hurricane to receive a bar to his D.F.C. on the Fall of France.

Tuesday 4 March

Sopley radar claims first kill.

The Type-15 mobile radar unit established in a field at Sopley, four miles north of Christchurch, on Christmas Day is fully operational and today celebrated the first kill of an enemy aeroplane to result from one of the aerial interceptions it has stage-managed.

The unit provides combat guidance to Blenheim Mark If fighters of 604 Squadron which operates from R.A.F. Middle Wallop.

Sunday 9 March

Another burn-up of the Studland beaches.

Last night the Studland "Sea Flame" experiment was repeated for the benefit of General Harold Alexander, Commander 1st Division, as the pipes of Project Fougasse ignited the sea with burning oil. A landing craft was towed through the flames to show the effect of the scorching.

Footnote: The Petroleum Warfare Department was authorised to install 50 miles of such barrages but shortages of steel piping would restrict "Sea Flame" to Deal, Dover, and Rye in the prime potential invasion area of Caesar's coast and Porthcurno, at the landfall of the transatlantic cables, in Cornwall.

Wednesday 12 March

Poole flying-boat 'Clio' fitted with gun turrets.

The former Poole "Empire" flying-boat *Clio* returned to service today after a refit by Short Brothers at Belfast to equip her with armour plating, bomb-racks on the wings, and four machine-guns in each of two Boulton-Paul turrets in the dorsal and tail. Radar apparatus completes her transformation into a military flying-boat of Coastal Command. Her new number is AX659.

Clio logged over 4,000 miles of civilian flights. Her next long-distance expeditions will be with 201 Squadron, from northern Scotland, to patrol the Iceland Gap.

Footnote: She would be lost on 22 August 1941.

Wednesday 12 March

Bombs shatter Winton houses.

Eight houses were destroyed tonight by German bombs which dropped on Portland Road and Morley Road, Winton, at 22.09 hours. Bournemouth rescue squads are digging people out of the debris.

Wednesday 12 March

Royal Blue blitzed in Bournemouth.

Royal Blue coach services were delayed tonight, with vehicle windows being blown out and damage caused to its depot beside The Square, after a near-miss from a high-explosive bomb. The company operates long-distance express routes to London, with 42 journeys each way per week, and across the West Country and South Coast, though the pre-war boast of "from Penzance to Plymouth" has been spoilt by the reality of wartime suspended services.

Friday 14 March

Re-equipped Warmwell squadron's first combat.

Improved Mark-II Spitfires, which have been issued to 152 Squadron at R.A.F. Warmwell to replace their Mark-I fighters, were scrambled today for their first combat patrol. They intercepted a Junkers Ju.88 reconnaissance aircraft, which was hit, but it escaped back across the Channel.

Friday 21 March

'Bournemouth II Crest' is the town's Spitfire.

54 Squadron, at R.A.F. Hornchurch, Essex, took delivery today of the Mark-Va Spitfire that will be known as *Bournemouth II Crest*. It has been paid for by public collections and war-weapons events in the town.

Footnote: Bournemouth II Crest would have a good war. It passed to 403 Squadron, and on to 332 Squadron, and then 164 Squadron in 1942. The next users were 602 Squadron. The Spitfire was then seconded to the 82nd Fighter Group of the United States Army Air Force on 8 November 1943. Then it went to 349 Squadron of the Royal Air Force before being passed between a couple of operational training units, and finally, as 5586M, being handed on by a succession of maintenance units. Finally it would cross the Channel and the R.A.F. relinquished ownership of *Bournemouth II Crest* to the post-war French Air Force.

Friday 21 March

'Glamour Puffer' is shell-shocked.

The "Glamour Puffer" as she is known — being a works train for the Royal Naval Cordite Factory on Holton Heath that brings young ladies from Christchurch, Bournemouth, and Poole — attracted the attention of a German raider as it steamed home this evening. It pulled out of Holton Heath Station at 17.19 hours.

Just as it crossed Rocklea Bridge, heading towards Hamworthy Junction, a stick of six bombs straddled the embankment beside the harbour backwater and blew out all the windows of the ancient non-corridor "bird-cage" stock. It kept going, into the semi-protected stretch of line through the sandy cutting, and then halted to wait for more of the same. The enemy aircraft did not return and the train was able to draw into the platform.

Apart from severe fright none of the ladies suffered anything worse than minor cuts.

Wednesday 26 March
Four bombs hit Warmwell Aerodrome.

A solitary Junkers Ju.88 crossed the Channel today and dropped four high explosive bombs on the R.A.F. station at Warmwell. There were no casualties and damage was limited to holes in the grass.

The station did, however, lose a flyer today. Pilot Officer L. D. Sandes, who held the Distinguished Flying Cross, was aged 28.

Thursday 27 March
Thirty-four killed by bomb at Branksome Gas Works.

The air-raid siren has sounded at Branksome almost every day this month, and sometimes more than once,

but today has been different. Despite the alarm, business continued as usual at Branksome Gas Works, where the staff were gathering in the canteen for lunch. It was at noon that a single enemy aircraft dived out of the clouds towards the viaducts in Bourne Valley.

Two bombs fell short of the railway and landed on the Gas Works. The first blew up the stores and the second smashed through the upper storey above the canteen and then wedged itself, protruding through the ceiling, to the horror of those seated beneath. There was only a matter of seconds to begin evacuating the crowded tables before the not-much-delayed fuse activated the bomb with deadly effect.

The explosion devastated the hall, killing 34 men, including Home Guard members Leonard Bartlett, Archibald Cherrett, and Herbert Williams. A further 23 were injured; some of them seriously. Anxious wives soon thronged at the gates as Royal Artillerymen helped the survivors to drag out their dead and wounded colleagues.

Thursday 27 March
Unexploded bomb at Winton.

In Bournemouth, a high explosive bomb that fell at Lowther Road, Winton, failed to go off.

BRANKSOME CARNAGE: THE SCENE OF TOTAL DEVASTATION AT BOURNE VALLEY GASWORKS ON 27 MARCH 1941 WHEN A DELAYED-ACTION LUNCHTIME BOMB FELL THROUGH THE CANTEEN CEILING AND PROTRUDED FOR SEVERAL SECONDS BEFORE EXPLODING. A.R.P. WARDENS AND ROYAL ARTILLERYMEN BEGIN TO DRAG OUT THE DEAD AND INJURED FROM THE DEBRIS. THREE OF THE 34 DEAD WERE MEMBERS OF THE HOME GUARD

Thursday 27 March
Lyme Regis pilot lost in action.

Wing Commander Edward Collis de Virac Lart, who was born in Lyme Regis in 1902 and has served as an R.A.F. pilot since he was 23, has failed to return to base. He was one of Britain's most experienced flyers. In the 1920s he flew with 60 (Bombing) Squadron in India.

Friday 28 March
Bournemouth's army of part-time firemen.

"Bournemouth has over 17,000 civilian fire-fighters," boasts the Bournemouth Times. Since a mass-meeting on 15 February 1941 the town has implemented the Fire Precautions (Business Premises) Order which requires all healthy men between 16 and 60, who are not otherwise involved in the war effort, to register for up to 48 hours duty a month as part-time firemen.

Stirrup pumps and whistles are being widely distributed and steel helmets will be ordered. Six-inch diameter steel piping is being laid on the pavements along the main roads in the centre of town to ensure a ready and repairable water supply. Underground mains pipes are much more liable to fracture, and usually impossible to repair, during night-time air-raids. Fire, the Government believes, is the most devastating aspect of aerial warfare.

During March
Canford Cliffs bomb for the bouncy Air Marshal.

One of the bombs that dropped on Canford Cliffs this month hit the home of Air Marshal Sir Philip Joubert, nominally the commanding officer of Combined Operations which is being set-up at Poole. In fact that job is a blind, for since 14 June 1940 he has been running the R.A.F.'s radar and signals intelligence system, right through the Battle of the Beams, and in effect he controls the Telecommunications Research Establishment at Worth Matravers.

It all couldn't have happened to a nicer chap — he must be the bounciest Air Marshal the R.A.F. has yet appointed.

During March
Wareham family has five sons in the R.A.F.

Aspiring to some sort of record, Mr and Mrs R. J. Brennan of the bakery at Worgret, near Wareham, have written to a local newspaper saying that all five of their sons have enlisted in the Royal Air Force. They are Samuel, Eric, Peter, Archibald, and Edwin, whose ages range from 20 to 33.

The other two Brennan children are girls.

ROASTED DISH: MRS DREW (LEFT) AND MRS SEATON SURVEYING THE REMAINS OF THEIR POOLE KITCHEN WITH THE ENGINE (FOREGROUND) OF A GERMAN RAIDER

Tuesday 1 April

German bombers kill ten at Warmwell.

Three Heinkel He.111s slipped low across the Dorset coast from Lyme Bay and followed the railway eastwards from Dorchester to the aerodrome at Warmwell. They had not been picked up by radar, or spotted by the Observer Corps, and the station had no warning of the attack. Ten were killed by the bombs, shortly after noon, and 20 injured.

Among the dead is Sergeant Pilot Fawcett, one of the Spitfire flyers of 152 Squadron, who was killed by a machine-gun bullet as he sat eating lunch.

A bomb crashed through the room of Eric "Boy" Marrs but the pilot was elsewhere — having the Distinguished Flying Cross, which was awarded last December, pinned on his uniform in Buckingham Palace by King George VI.

Similarly honoured, and also from 152 Squadron, was Pilot Officer Dudley Williams. Pilot Officer Marrs also had a shock at the weekend, hearing of the death of his best friend, Flying Officer Charles Davis D.F.C. of 238 Squadron from Middle Wallop. His Hurricane flew into a hill near Winchester, which was obscured by low cloud, on 26 March.

Friday 4 April

R.A.F. shoots down British bomber at Manston.

A British bomber, outward-bound on a mission to attack the German battle-cruisers *Scharnhorst* and *Gneisenau* at Brest, was shot down last night in the Blackmore Vale, two miles from Sturminster Newton. The twin-engined Whitley, T4299 of 51 Squadron, crashed on a hedge at Connegar Farm, half a mile north-west of Manston parish church.

The aeroplane had taken off from R.A.F. Dishforth, near Thirsk, Yorkshire, at 19.00 hours and was brought down at 21.20. This interception was the result of a misidentification and has been traced to a Hurricane night-fighter, V6960 of 87 Squadron, from R.A.F. Exeter.

Sergeant W. N. Brindley has been killed but the other four members of the crew are unhurt. For Pilot Officer M. E. Sharp and Sergeant L. J. Allum it was the second time they have baled out this year. The earlier escape was also from a Whitley, returning from a Bomber Command raid over Bremen, on the night of 11 February. They found themselves unable to pinpoint their position in deteriorating weather and abandoned the aeroplane above Bircham Newton, Norfolk.

Friday 4 April

Blenheim bomber crashes at Frampton.

An R.A.F. Blenheim, returning from Bomber Command's raid on the port of Brest, crashed last night at Frampton, five miles north-west of Dorchester. The three crewmen — Sergeants P. I. Burrows, G. B. H. Birdsell, and H. R. Perry — were killed instantaneously as the aeroplane exploded on hitting the ground.

T2439 belonged to 101 Squadron and had taken off from R.A.F. West Raynham, Norfolk, at 19.15 hours. It crashed while trying to chart a course to R.A.F. Boscombe Down, which is 45 miles to the north-east.

Saturday 5 April

Heinkel crash-lands on the Dorset ridgeway.

A Heinkel He.111 H-8 bomber is lying on its belly beside the coastal ridgeway to the east of Weymouth. Pilots from Warmwell Aerodrome have inspected the stranded aeroplane which had been attacking shipping off Portland. It is fitted with a curved tube which projects forward from the nose and extends from the top of one wing to the tip of the other. this refinement is to push barrage balloon cables aside and prevent them fouling the wings and engines.

The aircraft came into this predicament through navigational error. Its crew survived and have become prisoners. The sheep also had a fright.

Wednesday 9 April

152 Squadron quits R.A.F. Warmwell.

The familiar "UM" markings of Mark-IIa Spitfires of 152 (Hyderabad) Squadron disappeared today from the Dorset sky, as they headed west across Lyme Bay.

The squadron has left R.A.F. Warmwell for its new station, which is the newly-built Portreath Aerodrome in Cornwall.

This has been constructed by Richard Costain Limited and has four hardened runways. "Prepare to land on tarmac," 152 Squadron were told at their briefing, before their final take-off from the grass airfield that is R.A.F. Warmwell.

Thursday 10 April

Poole buildings destroyed by fire.

This evening's raid on Canford Cliffs and Parkstone has left incendiaries blazing on a number of buildings, including the Canford Cliffs Hotel, Tennyson Buildings, and Pinewood Laundry. The Tennyson Buildings are in a main shopping street, Ashley Road, and the laundry stands beside the Pottery Junction. Paintings have been removed from the blazing hotel but otherwise the inferno will be left to itself as there is no longer any water coming out of the hydrants.

Footnote: Canford Cliffs came out of it lightly as far as its residents were concerned; the following morning a Royal Engineers bomb disposal unit found and defused eight unexploded bombs in Haven Road.

Friday 11 April

Sleeping Bournemouth poet killed by German bomb.

Cumberland Clark, a familiar figure in central Bournemouth with white hair and walrus moustache, was killed in his sleep last night as a German bomb destroyed his flat in St Stephen's Road at three minutes past midnight. He was a prolific author with 67 books to his credit, many of them poetry, and his *War Songs of the Allies* have proved a tonic for the town's morale:

Down in our Air Raid Shelter
There's no cause for alarm,
It is so sure and strongly built
We cannot come to harm.

Let the bombs bounce round above us,
And the shells come whizzing by,
Down in our Air Raid Shelter
We'll be cosy, you and I!

The same enemy aircraft dropped an incendiary on Woolworths, in The Square, which burned fiercely for some time. The fire was brought under control at 02.20 hours and the All-clear sounded at 04.10 hours.

Seven women also died in the attack which destroyed several flats at Hampshire Court and in St Stephen's Road. A bomb that was dropped in Bodorgan Road failed to explode.

Footnote: Boots now stands on the site of the burnt-out Woolworths.

Saturday 12 April
Bombs fall on Upton.

Six high explosive bombs and a quantity of incendiaries fell on Upton, to the west of Poole, shortly after midnight.

Tuesday 15 April
Exeter's Roland Beamont to test-fly Typhoon.

Battle of Britain pilot Roland Prosper Beamont, who took part in many of the dog-fights over Lyme Bay and Portland in a Hurricane of 87 Squadron from R.A.F. Exeter, is being attached to Hawker Aircraft Company and will test-fly its latest aircraft. This machine, the Hawker Typhoon, is expected to be at the forefront of the next generation of dual-function fighter-bombers.

Beamont enlisted with the Royal Air Force on 1 October 1939, at the age of 19, and flew with the British Expeditionary Force in France. He was mentioned in despatches during the war over the Dorset coast through the summer of 1940. His new career as a test pilot is being restricted to what he terms "rest periods".

Footnote: Those working holidays would also extend to the trials of the Hawker Tempest. Wing Commander Roland Beamont finished the war D.S.O. and bar, D.F.C. and bar, and United States D.F.C., and was now the experimental test pilot for Gloster Aircraft Company. He went on to become Britain's most famous post-war aviator. In 1948 he was the first Briton to fly at the speed of sound. As English Electric's chief test pilot he was the first to take up Britain's first jet bomber. That was the Canberra and he put her into a climb of fighter-like steepness for a breathtaking display of manoeuvrability at the Farnborough Air Show of 1949. In 1954 he made the first flight of Britain's first supersonic fighter, the P1; later named the Lightning.

Wednesday 16 April
Poole flying-boat 'Cordelia' is armed.

Another "Empire" flying-boat from Poole, *Cordelia*, has been armed with gun turrets and bomb-racks and provided with radar during a major overhaul in Belfast. From today she is AX660 and will carry out anti-submarine depth charge trials with 119 Squadron.

Footnote: She returned to B.O.A.C.'s civilian fleet at Poole in September 1941 and would survive the war, being scrapped at Hythe on 6 March 1947.

Monday 28 April
Hurricane mishap at Christchurch.

Hurricane L1592, one of the three that are stationed at Christchurch Aerodrome to protect the Special Duty Flight which operates from there, crashed at 12.20 this afternoon when its port undercarriage failed to lock upon touch-down. The fighter spun across the grass but was not seriously damaged. The pilot was unhurt.

Footnote: L1552, L1562, and L1592 were the Christchurch Hurricanes. The latter, the one of the mishap, was in fact an unusually lucky aircraft. It survived this accident and the war to become part of the National Aeronautical Collection that is displayed by the Science Museum in London.

Monday 28 April
Rescue drama as Fairey Battle crashes off Hengistbury Head.

Fairey Battle fighter-bomber K9230 of the Special Duty Flight from Christchurch Aerodrome crashed with its crew of two into the sea off Hengistbury Head, Bournemouth, at 15.45 hours today. Pilot Officer A. C. James baled out shortly before the aircraft hit the water. His action was spotted by Second Lieutenant Andrew Page Watson of the Lancashire Fusiliers who was on top of the headland.

He immediately scrambled down the steep sandy cliffs, and swam out to sea, ignoring and defying the currents which are notoriously strong around this exposed promontory. Despite the water being bitterly cold and rough the soldier succeeded in reaching the pilot, who was entangled in his sodden parachute, and attempted to extricate him from the harness. His efforts, however, were unavailing, and he was ultimately compelled to release his hold through exhaustion as the pilot died.

In attempting to return to the beach, Second Lieutenant Watson was himself nearly drowned, and was only rescued by two of his comrades who dragged him ashore.

BÜCKER JUNGMANN: AIRCRAFT STOLEN FROM THE LUFTWAFFE NEAR CAEN AND FLOWN TO R.A.F. CHRISTCHURCH, 29 APRIL 1941

Footnote: In July Andrew Page Watson would be awarded the George Medal for heroism. As for the Fairey Battle, it was disliked by the R.A.F., Sergeant Fitter Bob Chacksfield recalls: "Useless aircraft, they shouldn't have been allowed in the war. Shameful aircraft — every time we started it, the thing began to catch light. It was totally underpowered."

Tuesday 29 April

Two Frenchmen fly to Christchurch in stolen Nazi plane.

Two young Frenchmen, former members of the Armée de l' Air, today landed at Christchurch Aerodrome in a German biplane, a Bücker Jungmann, they had stolen from an airfield near Caen.

They landed at 12.30 hours, after a flight of 75 minutes, and were spared some rounds of Bofors anti-aircraft fire through the quick thinking of Second Lieutenant H. G. Graham and Sergeant Gill of 229 Battery of the Royal Artillery who saw the swastikas on the plane but realised there was something unusual in a short-range aeroplane coming this distance. Messieurs Denys Boudard and Jean Hebert will be debriefed by Free French Forces.

Footnote: Hebert was lost over the sea in 1943 but Boudard was still flourishing in the 1980s.

During April

From Dunkirk to torture with Monty on Batcombe Hill.

Re-equipped, but with their commander, General Bernard Montgomery, calling them flat-footed, the Third Division of the British Army — veterans of the Dunkirk beaches — is coming to the end of seven weeks' intensive

training at a full-scale camp on Batcombe Hill, between Evershot and Cerne Abbas.

Biting winds, intense frosts, and the hard-slog of a route march from the Dorset Downs to the Avon valley are the memories that will last. The distance was 65 miles; being first to the Cerne valley, then crossing the Stour at Bryanston, and on to the River Avon at Fordingbridge, on the edge of the New Forest — then all the way back again. En route the men practised attacks on woods and hills and made assault-crossings of each stream and river.

Pre-war tourists among the soldiers teased their mates with descriptions of the Cerne Giant, as the field-force tramped towards Cerne Abbas, but he had disappeared. They then realised the hill-figure was probably camouflaged to deny the Luftwaffe an unmistakable direction finder.

During April

Commando unit formed at Poole.

Under the command of Captain Gustavus March-Phillips, an operational guerrilla unit of commandos known as the Small Scale Raiding Force has been formed at Poole, with its headquarters in the High Street, in the Antelope Hotel.

Their role, in Winston Churchill's words, will be to create "a reign of terror down the enemy coasts".

Thursday 1 May

Bailey Bridge tested at Christchurch.

The Experimental Bridging Establishment of the Royal Engineers, formerly known as the Bridge Company, has spanned the River Stour at Christchurch with a prefabricated steel bridge. It took shape almost instantly, taking 36 minutes from commencement, to the first lorry driving across.

This 70 feet structure was designed in 1939 by Donald Coleman Bailey. The bridge-building Sappers took over the former Horse Barracks beside the river in Barracks Road.

Footnote: Bailey Bridges would be taken to war in Tunisia and Italy. Then in the Normandy campaign, between 18-21 July 1944, they enabled British armoured divisions to cross the River Orne at five points to the north of Caen.

The length of the bridges grew to meet the size of the obstacle, such as 1,200 feet to cross the Chindwin in

Burma, and a record 4,000 feet plus at Gennep in the Netherlands.

Donald Bailey would be knighted in 1946. He retired to 14 Viking Close, Southbourne, Bournemouth.

Sunday 4 May
Junkers bomber crashes on Winfrith Heath decoy.

The decoy airfield at Winfrith Heath, which is rigged with flares and moving lights to draw air attack from Warmwell Aerodrome, today claimed a German bomber to add to the craters it has successfully attracted. The victim was a Junkers Ju.88 that had apparently been hit by anti-aircraft fire.

The crew had been able to bale out and are now prisoners of war.

Wednesday 7 May
German bomber crashes at Oborne.

A German bomber crashed into the hillside below Oborne Wood, to the east of Sherborne, in the early hours of the morning. The pilot baled out and gave himself up but the remainder of the crew, Feldwebel E. Ebert, Feldwebel H. Ottlick, and Unteroffizier T. Kowallik, died in the wreckage.

Footnote: Their bodies were buried the following day in the north-west corner of Oborne churchyard. Prayers were given. In 1963 the Volksbund removed the remains to the German war cemetery, Cannock Chase, Staffordshire.

Friday 9 May
All-clear at Weymouth — then six die.

After the All-clear sounded at Weymouth earlier this morning, Mrs Lilian Adnam and her daughters Dorothy, Margaret, May, Violet, and Vivian left their shelter and returned to bed. Then, at 04.30 hours, a single German bomber slipped over the town and dropped five bombs. The house received a direct hit and all six were killed. Two other daughters escaped with injuries.

Saturday 10 May
Christchurch Aerodrome bombed.

Christchurch Aerodrome and the factory buildings of Airspeed Limited, at Somerford, were bombed and machine-gunned early this morning, between 00.40 and 01.09 hours.

One of the Heinkel He.111 bombers dived to within 50 feet of the ground and bombs were dropped to within 20 yards of buildings. Of the thirteen that landed within the station, no less than nine failed to explode.

No air-raid warning had sounded and the attack, in full moonlight, came as a complete surprise.

Saturday 10 May
Bridport's Spitfire is 'The Brit'.

The Spitfire appeal in west Dorset, which raised nearly £6,000, has paid for Spitfire R7062 which was today handed over to 308 Squadron. It is being named *The Brit* after Bridport's river.

Footnote: The fighter was transferred to 403 Squadron, on 28 May 1941, and later to a training unit near Chester. It was lost in a flying accident on 21 December 1941.

Monday 12 May
Heinkel and flying-boat sink in Poole Harbour.

A Heinkel He.111 belonging to the 8th Staffel of the 3rd Gruppe, Kampfgeschwader 55, attacked the seaplanes on Poole Harbour in the moonlit early hours this morning and sank *Maia*, a B.O.A.C. Short "Empire" flying-boat, killing its watchman, off Salterns Pier.

The low-level attacker (G1+ES) was brought down with machine-gun fire from the ships in the harbour and land-

FRENCH ESCAPEES: FLYERS DENYS BOUDARD (LEFT) AND JEAN HEBERT (RIGHT) WITH FLIGHT SERGEANT PRITCHARD AT CHRISTCHURCH AERODROME, AFTER THEY HAD STOLEN A BÜCKER JUNGMANN FROM THE LUFTWAFFE AND FLOWN ACROSS THE CHANNEL FROM AN AIRFIELD NEAR CAEN, ON 29 APRIL 1941

Maia sunk: on 12 May 1941, in Poole Harbour, by a Heinkel bomber. She was no longer in tandem with the smaller Mercury float-plane (above) but that is how she will be remembered

based light anti-aircraft fire from Bofors Mark II guns firing 40-mm shells at the rate of 120 per minute. It plunged into the water off Patchin's Point, Arne.

Unteroffiziers Karl Scheuringer and Karl Rohl survived but the pilot, Willer Wimmer, and his other crewman are missing. Scheuringer, the flight engineer, received a punch in the mouth that sent him reeling back into the sea during the course of his rescue-cum-capture.

Maia, recently converted to a C-class flying-boat, had been a pioneering composite aircraft as the mother craft, having a cradle between her wings, for the *Mercury* mail-carrying floatplane.

Monday 12 May
Kennels and cafe hit by Somerford bombs.

A raid on Christchurch Aerodrome at 02.18 hours hit nearby civilian buildings, wrecking the bungalow at Somerford Kennels and smashing Bert's Cafe. There are four craters opposite the cafe and the Somerford Road is strewn with debris for a hundred yards. The family at the kennels are safe and have returned to look after their horses.

Monday 12 May
Bomb blasts Ashley Heath level crossing.

03.25 hours. The railway line from Ringwood to Wimborne has been blocked by a bomb crater at Ashley Heath level crossing. Twenty homes are damaged and the telephone wires down.

Wednesday 14 May
Swanage bomb hits Wesley's Cottage.

16.30 hours. Wesley Cottage, a picturesque stone-roofed dwelling in the High Street at Swanage, where John Wesley stayed on a preaching trip, has been badly damaged by a German bomb. It had been the town's 315th air-raid alert.

Footnote: The ruined cottage would be demolished. Its site is now marked by its original circular inscribed nameplate, returned to the town after a period in a Fontmell Magna rockery, with additional words about Wesley's 1774 stay and the 1941 bomb.

Thursday 22 May
Christchurch loses war trophy to London's War Weapons Week.

The German Bücker Jungmann biplane in which two patriotic Frenchmen escaped from Caen to Christchurch on 29 April has been dismantled and taken to London for display in the War Weapons Week.

Tuesday 27 May
'Dorsetshire' sinks the 'Bismarck'.

The county of Dorset will take special pride in the fact that today the cruiser H.M.S. *Dorsetshire* delivered the coup de grâce to the enemy battleship *Bismarck* at 10.36 hours this morning. The vessel had been pounded by Royal Naval gunfire and was ablaze from stem to stern, rolling in a heavy sea, when Captain B. C. S. Martin of the

Dorsetshire received the order to finish her off — with two torpedoes into the starboard side from 2,400 yards.

The cruiser then steamed around the battleship's bows to fire another torpedo into the port side, sending the great grey ship lurching and exposing her red-painted hull as she rolled over to sink within 15 seconds.

For a time the *Dorsetshire* stopped amongst the clusters of some 400 survivors but many were too weak to climb the rope ladders. A British midshipman jumped in fully clothed to help. He was nearly left behind as a total of 110 Germans had been dragged aboard the cruiser and the destroyer H.M.N.Z.S. *Maori*, when the humanitarian operation ceased because a submarine alert was received. Many exhausted sailors fell from the ropes and drowned as the cruiser gathered speed to leave the area.

So ended an epic of naval warfare in less than heroic fashion. The chase across the North Atlantic and into the South Western Approaches has been an expensive victory for the British. Three days ago the Admiralty announced the loss of the battlecruiser H.M.S. *Hood* without being able to offer any prospect of survivors beyond the three saved from its crew of 1,416.

During May
The wealthy hoard gold and butter.

Some of the best-heeled residents in the county have passed through the criminal courts in the past few months to face accusations of ignoring wartime restrictions. Sir John Sherlock of West Wings, Clarence Road, Dorchester, was fined £4,000 with £100 costs for concealing 3,647 sovereigns, 4,590 half sovereigns, and £499 in other gold. He was forced to sell his hoard to the Treasury.

Eyebrows were also raised when the county's premier political households, the Wimborne St Giles dynasty of the 9th Earl of Shaftesbury, the Lord Lieutenant of Dorset, and their neighbours at Cranborne Manor, represented by Viscount Cranborne, Member of Parliament for South Dorset, were charged with buying black-market butter.

At the other end of the social spectrum, Albert Bulley of the Bungalow at Owermoigne had the distinction of being the first in the county to be convicted for refusing to take in evacuee lodgers. He was fined £5.

During May
Minefield laid off Brownsea Island.

An electrically triggered anti E-boat minefield has been laid beside the passages between the scaffolding obstructions at the entrance to Poole Harbour. It is controlled from an observation post on Brownsea Island which is manned by a unit who have taken over the derelict Rose Cottage on the southern shore.

Friday 6 June
Convoy-hit Bf.109 crash-lands at Worth.

Hit by flak from an escort vessel, Oberleutnant Werner Machold, the Staffelkapitan of the 7th Gruppe of Jagdgeschwader 2 Richthofen, today turned his stricken Messerschmitt Bf.109 inland from the Channel convoy and crash-landed the White 15 among stone workings at Worth Matravers.

Machold is among the most famous of the Nazi flyers. He was credited with fighter wing Jagdgeschwader 2's hundredth victory over France and found himself being personally congratulated by Field Marshal Hermann Göring. When his comrades were upgraded to the Bf.109F he insisted on sticking with his old Bf.109E but had it improved with special Zusatz-gear to feed nitrous oxide to boost the engine power.

For this reason the crashed plane has been impounded on behalf of the Royal Aircraft Establishment, Farnborough.

Monday 9 June
'Dagmar' sinks off Swanage.

The steamship *Dagmar* was today sunk by a German bomber off Durlston Head, Swanage. One of the convoy escorts, the Free French Navy's gunboat *Chasseur 43*,

FATAL TORPEDOES: THE HONOUR FALLS TO THE CRUISER H.M.S. DORSETSHIRE TO DELIVER THE COUP DE GRÂCE THAT SINKS THE BATTLESHIP BISMARCK ON 27 MAY 1941

picked up survivors and took them to Poole Quay. Many were admitted to hospital.

Thursday 12 June
Poole family wakes up to a bomb in the kitchen.

A family in Bournemouth Road, Branksome, came downstairs to breakfast this morning to find an unexploded bomb in their kitchen. They had heard the explosions from a stick of bombs that were dropped across Layton Road but ignored their own lighter thud. A bomb disposal unit has pronounced it a dud.

Saturday 14 June
Warmwell Whirlwinds strafe Cherbourg airfields.

Four Westland Whirlwind fighter-bombers took off from R.A.F. Warmwell at 05.05 hours this morning on their first cross-Channel expedition. They were escorted by Spitfires of 234 Squadron and strafed two airfields on the Cherbourg peninsula. The operation was accomplished successfully and all the aircraft returned safely.

Sunday 22 June
Bournemouth buys another Spitfire.

Paid for by the town's Spitfire Week fund raising, the second of the town's Spitfires, the Mark-I *Bournemouth*, was today handed over to 457 Squadron at R.A.F. Baginton, Coventry.

Footnote: 457 Squadron flew to the Isle of Man in August 1941. *Bournemouth* left them in October to join a training unit at Grangemouth. It would be lost in a flying accident on 16 March 1942.

Sunday 22 June
Poole's Spitfire is 'Villae de Poole'.

Street collections and fund raising events in Poole have paid for Spitfire *Villae de Poole* which was handed over today to the newly formed 411 (Royal Canadian Air Force) Squadron.

Footnote: Sergeant Pilot S. W. Bradshaw was killed on 7 December 1941 when *Villae de Poole* crashed at Chester during a blizzard.

During June
Dorset supports 'Dig for Victory'.

Helping to take the message of "Dig for Victory" to the people is the Dorset County Produce Association which has been sponsored by the Ministry of Agriculture to help promote the vital cause of restocking the nation's larder. Similar associations are being set-up in other counties.

Each will in turn establish branch associations in the villages and towns to give technical advice and encouragement. More families must start keeping rabbits and hens in their gardens and be persuaded to turn over their lawns and flower beds to the growing of vegetables.

WAR WEAPONS: POOLE SAVINGS, THROUGH THE "WINGS FOR VICTORY" APPEAL (top), PAID FOR SPITFIRE R7126 IN 1941

CRUISER TANKS: AT GATEMERSTON AND BROOMS PLANTATION, SOUTH OF LULWORTH PARK, PREPARING TO FIRE SEAWARDS AT TARGETS ON BINDON HILL

During June

Lyme's £25 a head for a warship.

Lyme Regis has contributed no less than £69,222 "towards sending another ship to fight in His Majesty's Navy for the freedom of mankind from the Nazi thrall". This is £25.10s. per head from the 2,700 inhabitants.

Champion town crier Walter Abbott made the announcement of "this Empire's determination to guard our rightful place on the good Earth".

Footnote: The town's special warship would be the Bangor-class minesweeper H.M.S. *Lyme Regis*, a 650-ton vessel launched from Alexander Stephens and Sons' yard on the Clyde, 19 March 1942.

During June

Montgomery's infantry leaving Abbotsbury for Lulworth.

The infantry brigade of the Third Division, commanded by General Bernard Montgomery, is to be converted to armour and equipped with the new Churchill tank. The brigade is currently at Abbotsbury and has been holding its regimental sports at Bridehead, Little Bredy. Tank training is to begin at the Armoured Fighting Vehicles School at Lulworth and Bovington.

During June

Bere Regis boy clambers into the first Churchill.

Ten-year-old Fred Pitfield, of Bere Regis, has enjoyed one of the privileges that extreme youth can sometimes bestow. He has been allowed by armed guards to momentarily ignore the security restrictions and climb into the brand new

interior of one of the first three Churchill tanks that are en route to the Armoured Fighting Vehicles School at Bovington and Lulworth. The Driving and Maintenance Wing is at Bovington Camp and the Gunnery Wing is based at Lulworth Camp, with a coastal firing range on Bindon Hill and in the Arish Mell valley.

This tank is a winner; it has to be with a name like Churchill. Fred and his friends are used to all the tanks that Bovington can field but when these pulled on to the verge at Court Green, opposite the Royal Oak, they realised that here was the shape of things to come.

The 39-ton Churchill has evolved from specification A20 into A22 — designated the Mark-IV Infantry Tank — and is produced by Vauxhall Motors. It has 10-centimetre frontal armour and a 2-pounder gun.

Footnote: Three Churchills would also get as far as El Alamein for their testing. They were then armed with 6-pounder guns; the Lulworth crews having dismissed the 2-pounder as a pea-shooter.

Wednesday 2 July

234 Squadron re-equips with ungainly Spitfires.

The sleek lines of Dorset's Spitfires look somewhat compromised from today. The familiar fighters of 234 Squadron, operating from R.A.F. Warmwell, have been exchanged for Mark-II machines. Each of these has an un-jettisonable fuel drop-tank added to the centre section of the port wing.

CRUISER TANK: THE LONG-RANGE A13 WAS THE FIRST BRITISH CHASSIS TO USE CHRISTIE SUSPENSION. IT IS SEEN ON THE DORSET HEATHS IN 1941. THE SUSPENSION IDEA WAS DEVELOPED IN THE UNITED STATES AND SMUGGLED INTO BRITAIN, IN 1936, AS TRACTOR PARTS AND IN CASES LABELLED "GRAPEFRUIT"

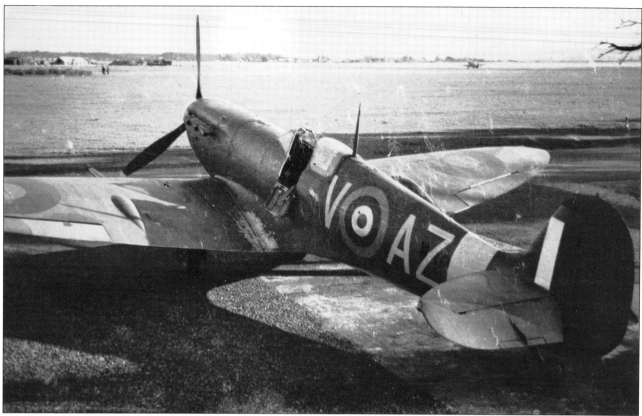

DORSET SPITFIRE: PILOT OFFICER DAVID GLAZER'S V FOR VIC, WITH THE "AZ" SQUADRON CODE OF 234 SQUADRON, AT DISPERSAL BESIDE WARMWELL AERODROME IN 1941

CO-PILOT BLACKIE: THE COCKER SPANIEL IS IN THE COCKPIT OF FLYING OFFICER DAVID GLASER'S SPITFIRE OF 234 SQUADRON AT R.A.F. WARMWELL

BREATHING KIT: FLYING OFFICER DAVID GLAZER WITH SPITFIRE "AZ" M FOR MONKEY OF 234 SQUADRON, PREPARING TO SCRAMBLE FROM R.A.F. WARMWELL

This has been devised to extend their flying range so that the fighters can go on escort duties for offensive operations over the Brest peninsula. Pilots, however, are unimpressed. The superb aerodynamics have been disturbed and will require delicate teasing of the rudder to compensate for the effect. There is also now the danger that when it returns with an empty tank the fighter may spin out of control on tight turns.

Thursday 3 July
Christchurch camouflage confusion.

As he inspected the camouflage at Christchurch Aerodrome, of make-believe roads encroaching through what are actually runways, Group Captain Shaw was told that it was effective enough to confuse both friend and foe. A Hampden bomber, due to visit the station's Special Duty Flight, had circled the aerodrome for a considerable time before departing because the pilot considered the main runway to be too short for landing.

234 Squadron: plus mascot, at R.A.F. Warmwell in July 1941, with Squadron Leader "Mindy" Blake beneath the propellor. They are beside the still aero-dynamic starboard wing of a Mark II Spitfire which had its port side adapted to carry an external petrol tank for cross-Channel flights

Thursday 10 July

Warmwell Spitfires escort Blenheims to bomb Cherbourg.

The Spitfires of 152 Squadron joined with those of 234 Squadron and flew from Warmwell Aerodrome today to link-up with a flight of twelve Blenheim bombers that were heading across the English Channel. These were from 21 Squadron at R.A.F. Watton, Suffolk, in 2 Group of Bomber Command. The fighters provided an escort for the bombers in a low-level raid on the harbour at Cherbourg. As it went into attack each Blenheim had a Spitfire on its port and starboard flanks and another following its tail.

Messerschmitt Bf.109s engaged the British formation and Squadron Leader Minden Vaughan "Mindy" Blake, the New Zealander commanding 234 Squadron, shot down two. He was then found to be missing, however, on the return journey.

The final sweep of the day came home with the report that Blake had been sighted, by Sergeant Pilot Peter Hutton Fox, alive and well and cheerily paddling his dinghy in the general direction of the Isle of Wight.

Footnote: Given he was helped by a following wind, but it was still a remarkable achievement, for "Mindy" Blake to propel himself from a point seven miles off the French coast to within a couple of miles of the Isle of Wight, before he was picked-up. He had been at sea for twelve hours.

Thursday 17 July

Bomb drops on boy saying his prayers.

The funeral took place today in Melcombe Regis cemetery of a ten-year-old Weymouth boy, Kenneth Polden, who was killed when a German bomb dropped on his house. Only a minute earlier his mother had told him: "Go to bed. Say your prayers and ask God to keep us safe."

The rescue squad found Kenneth beside his wrecked bed. His hands were clasped in prayer.

Thursday 17 July

Blenheim lost in strange encounter.

A Blenheim of the Special Duty Flight, from Christchurch Aerodrome, descended to take a closer look at a silvery shape that had been spotted floating in the English Channel, 33 miles south of St Alban's Head. The Blenheim, P4832, was on a calibration flight.

Its pilot, Flight-Lieutenant Douglas L. Rayment, was monitored by radio from the mainland. He was heard telling his wireless operator and gunner, Sergeant R. Sadler, that the mystery object seemed to be a weather balloon. Rayment's last words were: "There you are, have a go. You can't miss."

Two bursts of machine-gun fire followed. The aircraft's wireless then went dead.

Thursday 24 July
Warmwell's hero killed over Brest.

Pilot Officer Eric "Boy" Marrs of 152 Squadron from R.A.F. Warmwell was shot down today over the French coast while on one of the first long-range offensive missions undertaken by the station, which was the backbone of Dorset's defences in last year's Battle of Britain. They flew to Brest, as fighter escorts for 18 Hampden bombers of 44 Squadron and 144 Squadron, in a daylight raid on its German capital ships.

Marrs's Spitfire was hit by chance flak, bringing true a station prophecy that no German fighter pilot was going to take the "Boy". In December he had been award the Distinguished Flying Cross. A fortnight ago, on 10 July, he celebrated his 20th birthday.

Footnote: His body was recovered and interred in the military cemetery at Brest.

Friday 25 July
Warmwell's Jimmy Short taken prisoner.

Sergeant Pilot Jimmy Short of 152 Squadron, from R.A.F. Warmwell, parachuted into captivity yesterday when his Spitfire was shot down by Messerschmitt Bf.109s as he escorted Hampden bombers that were attacking the French port of Brest. The daylight raid, spearheaded by

Wellingtons of Bomber Command, targeted the German battlecruiser *Gneisenau* and the cruiser *Prinz Eugen.*

Eighteen Hampdens were given the fighter escort but the much larger contingent of 79 Wellingtons had to look after themselves. Ten Wellingtons were lost and two of the Hampdens.

During July
Purbeck howitzers withdrawn.

The 14th Super Heavy Battery, which has been stationed at Furzebrook in the heart of the Isle of Purbeck since 1 August 1940, is experiencing troubles with its two rail-mounted 12-inch howitzers. They are being taken to the Royal Artillery's main depot at Bulford on Salisbury Plain for trials. Though only fired a few times for practice shots the recoil system has failed and shattered the mountings.

Meanwhile, for their return, Royal Engineers and Southern Railway gangers are building two new sidings for railway-mounted guns. One is a half a mile on the Wareham side of Furzebrook and the other on Norden Heath, towards Corfe Castle.

Footnote: The project would soon be abandoned and no more rail guns were brought into Purbeck. The battery's locomotive, number 393, rejoined the Southern Railway on 9 August 1941.

AT READINESS: FLYING OFFICER DON SOGA IN A SPITFIRE OF 234 SQUADRON ON THE WESTERN EDGE OF WARMWELL AERODROME WITH SANDBAGGED DISPERSAL PENS VISIBLE BEHIND, SCREENED BY THE TREES OF KNIGHTON HEATH WOOD

During July

Shirburnian hits back at American presumptions.

An ex-Sherborne schoolboy, the distinguished mathematician and philosopher Alfred North Whitehead, has reminded Americans that "as a training in political imagination, the Harvard School of Politics and Government cannot hold a candle to the old-fashioned English classical education of half-a-century ago".

Footnote: A. N. Whitehead [1861-1947] was co-author with Bertrand Russell of the *Principia Mathematica* [1910-13]. He had been Professor of Philosophy at Harvard University [1924-37] and would die at Cambridge, Massachusetts [30 December 1947].

During July

Cinema show selected U.S. newsreels.

The March of Time, a monthly 20 minutes current events film magazine that began in 1935, is the most positive United States newsreel propagandising for American aid and munitions to be sent to Britain. It is widely shown here, with the emphasis on President Roosevelt's speeches — "We must be the great arsenal of democracy," is their theme — but never are there any clips from counter-blasts by his opponents. Neither is there any mention of the price being exacted from these islands for United States assistance.

Footnote: Throughout the war there would be nothing said about the liquidation of British dollar assets to pay for lend-lease.

Friday 1 August

Hurn Aerodrome handed over to the R.A.F.

R.A.F. Hurn, a new aerodrome of hardened runways, has been completed on the flat ground between the River Stour meadows and heathland north of Bournemouth. It has three concrete runways. The longest is 5,200 feet and the others are 4,800 and 3,400 feet. Seven large and ten small blister hangars have been provided for under-cover maintenance. The aerodrome was today handed over to the Air Ministry, which passed it to 11 Group, Fighter Command.

It was received on the Air Ministry's behalf by Wing Commander G. K. Horner of the Special Duty Flight, from Christchurch Aerodrome, who handed over interim command of R.A.F. Hurn to Flight-Lieutenant Theobald.

Wednesday 6 August

Shot-up Whirlwind force-lands at Hurn.

A shell-damaged Westland Whirlwind, with one engine out of action and the other leaking glycol coolant, force-landed at R.A.F. Hurn at 17.40 hours. Flight-Sergeant H. G. Brackley brought P6983 down on an obstructed runway and hit both wings in the process but was able to walk clear from the wreckage. It has been the aerodrome's first emergency landing.

Brackley claimed two Messerschmitt Bf.109s in a dog-fight off the Cherbourg peninsula when four Whirlwinds from the Filton-based 263 Squadron had been attacked by a formation of 20 enemy fighters.

Sunday 10 August

Pulling the plug on double Summer Time.

The second hour of British Summer Time ended today, to general popular relief, particularly among the old and those who have to rise early for work. They complained that it had become hard to live by the maxim "early to bed and early to rise" when it remained sunny until 11 o'clock at night. Those of younger years, however, will be disappointed to lose the evening daylight.

Wednesday 13 August

Telecommunications Flying Unit formed at Hurn.

Aircraft of the Fighter Establishment from R.A.F. Middle Wallop have landed today at R.A.F. Hurn where they will re-group as the Development Section of the Air Ministry's newly formed Telecommunications Flying Unit. Another technical research team, the Blind-Landing Detachment from the Royal Aircraft Establishment at Farnborough, is also moving to Hurn to become part of the new unit.

Wednesday 18 August

National Fire Service formed.

Local fire brigades which were organised by town councils are from today part of the National Fire Service. Number 16 District covers Hampshire and Dorset, with its two western divisions being based in Bournemouth and Weymouth.

Thursday 19 August

Group Captain takes over R.A.F. Hurn.

Group Captain P. J. R. King has taken charge of R.A.F. Hurn from Flight-Lieutenant Theobald.

During August

Warmwell mourns 'Bottled Gull'.

152 Squadron, based at R.A.F. Warmwell, has lost its top man. Squadron Leader Derek Boitel-Gill — affectionately known as "Bottled Gull" — has been killed in a flying accident. The great survivor of the Battle of Britain was among the longest serving fighter pilots. He enlisted in the R.A.F. in 1936.

Tuesday 9 September

Warmwell Pole is killed.

Pilot Officer T. W. Pytlak, flying a Hurricane with 302 (Poznanski) Squadron from R.A.F. Warmwell, has been killed in an aviation accident. He was aged 22. The Polish squadron was posted to Dorset four days ago.

LANCASTER BOMBER: NOTE THE PURBECK-DEVISED AND BOURNEMOUTH-MADE H2S RADAR POD BENEATH THE FUSELAGE, WHICH WOULD ENEABLE THE BLIND-BOMBING OF GERMAN CITIES AT NIGHT

GROUND MAPPING: AN H2S RADAR MODULE, DEVISED AT LANGTON MATRAVERS AND TESTED FROM HURN AERODROME IN 1941, THEN BEING MANUFACTURED IN BOURNEMOUTH

Footnote: He is buried in the R.A.F. plot at Warmwell churchyard. The squadron left Warmwell on 11 October 1941 and would return briefly, re-equipped with the Mark-Vb Spitfire, from 27 April to 1 May 1942.

Saturday 13 September
Poole commandos killed in Normandy.

A cross-Channel raid by No. 62 Commando from Poole was foiled last night by the Germans as it attempted an attack on the defences of the Atlantic Wall West. Though the commandos had killed the seven-man German patrol that came across them, and retreated to their wooden boat, it was then hit by a shell.

Three of the men were taken prisoner and one escaped. The others are dead, including their commander, Major Gustavus March-Phillips.

Tuesday 25 September
Wavell's Dorset partridges fly to Tehran.

The Daily Telegraph reports the following anecdote about General Sir Archibald Wavell. He had been shooting partridge in Dorset on a Friday and was departing on the Saturday with a couple of brace.

As he was leaving the country the following day his hosts asked the Commander-in-Chief India what he was going to do with the birds. "Eat them myself, of course," he replied. "In Tehran on Tuesday."

Saturday 11 October
Wellington bomber crashes off St Alban's Head.

Wreckage found off St Alban's Head, including parts of a wing and a wheel, has been identified as that of Wellington X9677 of 218 Squadron which took off from R.A.F. Marham, Norfolk, at 21.51 hours last night on a bombing mission to Bordeaux.

Three members of the crew have been picked up by the St Ives lifeboat but the other three are feared to have drowned. The St Ives boat has been brought from Cornwall, to Weymouth, to supplement hard-pressed Air-Sea Rescue coverage in the Portland sector.

Monday 20 October
Warmwell Spitfire shot down over France.

Sergeant Pilot Peter Hutton Fox, flying a Spitfire of 234 Squadron from R.A.F. Warmwell, has failed to return from a cross-Channel operation over Normandy. He is believed to have baled out on being shot down.

Footnote: He survived and was captured, being eventually liberated from a prisoner of war camp in Germany, on 16 April 1945.

Tuesday 21 October
Focke-Wulf 190 crashes at Lulworth.

There was a huge explosion at Lulworth today when a Focke-Wulf 190 flew in low from the sea and crashed into the side of Bindon Hill. The pilot was killed instantly. He had apparently misjudged his position and course.

Tuesday 21 October
Churchill on behalf of Turing: 'Action this day.'

Twenty-nine-year-old mathematical genius Alan Turing, as dishevelled now as in the days when he was at Sherborne School, is using his "Turing Bombe" to crack the cipher codes of the polyalphabetic German "Enigma" cryptographic teleprinter-enciphering machines which scramble their military radio commands and responses.

His work at the Government Code and Cipher School, Bletchley Park, Buckinghamshire, is providing what Winston Churchill calls the "golden eggs" from geese who never cackle. Having shown Churchill how cryptanalysts function, Turing today sent the Prime Minister a personal memorandum of demands that he sees as vital if full efficiency is to be achieved.

Churchill responds instantly, writing on the list of complaints: "Action this day. Make sure they have all they want on extreme priority and report to me that this has been done."

Footnote: Alan Turing designed the first programmed electronic digital computer in the world. His personal behaviour would also prove to be ahead of its time, a conviction in 1952 for gross indecency with another male causing him to take his life with a cyanine-dipped apple, in 1954. Sherborne School now acknowledges its greatest pupil with the Alan Turing Laboratories.

As the tonnage of "Enigma" decrypts are reappraised — thousands were produced at Bletchley each day — it has become clear that Alan Turing was the factor, as much as radar, that enabled victory in the Battle of Britain in 1940 and would turn the tide of the Battle of the Atlantic in 1942, at a time when the German U-boats were sinking ships faster than America could build them.

Thursday 23 October
King and Queen visit Bournemouth.

King George VI and Queen Elizabeth are in Bournemouth today to inspect Dominion airmen assembled at the Pavilion.

AIR INTERCEPTION: PERSPEX NOSE-CONE ON AN AI RADAR APPARATUS, DEVELOPED BY THE TELECOMMUNICATIONS RESEARCH ESTABLISHMENT IN THE ISLE OF PURBECK AND INSTALLED ON AN EXPERIMENTAL BEAUFIGHTER NIGHT-FIGHTER, IN 1941

RADAR ANTENNA: TYPE 15 IN OPERATION IN THE FIELD, MONITORING BOTH ENEMY INTRUSIONS AND BRITISH INTERCEPTIONS, AT R.A.F. SOPLEY, IN 1941-42. THE APPARATUS WAS TURNED BY PEDAL POWER, USING IMPROVISED BICYCLE PARTS, BY TWO AIRMEN ASSIGNED TO AIRCRAFT HAND GENERAL DUTIES. THEY BECAME KNOWN AS "BINDERS" - FROM THEIR CONSEQUENT LEVEL OF COMPLAINING - IN A WONDERFUL WARTIME WORD THAT WOULD BE IMMORTALISED BY THE WIRELESS PROGRAMME MUCH BINDING IN THE MARSH

LESLIE HOWARD: THE ACTOR WAS IN CHRISTCHURCH TO CO-STAR WITH THE SPITFIRE IN THE FIRST OF THE FEW

During October

Leslie Howard in Christchurch to make 'The First of the Few'.

Leslie Howard, the actor and film-maker, is staying at the King's Arms Hotel, Christchurch, to work on a motion picture, entitled *The First of the Few*. This will dramatise the legend of the Spitfire from its creation by Reggie Mitchell whose inspired designs first took to the air from Eastleigh Aerodrome, Southampton, on 5 March 1936. Prototype Supermarine monoplane K5054 was at the hands of Mutt Summers who was watched throughout by an already ailing and constantly stressful Mitchell.

A grass airfield is in keeping with the story, and R.A.F. Warmwell was selected, but Howard — who directs as well as acts — has decided upon the new concrete runways of R.A.F. Ibsley, two miles north of Ringwood. Not only has this become the look of modern aviation but it has advantages for the film-makers in providing smoother footage, rather than having to track the eight-gun fighters as they bounce across turf.

The film also stars Rosamund John and Major David Niven. Its music, the *Spitfire Prelude and Fugue*, is being composed by William Walton.

Sunday 2 November

Mayor trapped by rubble as three die in Weymouth.

Three died and eleven were injured yesterday at about 23.20 hours, when four high explosive bombs dropped around Abbotsbury Road, Weymouth. Among the 171 damaged buildings was the Adelaide Arms, at 182 Abbotsbury Road, which received a direct hit.

Publican John Goddard had a lucky escape from death but was trapped under the rubble until after midnight. He is the Mayor of Weymouth. His rescue was effected by mayoral mace-bearer Bill Docksey, who also managed to save the first citizen's chain of office and his medals from the Great War.

Wednesday 5 November
234 Squadron leaves Warmwell for Ibsley.

The Mark-IIb Spitfires of 234 (Madras Presidency) Squadron today left R.A.F. Warmwell but will still be regular visitors to Dorset skies. Their new home is Ibsley Aerodrome, between Ringwood and Fordingbridge, where they will be re-equipped with Mark-Vb Spitfires.

Thursday 6 November
Signals-probe Wellington lost over France.

Wellington T2565, being used by the Telecommunications Research Establishment but nominally attached to 109 Squadron, Bomber Command, has been abandoned whilst on a mission for the Special Duty Flight over France. The starboard airscrew fell off and the crew baled out; the seven are presumed to have been taken prisoner of war.

The Wellington took off from R.A.F. Boscombe Down at 18.30 hours. Contact was lost at 20.46 last night.

Footnote: One of the seven, Sergeant N. W. MacKenzie, was able to avoid capture.

Thursday 6 November
'Hurri-bombers' arrive at Warmwell.

The Mark-IIb "Hurri-bomber" variant of the Hawker Hurricane has arrived at R.A.F. Warmwell, bringing 402

(Royal Canadian Air Force / Winnipeg Bear) Squadron. They carry the code letters "AE" and have been adapted into ground attack aircraft, for cross-Channel offensive sweeps over Normandy and Brittany.

"We stand on guard" is the squadron's motto.

Monday 10 November
Special Duty Flight joins T.F.U. at Hurn.

The Special Duty Flight has moved from Christchurch Aerodrome to R.A.F. Hurn where it is now the Research Section of the recently formed Telecommunications Flying Unit. Christchurch has become the satellite airfield for Hurn.

A wide variety of ancient and modern aircraft are among the 23 single-engine machines and 33 twin-engine aeroplanes that the unit possesses. It also has two specialised communications aircraft. Among their functions are the provision of aerial test-beds for the radar scientists of the Telecommunications Research Establishment.

Tuesday 11 November
Crashing Hurricane kills pilot and two soldiers at Warmwell.

Two members of the Dorsetshire Regiment, on guard duty at R.A.F. Warmwell, were killed today when a Hurricane

MAYOR TRAPPED: LANDLORD JOHN GODDARD OF THE ADELAIDE ARMS, 182 ABBOTSBURY ROAD, WAS PINNED UNDER RUBBLE WHEN HIS PREMISES RECEIVED A DIRECT HIT AT 23.20 HOURS ON 1 NOVEMBER 1941. HE WAS RESCUED SHORTLY AFTER MIDNIGHT BY HIS MACE-BEARER, BILL DOCKSEY. THE FOLLOWING MORNING THE UNION JACK WAS RAISED DEFIANTLY, IF LIMPLY, ABOVE THE DEBRIS

marked with the "GZ" of 32 Squadron came down out of control and crashed into the station's ammunition dump. The pilot also died in the explosions that followed.

Monday 17 November
Buses and paper in short supply.

There are further restrictions on the omnibus services which will mean even longer crowds for the last ones. In fact the Regional Transport Officer is trying to discourage any idea of having a night out using public transport because in future no bus may leave after 21.30 hours. Fuel shortages are to blame.

Paper controls are also being tightened. There will be no Christmas cards this year and it is now illegal to use paper for advertising leaflets, posters, or the production of paper handkerchiefs. Efforts to recycle materials, such as waste-paper, scrap-iron, and pig-bin collections, are being intensified as the shortages become serious.

During November
Boffins in a Blenheim find that radar can map Bournemouth.

There was elation this month among radar scientists at the Telecommunications Research Establishment in Worth Matravers and Langton Matravers following a discovery made from a Blenheim bomber of the Telecommunications Flying Unit. It has taken off from Christchurch Aerodrome to test a theory — that it should be possible to devise an airborne radar system that can map the ground.

An A.I. (Airborne Interception) Mark-VII radar set was installed in the aircraft and its centimetric beam tilted towards the ground. The Blenheim climbed to 8,000 feet and the aerial was then spun at 30 revolutions per minute.

As had been predicted, the apparatus acted as an effective "Town Finder" for bomber navigation and returned varying signals from the streets and roofs of Bournemouth and its adjacent landscape of pinewoods, heath, and cliffs.

During November
R.A.F. Hurn is operational.

R.A.F. Hurn, which is already being used by 1425 Communications Flight and the Telecommunications Flying Unit, is due to receive 170, 296, and 297 (Army Co-Operation) Squadrons. It is now an operational aerodrome of No. 11 Group, Fighter Command.

Wednesday 17 December
Wellington bomber crashes at Powerstock.

When their starboard engine failed last night, five crewmen of Wellington X9785 baled out over Chilfrome, eight miles north-west of Dorchester. The pilot, Sergeant Vezina, successfully brought his crippled bomber to a crash-landing at Holm Farm, above West Milton, near Powerstock.

The Wellington, belonging to 218 Squadron, had taken off from R.A.F. Marham, Norfolk, at 18.40 hours to attack the German capital ships in the French Atlantic port of Brest.

Tuesday 23 December
Air Minister backs Dorset 'Blind Navigation' tests.

Upon hearing a report of last month's flight in which a Blenheim bomber had flown from Christchurch Aerodrome, and used a down-turned radar set to map the ground, the Secretary of State for Air, Sir Archibald Sinclair, today authorised a further six such flights. These are to "determine whether the signals obtained . . . could be definitely associated with ground objects".

The experiments are to be co-ordinated by Bernard Lovell, a young scientist in Professor Philip Dee's section at the Telecommunications Research Establishment in the Isle of Purbeck.

The ramifications of the discovery are considerable. B.N. (Blind Navigation) would enable bombers to find distant targets in poor weather at night. Bomber Command experiences extreme difficulty in finding the general area of German cities let alone in delivering a significant proportion of the bomb load to any specific location.

Monday 29 December
Beaufighter crashes at Pulham.

Beaufighter R2438 of 307 (Lwowski [Polish]) Squadron from R.A.F. Exeter force-landed at 15.15 hours today in a field 200 yards south-east of Pulham parish church. The port engine had cut out and the night-fighter, a Mark-III airframe carrying Air Interception radar, landed wheels-up.

Though the machine is extensively damaged it is to be categorised as repairable by contractors. Sergeant Pilot R. Sniezkowski and Sergeant Observer Z. Domanski walked uninjured from the wreckage.

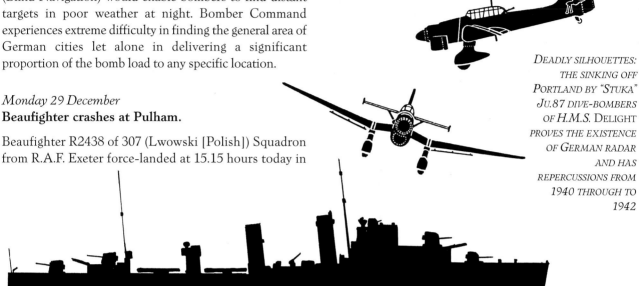

DEADLY SILHOUETTES: THE SINKING OFF PORTLAND BY "STUKA" JU.87 DIVE-BOMBERS OF H.M.S. DELIGHT PROVES THE EXISTENCE OF GERMAN RADAR AND HAS REPERCUSSIONS FROM 1940 THROUGH TO 1942

WARMWELL "HURRIBOMBER": SQUADRON LEADER R. E. MORROW OF 402 (ROYAL CANADIAN AIR FORCE) SQUADRON ASTRIDE HIS MARK IIB HURRICANE AS ITS BOMBS ARE ARMED AND LOADED IN THE WINTER OF 1941

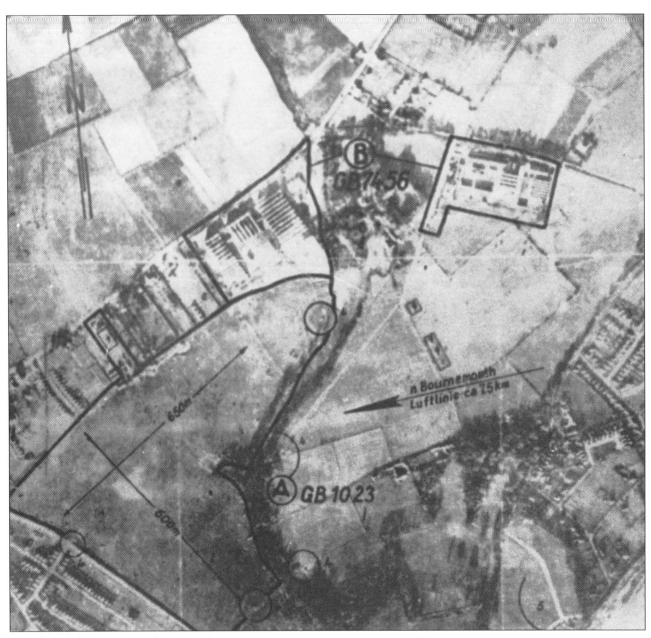

CHRISTCHURCH AERODROME: GERMAN AIR RECONNAISSANCE PHOTOGRAPH TAKEN IN 1941 BEFORE THE BUILDING OF THE MAIN RUNWAY. 'A' SIGNIFIES 'CHRISTCHURCH FLUGPLATZ' — 'CHRISTCHURCH FLYING LANDING-GROUND.' 'B' SHOWS TWO 'FLUGZEUGZELLEN REPARATURWERK' — 'AEROPLANE REPAIR WORKS'. HERE THE GERMANS UNDERESTIMATED THE IMPORTANCE OF THE SOMERFORD FACTORIES, FOR AIRSPEED WAS MANUFACTURING AIRCRAFT AND THE AIR DEFENCE RESEARCH AND DEVELOPMENT ESTABLISHMENT OF THE MINISTRY OF SUPPLY (KNOWN IN THE TOWN AS THE AIR DEFENCE EXPERIMENTAL ESTABLISHMENT) WAS ONE OF THE COUNTRY'S MAJOR PRODUCERS OF RADAR COMPONENTS, WORKING IN CONJUNCTION WITH SCIENTISTS OF THE AIR MINISTRY'S TELECOMMUNICATIONS RESEARCH ESTABLISHMENT AT WORTH MATRAVERS. THE ARROWED 'BOURNEMOUTH LUFTLINIE' SHOWS THE FLIGHTLINE FOR BOURNEMOUTH. NORTH IS AT THE TOP, AND THE RINGED POSITIONS SHOW 'KLEINKAMPFANLAGEN' (LIGHT MACHINE GUNS). THE FIGURE '5' AT THE BOTTOM RIGHT LOCATES 'SCHEINWERFERSTELLUNG' (SEARCHLIGHT POSITIONS)

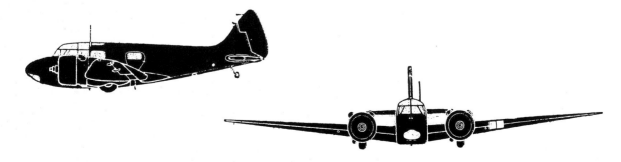

AIRSPEED OXFORD: TRAINER FOR THE R.A.F., MANUFACTURED AT SOMERFORD, CHRISTCHURCH

1942

Friday 9 January
Wellington crashes at Fifehead Magdalen.

Flak-damaged Wellington IV bomber Z1312 of 458 (Royal Australian Air Force) Squadron from Holme-on-Spalding Moor, Yorkshire, crashed in the early hours this morning in a field beside Fifehead Wood, Fifehead Magdalen. It hit electricity power lines as it was attempting a forced-landing.

The aircraft, which had its bomb-load intact, exploded on impact, killing Sergeants T. L. Brown, A. I. Hewish, P. H. Smith, and D. G. Taylor.

The pilot and co-pilot, however, were thrown forward through the windscreen and have survived, though with serious injuries. They are Bert Garland and Ian Higlett, who have been taken to Salisbury Hospital.

Footnote: The Wellington had been on a raid against the docks at Cherbourg where it encountered fog and flak. It was hit by anti-aircraft fire and had not been able to release any of its load of twelve 250-pound bombs. Four detonated on impact at Fifehead Magdalen.

The dead are buried in Brookwood Military Cemetery, Surrey. Sergeant Pilot Garland returned to Australia but would come back to Dorset to visit the crash site, at the age of 76 in September 1996, where he was given souvenir rounds from one of the bomber's machine-guns, by wartime local boy Peter Custard.

Tuesday 13 January
Tizard inspects Hurn and Christchurch.

A naval experimental party demonstrated a Walrus seaplane today to Sir Henry Tizard, the scientist on the advisory council of the Ministry of Aircraft Production, who visited the Telecommunications

CHANNEL DASH: THE GERMAN CAPITAL SHIPS SCHARNHORST, GNEISENAU (RIGHT), AND PRINZ EUGEN, MAKING FOR HOME ON 18 FEBRUARY 1942

Brunaval target: a German Würzburg radar, wanted for evaluation by the Telecommunications Research Establishment at Worth Matravers

Brunaval rehearsals: "C" Company of the 2nd Battalion of the Parachute Regiment, training for their evacuation after making a daring raid on the French coast, to capture German radar apparatus. They would land by air and leave by water. The latter part of the operation, joining their rescue flotilla was practised on Redcliff Point, Osmington, in February 1942. One of the lessons they had to learn was how not to roll the landing craft sideways on to the beach. Things went better on the night

Flying Unit at R.A.F. Hurn and its satellite station at Christchurch Aerodrome.

Sunday 18 January
Hurn is dispatch-point for Middle East Liberators.

1425 Communications Flight, which delivers long-range aircraft from the factories to overseas operational bases, is to ferry out Liberators from R.A.F. Hurn. The aircraft are being flown via Gibraltar, and across the Sahara Desert, to the Middle East.

The first Liberator landed at Hurn today and several are expected over the next few weeks. A detachment of 1425 Communications Flight will start ferrying operations from Hurn next month.

Footnote: The Liberator was the R.A.F. version of the bulky high-wing American Consolidated B-24 bomber which was powered by four Pratt and Whitney 1,200 horsepower Twin Wasp engines. Five Liberators left Hurn for the Middle East in February-March 1942. This

would become the largest single United States aircraft type of World War Two, with 18,482 being delivered, of which the R.A.F. received 1,889.

During January
The Yanks arrive — bringing good food.

The first American contingents have arrived to the tune of *Lilli Burlero*, the lively Ulster Protestant march. The American soldiers have found that it is a shilling a meal in the British Restaurants, but for what? They are much better fed in camp and for free.

The tendency to contrast the public menu with their own is being counteracted with a special U.S. Forces newsreel: "The best food in England is G.I., but don't keep rubbing in how good your food is."

The commentator then added: "And don't say you've come over to win the war!" Which, of course, they have.

Footnote: G.I. stands for General Infantryman. The Japanese attack on Pearl Harbor on the Hawaiian island of Oahu began at 07.50 hours Honolulu time, Sunday 7 December 1941 — "a date that will live in infamy," in President Roosevelt's words to Congress. There had been no declaration of war. Isolationist sentiment in America ceased to exist; the Japanese had stung a sleeping tiger. The United States declared war on Japan on Monday 8 December. The question of United States neutrality in the European war was conveniently settled by the Axis powers themselves, when Germany and Italy declared war on the United States, on Thursday 11 December 1941.

COMBINED OPERATIONS: MASTERMINDED FROM ANDERSON MANOR AND POOLE HARBOUR BY ACTING ADMIRAL LOUIS MOUNTBATTEN, IN 1942-43

Wednesday 18 February
The Channel Dash.

Three of the capital ships of the German fleet escaped today up the Channel from Brest to Kiel. They were the battleships *Scharnhorst* and *Gneisenau* and the battle-cruiser *Prinz Eugen*. The Times is anguished: "Nothing more mortifying to the pride of sea-power has happened in home waters since the 17th century."

The Admiralty assumed that the break-out would start in daytime and pass southern England during darkness. In fact the reverse has happened. Admiral Ciliax left last night and sailed up the Channel in daylight, despite the valiant efforts of Commander Esmonde and his Fairey Swordfish torpedo-dropping biplanes.

Friday 27 February
Bruneval raiders bring Worth a German radar.

Having practised off Portland and at Redcliff Point, Osmington, "C" Company of the 2nd Battalion of the Parachute Regiment has embarked on an audacious air, land, and sea commando operation to Bruneval, on the coast between Le Havre and Fécamp, to bring back a German Würzburg radar apparatus. The raiding party is led by Major J. D. Frost with technical expertise being provided by Flight Sergeant C. H. Cox.

They jumped from twelve Whitley bombers and landed on a 400-feet clifftop in deep snow to take their objective with complete surprise. The equipment was dismantled for removal by landing craft from the beach below. Its components will be examined by the Telecommunications Research Establishment at Worth Matravers. Only one important piece had to be left behind, despite only ten minutes being available for the technical side of the operation.

Wurzburg operates at 53 centimetres frequency (between 558 and 560 mHz) and is a coast defence radar apparatus with a range of about 40 kilometres. Its parabolic aerial had shown on air reconnaissance photographs of clifftop fields at Cap d'Antifer. The Biting Plan for the seizure of its aerial, receiver, and cathode-ray tube was organised by Combined Operations headquarters, at Anderson Manor and Poole, under Acting Admiral Louis Mountbatten.

During February

Hurn unit prepares for airborne landings.

Part of Hurn Aerodrome has been set aside for Number 3 Overseas Aircraft Despatch Unit. They will modify Halifax, Whitley, and Stirling bombers into tow-craft and muster a fleet of gliders for airborne landings.

Footnote: In 1943 the Whitleys were replaced by twin-engined Albemarles; the first British military aircraft with a tricycle undercarriage. The unit would remain at Hurn until D-Day. One Sunday evening four of its gliders crash-landed into the lane immediately west of the aerodrome that led to East Parley mission church.

MAKING NEWS: THE OFFICES AND PRINTING WORKS OF THE DORSET DAILY ECHO, IN WEYMOUTH, ON 2 APRIL 1942

Tuesday 3 March

175 Squadron formed at R.A.F. Warmwell.

"Stop at nothing" is the motto of 175 Squadron which came into existence today at R.A.F. Warmwell. It is being equipped with Mark-IIb Hurricanes and has been allocated the squadron code "HH".

They are taking over from 402 (Royal Canadian Air Force) Squadron, which has also been flying the "Hurri-bomber" on cross-Channel ground-attack missions.

Saturday 7 March

'Non-stop Luftwaffe attacks' on empty fields at Cerne and Milton Abbas.

German radio on Thursday 5 March was reporting continuous Luftwaffe attacks on England the previous night that had avenged the R.A.F. bombing of targets in Paris. Initially, the Air Ministry said it had "nothing to report", but later in the day it was confirmed that bombs had fallen in Dorset at Smacam Down and in Delcombe Bottom.

The national press were encouraged to follow up the reports and, unusually, to publish precise locations. They failed, however, to find Smacam Down, even though it is shown on the Ordnance Survey map as a spur of open grassland on the west side of the Cerne valley between Cerne Abbas and Nether Cerne. Its only features of note are some ancient earthworks.

Newspaper reporters had more success with the second location. To quote a Daily Mail reporter: "After an all-out search I tracked down Delcombe Bottom. At Milton Abbas, a picturesque downland village west of Blandford, I learned that Delcombe Bottom is a valley about a mile away.

"At the village inn, the Hambro Arms, at Milton Abbas, the 'blitz' was the sole conversation piece. The landlord was despondent. He had slept all night, and was slightly annoyed that the customary crowd of cronies drinking ale and smoking pipes was in its element.

"George Collis chuckled when told what the Germans were saying. 'Armed reckernizing, were they?' he said.

"A companion interjected: 'You know what I reckon, Jarge? We rattled 'ee wi' Warr-ships Week. There be only five 'undred of we, and we got two thousand five 'undred pounds. We 'it 'im 'aard and no mistake. 'Ee were after revenge.'

"'Never you mind,' said Jarge. ' 'Ee missed us and a miss be as good as a mile. One in a field, one in corn-patch, one in the 'ood, and last one — 'ee were in a bit o' field where there used to be potatoes. Not even a rabbit was 'urt.'

"One bomb fell a few hundred yards from the famous Church of England faith-healing centre established at the historic landmark of Milton Abbey. But Smacam Down remained a mystery. One farm labourer said: "Reckon 'twas a farmer as told 'em that.'"

Sunday 8 March

Woman machine-gunned as she reads at Christchurch Quay.

At 18.10 hours two Messerschmitt Bf.109s crossed Wick Hams at low level and then machine-gunned the Quay at Christchurch. Their single victim was a woman who sat reading on a riverside bench. Josephine O'Reilly of Iford Bridge Hotel has been admitted to Fairmile House with a shoulder wound. Her condition is described as fair.

Saturday 14 March

German raider escapes into the Atlantic.

There was intense naval activity off Dorset last night as the destroyer H.M.S. *Walpole* and the New Zealand destroyer H.M.N.Z.S. *Fernie* tried with 21 motor torpedo boats and four of the larger type of motor gun boats tried to block the English Channel. They were attempting to prevent the passage of the Nazi raider Schiff 28 *Michel*. She slipped through, however, towards the Atlantic, with the aid of five 1,300-ton light destroyers of the 5th T-boat Flotilla (*Falke, Jaguar, Kondor, Iltis,* and *Seeadler*) and nine minesweepers.

Sunday 22 March

New bomber arrives at Hurn for radar-mapping tests.

A new Halifax bomber — the type went into operational service on 11 March — has been delivered to the Telecommunications Flying Unit at R.A.F. Hurn. V9977 has been adapted by Handley Page Limited to the requirements of the Telecommunications Research Establishment. at Worth Matravers, and has a Perspex cupola covering the space which would normally house the nose gun-turret.

Here the scientists will install the magnetron section of a Mark VII A.I. (Airborne Interception) radar set, adapted into the first prototype of a version codenamed H2S, which is being developed for ground-mapping.

Monday 23 March

234 Squadron returns to R.A.F. Warmwell.

Now flying Mark Vb Spitfires, 234 (Madras Presidency) Squadron today flew into Warmwell Aerodrome, which was home for the squadron between February and November, 1941. This time, however, it is to be a short stay of just two weeks, after which it is due to move on to Cornwall.

During March

Royal Fusiliers guard Christchurch radar establishment.

The 12th Battalion of the Royal Fusiliers have been sent to Christchurch to guard the top-secret Air Defence Research and Development Establishment, at Somerford and Friars Cliff, against the possibility of the Germans staging a retaliatory Bruneval-style commando raid. The research plants, known locally as the Air Defence Experimental Establishment, work in conjunction with the Telecommunications Research Establishment at Worth Matravers and specialise in radio and radar counter-measures.

Wednesday 1 April
The King reviews 2nd Dorsets en route for Bombay.

The 2nd Battalion, the Dorsetshire Regiment, were today lined up along the Oxford Road at Banbury, Oxfordshire, for inspection by King George VI. 'A' Company then went through a jungle assault course in the trees above the officers' mess. The battalion is under orders to move to Liverpool from where it will sail to Bombay.

Thursday 2 April
Flying Fortress drops in at the Baker's Arms.

An American B-17 Flying Fortress bomber, returning from a cross-Channel mission, has made a successful emergency landing in a field opposite the thatch-roofed Baker's Arms at Lytchett Minster. The huge aeroplane had been attempting an approach towards the new aerodrome at R.A.F. Hurn, nine miles to the north-east, but lost too much height.

There was considerable local commotion as people heard or spotted the B-17's descent. "I was with a group of boys standing on the pillbox beside the railway bridge at Sterte," said nine-year-old. "We saw the plane getting lower and lower and it came down on Tatchell's Holding at Charity Farm."

The American crew congratulated their pilot on bringing them to ground outside a traditional English public house.

KING'S FAREWELL: KING GEORGE VI INSPECTS THE 2ND BATTALION OF THE DORSETSHIRE REGIMENT, ABOUT TO LEAVE FOR INDIA AND A JAPANESE EXPERIENCE, ON 1 APRIL 1942

It has been a shock, however, for Mrs Joan Hooper who is in the final stages of pregnancy at Tatchell's Holding, and there is concern that she may experience complications.

Footnote: The excitement induced the birth of a healthy daughter, Wendy, delivered by midwife Margaret Gibson the following day, on Friday 3 April 1942. Then the Americans arrived in force, by road, with outsized earth-moving machinery of an Engineer unit. They flattened the field into a

runway. Another team carried out minor repairs and checks on the B-17 which was then refuelled and made a smooth take-off for its home base.

Thursday 2 April
Twenty killed and Weymouth's newspaper blitzed.

21.00 hours. Twenty people are dead and 56 injured after Nazi dive-bombers indiscriminately swept across Weymouth. Only one of their bombs hit the central area of the town but this has devastated the Dorset Daily Echo offices and printing works. Only a few hours earlier, new hot-metal foundry equipment was being installed, and the current edition of the newspaper distributed for this Maundy Thursday.

The staff are returning to salvage what they can. Just one item of standing type has been found and that, ironically, carries the headline "Hitler's Nightmare!"

Footnote: The 8-page paper could miss Good Friday but it appeared again on Saturday 4 April, with 12,730 copies printed at Bournemouth. The Richmond Hill plant had already taken on the Southern Daily Echo when it was bombed out of its works at Southampton.

Sunday 5 April
Sinking of H.M.S. 'Dorsetshire'.

Japanese dive-bombers, coming out of the tropical sun at 13.40 hours this Easter Sunday in waves of seven, today sank the cruisers H.M.S. *Dorsetshire* and H.M.S. *Cornwall* in the Indian Ocean. The warships were hunting for surface raiders about 300 miles west of Colombo.

Footnote: The 1,100 survivors floated in clusters around two leaky whalers in which the worst of the wounded were tended. They were told by the *Dorsetshire's* captain, Commodore A. W. S. Agar V.C., to conserve their strength by making as little noise as possible and cover their heads against the equatorial heat. Rescue did not arrive for 33 hours, after they were sighted by a 'Stringbag', a Swordfish torpedo-reconnaissance biplane, of the Fleet Air Arm.

Monday 6 April
Churchill inspects Churchills at Lulworth.

Ranks of Churchill tanks, the first to go into service, received their namesake's approval today in Arish Mell valley on the Dorset coast. Prime Minister Winston Churchill made an Easter Monday tour of the Gunnery Wing of the Armoured Fighting Vehicles School at Lulworth Camp. Some of the Churchills have been refitted with 6-pounder guns to give them much increased fire-power. The first production version carries 2-pounders.

Friday 17 April
'Blind' Halifax spots Bournemouth from six miles.

The first version of an H2S town-finding radar set, intended for use in long distance bombers, today succeeded in giving scientists a convincing signal that could be identified as Bournemouth, detected from a height of 8,000 feet at six miles. Halifax V9977 carries the set behind a Perspex dome. This morning's flight, undertaken by the Telecommunications Flying Unit for the scientists of the Purbeck-based Telecommunication Research Establishment, then used the apparatus to distinguish between the outlines and land-forms of the adjoining towns of Poole and Christchurch.

DORSETSHIRE *SUNK: SURVIVORS IN THE INDIAN OCEAN, HAVING WAITED HOURS FOR RESCUE UNDER THE TROPICAL SUN, ON 13 APRIL 1942*

CHURCHILL'S INSPECTION: THE PRIME MINISTER VIEWING THE NEW TANKS BEARING HIS NAME, AT HALCOMBE VALE, ABOVE SEA VALE FARM, EAST LULWORTH, ON 6 APRIL 1942

Progress on several types of airborne radar operations has gathered pace since the start of 1942. Five important versions are now in production or being perfected:

A.I. (Airborne Interception) for night-fighters;

A.S.V. (Air to Surface Vessel), for Coastal Command, to detect submarines surfacing to charge their batteries;

Gee (renamed T.R. to indicate Transmitter Receiver, which it is not) concealing the fact it forms a grid-lattice map from synchronised pulses on a cathode ray tube in a colour-coded pattern that shows the aircraft's location when superimposed on a chart;

Oboe (navigation beam) to aid target marking for flare-dropping Pathfinders, as they became known;

H2S (ground-mapping radar) for Bomber Command to bomb blind, straight through the clouds.

Footnote: The latter prototype would have been tested on a similar flight in Halifax V9977 but the operator failed to find a concealed switch and the radar was not turned on. Scientists only spotted the switch after the bomber had landed back at Hurn.

Monday 20 April
Swanage hit by bombs.

Houses in Cornwall Road at Swanage have been destroyed by German bombs. There is also considerable damage to commercial buildings in Station Road.

CHURCHILL TANKS: GATHERED ON THE BINDON RANGE, EAST LULWORTH

During April

Weymouth scholarship boys meet again in Libya.

The war has brought about a surprise reunion for two of the brightest pupils of recent times from Weymouth Grammar School. A. E. Walkling and R. R. Head have had a brief encounter in the Western Desert. Between 1928 and 1937 they had competed at Weymouth for honours with both gaining scholarships and going to Oxford.

Lieutenant Alec Walkling has written to school-friend Norman Windust in Weymouth: "You will be amazed when I tell you who I ran into the other day. About a month after the campaign started, I was wandering the desert in a truck looking for Jerries. I spotted a large column early one morning and crept up on it as stealthily as an Army truck will allow.

"I was a friendly column, and out of the nearest vehicle popped a long thin figure with glasses. It was Head. I don't know which of us had the biggest surprise. It seems strange to me, but there was both of us, with more than our fair share of brains, yet we had nothing better to do than chase our fellow men around the desert."

Footnote: It would be their last meeting. Head's parents, at Queen's Street, Weymouth, were to hear that their son had been reported missing. As for Walkling, he went on to Burma where he was mentioned in despatches and not only survived the war but scaled his chosen profession, becoming Major-General and Colonel Commandant of the Royal Artillery, in 1974.

Thursday 14 May

Charmouth radar station slips down cliff.

A radio location [radar] station on the Dorset coast was lost at 08.00 hours today through natural causes when 300 feet of clifftop subsided in a landslip at Cain's Folly, to the east of Charmouth.

Footnote: The concrete building lies partly submerged in the lias clays in the undercliff, 75 feet below the edge, and was half visible in 1985 with its seaward side tiling upwards.

Tuesday 19 May

Germans lose two T-boats.

Two of the 1,300-ton craft of the German 5th T-boat Flotilla, *Iltis* and *Seeadler*, have been sunk off Dorset in recent days. They were intercepted by Portsmouth-based motor torpedo boats. The Royal Navy lost *MTB220* during the action.

Saturday 23 May

Luftwaffe ace Langar killed at Shaftesbury.

Luftwaffe ace Hauptmann Langar, the officer commanding the elite pathfinding Kampfgruppe 100, was killed today when his Heinkel He.111 flew into a hillside in low cloud. He had been intercepted by Squadron Leader John "Cat's Eyes" Cunningham, whose Beaufighter had been scrambled from Middle Wallop on the Hampshire Downs.

Cloud cover was dense and carried heavy rain. Langar dived in an attempt to evade the Beaufighter and then crashed into the hills near Shaftesbury. No shot had been fired.

The intruder was detected by a Type 15 radar antenna in the field near Christchurch that is R.A.F. Sopley. Its tented Operations Room directed the Beaufighter, of 604 Squadron, and brought about the interception. Sopley radar station is enabling fighters to operate in total darkness, as well as dense cloud, and has been given the codename "Starlight".

Monday 25 May

Brownsea decoy draws bombs from Poole.

The western end of Brownsea Island rocked to countless explosives in the early hours of this Whit Monday morning. Pathfinder bombers had dropped incendiaries nearly on target for the new Coastal Command base, at R.A.F. Hamworthy, and many of these landed with some high explosives in Rockley Road, Coles Avenue, and Hinchcliffe Road. Many bungalows were destroyed and five civilians killed, but fortunately for Hamworthy and Poole the fires were extinguished in time for the newly completed "Starfish" apparatus of the Major Strategic Night Decoy to come to light across the water on Brownsea Island.

The combination of wood, coal, and paraffin, plus flushes of water, produces white-hot flashes just like those of bursting bombs and lured the 55 enemy aircraft to unload 150 tons of high explosive harmlessly on to the uninhabited western extremity of the island. Only one bomb found a military target — a stray made a direct hit on Poole's Home Guard company headquarters in Lindsay Road, causing the unit's first death from enemy action, with the loss of Private W. J. Griffiths.

The bombers had come from the Pas-de-Calais and been tracked by radar to St Catherine's Point, Isle of Wight, from where they turned north-westwards.

Footnote: The Brownsea decoy would save Poole and Bournemouth from a total of 1,000 tons of German bombs.

Monday 25 May

Worth radar establishment evacuated.

The Telecommunications Research Establishment is being evacuated from Worth Matravers and Langton Matravers to Malvern College, Worcestershire, because of fears that the Germans might attempt their own Bruneval-style raid on the Purbeck coast.

In order to emphasise the danger, Dr. Reginald Jones and Hugh Smith arrived on the Dorset seaboard from Air Ministry Scientific Intelligence in London with revolvers ostentatiously strapped to their belts, when they came to inspect the enemy radar apparatus captured at Bruneval.

HEADQUARTERS SHIP: H.M.S. SONA CONTROLLED MARITIME MOVEMENTS FROM POOLE QUAY UNTIL SHE WAS DESTROYED BY A GERMAN BOMB ON 7 JUNE 1942

Monday 25 May
Telecommunications Flying Unit exits from Hurn.

As a result of the departure from the Purbeck coast of the Air Ministry's Telecommunications Research Establishment, because of fears of a German raid, its support team and their unusual collection of some 50 assorted aircraft were today flying from R.A.F. Hurn. The Telecommunications Flying Unit is on its way to Defford, near Worcester.

During May
Airman's body washed up at Bournemouth.

The body of R.A.F. Sergeant R. E. Heathway, who served with 107 Squadron of Bomber Command from Great Massingham, Norfolk, has been washed up on the Bournemouth coast.

He was lost with Boston bomber AL286 over the English Channel in a raid on the docks at Cherbourg on 25 April. The aircraft had been hit by flak. Subsequently, the pilot and another crewman have been reported prisoner of war, but the fourth airman is missing and presumed dead.

Monday 1 June
R.A.F. Hurn taken over by Army Co-Operation Command.

R.A.F. Hurn was transferred today from 11 Group Fighter Command to 38 Wing Army Co-Operation Command. The Air Officer Commanding, Air Marshal Sir Arthur Sheridan Barratt, inspected the aerodrome which is under the command of Group

Captain Harold John Granville Ellis Proud. The station will provide transport support for the 1st Airborne Division.

Monday 1 June
Fleet Air Arm aerodrome for Charlton Horethorne.

An airstrip to the north of Sherborne, at Sigwells Farm, Charlton Horethorne, which has been used as an emergency landing ground, is to become a satellite aerodrome for the Fleet Air Arm station at Yeovilton. Flight-Lieutenant H. C. V. Jollef was waiting today on the 600-feet limestone plateau to the north of the farm to meet an advance party from Exeter.

Thursday 4 June
Arne decoy blaze saves Holton Heath.

The Royal Naval Cordite Factory on Holton Heath was saved from a potentially devastating major raid last night by the swift ignition of half a ton of waste shell-propellant at its dummy factory on the other side of the Wareham Channel. Inspection of the Arne decoy site today revealed 206 craters and it is estimated that 50 or more bombs also fell into Poole Harbour.

Thursday 4 June
Germans nearly set Hamworthy ablaze.

A German raid on Hamworthy and Poole, by 50 bombers in the early hours this morning, was partly thwarted by heath fires started by the incendiaries of the pathfinder bombers in the gorse and heather at Rocklea. This drew

EMERGENCY WATER: PIPED AROUND THE KERB BESIDE BEALES DEPARTMENT STORE, FROM OLD CHRISTCHURCH ROAD INTO GERVIS PLACE (BACKGROUND) FOR USE IN WARTIME FIRE-FIGHTING. THE 6-INCH SURFACE MAIN, INSTALLED IN 1942, HAD THE ADVANTAGE OF BEING MUCH EASIER TO REPAIR, AFTER BOMB DAMAGE, THAN CONVENTIONAL UNDERGROUND PIPES. THEY WERE PROVIDED WITH THEIR OWN RESERVOIRS (below)

many of the bombers westwards from the urban area but it nearly created a disaster.

One of the bombs that exploded on Ham Common ruptured a giant tank of 100-octane aviation fuel concealed in the old claypits at Doulting's Pier. A million gallons flowed from it and formed lakes across the wasteland as fire teams could only pray that no one dropped a match, let alone a bomb, as the whole area began to reek with fumes.

Some of the bombs did find the urban areas of Hamworthy and the densely-packed Georgian terraces of the Old Town at Poole. A grocer's shop opposite the parish church was hit, as was Yeatman's Mill on Poole Quay.

Bolson's store at their Wessex Wharf shipyard was gutted, in Ferry Road, at Hamworthy. The yard manufactures twin-screw H.D.M.L.s (Harbour Defence Motor Launches) which are 72-feet vessels. There a firewatcher, Louis Pittwood, was fatally injured. The 55-year-old died today in the Cornelia Hospital, Longfleet Road, Poole. Twenty-three others are having their injuries tended.

Mrs Florence Diffy of Green Road and Victor Park, a six-year-old boy who was staying in Hamworthy, also died in Cornelia Hospital from injuries received in the raid.

The Royal Navy's Headquarters Ship for the port, H.M.S. *Sona* — which is berthed beside Poole quay — was sunk by a bomb. This dropped through the funnel and buried itself in the mud beneath the hull. As it did not explode, the sailors were able to escape, by scrambling up the quayside.

Friday 5 June
Whitleys arrive at Hurn for Resistance 'Special Duties'.

297 (Army Co-Operation) Squadron has flown into R.A.F. Hurn from Netheravon. Its Tiger Moth biplanes have been replaced by twin-engined Whitleys.

Their flights include Special Duties across the Channel to drop agents for the Special Operations Executive and supplies for resistance groups.

Saturday 6 June
Bournemouth is bombed.

High explosive bombs have damaged a total of 454 properties in Bournemouth. One landed on a railway siding, beside Southcote Road, to the east of the Central Station. Others dropped near St Peter's Church, on the Anglo-Swiss Hotel, and at Hill House in Parsonage Road.

The bodies have been brought to Bournemouth of three Canadian airmen who lost their lives in a flying accident. They are 23-year-old Pilot Officer N. R. Bailey; 30-year-old Pilot Officer J. W. Morgan; and 25-year-old Wireless Operator / Air Gunner J. A. Epp.

Sunday 7 June
Delayed bomb destroys the Navy's Poole headquarters.

00.52 hours. The bomb which sank the Royal Navy headquarters ship at Poole Quay, H.M.S. *Sona*, but failed to explode, has now detonated itself and completely destroyed what was left of the vessel. It also brought down the frontages of several quayside buildings. The area had been roped off and there were no casualties.

Sunday 7 June
Hurn Halifax crashes in the Welsh Marches.

Halifax V9977, which operated with the Telecommunications Flying Unit from R.A.F. Hurn, has been lost while carrying out a secret experimental test from its new base at Defford, Warwickshire. It crashed at 16.20 hours, in the Welsh borders, with the loss of everyone on board. The scientists included 38-year-old Alan Blumlein of Electrical Musical Industries, who revolutionised electronics by filing 128 electronic patents including key discoveries for multiple telephone circuitry, stereo-optical sound, 405-line television transmission, and video waveform.

They were comparing prototype H2S magnetron equipment, being used in ground-mapping radar sets, with a klystron version produced by E.M.I. Prime Minister Winston Churchill has expressed concern that the magnetron is virtually indestructible, and therefore inevitably bound to fall into enemy hands if used over Germany, whereas a klystron could be destroyed.

Footnote: Churchill was right, in that the magnetron would be the only piece of equipment to survive the crash of V9977, though this and the death of Alan Blumlein would not be announced until after the end of the war. In effect the H2S set had caused the loss of the Halifax. The starboard outer engine of the four-engined bomber had failed after an inlet valve fractured, from metal fatigue. This engine was driving a generator to power the H2S apparatus.

Rather than feathering the propeller, the crew attempted re-starting the engine, which then caught fire. Extinguishers were found to be empty. Control of the stricken aircraft was lost, at 2,500 feet, and it dropped into the Welsh hills.

Monday 15 June
Mustangs arrive at R.A.F. Hurn.

Mustangs of newly formed 170 (Army Co-Operation) Squadron have flown into R.A.F. Hurn from Weston Zoyland, Somerset. They are to provide fast forward-reconnaissance in an Army support role and are both highly manoeuvrable and toughly armed.

More Whitleys are arriving from Netheravon with the redeployment to Hurn of 296 (Army Co-Operation) Squadron. Routine exercises for this and the existing Hurn-based 297 Squadron will include paratroop drops over Salisbury Plain.

Thursday 18 June
Royal Navy puts into Bournemouth for repairs.

Coastal forces of the Royal Navy have anchored and tied up around the remnants of Bournemouth Pier. Its central section was broken in 1940 to prevent it being used by German invaders. The visiting vessels have put in for running repairs before leaving for Portland.

The damage to the War Programme light destroyer H.M.S. *Albrighton* and two special gun-boats, *SGB6* and *SGB8*, was sustained whilst trying to stop an Axis convoy. Four German, Italian and Finnish ships were being escorted by the 1st Schnellboot Flotilla. One of the four enemy transports was sunk, for the loss by the Royal Navy of a special gun-boat, *SGB7*.

During June
Campaign to replace the 'Dorsetshire'.

The H.M.S. *Dorsetshire* Replacement Campaign, launched by the Earl of Shaftesbury, aims to double the level of War Savings in the county and raise £2,700,000 in the six months to the end of the year.

Tuesday 9 July
Battle of Lyme Bay.

This has been the Battle of Lyme Bay. The German 1st Schnellboot Flotilla attacked Allied Coast Convoy E/P 91 and caused the loss of 12,192 tons of merchant shipping with the sinking of the tanker SS *Pomella* and four freighters. One of the British escort vessels, the armed trawler HMT *Manor*, has also gone down.

The E-boats involved were *S48*, *S50*, *S63*, *S67*, *S70*, *S104* and *S109*.

Monday 13 July
Bomb damage in Swanage.

Three people have been injured and houses damaged in an air-raid at Swanage. Most of the destruction is in the vicinity of Park Road.

Wednesday 22 July

Germans lay more mines in the Channel.

The central part of the English Channel has been heavily mined by the Germans over the past three days through the efforts of Operation Rhein and Operation Stein. The 3rd T-boat Flotilla of Torpedoschulboote (*T4*, *T10*, *T13* and *T14*) have been depositing the mines through their torpedo tubes.

Wednesday 29 July

H.M.S. 'Poole' adopted by the town.

H.M.S. *Poole*, a new Bangor-class fleet minesweeper of 750 tons, with a complement of 60, has been formally adopted by the town. A civic reception took place on the edge of the harbour at Poole Park. She joins a total, so far, of 35 vessels, with H.M.S. *Bridport* and H.M.S. *Lyme Regis* also financed by Dorset savers.

During July

Americans fly into R.A.F. Warmwell.

British-made Spitfires returned to Warmwell Aerodrome this month but they are being flown by a detachment of the 31st Fighter Group of the Eighth United States Army Air Force.

During July

Hurn Aerodrome to house Churchill's Liberator.

A purpose-built V.I.P. hangar is being constructed at R.A.F. Hurn to house Prime Minister Winston Churchill's personal Liberator transport and other special aircraft. This hangar will have blast-walls at the sides but be left open at each end to avoid containing the blast from any explosion.

Footnote: The hangar survives, plus door but no longer with blast-walls, and was handling millions of kilos of air-freight each year, by the 1980s.

Sunday 2 August

More German mines sown in the Channel.

Once again the 3rd T-boat Flotilla (this time deploying *T10*, *T13* and *T14*) has been sowing German mines in the Channel sea-lanes, in Operation Masuren.

Wednesday 5 August

Plane explodes off Bournemouth.

An unidentified aeroplane approached Bournemouth from the sea shortly before 03.00 hours with its navigation lights on. It then blew up with a tremendous flash.

VALENTINE TANK: MOUNTING A 6-POUNDER ANTI-TANK GUN, AT LULWORTH CAMP IN 1942

GENERAL GRANT: THE NEWLY INTRODUCED AMERICAN TANK BEING PUT THROUGH ITS PACES AT LULWORTH CAMP IN APRIL 1942

Wednesday 5 August

No. 4 Commando rehearses Dieppe Raid at Lulworth.

No. 4 Commando, brought up to full strength and now fielding 1,000 men, has returned to south Dorset, where it was formed in July 1940. It is preparing for the Dieppe Raid, with training at Weymouth and Lulworth to include coastal landings at Lulworth Cove and nearby bays, in a full-scale rehearsal before being tasked to attacking the German's Atlantic Wall. Their Commanding Officer is 31-year-old Lieutenant-Colonel Simon Fraser, the 17th Baron Lovat.

Thursday 6 August

Portland radar test plays on German nerves.

A test off Portland that amplified the enemy's radar echo, from a formation of eight Defiant fighters, caused the Luftwaffe to think that a major attack was in prospect. Thirty fighters were scrambled from airfields on the Cherbourg peninsula to meet the phantom force.

Wednesday 12 August

Tarrant Hinton flyer shot down over Malta convoy.

Michael Hankey, a young fighter pilot in the Fleet Air Arm, was killed in combat today whilst trying to protect a

Malta convoy. He was the son of the rector of Tarrant Hinton, Rev. Basil Hankey, and grew up in the Cranborne Chase village in the 1930s.

Monday 17 August

Eight killed in Swanage air-raid.

Eight people have been killed and 39 injured in a hit-and-run raid by the Luftwaffe that has caused considerable damage in central Swanage. The Westminster Bank at 1 Institute Road suffered a direct hit and was destroyed. Miss Helen Muspratt's photographic studio at 10 Institute Road was badly damaged, as was Hayman's Cafe.

Bombs also fell in The Narrows, destroying the southern line of the old terraced cottages that constricted the middle of the High Street, and in Chapel Lane and Church Hill.

Cottages opposite the old parish churchyard were ruined and part of the tile roof taken off St Mary's parish church. There was also damage to the nearby Tithe Barn.

Monday 17 August

No. 4 Commando leaves Weymouth to land at Dieppe.

No. 4 Commando are sailing today from Weymouth towards a gathering point in the English Channel from which they will proceed toward the enemy shore to land just before dawn on Wednesday, in an attempt to breach the defences at occupied Dieppe. The purpose of the Operation Jubilee assault reconnaissance is to test the strength of the German West Wall.

Footnote: Theirs would be the only completely successful operation of that bloody day, as Major James Dunning of the Commando Association reminded me at the 50th anniversary commemorations of the battalion's formation, held in Weymouth on 17 October 1990. They were given the right flank of the attack, codenamed Orange Beach, west of Dieppe between Varengeville-sur-mer and Quiberville, where they silenced the Hess Battery.

Frenchmen offered them wine but the celebration was premature as the Canadian sector was being pinned down on the beaches and forced to take cover behind their own dead. No. 4 Commando withdrew as heroes with their Commanding Officer, Lord Lovat, being awarded the Distinguished Service Order, and decorations for his men including the Victoria Cross, to Patrick Porteous.

Monday 17 August
First crash at Charlton Horethorne aerodrome.

The first squadron using the new Fleet Air Arm aerodrome at Charlton Horethorne, near Sherborne, has left for St Merryn, Cornwall. Departing 887 Squadron is being replaced by 790 Squadron and the Sea Hurricanes of 891 Squadron.

One of the latter crashed on landing. This was the first mishap at the aerodrome. Only slight damage was done to the fighter and the pilot was uninjured.

Sunday 23 August
Five killed and terracotta cow destroyed at Swanage.

Five people were killed and nine wounded when German bombs caused extensive damage to commercial buildings around The Square in Swanage. The most dramatic casualty was the terracotta cow centrepiece of the facade to Swanage Dairies which is now lying in pieces amid the rubble of the collapsed building. The adjoining Ship Inn also suffered considerable damage.

Monday 24 August
Poole and Weymouth boats at Dieppe.

Boats from Poole and Weymouth have for the past week been operating as support vessels for Operation Jubilee. The Dieppe Raid returnees have brought back stories of amazing escapes and days of contrast which started with Frenchmen uncorking wine in the belief that they had been liberated and ended with the Canadians setting up machine-guns on parapets comprised of their own dead.

Monday 31 August
Australians fly into Hamworthy.

Nine Short S.25 Sunderland Mark III flying-boats of 461 (Royal Australian Air Force) Squadron today landed in Poole Harbour from Mount Batten, Plymouth. Squadron Leader R. C. Lovelock heads a complement of 132 men. The new base at Hamworthy was established as R.A.F. Poole at the start of the month and renamed R.A.F. Hamworthy only a week later.

Squadron headquarters are being established on the north-eastern shore of Poole Harbour in the Harbour Yacht Club buildings at Lilliput. The Australians are flying anti-submarine patrols in the South-Western Approaches and the Bay of Biscay where U-boats have been caught napping by airborne radar and are now under orders to surface only for the recharging of their batteries.

During August
Bovington's remaining Great War tanks rescued for a film.

The old tanks from the Great War that were used as pillboxes around Bovington in the anti-invasion defences of 1940 have come back to life for the making of a movie, entitled *Victory*, by the Crown Film Unit. It has realistic scenes, shot on the Dorsetshire heaths at Turners Puddle and Gallows Hill, of British light tanks advancing under heavy enemy artillery bombardment in trench warfare on the Western Front, in 1918.

During August
Midget submarine X-3 tested at Portland.

Captain Willie Meeke D.S.C. has completed a series of dummy attacks in Portland Harbour, using a midget X-craft submarine, the *X-3*. Launched in March, the 22-ton boat is 43 feet long and has a crew of three. It can make 6 knots on the surface, and 5 knots underwater, while carrying delayed-action side charges of two tons of explosive attached to each side.

The idea for these innovative craft came from Commander Cromwell Varley, a retired submariner of the Great War, who conceived the hazardous plan for miniature submarines to slip through harbour barriers and natural obstacles to lay massive charges beneath anchored enemy warships.

X-3 has now been loaded on a railway wagon for the first stage of its journey to an operational unit, the 12th Submarine Flotilla, which has been established at shore-base HMS *Varbel*, in the Hydropathic Hotel, Port Bannatyne, on the Isle of Bute. She will be unloaded at Faslane and towed from there, by sea, to Loch Striven.

Footnote: A year later, X-craft of the 12th Submarine Flotilla would carry out Operation Source, in September 1943, and succeed in badly damaging the German battleship Tirpitz in her apparently secure refuge in a Norwegian fjord. Two of the Royal Navy's submariners,

Lieutenant Donald Cameron in *X-6* and Godfrey Place in *X-7*, won the Victoria Cross for their part in what had been regarded at times as an impossible mission.

Captain Meeke had meanwhile moved on to Trincomalee, Ceylon, for patrols in the Indian Ocean with the 2nd Submarine Flotilla. He would be appointed MBE for his part in the X-craft project, as he was winning a Bar to his D.S.C. in those warmer waters.

Tuesday 3 September
Poole Commandos raid the Channel Islands.

A successful raid has been carried out on a German U-boat signalling station, in the Casquets Lighthouse, in the Channel Islands. This stands in the English Channel eight miles west of Alderney. The attack was carried out last night by No. 62 Commando, attached to Combined Operations, which is based at Anderson Manor near Bere Regis and operates from Poole Harbour.

Code-books have been captured along with seven German wireless operators, who were taken completely by surprise, and found themselves in Poole at 04.00 hours this morning as prisoners of war.

Footnote: The leader of the Small Scale Raiding Force, Geoffrey Appleyard, was promoted to Major and awarded the Distinguished Service Order.

Tuesday 3 September
Prayers for the third anniversary.

Today, the third anniversary of the declaration of war, churches have been packed for the national day of prayer. Services have also been held at places of work including the Bournemouth department stores of Allens and Beales.

Wednesday 9 September
Warmwell Whirlwinds sink two armed trawlers.

An idea first suggested a year ago, by Squadron Leader T. Pugh, was successfully put to the test today with the fitting of bomb-racks to Westland Whirlwinds of 263 Squadron at R.A.F. Warmwell.

Modifications were duly made so that a single 250-pound or 500-pound bomb can be carried under each wing. In the trial operation today two sections of Whirlwinds were thus turned into bombers and provided with an escort of Spitfires, as they crossed the Channel to attack four armed trawlers steaming westwards from Cap de la Hague, towards Alderney.

Two were sunk. No bomb-sight was used and the Whirlwinds dropped their loads from 50 feet, utilising delayed action fuses.

Wednesday 9 September
Squadrons change at Charlton Horethorne.

891 (Fleet Air Arm) Squadron today left Charlton Horethorne for St Merryn, Cornwall, and are being replaced by 893 Squadron. The aerodrome is being used for working-up training, with Sea Hurricanes practising on target-towing Martinets.

Friday 11 September
Lone raider kills five in Parkstone.

A single German bomber ignored the Bofors guns at Canford Cliffs today to come in from the bay and drop a bomb that killed five people in three adjoining roads at Parkstone. The dead are Rev. William Russell and his son Frank at 11 Marlborough Road; Mrs Winifred Phillips and her 11-year-old daughter June at Woodgrove in Bournemouth Road; and Mrs Annie Watts at 12 Earlham Drive.

Monday 14 September
Twenty-one killed on Poole flying-boat.

The "Empire" flying-boat *Clare*, outward bound from Poole Harbour for Bathurst, West Africa, radioed soon after take-off to report engine trouble. Half an hour later this had become a fire and she was attempting to make an emergency landing in the English Channel to the south-west of Lyme Bay. The flying-boat, with six crew, was carrying 13 passengers.

Footnote: Nothing more was heard or found.

Thursday 17 September
Piddletrenthide man found shot dead.

In the early hours this morning the body of farmworker Louis Aubrey Stickland, aged 42, was found lying beside Chapel Lane at Piddletrenthide. He had a single gunshot wound in the chest.

Stickland enlisted with the Home Guard two months ago. Last evening he went to the Golden Grain Bakery for cigarettes but did not return home. His wife was unconcerned because she assumed he was having a long chat, with the baker, Frederick Davis.

Mrs Stickland did not report her husband missing until 00.30 hours today. His body was found by the local magistrate, Henry Levi Green, in a spot known to the locals as Darkie Lane. It is called Chapel Lane on the map.

Footnote: The story is set to continue, with November and December entries.

During September
Coastal Command aerodrome at Holmsley.

R.A.F. Holmsley South, an aerodrome with concrete runways earmarked for the Wellingtons of Coastal Command on anti-submarine patrols, has been constructed across the flat expanse of heather and gorse at Plain Heath on the south-western edge of the New Forest.

Footnote: In 1943 they would be joined by four-engined Halifax bombers, as the tugs for troop-carrying gliders.

During September

Aerodrome being built at Tarrant Rushton.

Work is in progress on the construction of a major aerodrome for the R.A.F., with hardened runways, on flat-topped sheep downs between Badbury Rings and the valley at Tarrant Rushton, four miles east of Blandford. Its north-south runway is to be 2,000 yards with intersecting north-west to south-east and south-west to north-east runways of 1,500 yards each.

During September

Poole baker raised £3,600 for Soviet Russia.

Joe Bright, the Mayor of Poole and the man voted "Best Baker in Britain", has raised £3,600 in aid for Uncle Joe. To help Stalin's heroic struggle and relieve some of the appalling suffering on the Eastern Front he has been working tirelessly for the Medical Aid to Russia and China Fund which he founded. Bright's Bakery is at 117 High Street, Poole.

Thursday 1 October

Sherborne postman loses his arm in a propeller.

Levelling off runways and the rolling of relayed turf has led to some changes in the usual pattern of aircraft movements at the Fleet Air Arm station near Charlton Horethorne. One of these caused a serious accident at 09.00 hours today when a Fulmar of 790 Naval Air Squadron, being moved by Lieutenant Commander Hodgson, was involved in an accident on the ground with a postman from Sherborne.

W. J. John was riding a Post Office combination motor-cycle when he collided with the Fulmar, hitting the propeller, which severed his right arm at the shoulder. He was taken to the Royal Naval Hospital at Sherborne, in a state of severe shock, but is expected to recover.

Wednesday 7 October

Hamworthy becomes a landing craft base.

The Admiralty today commissioned The Lake camp-site at Hamworthy and the adjoining Hamworthy Common, plus Round Island two miles away towards the opposite shore of Poole Harbour, for a new shore-base which is being named H.M.S. Turtle. It will be tasked with training British, Canadian, and American crews in the handling of landing craft at sea and their use in beach assaults.

Saturday 10 October

175 Squadron departs from R.A.F. Warmwell.

The Hurricanes of 175 Squadron are today leaving Warmwell Aerodrome which has been their first home since being formed in March. They are off to R.A.F. Harrowbeer, Devon, which opened in August 1941 as a satellite station to R.A.F. Exeter.

Wednesday 14 October

German merchant raider sunk in Channel battle.

Last night a reconnaissance aircraft of Coastal Command, from Calshot, spotted the German auxiliary cruiser Schiff 45 *Komet* attempting to break out from Le Havre, westwards into the Atlantic. She was being escorted by the 3rd Schnellboot Flotilla and German minesweepers.

The Royal Navy proceeded to intercept them with a flotilla of Hunt-class destroyers (H.M.S. *Cottesmore, Esdale, Glassdale, Quorn*) and motor torpedo boats (*MTB55, MTB84, MTB95, MTB229, MTB236*), plus another destroyer, HMS *Albrighton*. The engagement took place five miles north of Cap de la Hague where *Komet* was sunk with the loss of all her crew. She had been hit by two torpedoes fired from *MTB236*.

From Portland a supporting force set sail. This comprised the British destroyers H.M.S. *Brocklesby* and *Tynedale* with the New Zealand destroyer H.M.N.Z.S. *Fernie* and the Polish destroyer *Krakowiak*. They tangled with the German E-boats with *Brocklesby* taking a large number of casualties though she survived the action. In a separate incident the armed trawler H.M.T. *Jasper*, making for Portland from Drover, was sunk by German Schnellboot *S81*.

Saturday 17 October

Fuel shortages stop Royal Blue coaches.

Royal Blue express coach services to London finally ceased operation today, after months of steadily slimmer timetables, as a result of the gravity of the national fuel shortages. Half of the familiar dark-blue fleet is already reserved for manoeuvres and other military uses.

Just a few coaches, however, will still be seen with civilian passengers, as the Ministry of Transport has licensed five services to run seven days a week. They amount to 370 hours of driving time. This concession has been granted because it is accepted that alternative ordinary bus services and rail facilities are less than adequate in many parts of Dorset. These are the surviving Royal Blue routes:

Service 400. Bournemouth — Southampton. Four journeys each way of 88 minutes.

Service 402. Bournemouth — Dorchester — Bridport — Exeter. Two journeys each way of 250 minutes. Re-booking will be necessary at Dorchester as through tickets cannot be issued. The licence for the run specifies two separate stages (Bournemouth — Dorchester and Dorchester — Exeter).

Service 403. Bournemouth — Blandford — Sherborne — Yeovil. One journey each way of 136 minutes.

Service 404. Honiton — Crewkerne — Yeovil — Sherborne — Shaftesbury. One journey each way of 167 minutes.

Service 405. Bournemouth — Blandford — Shaftesbury — Trowbridge. Two journeys each way of 215 minutes.

Footnote: Fuel shortages would continue after the war and the coach express service to London did not resume until 15 April 1946.

Sunday 25 October
Army Co-Operation Squadrons leave Hurn.

The Mustangs of 170 (Army Co-Operation) Squadron and the Whitleys of 297 (Army Co-Operation) Squadron have departed from R.A.F. Hurn for Thruxton on the Hampshire Downs. The other Hurn Whitleys, those of 296 (Army Co-Operation) Squadron, have left for nearby Andover. Hurn is being evacuated so that it can be used as the springboard for a major overseas operation.

Saturday 31 October
Eisenhower and staff fly into Hurn.

Six Boeing B-17 Flying Fortress bombers of the 97th Bombardment Group of the United States Army Air Command touched down at R.A.F. Hurn today with a large contingent of top-ranking American officers. They are led by Lieutenant-General Dwight D. Eisenhower who is the Commander of Allied Forces North-West Africa.

During October
Weymouth's famous aviator killed in Middle East.

The latest casualties in the Middle East include George Stainforth, an old boy of Weymouth College, who rose to fame in 1931 when he took the world air-speed record in Schneider Trophy flights. He pushed his Supermarine S-6B round the Spithead course at an average speed of 340 miles per hour and then raised the world's absolute speed record to 379.05 m.p.h. Other records included flying upside-down for a duration of 11 minutes 7 seconds. He was also the R.A.F. revolver champion.

As a Wing Commander in the Middle East he was the oldest fighter pilot serving in that theatre. He was shot down in night-fighting which he had made his particular forte.

Tuesday 3 November
V.I.P. Fortresses take-off from Hurn for Gibraltar.

Lieutenant-General Dwight D. Eisenhower, the Commander of Allied Forces North-West Africa, has flown out from Hurn today with his staff officers and a British contingent for a conference in Gibraltar to discuss Montgomery's break-out into the Western Desert from El Alamein and the advance towards Algiers. They are aboard five Flying Fortress transports; a sixth had to abort its take-off when the undercarriage hydraulics failed.

The top-brass include General Kenneth Anderson, the Commander of the British 1st Army; Major-General Mark Wayne Clark, the co-ordinator of the secret moves to see whether the Vichy French will defend North Africa; and Brigadier Lyman Lemnitzer. Their transit to

TURNING POINT: THE WAR, FOR THE BRITISH, WOULD GO FROM DEFENCE TO ASSAULT NEAR THE HALT ON THE EGYPTIAN RAILROAD AT EL ALAMEIN, WHERE THE BREAK-OUT INTO THE WESTERN DESERT TOOK PLACE FROM 31 OCTOBER TO 3 NOVEMBER 1942

Gibraltar, off Cape Finisterre and down the coast of Portugal to Cabo de Sao Vicente, is codenamed Operation Cackle.

Footnote: Eisenhower's pilot was Major Paul Tibbets. He would end his and the world's war by flying B-29 *Enola Gay*, named for his mother, in the first operational use of the atomic bomb, on Hiroshima in August 1945.

Wednesday 4 November
Sixth Fortress flies out from Hurn.

Brigadier-General Jimmy Doolittle, the aviator who set the world air-speed record in 1932, flew from Hurn today to Gibraltar aboard the Flying Fortress that experienced wheel-jamming yesterday and was left behind. Doolittle is Commander of United States Air Forces in North Africa.

Troop-carrying American C-47 Dakota transports will also be leaving for Gibraltar via R.A.F. Hurn. The 39 Dakotas of 31 Wing Troop Carrier Group of the 12th United States Army Air Force are currently assembling at Hurn. Their crews are being briefed in connection with the planned landing in North Africa. More aircraft are expected shortly for Allied air Operation Cackle.

Today's news from General Bernard Montgomery, the desert Commander of Britain's 8th Army, that Erwin Rommel's Afrika Korps is in full retreat. The battleground at El Alamein takes its name from a coastal railway halt only 60 miles from Alexandria. Rommel had been poised to attack the Nile delta of Lower Egypt.

HURN VISITORS: BRIGADIER-GENERAL JIMMY DOOLITTLE (left) AND LIEUTENANT-GENERAL DWIGHT D. EISENHOWER, MAKING PLANS AT THE AERODROME, FROM 31 OCTOBER TO 3-4 NOVEMBER 1942

Saturday 7 November
Next Sunday the bells will ring.

National jubilation continues. Hearing that the 8th Army has taken 30,000 prisoners, following the Battle of Alamein, Prime Minister Winston Churchill has told the country to celebrate a week tomorrow by ringing church bells — the first time they have been heard since the outbreak of war. Until now their sound would have warned of German invasion. He said he would like them to have rung this Sunday but there was insufficient time to mobilise decommissioned campanologists.

The prisoners in Egypt include nine generals. Only the rains of the past two days have saved the enemy from utter annihilation.

General Montgomery is to be knighted.

Footnote: There remained a psychological restraint. Rommel's reputation inhibited what should have turned into a British stampede across the desert. The reality was even better than anyone could have predicted, for by now there was nothing that could have stopped them — on 9 November 1942 the Afrika Korps would not only be down to ten fighting tanks but lacked sufficient petrol to field even this number in combat.

Sunday 8 November
Eisenhower takes over North Africa as Dakotas return to Hurn.

A combined British and American force involving a total of 107,000 men has landed across French North Africa at Casablanca, Oran, and Algiers. Operation Torch is under the overall command of Lieutenant-General Dwight D. Eisenhower and has 500 transport craft that are being shepherded by 350 naval vessels.

Back home, rounding off Allied air Operation Cackle, 51 Dakota troop transports returned empty to R.A.F. Hurn, where debriefings have been attended by Major-General Frederick Browning, General Officer Commanding 1st British Airborne Division. A total of 180 transport aircraft passed through Hurn during the build-up for the operation. They included 61 Boeing B-17F Flying Fortress bombers.

Operation Cackle, the Hurn-Gibraltar air ferry service, has been successfully completed without a single casualty.

Friday 13 November
Accused man's wife exhumed at Piddletrenthide.

Following the charging of Frederick Davis with the murder of a fellow Piddletrenthide villager, Louis Stickland, on the night of 16 September, police today exhumed the remains of the accused man's 32-year-old wife. Freda Davis died in August with an illness described as ulcerative colitis.

Her coffin was removed to the County Hospital, Dorchester, where it is to be opened for an autopsy by Sir Bernard Spilsbury, the chief Home Office pathologist. The accused man watched at the graveside as it was lifted and soil samples were taken.

Footnote: Sir Bernard found no evidence of foul play.

Wednesday 25 November
Weymouth Home Guard grenade accident.

Major-General A. A. Dowler of Southern Command reports that during an N.C.O. battle practice by the 5th Dorset (Weymouth) Battalion of the Home Guard a member accidentally burst a No. 76 (S.I.P.) grenade over himself. He would probably have been incinerated but for the prompt action of Q.M.S. W. Marsh and Sergeant W. Andrew in removing his burning clothing.

During November
Cannon-fire is the Creekmoor sound.

Aircraft cannon-fire is now being heard incessantly on the heathland north of Poole, in the vicinity of Fleet's Corner, but the noise comes not from the sky but the ground. The local munitions factory, in Soper's Lane at Creekmoor, makes Oerlikon machine-guns. These are fitted to the latest version of the Spitfire and other fighters.

Production continues around the clock and test-firing has to be carried out every day.

Thursday 3 December
H.M.S. 'Penylan' sunk off Dorset.

The German 5th Schnellboot Flotilla, comprising *S81*, *S82*, *S115* and *S116*, today attacked two British convoys in the English Channel. One was in the area off Bournemouth and the Isle of Wight and the other in the vicinity of Start Point and Lyme Bay. In the latter skirmish a War Programme escort destroyer, 1941-built H.M.S. *Penylan*, was sunk though 115 members of her crew have been rescued. A freighter has also been lost.

Friday 4 December
Barnes Wallis bomb fails to bounce across The Fleet lagoon.

Barnes Neville Wallis, the assistant chief designer at the aviation section of Vickers-Armstrongs Limited, flew today from their Weybridge works in Surrey to the Chesil Beach Bombing Range. He was in Wellington BJ895, code letter 'G' for George — an aeroplane he designed — and acted as the bomb aimer when the firm's Chief Test Pilot, Captain Joseph J. "Mutt" Summers of Spitfire fame, came in low over the flat waters of The Fleet lagoon between the offshore pebble bank and the inshore coast of Langton Herring and Abbotsbury.

Captain R. C. Handasyde acted as the observer. Two steel spheres were dropped, with the hope that they might bounce along the surface of the water, but both burst upon impact. Neither carried explosives.

Thursday 10 December
Poole port gets a Seamen's Mission.

Admiral Sir Reginald Aylmer Ranfurly Plunkett-Ernle-Erle-Drax of Charborough Park, who fought in H.M.S. *Lion* at the Battle of Jutland and headed the diplomatic mission to Moscow in 1939, today opened a Mission to Seamen at Poole. It is based in the Mansion House in Thames Street. It is a mark of

Hurn planned: Eisenhower's landings in Morocco, on 8 November 1942

Poole's restored status as a port that it should be provided with a Seamen's Mission.

Sunday 13 December
Cruel sea engulfs a hundred Portland homes.

Shortly after 11.00 hours this morning the sea started to seep through the pebbles of the Chesil Beach at Portland. By noon the first waves were splashing over the top. Initially a shallow layer of water spread across Victoria Square but it soon surged to a depth of over five feet. The postbox was almost totally covered and the mail floated out on the tide.

More than 100 homes in Chiswell were inundated as both the rail and road links between Portland and the mainland were dislocated. The stout stone wall beside the beach road has been reduced to rubble at many points and the railway embankment breached for several yards. Sleepers were swept away and the rails buckled.

The water also put the island's Gas Works out of action. A slimy trail of mud, clay, shingle and boulders lie across the low-lying parts of Chiswell. Many of those rendered homeless have been told that their ruined cottages will have to be demolished.

Portland branch of the Women's Voluntary Service were soon in action with hot dinners, bedding and clothes — at least help comes fast when there is a war on — and by this evening the extensive damage caused by chest-deep water to the Cove House Inn had been cleared sufficiently for it to open punctually at seven o'clock.

England's motto is business as usual. In Portland that defiance has been extended to an older enemy — the sea.

Monday 14 December
Welder killed as Tank Workshop is strafed at Lulworth.

The Workshop of the Gunnery Wing of the Armoured Fighting Vehicles School at Lulworth Camp was devastated today in a surprise attack by two German fighter-bombers. The first one passed over the camp without incident but the second dropped a 1,800-kilogram high explosive bomb. It landed at the road junction at the edge of the camp. Though it embedded itself in the concrete, leaving several feet of casing and fins standing in the air, it failed to explode.

Then the second aircraft returned low across the camp and raked the Workshop with 20-mm cannon fire. The welder, Sergeant Jack Stevens, was fatally wounded in the head, and three other soldiers were injured. The building is an utter shambles.

The aircraft had come from the east, across the Tank Park, and then turned south-west, disappearing over Lulworth and out to sea.

Tuesday 15 December
Second bouncing-bomb test is also a failure.

Wellington BJ895 put down at Warmwell Aerodrome en route for further testings of a bouncing-bomb designed by scientist Barnes Wallis of Vickers-Armstrongs. As with the first test, on 4 December, both drops failed.

It was decided to try again after Christmas.

Wednesday 16 December
Lunchtime bombs kill four at Poole.

A Dornier Do.217 bomber swept low over Poole Quay at lunchtime today and dropped a stick of five bombs. They have fatally injured 14-year-old William Matthews and a member of the Home Guard, George Davis, who was working at Poole Iron Foundry in Thames Street.

There were casualties from other blasts, at the Gas Works, in Barbers Piles, and at Newman's Shipyard. A worker died as a result of the latter blast.

The fifth explosion sank a Royal Navy harbour patrol vessel, at its mooring, and killed the only rating aboard.

Thursday 17 December
Airman's prophetic farewell to Came Wood.

Sergeant-Pilot Marcel Fussell of Monmouth Road, Dorchester, has been killed in action. Shortly before he died he wrote about Came Wood — autobiographical, though presented in the third person — prophetically appreciating Winterborne Came "for the last time, for tomorrow he was to leave his native life, his home, the fields and woods, where he had spent his life as a boy . . . to join the Air Force and serve his country."

At the top of the paper he had written one word: "Farewell."

Monday 21 December
French gunboat sinks off Swanage.

The sea was the villain today in its age-old war against those who take it for granted. The Free French Navy's gunboat *Chasseur* underestimated the tide-flow and rough waters off Durlston Head, Swanage, and sank after capsizing.

Friday 25 December
Bells are enjoyed once again.

First to celebrate the Battle of El Alamein, and now for their traditional purpose this Christmas Day, we have been treated to a rare sound. The bells of Christchurch Priory were put through their paces. It is an unusual and joyful treat, not that their silence over the past three years has been in any way unwelcome — had they tolled, it would have been to warn of German invasion.

Thursday 31 December
Poole machine-gunner brings down a Dornier.

New Year's Day at Poole belongs to Sergeant William Hanbury who was manning a waterside searchlight post. He illuminated a Dornier Do.217 bomber as it came at low level across the sea and sprayed it with his Lewis machine-gun. The pilot veered away but struck a gasometer and lost control and crashed into Poole Harbour.

Another raider was more successful. Its bomb destroyed Bradford's store on Poole Quay which had just been completely rebuilt after being hit on Whit Sunday.

During December
Piddletrenthide baker acquitted of murder.

Summing up at the trial for murder of Piddletrenthide baker Frederick Davis, Mr Justice MacNaughton said that in his opinion there was a matter of real doubt for the jury to consider; he put it to them that the defendant's story might be true.

Frederick Davis maintained that he had been at home with Louis Stickland at the Golden Grain Bakery, examining a loaded gun, which misfired and discharged a single shot into Stickland's chest: "When I found I had killed my best friend I was frightened. I was afraid of being found in the house with a dead man. On the impulse of the moment I moved the body."

After being out for only 45 minutes the jury returned to the Assize Court at Winchester with their verdict: "Not guilty."

During December
Swordfish fly from Hurn to search for E-boats.

Torpedo-carrying Swordfish biplanes of 811 and 816 (Fleet Air Arm) Squadrons, from Thorney Island Royal Naval Air Station, have been flying from R.A.F. Hurn to widen their patrols against German E-boats. Six aircraft are taking part in this attempt to counter the growing menace from these fast attack vessels.

Hurn has also hosted the Halifax bombers of 138 and 161 (Special Duty) Squadrons, usually based at R.A.F. Tempsford, Bedfordshire, which runs flights deep into occupied Europe for the Special Operations Executive.

The Mustangs of 239 Squadron arrived from R.A.F. Odiham, Hampshire, on 7 December; one of the fighters was involved in a collision with a Lancaster bomber.

1498 Gunnery Flight was formed at Hurn on 10 December. Its Lysander and Martinet light aircraft will provide realistic bursts of air-firing to accompany glider-towing exercises.

Ventura and Boston light bombers visited Hurn on 11 December to provide the smoke-screen for a practice landing in Studland Bay.

Later that day, the twin-engined Whitleys of 297 (Army Co-Operation) Squadron returned from Andover with almost all their personnel and equipment following in tow, in seven Horsa gliders. They had been ousted from Hurn to provide space for the massive movements in Operation Cackle.

During December
No. 5 Commando are based in Boscombe.

Back from Madagascar, which they helped to recapture on behalf of Free French Forces, the men of No. 5 Commando, Combined Operations, are being billeted in Boscombe and Bournemouth. Their base is at Broughty Ferry Hotel in Boscombe.

Footnote: They would be amalgamated with No. 1 Commando, and 42 Company and 43 Company of the Royal Marines, to form the 3rd Special Services Brigade.

During December
Spies for France fly from Christchurch.

Christchurch Aerodrome has been used by the Westland Lysanders of the Special Operations Executive for several cross-Channel missions. They have been landing and recovering agents in occupied France.

WARTIME FILM: THE BRITISH PROPAGANDA MOVIE VICTORY WAS SHOT ON HEATHLAND AROUND BOVINGTON CAMP IN 1942, USING VETERAN TANKS FROM THE GREAT WAR

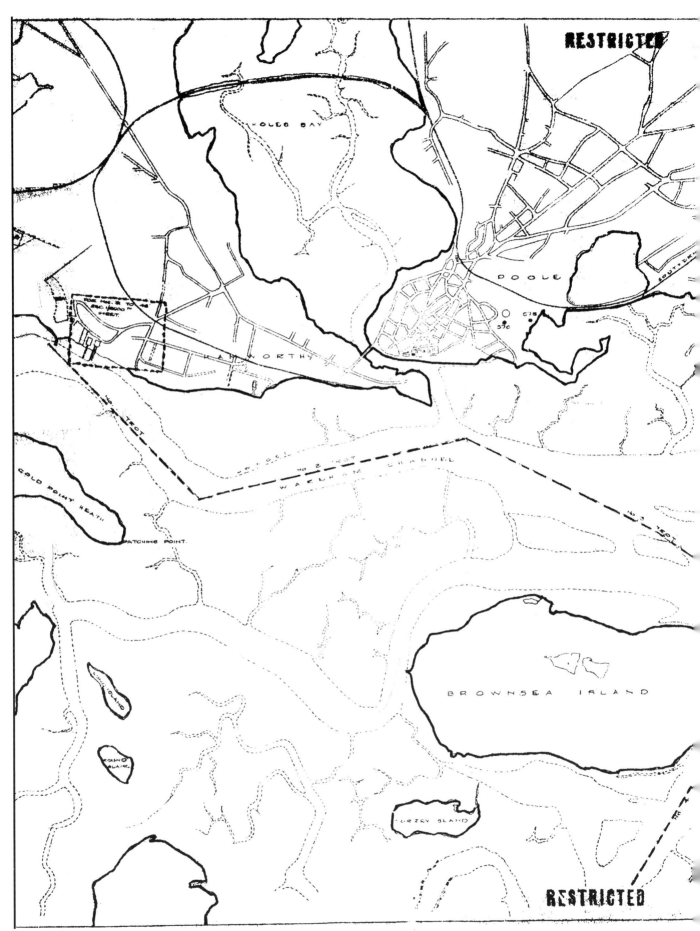

POOLE HARBOUR: THE FLYING-BOAT 'TROTS'. THESE ARE THE STRAIGHT PECKED LINES ACROSS THE CENTRE OF THE MAP. THEY ARE THE
WATER-RUNWAYS USED BY R.A.F. COASTAL COMMAND AND BRITISH OVERSEAS AIRWAYS CORPORATION FLYING-BOATS IN LANDING AND
TAKING OFF. NO. 1 TROT IS OFF THE LAKE AREA OF HAMWORTHY; NO. 2 TROT IS OFF LOWER HAMWORTHY; NO. 3 TROT OFF PARKSTONE
BAY AND LILLIPUT; NO. 4 TROT BETWEEN BROWNSEA ISLAND AND THE SANDBANKS PENINSULA

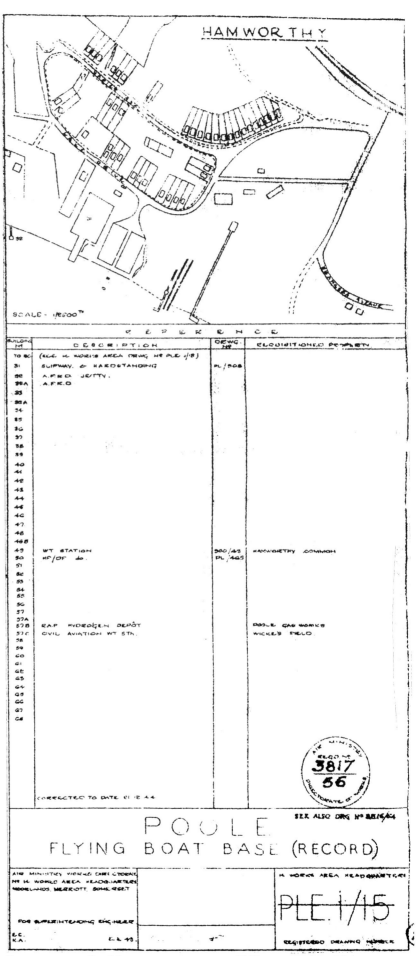

BASE MAP: FROM AIR MINISTRY RECORDS, DATED 1942, SHOWING (top right) – AND INSIDE A RECTANGLE ON THE MAIN MAP – THE SLIPWAY, JETTY AND HARDSTANDING THAT COMPRISE R.A.F. HAMWORTHY

CHANNEL SHIPPING: IN THE EARLY YEARS OF THE WAR THIS BLENHEIM BOMBER WOULD HAVE BEEN WITNESSING YET ANOTHER BRITISH LOSS, WITH LUFTWAFFE DIVE-BOMBERS OPERATING FROM THE CHERBOURG PENINSULA

1943

Saturday 9 January
Third bouncing-bomb test also a disappointment.

Two more steel spheres were dropped today by Wellington BJ895, from the Vickers-Armstrongs works at Weybridge, on the Chesil Beach Bombing Range. The tests were once again a failure. The aim of aircraft designer Barnes Wallis is to devise a bomb that can bounce across water and have a dam-breaking capability.

So far, of the six dummy bombs that have been dropped, five have fragmented on touching The Fleet lagoon and the other was incorrectly released and hit the land.

Sunday 10 January
At last, Barnes Wallis bounces his bomb!

Vickers-Armstrongs scientist Barnes Wallis last night carried out modifications to one of his prototype bouncing-bombs at Warmwell Aerodrome. The aviation firm's Chief Test Pilot, Captain Joseph J. "Mutt" Summers then took it in Wellington BJ895, heading south-westwards for their fourth low-level drop over The Fleet beside the Chesil Beach Bombing Range, on the coast at Langton Herring.

The boffin and his team are jubilant. For the first time their dummy bomb, which had been strengthened, skimmed the lake-like surface of the lagoon. It spun for 50 feet and then shattered. Despite that, the principle had been proved: "It works!"

Wednesday 13 January
Dorchester anxiety at ploughing of public paths.

The Rights of Way Committee of Dorchester Rural District Council has expressed anxiety that public paths are being lost in the emergency ploughing of grasslands for grain production. "With regard to the temporary ploughing up and diversion of rights of way consequent upon the service of directions under the Cultivation of Lands Order, the committee were extremely anxious that, during hostilities, the existence of rights of way should not be lost, and their chief anxiety was lest at the cessation of hostilities the formerly existing rights be not restored to the public."

Friday 15 January
H.M.S. 'Dorsetshire' appeal tops £3 million.

Dorset's county savings campaign, through the War Loan scheme, to raise enough money to buy the Royal Navy a cruiser to replace H.M.S. *Dorsetshire* is well ahead of its original £2,750,000. This has been exceeded by £307,703 and stands at £3,057,703.

Monday 18 January
Lindbergh Road has to go.

Lindbergh Road, a short street a stone's throw from Castle Lane in the suburb of Moordown, Bournemouth, is having its name changed. This was chosen originally as a tribute to the pioneer aviator Colonel Charles Augustus Lindbergh whose *Spirit of St Louis* had just made the first solo non-stop crossing of the Atlantic in 1927.

Now, however, the memory has soured, with Lindbergh expressing pro-Nazi sentiments. Bournemouth town councillors have therefore decided to re-name it Franklin Road — honouring the United States President, Franklin Delano Roosevelt.

Saturday 23 January
Barnes Wallis bomb bounces 13 times.

Wellington BJ895 today dropped a wooden version of the bouncing-bomb devised by Vickers-Armstrongs designer Barnes Wallis. It achieved 13 bounces on the inshore lagoon of The Fleet to the east of Langton Hive Point, Langton Herring, on the landward side of the R.A.F.'s Chesil Beach Bombing Range.

Sunday 24 January
Bouncing-bomb jumps a boom at Langton Herring.

Twenty bounces were recorded this morning by scientist Barnes Wallis as his revolutionary bomb zipped across The Fleet lagoon at Langton Herring. Once again it had been dropped by Wellington bomber BJ895 which then flew back to Warmwell Aerodrome.

The ground support team from the Vickers-Armstrongs works at Weybridge then prepared a boom across the shallow waters. This is intended to simulate the wall of a dam.

The evening saw another successful trial when the Wellington returned to the Chesil Beach Bombing Range. It again turned over the sea and came in across the lake-like waters of The Fleet. The bomb was dropped, and bounced, and proceeded to jump the boom.

Sunday 24 January
Halifax bomber crashes at Kingston Lacy.

A four-engined Halifax bomber from R.A.F. Holmsley South, on Plain Heath at the south-west edge of the New Forest, faltered today shortly after take-off at 13.30 hours. It made two circuits of the aerodrome and was 15 minutes into a transit flight to Talbenny, Haverfordwest, when it lost height over Wimborne and descended towards parkland beyond the town.

Bomber DT684, belonging to 58 Squadron, crashed 200 yards north-north-east of Kingston Lacy House. All the crew were killed and a terrified stag jumped through one of the ground floor windows of the elegant country house which is the seat of Ralph Bankes.

The dead are Flying Officer M. A. Legg of the Royal New Zealand Air Force (aged 32); Flying Officer G. R. Pringle, an air observer of the Royal Canadian Air Force (aged 29); Warrant Officer L. E. Gilpin of the R.C.A.F. (aged 21); and Warrant Officer S. J. Prince of the R.C.A.F. (aged 25). The latter two officers were wireless operators and gunners.

BOUNCING BOMB: THE MOVIE VERSION OF BARNES WALLIS WATCHING FILM FOOTAGE OF HIS SPHERICAL DEVICE BEING DROPPED FROM A WELLINGTON OVER THE FLEET

DAMBUSTING BOMB: ACTUALITY, BEING DROPPED FROM THE WELLINGTON, OVER THE FLEET LAGOON, WITH THE CHESIL BEACH VISIBLE IN THE BACKGROUND WITH WATER EITHER SIDE IN JANUARY 1943. LINES ON THE BEACH IDENTIFY THE SPOT AS BEING OFF LANGTON HIVE POINT

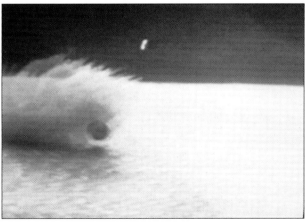

IT BOUNCES: THE PROTOTYPE BOMB FOR ATTACKING THE RUHR DAMS IS PROVED TO WORK, ACROSS THE FLAT WATERS OF THE FLEET IN JANUARY 1943

Footnote: The four Dominion airmen are buried in Bransgore churchyard, Hampshire, a mile from the now disused Plain Heath Airfield.

Sunday 31 January

H2S works — thanks to Langton, Christchurch, Hurn and West Howe.

Bomber Command last night used H2S airborne radar sets, operationally, for the first time. They were deployed in a raid over Hamburg and enabled Pathfinder flares to be dropped on their target. The need for this apparatus has been apparent since of the night of 9 March 1942 when Bomber Command, in its Chief's words, "attacked Hamborn in mistake for Essen". Sir Arthur Harris, Commander-in-Chief Bomber Command, has enthusiastically backed the development of H2S — promised for last autumn — which takes its name from the chemical formula for the obnoxious gas hydrogen sulphide, because Churchill's chief scientific adviser, Professor Frederick Lindemann, hearing of it from the Telecommunication Research Establishment said: "It stinks that we haven't thought of it before!"

The invention was the product of Group 8, working from a Nissen hut in the grounds of the Establishment's eastern out-station, Leeson House, at Langton Matravers.

"TF" was its earlier code but this was reckoned to be a give-away [try for yourself; the answer is in the footnote] and it came into being after J. T. Randall and H. A. H. Boot invented the centrimetric cavity magnetron which was put into the new Beaufighter. Giving power on a short wavelength it provided an image on a screen that showed features of the ground below. This was initially tested by a Blenheim bomber at 8,000 feet above the Air Defence Establishment beside Christchurch Aerodrome.

Six more flights were made and then Halifax bomber V9977 was drafted to the new aerodrome at R.A.F. Hurn for fitting with the first specially designed unit shielded in a cupola protruding from the belly which made the aeroplane seem ungainly and pregnant. The casing is Perspex. V9977 would be lost, along with the inventor of Airborne Interception radar, 38-year-old Alan Blumlein, in a test flight from R.A.F. Defford on 7 June 1942.

Air Commodore Donald "Pathfinder" Bennett tried the apparatus with the result that Winston Churchill agreed it should be in production by the end of 1942. The Prototype Research Unit is making the sets — which have been perfected by Philip Gee and Bernard Lovell at Worth Matravers — in a factory beside Northbourne Golf Links at West Howe, Bournemouth.

Footnote: "TF" stood for "Town Finder". The factory at West Howe that produced H2S went on to make real smells for Max Factor cosmetics.

In practice, H2S was to create its own disaster, as the Germans realised that not only could it be jammed but that advanced technology would enable exploitation of

WAR RELIC: WHEEL-LIKE SPHERE OF ONE OF BARNES WALLIS'S STEEL AND CONCRETE BOUNCING BOMBS, SUBSEQUENTLY SERVING AS A MOORING AT LANGTON HIVE POINT, LANGTON HERRING

the signals. Luftwaffe fighters began to find their targets by homing in upon waveforms radiating from the bombers. This again accelerated the rate of losses. On 30 March 1944 a total of 94 British bombers were shot down in a night raid on Nuremberg and of those that made it home 71 were damaged.

During January
B.O.A.C.'s land-based operations now at Hurn.

Hurn Aerodrome has become a multi-tasked military and civilian airfield with the transfer of British Overseas Airways Corporation's dry-land flights — as distinct from the Poole flying-boats — from Lyneham in Wiltshire.

During January
Spitfire pilot rescued from Poole Bay.

The Poole Air-Sea Rescue launch *Commodore* picked-up a Spitfire pilot who fighter ditched in Poole Bay.

Friday 5 February
Bombs bounce 4,000 feet across The Fleet.

The trials of wooden prototypes of Barnes Wallis's bouncing-bomb resumed on The Fleet today. They were dropped from Wellington BJ895, coming from Weybridge and operating for the day out of Warmwell Aerodrome. The bomber is now making faster approach runs.

It swept in across the Chesil Beach Bombing Range at 300 miles per hour and succeeded in sending bombs jumping across the sheltered and wave-less inshore water for distances in the region of 4,000 feet.

Thursday 11 February
Blandford Camp Commandant dies in raid.

The Commandant of the Battle Training Camp at Blandford, Brigadier Harold Woodhouse of the local brewing firm, has died from a heart attack induced by the exertion and stress caused by a stick of German bombs. A single bomber attacked the camp. The only blast damage was to one of the cookhouses.

HEART ATTACK: THE CAUSE OF DEATH FOR BRIGADIER HAROLD WOODHOUSE DURING AN AIR-RAID ON BLANDFORD CAMP, 11 FEBRUARY 1943

NOT TO BE PUBLISHED

"The Advance Post"

Published by the British Army in the Field

No. 1   1 MARCH, 1943   Free Issue

ON TO EASTLAND!

OUR ADVANCE CONTINUED

Enemy Infiltration from the North?

Waiting for Zero Hour

The following official communique was issued at Headquarters of the British Expeditionary Force in SOUTHLAND to-day:

Operations by the British Expeditionary Force in SOUTHLAND are proceeding according to plan.

During the past few days there has been increased air activity on the EASTLAND border.

On the 24th February our fighters and fighter-bombers attacked enemy M.T. and troops approaching the frontier. Considerable enemy fighter opposition was encountered. Successful reconnaissance flights have been made over enemy territory.

From these operations one of our aircraft is missing.

The civilian population of SOUTHLAND continues friendly and co-operative, and our forces are received with acclamation wherever they go.

HERE is the story of the Exercise on which we are engaged.

In theory the island of GREAT BRITAIN is

(Continued overleaf)

A NAME TO LIVE UP TO

SPARTAN   1943

We are all about to take part in an exercise which will be a test of endurance. It will need the most strenuous efforts from everybody to make it a success.

The name of the Exercise has been carefully chosen. It is "SPARTAN": a name to live up to. In ancient Greece, the battle of Thermopylae, was a heroic and successful defence by 4,000 fighting Spartans against ten times as many Persians.

We are not on the defensive; we are passing to attack, but if we carry the Spartan determination in defence into attack, then the battle will be won.

We are all well trained men, hardened and fit; so let us go forward into "Exercise Spartan" so that the lessons we learn will help us to take our places at the side of our fighting comrades elsewhere.

Finally, in words which echoed through the Eighth Army before El Alamein. . . . ." there will be no belly-aching. And to these we add. . ."BE A SPARTAN."

R.A.F. OVER EASTLAND AGAIN

BRING BACK VITAL INFORMATION FOR ARMY

GROUND AND AIR TARGETS SUCCESSFULLY ATTACKED

THE Royal Air Force will be playing its part in full in co-operation with the Army throughout this Exercise. There will be fighters, bombers and reconnaissance aircraft constantly in the air by day and by night.

Already many "Spartan Sorties" have been made by our own aircraft, flown by young veterans of many a battle over this country and enemy territory. The Spartans of old have taken wings, and the same Spartan endurance which will be shown on the ground will also be in evidence in the air.

The R.A.F. has taken every advantage of good weather to make reconnaissance reports and follow the movements of the enemy, and also to hamper his motor transport and troop convoys.

Surveys have been made deep into the enemy lines despite the determined opposition of his fighter aircraft, and the only deterrent to the work of the flying men has been fog on the Eastland frontier and further into enemy territory.

Reconnaissance pilots have been able to bring back valuable information, and some of them have seen repeated signs of friendliness on the part of the civilian population, workers in the fields waving to them as they flew over northern Southland on their way to Eastland.

The enemy has shown his concern about our inquisitiveness by sending up strong formations of fighters to try to intercept our aircraft. On the afternoon of 24 February our fighters and fighter-bombers, strafing enemy troops as they moved towards the frontier, encountered more than 50 fighters.

THE AIRCRAFT IN THE BATTLE

THE value of air support and cover in present-day warfare cannot be over-estimated. This has been proved time and time again and the lessons learned in those earlier encounters, both offensive and defensive, will prove invaluable in this exercise.

Immediate recognition of our own and enemy aircraft is vital. Our own fighters, fighter-bombers and reconnaissance aircraft will carry NO special markings, and our light bombers will be Bostons.

The enemy fighters, fighter-bombers and reconnaissance craft will have the under side of the port wing treated with black wash, while his light bombers will be largely Venturas with possibly a few Mitchells in addition.

Throughout the exercise all aircraft will be acting in a realistic manner, flying at operational heights and speeds, and you will have no difficulty in knowing by their actions whether or not you are coming under fire.

Light bombers when attacking from high or medium levels will fire Verey lights, and when bombing from low levels will come in with their bomb doors open.

Fighters will give no visible notification of attack, but their markings will be clearly distinguishable when flying low, and the action of the aircraft themselves will indicate when an actual attack against a ground target is being carried out.

Remember, when an air attack develops, it takes place and is over, all in a matter of seconds, so keep on the alert.

SPARTAN'S NEWSPAPER

Army field newspapers are not unknown, but "THE ADVANCE POST" is the first daily newspaper of its kind to be printed specially for the purpose of a military exercise in this country.

Written and produced by a staff of soldier-journalists—some of them not undistinguished in their peace-time professions—its aims are:—

1. To put you in the picture and keep you there, day by day, as the "battle" develops.

2. To increase and widen the range of your outlook on the scheme.

3. To try to simplify your own particular job by giving you what we hope will be useful tips on what you should or should not do.

Our readers may note a certain unusual character about "THE ADVANCE POST." This arises from the unusual composition of the Southland Force itself—we have troops from the United Kingdom and from Canada, and the latter of course include French-Canadians. All three sections go to make up our reading "public"; our staff, and the appeal of their work, are designed accordingly.

Where We Stand To-day—March 1st

(Shaded part is territory already occupied by British).

WORLD WAR NEWS

TUNIS.—German retreat from Kasserine continues. Enemy landing grounds strafed by fighter-bombers. Enemy counter-attacks beaten off; 850 prisoners taken.

RUSSIA.—German counter-attacks in Western Donetz basin driven off with loss of 30 tanks.

AT HOME.—No enemy air activity over this country in daylight.

R.A.F.—Air offensive over France and Holland continues. Mines laid in enemy waters.

FAR EAST.—Japanese transport and corvette bombed by U.S. planes and left blazing.

U.S.A.—New aircraft carrier and four destroyers launched.

EXERCISE SPARTAN: MARKING THE CHANGE FROM DEFENSIVE TO OFFENSIVE WAR WITH THE APPEARANCE OF THE "FIRST DAILY NEWSPAPER OF ITS KIND TO BE PRINTED SPECIALLY FOR THE PURPOSES OF A MILITARY EXERCISE IN THIS COUNTRY". SALISBURY FALLS TO THE ATTACKERS IN MARCH 1943. PARTICIPANTS ARE CAUTIONED TO KEEP OUT OF PUBLIC HOUSES AND AWAY FROM R.A.F. WIRELESS STATIONS, IN CASE THIS INTERFERES WITH RADAR RECEPTION AND THE REAL WAR

No.1.   The BULLDOG.   No.1.

THIS CONCERNS YOU!
No Visits To 'The Local' During Spartan.

You'll probably think this really is a spartan war, but during the period of the exercise you are strictly forbidden to make any purchase outside home stations at shops, canteens (including mobile canteens), hotels and public houses.

There are several very good reasons for this order. One of them is that the exercise must be made as realistic as possible and there would be very little to buy in the shops of an invaded country.

Reason number 2 : One of the objects of the exercise is to test the supply arrangements in an overseas operation; and the third reason, and one which all will admit is fair and reasonable, is that local inhabitants will suffer hardship if the limited supplies in the shops are all bought up by troops taking part in the exercise.

This order applies to all ranks and will be strictly enforced.

Cigarettes and tobacco will be available but you will have to control your thirst until you have disposed of the enemy.

NO LEAVE DURING SPARTAN.

Privilege will not be granted during the period of the exercise, but all personnel due to begin leave during the exercise will be granted privilege leave on its termination.

It has also been decided that a maximum of 3% instead of the normal 1½% of unit personnel may be sent on leave after the exercise until all personnel whose leave was postponed have been despatched. The usual regulation will apply - no travelling on Saturday or Sunday.

BRITISH ARMY IN SOUTHLAND
(Continued from Page 1. Col.1.)

This they did shortly after the fall of their capital, Salisbury.

Since the fall of Salisbury, the invading force has made rapid headway. The shaded portion on the map shows the areas now occupied by the British. The interstate boundaries between Eastland and Westland and Southland are also shown.

It is learned in reliable diplomatic circles that Westland's government has declared her intention of remaining neutral and is prepared to defend her neutrality against any aggressor.

A large scale battle is undoubtedly imminent.

B.B.C. NEWS SUMMARY

There is no official news from Central and Northern Tunisia to-day (1300 hrs Sunday).

In the South the 8th Army is continuing its probing of the Mareth Defences.

The Russians are still meeting strong German counter-attacks at the Western end of the Donetz Basin.

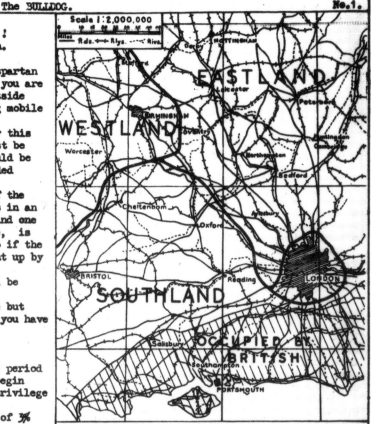

SITUATION MAP. For security reasons it is not possible to indicate the actual locations on this map, which will be published daily, but it will show the general situation and will assist you to follow the progress of the battle.

YOU CAN'T FIGHT WITHOUT FOOD.
(Continued from Page 1. Col. 1.)

All vehicles, especially armoured fighting vehicles, should avoid operating, or coming to rest within 400 yards of R.A.F. wireless stations. The R.A.F., you know, will probably be engaged with the real enemy and we want to avoid interfering with their functional efficiency.

With regard to digging and wiring, the orders are that the digging of weapon slits, gun-pits etc. and the erection of wire obstacles will be carried out at all times as in actual battle. Where the ground and tactical siting permit, digging should take place, if possible, along the line of hedges and fences.

All units should take full advantage of the facilities provided, and these special arrangements will add greatly to the realism and training value of the exercise, but the army must demonstrate that it is possible to apply sound common sense to the use of land under these conditions without abusing the facilities provided.

Aircraft of Bomber Command laid mines in enemy waters and bombed objectives in Western Germany.

The Prime Minister has sent a message of good wishes to the Wings for Victory Campaign.

Sunday 28 February

Germans sink four ships off Dorset.

In the past four days the 3rd Schnellboot Flotilla has been harrying a Channel convoy in Lyme Bay and onwards between Portland and the Isle of Wight. Two of the escorts protecting Convoy CHA172 have been sunk. These were the armed trawlers H.M.T. *Harstad* and H.M.T. *Lord Hailsham*.

The 4,858-ton freighter *Modavia* has also gone down, together with a new 658-ton tank landing craft, LCT381.

During February

Evelyn Waugh oversees Special Services at Canford.

Rifle-range shooting by the 2nd Special Services Brigade is being carried out on Canford Heath. It is being overseen by the author Evelyn Waugh who last year published *Put Out More Flags*. He is Staff Officer to Acting Admiral Louis Mountbatten, Commander of Combined Operations, which has its country house headquarters at Anderson Manor, near Bere Regis.

The brigade is also training with landing craft in assaults on Brownsea Island and Shell Bay and Studland beach. These have now been cleared of their anti-invasion scaffolding and mines.

During February

Dornier bomber shot down at Beaminster.

A Dornier Do.17 bomber, shot down at night over South Buckham Farm, Beaminster, has been claimed by Wing Commander Rupert Clarke, flying a Beaufighter of 125 (Newfoundland) Squadron from R.A.F. Fairwood Common, Glamorgan.

During February

Five rescued from bomber off Hengistbury Head.

The five-man crew of a R.A.F. Whitley bomber were plucked from the eastern side of Poole Bay, four miles south of Hengistbury Head, after they had crashed into the sea. The rescue was carried out by the Poole Air-Sea Rescue launch *Commodore*.

Monday 1 March

Cattistock man jumped out of a safe job.

Sergeant-Navigator Robert Paull of Cattistock has been reported missing after a bombing raid. He previously had a safe reserved occupation as an inspector of "Predictor" work in an aircraft factory but insisted upon volunteering for the Royal Air Force.

Monday 1 March

'The Advance Post' on the Wessex front-line.

Such is the growing sophistication of this Second World War that the present major military game, Exercise Spartan, has been marked by the appearance of the "first daily newspaper of its kind to be printed specially for the purpose of a military exercise in this country".

The hypothetical cause had been the invasion of southern England by the British Expeditionary Force. But for southern England one should read northern France for the war is moving ahead. "On to Eastland," as the headline puts it. "We are not on the defensive; we are passing to attack, but if we carry the Spartan determination into attack, then the battle will be won."

This unusual newspaper is "Not to be published". There is a reminder that those taking part in the exercise must leave R.A.F. radar stations in peace so that they can carry on with the real war: "All vehicles, especially armoured fighting vehicles, should avoid operating, or coming to rest within 400 yards of R.A.F. wireless stations. The R.A.F., you know, will probably be engaged with the real enemy and we want to avoid interfering with their functional efficiency."

Monday 8 March

Navy lands rescued Germans at Mudeford.

E-boats failed to ambush a coastal convoy off Devon and escaped eastwards pursued by the Polish destroyer *Krakowiak* until she had to pull into Poole to refuel. Six-inch coast defence batteries then opened up from Brownsea Island, Hengistbury Head, and Mudeford, aided by 3.7-inch dual anti-air and anti-ship emplacements and the 40-mm Bofors anti-aircraft guns along the Bournemouth cliffs.

There were German losses in Poole Bay. Two bodies and four survivors have been brought to Mudeford Quay by the picket-boat *Robert T. Hillary*. This former lifeboat is crewed by the Royal Navy Volunteer Reserve.

Tuesday 9 March

Bouncing-bombs upset the Abbotsbury swans.

Carrying concrete-filled full weight versions of the prototype bouncing-bomb devised for dam-busting operations by designer Barnes Wallis of Vickers-Armstrongs, Wellington BJ895 returned yesterday to Warmwell Aerodrome and the Chesil Beach Bombing Range. An extended series of trial runs has taken place over The Fleet lagoon. Dummy bombs have been skimming the water with the precision that suggests their use as an effective weapon may now be feasible.

These trials concluded this evening. Locally, there have been complaints that the Wellington's approach flight — at 300 miles per hour over the West Fleet towards Langton Hive Point and the uninhabited Herbury peninsula — has been upsetting mating and nest-building at the famous Abbotsbury Swannery.

Footnote: The next full set of tests, to determine the handling behaviour of the bomb on choppier water, would take place off Reculver, Kent. One or two of those deposited off the beach at Langton Herring would come in useful as boat moorings.

Thursday 18 March
Hanging parachutist killed in Poole Harbour.

A Royal Artillery officer today fouled his parachute on the airframe of a Dakota in a jump that went tragically wrong. He found himself hanging from the aircraft, which was from R.A.F. Broadwell, and the pilot headed for the South Coast and the nearest area of calm sea.

He chose Poole Harbour and circled at 1,000 feet over the Wareham Channel before coming in low, to within 50 feet of the harbour, at which point the soldier dropped off. It was to no avail as the gunner died upon impact with the water.

Sunday 21 March
Australian Sunderland wrecked in Poole Harbour.

Sunderland flying-boat T9111 of 461 (Royal Australian Air Force) Squadron was wrecked at 20.55 hours today off R.A.F. Hamworthy. The pilot, Flight-Lieutenant Manger, had begun lifting off from the "Trots" — as the sea runways are called — when he found himself losing power.

The flying-boat careered into the mud-flats of Poole Harbour and is a total loss but the pilot and his eleven crewmen were able to clamber free and stagger to the shore. They have only superficial injuries.

Tuesday 23 March
Three die as a B.O.A.C. Catalina is wrecked in Poole Harbour.

Having successfully returned to Poole Harbour on the last leg of a trip from Lagos, Nigeria, B.O.A.C. Catalina flying-boat DA took off again for a training flight.

Everything was routine until her second homecoming of the day. This time, however, it turned into a disaster. For the second time in the week a flying-boat has been lost in landing though the circumstances are quite different. The Catalina ploughed into a dense raft of flotsam and crumpled into a mass of wreckage with the loss of three crewmen.

Tuesday 30 March
1st Dorsets leave Malta.

The siege of Malta has been lifted and the 1st Battalion of the Dorsetshire Regiment today sailed for Egypt. It is part of the 1st Malta Brigade which is to be renamed the 231st Infantry Brigade.

Footnote: They would be welcomed at Fayid by General Sir Bernard Montgomery. "This morning I have seen some magnificent soldiers," he said. "These fine Regular battalions who have been shut up in Malta, and have now joined us, will be an asset to the 8th Army."

During March
Hurricane comes down off Green Island.

A Hurricane has crashed off Green Island into Poole Harbour. Its pilot was picked-up by the Air-Sea Rescue launch *Commodore*.

During March
Rabbits replace cage and aviary birds.

Children visiting the aviaries in the Pleasure Gardens at Bournemouth can now watch the rabbits. For gone are most of the exotic birds of the jungle for which these cages used to be renowned. Parks department staff are supplying bunnies to British Restaurants in the town though so far supplies have not been sufficient to put rabbit pie on the menu.

Likewise, throughout the suburbs, animal husbandry is taking over where the tedium of spade-work caused relapses into boredom for those who only reluctantly responded to C. H. Middleton's "Dig for Victory" exhortations in his famous wireless broadcasts. Chicken and even the occasional pig now root around beneath rabbit hutches.

From cock-crow onwards Bournemouth resonates with sounds of the farmyard. There is also a revival of the Victorian allotment movement. Gardeners have taken over open spaces and potential building sites and here, at least, Mr Middleton's words are heeded: "These are critical times, but we shall get through them, and the harder we dig for victory the sooner will the roses be with us again."

Thursday 1 April
'Sweets removed from rationing' — April fool!

Tiring of the usual pranks, such as swapping over householders' gates and front-door mats, some Bournemouth-bound schoolboys played a more contemporary wheeze on their mates this All Fools Day.

They spread the rumour around the bus that sweets and chocolates had been removed the food ration and would no longer require coupons. "I bet dozens of chaps will run into the shops," said the joker. He was proved correct.

Saturday 17 April
Poole Catalinas leave for Trincomalee.

Repainted with the white and blue roundels of the South-East Asia theatre, two B.O.A.C. Catalina flying-boats are en route from Poole Harbour to Trincomalee, Ceylon, where they will be handed over to the Royal Air Force.

Catalina FM left Poole on 11 April and Catalina FL lifted off today for the same destination.

Footnote: They would survive to become named peacetime flying-boats *Altair* and *Vega*.

EXERCISE DEMON: FIREMEN ARRIVE IN NEWLAND, SHERBORNE, AFTER A BOUT OF STREET FIGHTING ON 9 MAY 1943

TEA BREAK: THE ARRIVAL OF THE WOMEN'S VOLUNTARY SERVICE (RIGHT) WITH SUPPORT FACILITIES FOR THE STREET FIGHTERS IN OPERATION DEMON AT NEWLAND, SHERBORNE, ON 9 MAY 1943

REALISTIC CASUALTY: THANKS TO A DETACHED EYE (COURTESY THE BUTCHER) IN NEWLAND, SHERBORNE, FOR EXERCISE DEMON ON 9 MAY 1943

The Observer Corps, incidentally, was awarded the "Royal" cachet on 11 April 1941.

Sunday 9 May

Exercise Demon in Sherborne's wrecked street.

Bomb-damaged Newland in Sherborne, one of the streets devastated by the Luftwaffe on 30 September 1940, has provided a realistic setting for Exercise Demon. Spectators watched from rows of seats on the rise that looks down towards the Black Horse Hotel at Castleton as troops, firemen, A.R.P. wardens, and the Women's Voluntary Service practised their crafts — from street warfare to the arrival of W.V.S. tea urns.

Wednesday 21 April

Australian flying-boats leave Poole for Pembroke.

461 (Royal Australian Air Force) Squadron today left R.A.F. Hamworthy and took their Sunderland flying-boats to Pembroke Dock in South Wales.

They are to be replaced by 210 Squadron which is flying military Catalinas.

Wednesday 21 April

Mine-damaged vessel puts into Christchurch.

The United States Coastguard Service vessel *Apache*, bound for Cowes from Boston, Massachusetts, has been forced into the River Avon at Christchurch for repairs after having hit a mine in the English Channel.

Sunday 16 May

Hurn Halifax crashes at Bransgore.

A four-engined Halifax bomber, DG390 of 295 Squadron, crashed today whilst on a flight from R.A.F. Hurn to the nearby R.A.F. at Holmsley South on the edge of the New Forest. Only a mile short of its destination, at Bransgore, it dived to starboard from 1,200 feet and two of the crew were killed on impact. They were 21-year-old Flying Officer M. W. Collins of the Royal Canadian Air Force and Flying Officer P. S. Thomas, an R.A.F. air gunner.

A third crewman, 21-year-old Canadian Flying Officer D. J. Smith, was dragged out of the wreckage alive but has died in Boscombe Hospital.

Footnote: They are buried in Bransgore churchyard.

Wednesday 28 April

German craft sunk off St Alban's Head.

Last night a German VJ submarine-chaser, *140Z*, was sunk by Hunt-class destroyers of the Royal Navy's main coast protection flotilla from Portsmouth. It was trying to guard Axis Convoy code 37K/MS and went down off St Alban's Head.

Saturday 1 May

American daylight raiders cross Dorset.

Elements of the first massed United States Air Force daytime bombing raid against Germany have crossed Dorset on their way to the Channel. The Royal Observer Corps log at Dorchester records: "09.30 hours. 20 Liberators spotted south-west. 10.45 hours. 47 Fortresses flying south." The aircraft returned individually through the afternoon.

GERMAN PRISONERS: WELL, THE UNIFORMS WERE AUTHENTIC EVEN IF THE CONTENTS SPOKE BROAD DORSET, AS EXERCISE DEMON MOPPED UP RESISTANCE IN NEWLAND, SHERBORNE, ON 9 MAY 1943

BOUNCING BOMB: DAMBUSTING, FIRST PRACTISED AT LANGTON HERRING AND EFFECTED ON THE GRAND SCALE IN THE CASE OF THE MÖHNE DAM, 17 MAY 1943

RUHR FLOODS: THE BREACH IN THE MÖHNE DAM, PRECISELY IN THE CENTRE, ON 17 MAY 1943

Monday 17 May

R.A.F. moves into Tarrant Rushton.

An advance party has taken control of the aerodrome which from today is R.A.F. Tarrant Rushton. They are the Station Admin. Officer, Squadron Leader T. H. W. Pearce; Equipment Officer, Flight-Lieutenant S. N. Wright; Accounting Officer, Flight-Lieutenant C. F. N. Harrison; and 43 other ranks.

The station is operating as part of Army Co-Operation Command, through 38 Wing, but the aerodrome is not yet operational. The Wing is responsible for training aircrew in an Army airborne-support capacity.

Monday 17 May

Dambuster bombs were tested in Dorset.

The earliest versions of the bouncing-bombs that were dropped last night by Lancasters of 617 Squadron, to breach the Möhne and Eder dams in the Ruhr, were tested in Dorset. Prototypes of the weapon had been developed on a freelance basis by Barnes Wallis of Vickers-Armstrongs, working mainly at weekends outside the official Ministry of Aircraft Production's armament programme.

They were carried by a Wellington, flown by Captain Joseph J. "Mutt" Summers, and dropped from 60 feet on to the flat waters of the inshore Fleet lagoon near Langton Herring. This part of the Chesil Beach Bombing Range was used to ascertain that the bombs worked in principle, skimming across the calm waters like a well-thrown stone, though the actual practice runs for Operation Chastise were undertaken by the Lancasters of 617 Squadron over the Elan valley reservoir in the mountains of mid-Wales.

Footnote: Air Marshal Sir Arthur Harris, Commander-in-Chief Bomber Command, recalled that he "rang up Washington, where Churchill and Portal were at the time, to give them the news. The telephone personnel seemed never to have heard of the White House, and there was some little difficulty. When I did get through I was intercepted and asked for an assurance that the person I was calling was reliable. I don't know whether she was persuaded that Winston Churchill came into that category, but I got through to Portal in the end and told him that two dams had gone."

Eight of the 19 Lancasters failed to return. The main aim had been to cause a shortage of water for industrial purposes in the Ruhr, rather than sweeping everything away in a flood, which is how we tend to remember the exploit. Not that there were many happy farmers in Kassel when 330 million tons of water spread across their fields. Several hundred Russian prisoners-of-war were among the 1,294 people who drowned.

Psychologically, and as a momentous example of what could be achieved by a defiant combination of personal initiative and precision flying, it will retain pre-eminence among the achievements of aerial warfare. Wing Commander Guy Gibson D.S.O., D.F.C. was awarded the Victoria Cross.

Thursday 20 May

Another Halifax crashes at Holmsley.

Another Halifax bomber has crashed in the New Forest. Having taken off from R.A.F. Holmsley South, on a flight path towards Cranborne Chase, it was towing a Horsa glider. This was successfully cast-off but the aircraft then faltered, and fell from the sky near Fordingbridge, nine miles north-west of the airfield.

All the crew were killed. The pilot, Flying Officer R. M. Reisner, was Canadian.

Sunday 23 May

101 killed in Bournemouth's worst air-raid.

This has been Bournemouth's worst air-raid. Beales department is a burnt-out shell; West's Picture House in the former Shaftesbury Hall in Old Christchurch Road is destroyed; the Central Hotel in The Square is in ruins; facing it the drapers Bobby and Co. Limited has a frontage shattered by blast damage; the omnibus standing area beside the Bus Station in Exeter Road is covered in glass from 25 Hants and Dorset buses that lost all their windows; Punshon Memorial Church, on Richmond Hill, is ripped apart; and the Metropole Hotel at The Lansdowne has collapsed; the Shamrock and Rambler coach depot in Holdenhurst Road has been devastated.

Bombs also fell into residential areas at Bethia Road, Cotlands Road, Dean Park Road, Drummond Road, Howeth Road, Lansdowne Road, Vale Road, Queen's Park South Drive, and between Pokesdown and Iford Bridge. Of the 3,481 buildings that have been damaged it is estimated that about 40 will have to be demolished.

Seventy-seven civilians are dead and the bodies of 24 Empire airmen and other military personnel have been recovered from the debris of the Metropole Hotel. Firemen of National Fire Service, with a new 100-feet turntable ladder, rescued a further 35 airmen who were trapped on the upper floors of the elegant Victorian building, dating from 1893, which occupied the triangular corner between Holdenhurst Road and Christchurch Road. There are a total of 196 people being treated for their injuries.

All this happened within about five minutes, at 13.00 hours, when 22 Focke-Wulf FW190s swept in low from the sea and bombed the central shopping areas of The Square and Lansdowne. But for the fact that the attack coincided with Sunday lunchtime the casualty figures could have been much higher.

Two hours later the conductor of the B.B.C. Orchestra, Sir Adrian Boult, took the Bournemouth Municipal Orchestra through the Nimrod passage from Sir Edward Elgar's *Enigma Variations* in memory of those who had died. The bombs marred what had been intended as a celebratory concert to mark the 50th anniversary of the Bournemouth Orchestra.

Meanwhile, at 14.20 hours, Bournemouth A.R.P. Control Centre requested rescue parties from Christchurch and Poole. A major fire was still burning

BEALES BLITZED: WITH ITS CLOCK BROUGHT DOWN INTO OLD CHRISTCHURCH ROAD, BOURNEMOUTH, BY THE FIRE THAT FOLLOWED THE BOMBING IN THE MIDDLE OF THE DAY ON 23 MAY 1943. BEHIND THE FIREMEN (RIGHT) IS BRIGHTS DEPARTMENT STORE

TANGLED REMAINS: BURNT-OUT BEALES AFTER BOURNEMOUTH'S MOST DEVASTATING AIR-RAID, ON 23 MAY 1943, WITH ST PETER'S CHURCH IN THE FOREGROUND (LEFT) AND THE STORE OF J. J. ALLEN (BELOW, RIGHT)

BLAST DAMAGE: BOBBY'S LIMITED DRAPERY STORE IN THE
SQUARE AT BOURNEMOUTH, RIPPED APART IN THE AIR-RAID OF 23
MAY 1943

SNAKING HOSES: PUMPING WATER FROM THE BOURNE STREAM TO
FIGHT THE FIRE THAT WAS CONSUMING BEALES DEPARTMENT
STORE ON THE AFTERNOON OF 23 MAY 1943

CENSORED ACCOUNT: THIS BEING "A METHODIST CHURCH, HIT IN
SUNDAY'S RAID ON A SOUTH COAST TOWN" ACCORDING TO THE
CONTEMPORARY CAPTION. THE PICTURE SHOWS THE PUNSHON
MEMORIAL CHURCH, RICHMOND HILL, BOURNEMOUTH, WITH
THE DEBRIS OF THE CENTRAL HOTEL IN THE FOREGROUND, AS A
RESULT OF THE LUNCHTIME RAID ON 23 MAY 1943

around Beales, where the bombs fractured a gas main, and at one time threatened the adjoining department store of J. J. Allen and St. Peter's Church. Pumping parties dragged multiple snakes of hoses to the Bourne Stream to supplement the reservoir-fed gutter network of the emergency on-ground water supply. Others formed a chain to pass buckets of water up the slope.

Not only the concert proceeded as planned. Window-less buses went back into service during the afternoon with sacks tied across the front of the vehicles to reduce draughts.

Five FW190s were reportedly shot down. One crashed beside St. Ives Hotel, at 34 Grove Road, with an unexploded bomb still attached. The pilot, Unteroffizier F. K. Schmidt, was killed. Though the bomb failed to explode, the aircraft caught fire and the hotel was gutted. Another kill was seen to crash in the bay and has been credited to a machine-gun post of the 87th Light Anti-Aircraft Regiment of the Royal Artillery which was emplaced on the former flat roof of J. E. Beale Limited. Its triple Lewis guns were manned by Lance-Bombadier John Howard and Lance-Bombadier Norman Lawrence.

Footnote: R.A.F. figures show the five destruction claims against the FW190s as overstated. Two had been destroyed, as described, and two more were damaged.

Falling masonry would kill one of the men who finished the demolition of Beales. The principal buildings would remain as bomb sites for more than a decade. West's Picture House is now the Burlington Arcade. Beales was replaced and Bobby's repaired. The lost landmarks have been replaced by shops and offices.

The following servicemen were buried in the military plot at the North Cemetery:

Flight Sergeant W. G. Abbott of the Royal Canadian Air Force (aged 21);

Flight Sergeant G. Assaf of the Royal Canadian Air Force;

Sergeant D. R. Chalmers of the Royal Canadian Air Force (aged 38);

Sergeant R. R. Courtney of the Royal Canadian Air Force (aged 39);

Flight Sergeant C. B. Crabbe of the Royal Australian Air Force (aged 23, from Fiji);

Aircraftman R. Crawshaw of the Royal Air Force (aged 34);

Flight Sergeant R. F. Fenton of the Royal Australian Air Force (aged 20);

Leading Aircraftman E. O. M. Gilbert of the Royal Canadian Air Force (aged 26);

Sergeant N. M. Gray of the Royal Australian Air Force (aged 19);

METROPOLE HOTEL: MORE THAN 24 CANADIAN AND OTHER EMPIRE AIRMEN WERE KILLED BY A DIRECT HIT ON THIS SEVEN-STOREY BUILDING AT THE LANSDOWNE, AT LUNCHTIME ON 23 MAY 1943

SOLEMN CELEBRATION: THE 50TH ANNIVERSARY CONCERT OF THE BOURNEMOUTH MUNICIPAL ORCHESTRA, WITH GUEST CONDUCTOR SIR ADRIAN BOULT (CENTRE) ONLY HOURS AFTER THE TOWN'S WORST AIR-RAID, ON 23 MAY 1943

Leading Aircraftman J. Howlett of the Royal Air Force;

Lieutenant J. St. A. Jewell of the Royal Navy Volunteer Reserve;

Flight Sergeant A. J. Kerrigan of the Royal Australian Air Force (aged 24);

Aircraftman A. J. P. Lohoar of the Royal Air Force (aged 57);

Flight Sergeant J. F. McMahon of the Royal Australian Air Force (aged 28);

Sergeant A. C. Matheson of the Royal Canadian Air Force (aged 20);

Sergeant F. J. Matier of the Royal Canadian Air Force (aged 32);

Sergeant G. A. Mills of the Royal Australian Air Force (aged 23);

Aircraftman J. J. Morrissey of the Royal Air Force (aged 39);

Corporal R. F. Pelrine of the Royal Canadian Air Force (aged 20);

Flight Sergeant V. L. Pope of the Royal Canadian Air Force (aged 19);

Sergeant J. L. Soos of the Royal Canadian Air Force;

Corporal W. G. Wood of the Royal Canadian Air Force (aged 29);

Sergeant R. C. Woods of the Royal Canadian Air Force (aged 25);

and an unidentified R.A.F. airman.

Wednesday 26 May

Three Mustangs fly into Smedmore Hill.

Ten North American P-51 Mustang Mark XV fighter-bombers of 2 Squadron Royal Air Force, based at R.A.F. Sawbridgeworth, Hertfordshire, took off from Thruxton in Hampshire at 16.50 hours this afternoon on Ranger Operation Asphalt. The cross-Channel offensive action was to have been against rail movements in the Rennes-Laval area.

They flew south-west in line abreast formation until reaching a wall of fog between Kimmeridge and St Alban's Head. The order to climb was given by Flight-Lieutenant G. Kenning at 17.35 hours.

Seven of the aircraft were able to clear Smedmore Hill but the other three — code letters U for Uncle, W for William, and Y for Yorker — crashed into the northern slope. Their three pilots were killed — Flying Officer N. J. Miller, Flying Officer D. Hirst, and Pilot Officer J. B. McLeod.

The remaining Mustangs returned to Thruxton after having failed to locate the missing aircraft. Flying Officer M. P. Dunkerley returned later with hydraulic failure but was able to effect a safe landing. The operation was then cancelled.

During May

Warmwell Whirlwinds to 'work on the railway'.

Westland Whirlwinds of 263 Squadron, turned into bombers with racks fitted under each wing, have been crossing the Channel to "work on the railway" in northern France. Bomb loads are being delivered from 50 feet or less, and they are now proving to be formidable fighter-bombers, using the aircraft's four 20-mm Hispano cannon as they press home their attacks on trains.

Their named Whirlwind P7094 *Bellows* was a war weapons donation from the *Bellows* Fellowship of 70,000 wealthy British expatriates in South America. It has been joined by others from the same sub-continent with P7116 being named *Bellows Argentina* and P7121 *Bellows Uruguay No. 1.*

During May

Catalinas takes over R.A.F. Hamworthy.

Catalina flying-boats of 210 Squadron of Coastal Command have moved into the seaplane base at R.A.F. Hamworthy and are operating long-range flights into the Atlantic in the battle against the U-boats.

During May

Hambro heir killed in Tripoli.

It is reported that Major Robert Hambro, the only son and heir of Captain Angus Hambro of Merley House,

Wimborne, was mortally wounded whilst serving in a reconnaissance regiment of the 8th Army. He died at Tripoli. Major Hambro was born in 1911.

Tuesday 1 June
10 Group gets Tarrant Rushton.

Administrative control of the new Tarrant Rushton Aerodrome has been transferred to 10 Group Fighter Command but No. 38 Wing remains the operating formation.

Saturday 12 June
Germans lay another 321 mines off Dorset.

A total of 321 German mines and 84 barrage protection floats have been laid off Dorset and the Isle of Wight in the past week through the combined efforts of the German 2nd, 4th, 5th and 6th Schnellboot Flotillas. The Royal Naval Mine Sweeping Service has simply noted the areas concerned and is making arrangements to have them cleared as soon as resources and weather conditions allow.

Wednesday 23 June
Dutch vessel blows-up in Poole Bay.

A Dutch craft, the *Leny*, was blown up today by a mine near the Swash Channel at the entrance to Poole Harbour. Only two of its crewmen have been rescued.

Friday 25 June
Bungalow landing for Christchurch pilot.

19.54 hours. A Royal Navy Seafire, being flown into Christchurch Aerodrome from Donibristle, Scotland, has overshot the runway and crashed into a bungalow, "Musoka" in Caroline Avenue at Stanpit. The aircraft is number MB315, piloted by Sub-Lieutenant P, M. Lamb who has been taken to hospital with head injuries.

Footnote: Lamb was stitched-up, though he had to let his hair grow to cover the scars. "Not my best landing," he wrote in his log. "Engine tired of living. Fortunately I didn't join it." Seafires were frequently seen over Christchurch as the Airspeed factory converted 160 of them, from standard Spitfires, for use by the Fleet Air Arm.

P7094 BELLOWS: THE WESTLAND WHIRLWIND OF 263 SQUADRON CARRIES THE NAME OF FLIGHT-LIEUTENANT H. K. BLACKSHAW BUT WAS LOANED FOR THESE PHOTOGRAPHS AT R.A.F. WARMWELL IN 1943 TO 22-YEAR-OLD FLYING OFFICER J. P. COYNE OF MANITOBA WHO HAD JUST BEEN AWARDED THE DISTINGUISHED FLYING CROSS

RESCUE DINGY: TO BE DROPPED, THE ORIGINAL CAPTION STATES, TO AIRMEN "IN THE DRINK". AIR-SEA RESCUE SPITFIRES OPERATED FROM R.A.F. WARMWELL. MARK II P8131, AS "AQ" C FOR CHARLIE, BELONGED TO 276 SQUADRON IN 1943

BURMESE PILOTS: AT R.A.F. WARMWELL, WITH 257 SQUADRON, IN JANUARY 1943. PILOT OFFICER M. H. YI OF PEGU, AND T. CLIFT FROM SHAN STATES HAD BEEN TRAINING IN INDIA WHEN THE JAPANESE INVADED THE BRITISH COLONY

263 Squadron: Empire unit line-up beside Westland Whirlwind Bellows. From left to right are Flight-Lieutenant E. C. Owens (Adjutant), Squadron Leader G. B. Warnes (Commanding Officer), Sergeant S. D. Thyagarajan (from India), Flying Officer C. P. King D.F.M. (British West Indies), Flight Sergeant F. L. Hicks (Australia), and Flying Officer J. P. Coyne (Canada). They are photographed at dispersal beside Knighton Heath Wood at R.A.F. Warmwell in 1943

During June

Thousand rockets pound Studland beach in 30 seconds.

The RCL, a tank landing craft that has been modified at Poole to carry batteries of rocket launchers, has been tested in live-fire exercises at Studland Bay and Kimmeridge. It fires more than 1,000 explosive rockets in about 30 seconds, delivering them to a small area of the beach. The aim is to annihilate enemy strong-points with firepower that is devastatingly concentrated.

During June

Gliders leave Hurn: destination Sicily.

No. 3 Overseas Aircraft Despatch Unit is co-ordinating a massive shuttle service from R.A.F. Hurn. No. 13 Maintenance Unit is fitting out Halifax bombers as tow-craft for the Horsa troop-carrying gliders which had been made ready by No. 1 Heavy Glider Maintenance Unit. That unit has moved to Netheravon, Wiltshire, and the Halifaxes of 295 Squadron are taking the gliders, built by Airspeed at Christchurch, to Portreath, Cornwall.

Meanwhile, 296 Squadron has been flying its Albemarle paratroop carriers out of Hurn since 3 June.

Twenty-eight had left by 21 June. The squadron was equipped with Albemarles in February and has been training with the Rebecca radio navigation system.

From Cornwall, the Albemarles and Halifax-Horsa combinations are flying out, in Operation Beggar, to Sale in Morocco. They are then being moved eastwards to Kairouan, in Tunisia, where they will be taken over by the 1st Air Landing Brigade Group, who are preparing for Operation Husky.

This will be the invasion of Sicily, into the "soft under-belly of Europe", as Churchill puts it.

Monday 5 July

1st Dorsets sail for Sicily.

The 1st Battalion of the Dorsetshire Regiment has sailed into the Mediterranean aboard the ex-Peninsula and Orient liner *Strathnaver* among the armada bound for the beaches of Sicily.

The 1st Air Landing Brigade Group, with aircraft from Hurn and Christchurch-made gliders, are tasked to begin the invasion of Sicily between 22.10 and 22.30 hours on Friday with a drop west of Siracusa to capture the Ponte Grande over the Anapo River, take out the coast batteries

SOPLEY "STARLIGHT": REVOLVING TYPE 7 RADAR AERIAL ABOVE A BUNKER KNOWN AS THE "WELL", INSTALLED IN 1943 AND FUNCTIONING AS THE EYES FOR BEAUFIGHTERS AND OTHER SPECIALLY ADAPTED NIGHT-FIGHTERS. THE KEY COMBAT RADAR STATION FOR CENTRAL SOUTHERN ENGLAND LIES IN FLAT FIELDS TO THE NORTH OF CHRISTCHURCH

companies then landed to establish themselves inland.

Footnote: The Royal Navy lost two submarines in the Sicilian invasion. One was H.M.S. *Saracen*, commanded by Lieutenant M. G. R. Lumby of South Eggardon Farm, Askerswell, who was taken prisoner with his crew.

Saturday 10 July

German E-boat sunk and H.M.S. 'Melbreak' damaged.

to the north, and also attack a seaplane base. Seaborne landings are to follow with the commandos arriving four hours later and then the main force of 13 Corps.

Footnote: The airborne operation on 9 July was disrupted by high winds. Some gliders came down in the sea and many paratroops fell considerable distances from the objective. Few reached the Ponte Grande but they held the bridge heroically for 18 hours. Fortunately the seaborne assault proved to be a complete success.

Saturday 10 July

1st Dorsets take Marzamemi.

"C" Company of the 1st Battalion the Dorsetshire Regiment, under Captain A. C. W. Martin, went over the side of the troopship *Strathnaver* at 03.00 hours to effect a scramble-landing on a rocky promontory at the right-flank of the projected bridgehead in Sicily. They took the village of Marzamemi and were able to secure the proposed landing beach to the south.

Tracer shells fired vertically from a Bren gun was the dawn signal of success to the Commanding Officer offshore. The battalion's "A" and "B"

An engagement took place last night off the Dorset coast, south-westwards towards the Channel Islands and Ushant, between Hunt-class destroyers from Portsmouth and the German 2nd Schnellboot Flotilla. The latter, on convoy protection duty, lost minesweeper *M135*. Among the British destroyers, H.M.S. *Melbreak* sustained serious damage, but was able to return to port.

Saturday 10 July

Spitfires at Hurn to escort Flying Fortresses.

Thirty-eight Spitfires of 66 Squadron, 131 Squadron, and 504 Squadron, flew into R.A.F. Hurn today as cross-Channel escorts for American Flying Fortress bombers. Spitfire EB687 was wrecked on arrival when it collided with a parked Whitley bomber.

Footnote: The fighters were led by Wing Commander C. E. Malfroy D.F.C. who would bring the Wing back for similar escort duties on 14 July.

GAS BOMB: DROPPED BY A LYSANDER BIPLANE ON A SHERMAN TANK, IN AN EXERCISE NEAR EAST LULWORTH IN 1943, TO AN INSTANTLY RECOGNISABLE BACKDROP OF THE PURBECK HILLS

Monday 12 July

Poole's 'Apple' killed in Sicily.

One of the heroes who was able to thrill the nation with daring exploits in desperate times, Major Geoffrey Appleyard D.S.O. of the commando unit from Poole, is missing presumed dead. The 26-year-old officer, known in Combined Operations as "The Apple", was deputy commander of the 2nd Special Air Service Regiment.

They were taking part in the invasion of Sicily, having been seconded to the North African Forces, where the unit was known as the 1st Small Scale Raiding Force.

Tuesday 13 July

Turin Lancaster just makes it to Christchurch.

This morning a Lancaster bomber of 49 Squadron, returning from the mass raid over Turin, crossed the English Channel on an almost empty fuel tank. Pilot Officer B. S. Tomlin then put JA851 down on to the 2,400 feet of grass that is Christchurch Aerodrome.

He brought his aircraft and its six crew to a perfect landing. Two-and-a-half hours later they were refuelled and airborne again, after an excellent short take-off, en route to R.A.F. Fiskerton, Lincolnshire.

Bomber Command strays are not uncommon in Hampshire and Dorset but it is the first time anyone can recall a four-engined bomber arriving at Christchurch.

Sunday 25 July

Worth's 'Window' is opened at last.

"Let us open the Window," Winston Churchill decided and last night it was done — this being the codename given by the Telecommunications Research Establishment's A. P. Rowe, to what was the parting shot of the Worth Matravers scientists to the war effort before their radar laboratories were moved from Purbeck to Malvern. It is deployed from the air in the form of millions of thin strips of aluminium foil that create a smoke-screen effect upon enemy radar scanners at the onset of a mass bombing raid.

"Window" was perfected in Dorset over a year ago but opposition from Fighter Command and Robert Watson-Watt, radar's British pioneer, blocked its operational use. It had been feared that it might give the Germans the idea at a time when they were liable to carry out major attacks against Britain.

The scientists and Bomber Command are elated with the results of "Window" in causing confusion and consternation to the German defences. Forty tons of "Window" were dropped, which is a total of 92 million strips, and all but twelve of the 791 bombers returned from the raid on Hamburg. Losses which statistically should have been about 6.1 per cent have been reduced to 1.5 per cent.

"Window" last night saved 36 aeroplanes and their crews.

During July

Crew killed as Whitley crashes at Hurn.

The crew of a Whitley tug-plane were killed when it stalled on take-off and crashed inside the perimeter fence at R.A.F. Hurn. The aircraft was on what should have been a routine training circuit.

During July

Advanced Landing Ground at Winkton.

Hedges and ditches have been removed across an area of flat farmland to the north-east of Sopley, beside the lane from Winkton to Ripley, for a temporary Advanced Landing Ground. This will enable additional fighter capacity to be

ITALY INVADED: 13 CORPS LANDING IN SICILY AFTER A NIGHT ASSAULT BY "C" COMPANY OF THE 1ST BATTALION THE DORSETSHIRE REGIMENT, ON 10 JULY 1943

brought into the Christchurch area for protection of the Channel convoys and the build-up of invasion shipping, plus cross-Channel ground-attack missions.

The runways of R.A.F. Winkton have been laid as sheets of steel mesh directly on to the grass. There are two runways, one north-south from east of Parsonage Farm to west of Clockhouse Farm, and the other east-west from the Ripley road to within a third of a mile of the cottages at Bransgore village.

Footnote: It would not be officially in use until March 1944 and was then handed over to the United States Army Air Force, though nominally controlled by 11 Group R.A.F. Fighter Command. Used as a satellite airfield to Christchurch. Closed when the war began to move into Germany in January 1945.

Monday 9 August
French bombers make it to safety at Hurn.

The Free French bombers of 88 Squadron, flying Bostons alongside those of 107 Squadron and 342 Squadron, headed back across the Channel this morning to the safety of R.A.F. Hurn. The three squadrons had been in action over Rennes, in Brittany, where they had lost two aircraft.

The 21 surviving bombers were short on fuel when they landed at Hurn.

Thursday 12 August
Thirteen killed in Bournemouth raid.

Gas-mains were set alight, water pipes fractured, and 1,455 properties damaged at about 01.10 hours today when eight high explosive bombs dropped on Bournemouth. Thirteen people are dead and 21 receiving hospital treatment.

The bombs fell at the corner of Firs Glen Road and Woods View Road; at the junction of Boundary Road with Beswick Road; at the corner of Wilton Road and Gloucester Road; in Spring Road; Charminster Avenue; and Shelbourne Road.

Thursday 12 August
Christchurch bomb damage.

There was an explosion near the railway, close to Christchurch Station, at 01.10 hours. Another high explosive bomb caused widespread damage in Ringwood Road, Walkford, at 01.15. Many houses were shattered and one bed-ridden lady is homeless. Three people were injured. There are also reports of unexploded bombs.

Saturday 14 August
Anti-Aircraft Squadron at Tarrant Rushton.

The main body of No. 2851 Anti-Aircraft Squadron have arrived at Tarrant Rushton Aerodrome from R.A.F. Friston, Sussex. Their advance party came to Dorset on Thursday.

Tuesday 24 August
Eight die as Catalina hits Round Island.

Pilot Officer Duff died with seven of his crew when he brought a military Catalina of 210 Squadron back to Poole Harbour at 04.25 hours. They descended into thick fog and the flying-boat missed the clear waters of the "Trots" in the channels of the northern harbour.

Instead it ploughed into the cord-grass salt-marshes that surround Round Island which is on the Purbeck side of the harbour — a mile south of the safe clear-way off R.A.F. Hamworthy. Ratings from the island's naval camp dragged bodies and survivors from the debris. Only four crewmen were rescued from this tragic training flight.

Saturday 28 August
'Second Front' — Eden, Brooke and Mountbatten fly into Poole.

The Secretary of State for Foreign Affairs, Anthony Eden, together with General Sir Alan Brooke, Chief of the Imperial General Staff, and Admiral Louis Mountbatten, Chief of Combined Operations, landed at 14.00 hours today in Poole Harbour. They were aboard the B.O.A.C. Boeing Clipper *Bristol* and had returned across the Atlantic from the Quebec Conference which set the location and timetable for launching the Second Front.

The decision has been taken to go for the beaches of Normandy and forgo the need to capture a port by towing across prefabricated concrete caissons, codenamed Mulberries, to make two instant harbours. The provisional date for the invasion of Europe is 1 May 1944.

Tuesday 31 August
Echo of Sedgemoor.

The Daily Telegraph reports that a Lyme Regis hotelier received a stamped addressed postcard from an anxious prospective visitor asking for "the date of the last enemy attack on your town".

The manager sent the card back with the year — "1685".

Wednesday 8 September
Dorset mailbag leads the rearguard into Italy.

Support landings at Pizzo, on the Toe of Italy, were carried out just before dawn to establish a rearguard to ease pressure on the Allied troops in the Reggio beachhead. The commandos went astray, however, and the first craft to beach contained the headquarters unit of the 1st Battalion the Dorsetshire Regiment.

The landing was led — not that he realised his bravado at the time — by an N.C.O. with a mailbag slung nonchalantly over his shoulder.

That moment passed uneventfully but later the battalion's "B" Company came under heavy counter-attack on the nearby coast road. Though the Dorsets knocked out a Panzer Mark IV tank, with one of their 6-

pounders, they had two anti-tank guns destroyed and many crews became casualties.

Without any gunnery to support him, Sergeant M. Evans single-handedly immobilised an approaching armoured car, which was leading an enemy column. He tossed in a grenade and killed all the crew with the exception of a German officer. Sergeant Evans then shot the survivor as he tried to bale out. The other enemy vehicles reversed and withdrew.

The company's left-flank was under infantry attack. This was held off by Lieutenant L. G. Browne's platoon in fierce hand-to-hand fighting which left 20 enemy dead.

At one point the Brigade Commander called up air support. Kittyhawk fighter-bombers duly arrived on time but they then confused the British positions for those of the enemy and proceeded to bomb and strafe them. Several vehicles were destroyed. It has been that sort of day.

Footnote: Some honour emerged from the chaos. Sergeant Evans won a bar to his Military Medal and Lieutenant Browne was awarded the Military Cross.

Wednesday 22 September
Twelve Venturas arrive at Tarrant Rushton.

The last of nine Ventura aircraft from R.A.F. Sculthorpe, Norfolk, arrived today at Tarrant Rushton Aerodrome. Two came yesterday and the main flight of six arrived the day before. Three other Ventura landed on Monday from R.A.F. Stoney Cross, in the New Forest, so the total now at Tarrant Rushton is twelve.

Thursday 23 September
First Albemarle tow-plane lands at Tarrant Rushton.

A prototype Albemarle Mark IV transport was brought into R.A.F. Tarrant Rushton today by Group Captain T. B. Cooper D.F.C. Its potential is to be assessed in towing trials with a view to using the aircraft as a tug-plane for troop-carrying gliders.

During September
Great Panjandrum tested at Clouds Hill.

One of the more bizarre weapons of war, a Great Panjandrum rocket-fired assault wheel, has been tested by commandos of Combined Operations from Poole on their explosives firing ground at Clouds Hill, near Bovington Camp. The cylinder at the centre of two 10-feet high wheels contains 4,000 pounds of high explosive.

The rockets are intended to send the wheel out of an invasion landing craft and up the beach to blow a hole in the 10-feet concrete of the German Atlantic Wall defences. The rocket propulsion was tried out on the sands of Westward Ho! and Instow, Devon, on 7 and 8 September with unpredictable results. Nevil Shute Norway, the aeronautical engineer and writer, figured out the size of the charges needed to breach the Atlantic Wall and is taking part in the experiments.

Footnote: A final trial took place at Westward Ho! in January 1944. It was filmed by motor-racing photographer Luis Klemantaski who had to run for his life as the machine reached 100 miles per hour and

PIZZO ARRIVAL: SERGEANT W. E. EVANS OF THE 1ST BATTALION THE DORSETSHIRE REGIMENT SHOWN WINNING A BAR TO HIS MILITARY MEDAL, IN THE TOE OF ITALY ON 8 SEPTEMBER 1943, AS SKETCHED BY BRYAN DE GRINEAU FOR THE LONDON ILLUSTRATED NEWS

suddenly veered towards him. Onlookers tried to escape up the beach and became entangled in anti-invasion barbed wire. The Panjandrum, meanwhile, wobbled seaward again as rockets spiralled across the beach; one being chased by an Airedale hound, Ammanol.

With this the project was abandoned, though it had served its purpose as a feint, by demonstrating that there were active plans to attack the concrete coast between the Seine and Calais, rather than the soft sands of Normandy. Hence the unprecedented testing of a "secret" weapon before an audience in a holiday resort; it was a deception that the public and the Germans could hear about. Few, if any, of those involved would have been privy to the ruse.

One of the wheels of the Great Panjandrum at Clouds Hill was rediscovered in 1946-47 by Bere Regis scouts who were camping nearby in Sare's Wood. Fred Pitfield, then aged 15, recalls the terrific fun they had rolling it up and down the hills adjacent to the camp. Though unpowered it still managed to demolish tents, bicycles, and billie-cans.

Saturday 9 October
Sandbanks Air Station closes.

The Royal Navy's seaplane training school at Sandbanks was today disbanded.

Sunday 10 October
P-o-Ws sent cigarettes.

The following card, written in a camp at M. Stammlager, is typical of those being received by the Society of Dorset Men:

"Kriegsgefangenenlager. Dear Sir, Thank you very much for your letter of September. I have today received a parcel of 200 cigarettes. I believe they are from the society. Cigarettes mean such a great deal. I am a Dorset man, born and bred, and to me it is still the finest little place in the world. Thanking you once again. Yours sincerely, G. W. Harris, 6848.

Monday 11 October
India's Viceroy flies from Poole to Bombay.

Field-Marshal Sir Archibald Wavell, Viceroy of India and Supreme Commander Allied Forces in India and Burma, today left Poole Quay by launch to board a B.O.A.C. flying-boat bound for Bombay.

Monday 11 October
298 Squadron to be formed at Tarrant Rushton.

No. 38 Wing of the Royal Air Force, comprising the support units for British airborne forces, today changed its name to HQ 38 Group. The week also started with movements on the ground between its two aerodromes in Dorset, from R.A.F. Hurn to R.A.F. Tarrant Rushton.

An advance party from "A" Flight of 295 Squadron moved with its Halifax tow-craft, into Tarrant Rushton,

where they will soon cease to be part of that unit. They are to form the nucleus of the new 298 Squadron which is to be based at Tarrant Rushton. They will be joined by the Sterlings of 196 Squadron.

Friday 15 October
Halifax tug-planes arrive at Tarrant Rushton.

Four-engined Handley Page Halifax bombers, converted for use as tug-plane transports for troop-carrying gliders, have started to arrive at Tarrant Rushton Aerodrome. Their operatives, "A" Flight of 295 Squadron from R.A.F. Hurn, will soon make themselves at home. The main party arrives on Sunday and the rear party follows on Wednesday. They will then become 298 Squadron.

Wednesday 27 October
Exercise Thresher takes gliders to Wiltshire.

Newly-formed 298 Squadron at R.A.F. Tarrant Rushton took to the sky today for Exercise Thresher. Three gliders were towed by their Halifax tug-planes and released to land at Netheravon Aerodrome in Wiltshire.

Thursday 28 October
Damaged bomber lands at Tarrant Rushton.

A Mitchell bomber, damaged by German flak off Cherbourg, made a successful emergency landing today at R.A.F. Tarrant Rushton. It was flown by Lieutenant Loeffe of 320 Squadron, from Lasham Aerodrome, near Alton, Hampshire.

Monday 1 November
Bournemouth hit by 23 bombs.

A total of 23 high explosive bombs fell on Bournemouth at tea-time. The raid took place at 17.45 hours and left 1,284 properties damaged. The casualty toll, however, was light, with just one person killed and 27 injured.

Widespread damage is reported from Cecil Avenue, Howard Road, Campbell Road, Borthwick Road, Avon Road, Chatsworth Road, Bennett Road, Orcheston Road, Shaftesbury Road, and Shelbourne Road. Bombs at Queen's Park Avenue did little more than crater the golf links.

Saturday 6 November
First home leave for 1st Dorsets since 1936.

Dorset's Regular Army soldiers, the 1st Battalion the Dorsetshire Regiment, disembarked on the Clyde at Gourock today from the troopship Durban Castle. They were played ashore by a Highland band.

The survivors of the Malta siege and assault landings in Sicily and Italy are looking forward to their first home leave in seven years — they have been overseas since their transfer to the North-West Frontier Province of India in 1936.

Saturday 13 November

Fighter Command becomes A.E.A.F.

Psychologically, at least, the war takes its turn today from defence to the offensive. Fighter Command has ceased to exist and is now part of the Allied Expeditionary Air Force, which is the umbrella command for all British, American, and other Allied fighting aircraft and air stations in the United Kingdom. Its Commander-in-Chief is Air Chief Marshal Sir Trafford Leigh-Mallory.

Saturday 13 November

Adjutant at Boscombe alive by an inch.

There was a shock last night for the Adjutant at the headquarters of the 7th (Boscombe) Battalion of Hampshire Home Guard. A shooting incident occurred shortly before 21.00 hours, as Sergeant G. A. Miller of 28th Platoon, Headquarters Company, has reported to his commanding officer:

"When rifles were being loaded, previous to proceeding to the Operational Patrol, one round was accidentally fired by a member of the patrol, Private G. H. Thomas. The round passed through the ceiling of the guardroom and lodged in the wall of the room above. I am able, fortunately, to report that no one was hurt. The bullet passed within one inch of the Adjutant who was sitting in the room above."

Monday 15 November

Hurn now has three squadrons of Albemarles.

Three Albemarle squadrons are now based at R.A.F. Hurn with the formation there today of 570 Squadron. "We launch the spearhead," is the motto chosen for the taxi service of the Airborne divisions.

The station's existing 295 Squadron has been re-equipped with Albemarles and reunited with those of 296 Squadron returning from Italy. Three squadrons will co-operate in paratroop drops and in exercising towing Horsa gliders.

A detachment from 570 Squadron is to be based at R.A.F. Stoney Cross in the New Forest.

Tuesday 16 November

Ten square miles requisitioned in Isle of Purbeck.

Major-General Charles Harvey Miller, the officer commanding administration at Southern Command, today issued eviction noticed to all persons living in an area of ten square miles of western Purbeck. The entire 3,003-acre parish of Tyneham has been requisitioned along with considerable areas of heath and downland in the adjoining parishes of East Lulworth, East Stoke, East Holme, and Steeple.

The village of Tyneham and hamlets of Povington and Worbarrow will have to be evacuated by 19 December, as will many isolated farms and cottages.

The land is to be used as a live-fire battle training area for the tanks of the United States Army as well as the Gunnery Wing of the Armoured Fighting Vehicles School which has its ranges at Lulworth Camp, next to the requisitioned area.

Practising tank warfare has become a top priority since August, when the Quebec Conference decided that the Overlord plan for the so-called "Second Front" invasion of Fortress Europe should be launched against Normandy, with the target date being the spring of 1944.

Tuesday 16 November

Paratroops drop near Sixpenny Handley.

Eight Halifax transports from Tarrant Rushton Aerodrome today carried out their Exercise Fledgling in which 298 Squadron dropped men of the 8th Battalion the Parachute Brigade on Cranborne Chase. They jumped over Thorney Down, beside the A354, two miles south of Sixpenny Handley.

Wednesday 24 November

Exercise Cumulus puts cloud over Studland Bay.

Studland Bay disappeared in a cloud of smoke today. This was Exercise Cumulus in which landing craft were obscured by a dense smoke-screen.

Thirteen Mitchell and 24 Boston bombers dropped the canisters. They operated for the day from R.A.F. Hurn. Four Typhoons of 181 Squadron came low across the sea to test the effectiveness of the screen against attacking fighters.

Wednesday 1 December

Hurn and Tarrant Rushton gliders in joint exercise.

Halifax tug-planes pulling Horsa gliders from 298 Squadron at R.A.F. Tarrant Rushton today met up in aerial formation with similar combinations from their previous aerodrome as 295 Squadron from R.A.F. Hurn joined them for Exercise Stickies. This also involved aircraft and gliders from R.A.F. Stoney Cross in the New Forest.

Wednesday 8 December

Americans arrive at Blandford.

The 184th Auxiliary Anti-Aircraft Gun Battalion is the first unit of the United States Army to arrive at Blandford Camp. It has 716 enlisted men and 25 officers. Their task will be to provide protection around the beach landing assault area at Studland.

Friday 17 December

Loaded Horsa gliders airborne from Tarrant Rushton.

Glider lift-offs for the pilots of 298 Squadron at Tarrant Rushton Aerodrome came close to reality today in Exercise Hasty. Their converted Halifax bombers pulled loaded Horsa gliders into the sky.

Friday 17 December
Bournemouth's £2 million 'Wings for Victory'.

Lord Brabazon, until last year the Minister of Aircraft Production, was the principal speaker today at a ceremony in the Town Hall, Bournemouth, to present a plaque and certificate of merit on behalf of the National Savings Campaign.

The town collected £2,033,894 in the "Wings for Victory" week, held from 8 to 15 May. The award of the plaque was made by Group Captain Hutchinson of the Royal Canadian Air Force.

Councillors and collectors were told that the money had been invested in a flight of six Sunderland flying-boats; three squadrons of 15 single-engine fighters; three squadrons of twelve 4-engine bombers; plus three 2-engine bombers. That is a grand total of 90 aircraft — at an average price of £22,598 each. Well done Bournemouth!

Sunday 19 December
Tyneham villagers are evicted.

Ralph Bond, the platoon commander of Tyneham Home Guard and a Purbeck magistrate, has been evicted from his Elizabethan mansion along with his servants, farm labourers, and the fishermen of Worbarrow Bay. The whole of the parish of Tyneham plus other land on either side of the Purbeck Hills has been depopulated by order of the War Cabinet.

GREAT PANJANDRUM: SPOOF WEAPON OF THE SECRET WAR, TESTED AT CLOUDS HILL IN SEPTEMBER 1943 AND RELEASED FOR PUBLIC CONSUMPTION ACROSS THE BEACH AT WESTWARD HO! IN JANUARY 1944. IT WOULD HELP TO DECEIVE THE GERMANS INTO THINKING THAT THE FORTHCOMING INVASION WOULD BE AGAINST THE CONCRETE OF THE CALAIS COAST RATHER THAN THE SOFT SANDS OF NORMANDY

The area will become a firing range for American Sherman tanks of the Second Armored Division which is the backbone of V Corps of the First United States Army. No mention of this extension of the Lulworth Ranges has been permitted in the press. Neither was there any consultation with local councils.

Tenancies are, however, being maintained and each occupant has been reassured: "This means that when the War Department has no further use for the property and it is handed back, you have every right to return to your property. It should not be assumed by you that, because the War Department has turned you out, you lose the right of occupying the premises again."

The prohibition of editorial mentions of the military take-over has not been extended to the advertising columns. On 2 December the Dorset County Chronicle

SOUTHERN COMMAND

TRAINING AREA, EAST HOLME, Nr. LULWORTH

IN order to give our troops the fullest opportunity to perfect their training in the use of modern weapons of war, the Army must have an area of land particularly suited to their special needs and in which they can use live shells. For this reason you will realise the chosen area must be cleared of all civilians.

The most careful search has been made to find an area suitable for the Army's purpose and which, at the same time, will involve the smallest number of persons and property. The area decided on, after the most careful study and consultation between all the Government Authorities concerned, lies roughly inside of the square formed by EAST LULWORTH—EAST STOKE—EAST HOLME—KIMMERIDGE BAY. *Including your properties – see overleaf.*

It is regretted that, in the National Interest, it is necessary to move you from your homes, and everything possible will be done to help you, both by payment of compensation, and by finding other accommodation for you if you are unable to do so yourself.

The date on which the Military will take over this area is the 19th December next, and all civilians must be out of the area by that date.

A special office will be opened at Westport House, WAREHAM, on Wednesday the 17th November, and you will be able to get advice between the hours of 10 a.m. and 7 p.m., from there on your personal problems and difficulties. Any letters should be sent to that address also for the present.

The Government appreciate that this is no small sacrifice which you are asked to make, but they are sure that you will give this further help towards winning the war with a good heart.

C. H. MILLER,
Major-General i/c Administration,
Southern Command.

16th November, 1943.

S.C.P. 24. 400. 11/43 S.P. 92944

EVICTION NOTICE: ISSUED TO EVERYONE LIVING BETWEEN EAST LULWORTH AND KIMMERIDGE BY MAJOR-GENERAL CHARLES MILLER OF SOUTHERN COMMAND, ON 16 NOVEMBER 1943. THOUGH NOT MENTIONED, THEY INCLUDED ALL THE INHABITANTS OF THE PARISH OF TYNEHAM. "THE GOVERNMENT APPRECIATE THAT THIS IS NO SMALL SACRIFICE WHICH YOU ARE ASKED TO MAKE, BUT THEY ARE SURE YOU WILL GIVE THIS FURTHER HELP TOWARDS WINNING THE WAR WITH A GOOD HEART."

published notices that the following farmers were quitting: S. G. Churchill (Tyneham Farm); A. E. Cranton (Lutton Farm, Steeple); A. J. Longman (Baltington Farm, Tyneham); J. H. House (North Egliston Farm, Tyneham); R. J. Cake (West Creech Farm, Steeple); T. W. Wrixon (Povington Farm, Tyneham); Arthur Cooper (Searley's Farm. Povington, Tyneham); J. Cooper (Jiggiting Corner, Povington, Tyneham); Mrs Vonham (Weld Arms Farm, East Lulworth); Mrs S. P. Damen (The Cat, East Lulworth); H. J. Sampson (Whiteway Farm, East Lulworth); H. C. George (Broadmoor Farm, West Creech, Steeple); Frank Cranton (Rookery Farm, West Creech, Steeple); A. E. Swain (Hurst Mill Farm, West Creech, Steeple).

Appended to the listings was this note: "The Auctioneers wish to draw special attention to the before mentioned sales and sincerely trust that all farmers from over a wide area will endeavour to attend as many as possible, to assist in the dispersal of the stock on offer, all of which is thoroughly recommended by the Auctioneers."

Footnote: Post-war pressure for honouring the wartime pledge failed to achieve the return of former residents. Instead all of Tyneham remains inside the country's premier tank gunnery ranges and has made a remarkable reversion into a natural wilderness with more wildlife potential than anywhere else on the South Coast. Buildings used to be regularly damaged, plundered, or even totally demolished, but many are now the subject of conservation projects.

Campaigning did, however, achieve public access on an unprecedented scale for a military firing range. A path network extends along the cliffs and across the hills from West Lulworth to Kimmeridge. These Lulworth Range Walks embrace Dorset's most stunning scenery and are available for public use most weekends and through the Christmas and Easter holidays, as well as during the Army's block-leave in August. The story of how Rodney Legg founded Tyneham Action Group, in 1968, is told in the present author's *Tyneham Ghost Village* which is currently being updated as *Tyneham*, with these books containing nostalgic before and after photographs of historic homes and their setting. Tyneham is the unique then and now.

Saturday 25 December
Glider pilots posted to Tarrant Rushton.

As a Christmas present for the 1st Battalion the Glider Pilot Regiment, it is arriving back in England today, from Taranto, Italy. The flyers are to be re-united with their Hamilcar gliders and the four-engined Halifax towing-craft of 298 Squadron and 644 Squadron at R.A.F. Tarrant Rushton, on the edge of the Cranborne Chase chalklands between Wimborne and Blandford.

Sunday 26 December
Puddletown farmer becomes an international broadcaster.

Ralph Wightman, known to the press as "the Dorset farmer" though he never actually farmed, has progressed from his career as Dorset's senior agricultural adviser to being the worldwide voice of the English countryman. He talks into the microphone as if he were having a chat among friends in the village inn, the King's Arms Hotel, at Puddletown, where he lived in a 16th-century stone-built thatched house.

TYNEHAM EVACUATED: THE ENTIRE PARISH OF TYNEHAM HAS BEEN REQUISITIONED FOR AN EXTENSION OF THE TANK-FIRING LULWORTH RANGES INTO THE HILLS AND HEATHS OF WESTERN PURBECK. EVICTION NOTICES ARE DATED FOR 19 DECEMBER 1943

Last year he was heard on the wireless, in the *Country Magazine*, with established rural pundits such as A. G. Street and S. P. B. Mais. Wightman's dulcet tones, warm humour, and practical down to earth common-sense immediately appealed to listeners. He found himself invited back by the B.B.C. to "star" in the programme.

Tonight he has been given the honour of delivering the Sunday *Postscript* which will be relayed by the Forces Broadcasting Network to all theatres of war, as well as across the British Empire and North America.

Footnote: Ralph Wightman went on to do 290 consecutive weekly broadcasts, describing the countryside at war and into the peace, for listeners in the United States. He was to compere the bulk of the *Country Magazine* series as well as make regular appearances in *Country Questions, On the Land,* and *Any Questions*.

For those who grew up with the wireless he was the best known Dorset man of his generation.

Monday 27 December
Paratroops exercise at Tarrant Rushton.

For R.A.F. Tarrant Rushton it has been a Christmas in and out of the clouds. The festivities were put on hold, having to wait until completion of Exercise James, on Christmas Eve. Paratroops were then grounded for all of two days.

Airborne troops were once more floating down today, in Exercise Wizzer, and the year is to end with more of the same, as Exercise Novice follows on Thursday.

Wednesday 29 December
Cross-Channel air activity knocks out eight V-1 'Ski-sites'.

Thirty-seven P-47 Thunderbolt fighter-bombers of the United States Army Air Force landed at R.A.F. Hurn today on their return from offensive operations over northern France. So too did two flak-damaged B-17 Flying Fortress bombers. The Thunderbolts had been protecting Liberator bombers that were also returning from raids.

There has been intense activity over the Cherbourg peninsula this months in which Hurn played its part. On 22 December there were 24 Spitfires at the station, from 131 Squadron and 165 Squadron, to escort bombers to Triqueville.

Eight "Ski-sites" have been accounted for in the vicinity of Cherbourg. These were being prepared for the new terror weapon, the FZG76 (Flakzielgerät = Anti-aircraft target device) or Vergeltungswaffe I (V-1 = Retaliation weapon 1) as the Germans have started to call it. The V-1 is a flying bomb which requires a concrete ramp — vulnerable to air attack — if it is to be launched with any accuracy.

During December
Flying-boats give way to landing craft.

The Catalinas of 210 Squadron have left R.A.F. Hamworthy to enable its concrete slipway to be used in training exercises to load landing craft with tanks and other heavy vehicles. There is a gathering armada of these vessels dispersed along the creeks and estuaries of the South Coast.

During December
Tanked-up in a Longham bar.

A heavy tank proceeding through the east Dorset village of Longham, between Ringwood and Poole, skidded off the road and careered into the public bar of the King's Arms Inn. The side of the building would have collapsed but for the turret of the tank which ended up supporting the bedroom floor and the bed of Michael Weaver, recovering from a bout of influenza. He is the son of landlord Leslie Weaver.

One soldier in the tank was slightly hurt but all the occupants of the bar, in the process of leaving at closing time, had remarkable escapes.

During December
Bridport man picked-up after a week in the drink'.

Perhaps the kindest sequel to a war story in the past few months has been that of R.A.F. Sergeant Ronald Foss, from Bridport, who was on a Coastal Command flight over the Bay of Biscay. The first person to know he was missing happened to be his wife, whom he married in April 1942, as she was serving in the operations room of the same air station. Ronald. in fact, was still alive, and would be picked-up from the sea a week later with enough experiences of the war to fill a book.

Footnote: Ronald Foss had in him not just one book but three. *In the Drink* would be followed by *Three of us Live*, and *Famous War Stories*. He was to enjoy a long retirement, with his wife, in London, Ontario.

During December
Portland insult provokes fatal shooting.

Some boys at Portland Royal Navy dockyard mocked a decent, self-respecting soldier, of the Buffs, and told him he was no better than a Home Guard. Instantly, in a fit of pique, the sentry shot dead 17-year-old John Groves of Williams Avenue at Wyke Regis. It was silly and unintentional, manslaughter rather than murder, and the situation rather than the participants was to blame. Give a man a gun and he may defend his pride as well as his country.

During December
Eisenhower's deputy is an Old Dorset.

Air Marshal Sir Arthur Tedder, who is General Eisenhower's Deputy Supreme Commander of Allied Forces Western Europe, began his military career with the Dorsetshire Regiment in the Great War. He served in France in 1915 and transferred to the Flying Corps in 1916, rising to become Vice-Chief of the Air Staff in November 1942.

1944

Wednesday 5 January

Battered Flying Fortress makes it to Tarrant Rushton.

A flak-damaged B-17 Flying Fortress of the United States Army Air Force limped back across the Channel today after sustaining 30 hits over Merignac airfield at Bordeaux.

The pilot proudly showed off his shell-shot bomber after he brought it down in a successful forced-landing at R.A.F. Tarrant Rushton. He found himself among the gliders that are preparing for Exercise Nox. This is a major training programme that is to run for almost a week.

Thursday 13 January

Military flying-boats return to Hamworthy.

R.A.F. Hamworthy is operating flying-boats once more, this time as a station of 44 Group Transport Command. British Overseas Airways Corporation crews are flying on military secondment.

Their Sunderlands are tasked to operate to Karachi — via Gibraltar, Tunis and Cairo — and will carry aircrew and other R.A.F. personnel who are needed in India and Burma.

Friday 14 January

Thirteen Tarrant Rushton Halifaxes cross the country.

Exercise Spook took place at R.A.F. Tarrant Rushton today; or, rather, it began there. Thirteen Halifax bombers of 298 Squadron practised long-distance troop carrying. They flew across England at its widest point, to Winterton on the North Sea, where 115 men parachuted on to a dropping zone.

The Dorset aerodrome has also been busy, from 5 to 11 January, with Exercise Nox.

Tuesday 18 January

Montgomery finds friends in Bridport.

"It is true you have made a score of enemies," General Sir Bernard Montgomery was told by a friend when he returned to England, after visiting Prime Minister Winston Churchill, in Marrakech. "But," he continued, "you have made hundreds of thousands of friends as well."

He found plenty of them lining the streets when his mid-month tour of the 21st Army Group, brought together as the British invasion forces for opening the Second Front, saw him being driven through Bridport. "Drive slowly," General Montgomery ordered his driver, as he realised that East Street was crowded with cheering civilians.

One lady pushed forward and succeeded in reaching his car. She thanked him for the "wonderful job" he had done in North Africa and Italy. Then she reprimanded the policeman who had tried to restrain her: "Constable, you cannot stop me from thanking the man who has saved his country!"

The general grinned broadly. He is returning to his old school, Saint Paul's at Hammersmith, which is his headquarters. There he will revise the top-secret "Cossack" plans for the invasion of Normandy. He first saw the details of Operation Overlord, of which he is overall land forces commander, whilst sitting beside Churchill's bed in Morocco on New Year's Day.

Thursday 20 January

Fog-bound Sunderland lands off Swanage.

The coast of southern England was fog-bound this morning as a Sunderland flying-boat arrived from Gibraltar. Flight-Lieutenant Satchwell had not received a message for him to divert from Poole Harbour to Pembroke Dock, in South Wales.

Instead, realising the impossibility of a harbour landing, he brought the Sunderland down in the sea, four miles off Swanage. Here she was located by a launch from Poole which acted as pathfinder for the final ten miles of the journey. The flying-boat slowly taxied towards Poole for four hours and was put on its mooring at 13.20 hours.

Thursday 20 January

B.O.A.C. airliner comes to Hurn.

British Overseas Airways Corporation is transferring its land-planes — as distinct from the flying-boats operating from Poole Harbour — to R.A.F. Hurn. Hitherto its solid-runway aircraft have been based at R.A.F. Lyneham in Wiltshire.

Today a Mark I Lancaster transporter arrived at Hurn for evaluation as an airliner in tests with a Development Flight unit. G-AGJI is the first civilian-flown Lancaster in Britain. It is without gun-turrets though it retains wartime camouflage.

Trans-Canada Air Lines operate a similar converted bomber and B.O.A.C. is developing a specification for the manufacture of a version of the Lancaster for peacetime needs.

Footnote: As a result, the first of the post-war civilian Lancasters, to be known as the Lancastrian, would be ordered in September 1944.

Thursday 20 January

Tarrant Rushton lifts off Canadians and tanks.

Both specialities of airborne warfare were brought together today, at R.A.F Tarrant Rushton, for Exercise Manitoba. It took its name from the participants. Firstly, eight Halifax aircraft of 298 Squadron carried the 1st Canadian Paratroop Brigade to a dropping zone. Then ten Halifaxes, from the same squadron, pulled Hamilcar gliders into the sky.

These were loaded with Tetrarch Mark VII light tanks which only just fit into a glider. Now too thinly armoured for normal tank warfare, this 7.5 ton vehicle has a two-pounder gun and a 7.92 mm Besa machine-gun, which were all that was considered necessary for taking on German tanks when it was made in 1939. In the scenario of an airborne landing, hopefully, it would be more likely to find itself in armoured reconnaissance or infantry support roles rather than facing the enhanced fire-power of front-line Panzers.

The gliders were released at 1,000 feet. One Hamilcar and its Tetrarch cargo overshot the landing area and split a Nissen hut apart as the tank shot forward from the debris. Both vehicle and driver survived.

Wednesday 26 January
Halifax crashes beside Bournemouth Pier.

Wreckage is being dragged ashore from a four-engined Halifax tug-plane, from R.A.F. Hurn, which crashed today beside Bournemouth Pier.

Friday 28 January
Horsa glider lands on a wet flare-path.

Two disorientated Glider Regiment pilots of the British 6th Airborne Division were relieved to spot a double line of flares at 20.00 hours this evening. They proceeded to bring their Horsa glider down on to the flare-path of the western "Trot" in the waters of Poole Harbour off R.A.F. Hamworthy.

A B.O.A.C. Sunderland flying-boat, waiting to take-off, radioed for a launch to come and rescue the pilots. Their glider, which had been released on a night-flying exercise, was then towed from the Wareham Channel by a B.O.A.C. pinnace. It was beached on the slipway at Hamworthy.

During January
U.S. Army hospitals built at St Leonards and Kingston Lacy.

An extensive General Hospital of the United States Army is being built on 20 acres of heathland to the south of the main road, the A31, between Ferndown and St Leonards, near Ringwood. It is being prepared for use as a major surgical centre for casualties brought out of France after the planned invasion of Europe.

Another American General Hospital is being established in the grounds of Kingston Lacy House, at Pamphill, to the north-west of Wimborne.

During January
Poole yards produce a landing craft per day.

Round the clock production in the three yards of shipbuilders J. Bolson and Son Limited at Hamworthy, Poole, brings about the completion of one assault landing craft every day. The LCAs are being tethered in Holes Bay.

The yards, formerly the Skylark boat business which made yachts and other pleasure craft, also produce Air-Sea Rescue speedboats and Royal Navy minesweepers, as well as carrying out repairs on tank landing craft.

Work practises have been revolutionised. One squad is responsible for the complete production of a single vessel and this has helped Bolson's into their premier position — the largest assault landing craft manufacturers in Britain.

Tuesday 1 February
Hurn and Tarrant Rushton are A.E.A.F. stations

R.A.F. Hurn and R.A.F. Tarrant Rushton are among the many southern aerodromes where the Allied Expeditionary Force has an inter-service dimension. Joint service chiefs today presented the Supreme Commander, General Dwight D. Eisenhower, with their "Initial Joint Plan" at Bushy Park, Teddington, Middlesex, which is the Supreme Headquarters, Allied Expeditionary Force.

Hurn and Tarrant Rushton come under the R.A.F.'s 38 Group which is now part of the Allied Expeditionary Air Force, controlled from Stanmore, Middlesex, and Norfolk House in St James's Square. This is the headquarters of the Air Officer Commanding-in-Chief, Air Chief Marshal Sir Trafford Leigh-Mallory.

Likewise the 2nd Tactical Air Force of the R.A.F. is working with the Second British Army, which includes the 6th Airborne Division, in the plans for Operation Overlord. British airborne troops are commanded by Lieutenant-General Frederick Browning, the husband of novelist Daphne du Maurier. Overall Army strategy for the invasion of Europe is being prepared by General Sir Bernard Montgomery who has proposed an assault front comprising two armies with the First United States Army (two divisions) on the west flank and the Second British Army (three divisions, including the First Canadian Army) on the eastern side.

Saturday 5 February
Germans lose M156.

Enemy boat M156, a Minensuchboot or minesweeper, is effectively out of the war for some time to come having been seriously damaged last night in a lengthy engagement with British destroyers H.M.S. *Brissenden*, *Tantside*, *Talybont*, and *Wensleydale*. She has been towed by a Vichy French craft into the estuary of Aber-Vrach.

Footnote: M156 was still not safe. At Aber-Vrach she was further damaged by bombs, from aircraft of Coastal Command, operating from Calshot.

Saturday 5 February
Amphibious landings on Weymouth sands.

The 1940 invasion defences provided an authentic backdrop to the bizarre spectacle of a practice attack by the most unseaworthy collection of craft ever to beach on Weymouth sands. They arrived in a fleet of LSTs, landing ships for tanks, and splashed down the ramps to wade ashore. The vehicles had to reach land in six minutes. The sea was obligingly flat.

Wednesday 9 February
Twenty flotillas planned for Portland and Weymouth.

Between them, Weymouth and Portland harbours could provide accommodation for a total of 20 flotillas of assorted landing craft for British assault force G (for Gold).

Held today at Portland Naval Centre, a top secret conference heard that the detailed preparations for Operation Overlord anticipate eleven flotillas of larger landing craft gathering at Portland and nine flotillas of assault landing craft at Weymouth.

Saturday 12 February
Leigh-Mallory visits R.A.F. Tarrant Rushton.

Air Chief Marshal Sir Trafford Leigh-Mallory, Commander-in-Chief of the Allied Expeditionary Air Force, today visited Tarrant Rushton Aerodrome. He saw preparations for airborne landings and also relevant German aircraft equipment which has been assembled at the station to show flying crews some of the enemy's innovative methods and ideas.

Tarrant Rushton hosts No. 38 Group, Airborne Forces, which was formed from No. 39 Wing, Army Co-Operation Command, on 11 October 1943. Its headquarters are at Netheravon, Wiltshire.

Wednesday 23 February
King George visits the 1st Dorsets.

His Majesty the King today visited the 1st Battalion of the Dorsetshire Regiment who are undergoing training at Halstead, Essex. He watched a company attack on a strongpoint supported by an assault pioneer platoon under Lieutenant W. F. Scott.

During February
Eisenhower and Monty at Bournemouth's Carlton Hotel.

The Carlton Hotel on Bournemouth's East Cliff is one of the perquisites of the United States Army's occupation of this holiday coast — they would call it a perk. It is host to the American Forces Bureau of Investigation and some crews of self-propelled guns but still manages to rise to occasional moments of style.

General Dwight D. Eisenhower, Supreme Commander Allied Forces Western Europe, and General Sir Bernard Montgomery, effectively commander-in-chief Allied land forces, though there is no such formal title, have used its facilities and the convenient clifftop view of rehearsals for invasion taking place in the bay below.

INVASION TALK: GENERAL DWIGHT D. EISENHOWER AND GENERAL BERNARD MONTGOMERY AT THE CARLTON HOTEL, BOURNEMOUTH, IN FEBRUARY 1944

These, sadly, have not been without their casualties including soldiers aboard several Valentine DD [Duplex-Drive] tanks which are both amphibious and land vehicles; failings in their "skirts" whilst carrying out the former role being the cause of the sinkings. These swimming tanks have canvas screens and propeller shafts at the rear. Hundreds of Shermans are being converted into DD tanks for the invasion assault.

Landing craft are now everywhere, including the backwaters of Poole Harbour, Christchurch Harbour, and the inlets of the Solent, such as Beaulieu River which also conceals the sunken sections of Mulberry Harbours. Most of the sand for making these caissons has come from pits at Stephen's Castle, Verwood.

During February
Massive airfield expansion at R.A.F. Hurn.

The two main runways at R.A.F. Hurn have been increased in length by half as much again and a square mile of heathland on the north and east sides has been churned into a moonscape of yellow sand, crossed by the curves and frying-pan shapes of a complex network of dispersal areas.

These are being prepared for an armada of day and night-fighters, transport aircraft, tug-planes, and gliders.

Wednesday 1 March
644 Squadron formed at Tarrant Rushton.

Personnel transferred from 208 Squadron, under the interim command of Squadron Leader A. G. Norman, have formed the new 644 Squadron at R.A.F. Tarrant Rushton. As with their present squadron they will fly Halifax tug-planes with glider combinations in an airborne assault role.

Friday 3 March
American paratroops in Tarrant Rushton glider exercise.

A detachment of 181 paratroops from the United States 101st Airborne Division are taking part in Exercise Sailor from R.A.F. Tarrant Rushton. They will be glider-borne with full operational equipment, including 17 trucks, 19 trailers, two jeeps, and 100 gallons of petrol.

Tuesday 7 March
American flyers take over Station 416, A.L.G. Christchurch.

A temporary wire-mesh runway has been laid across the grass at Christchurch Aerodrome which is now designated as an Advanced Landing Ground. It has become Station 416 of the United States Army Air Force. Nearly a thousand officers and men of the 405th Fighter Bomber Group have begun arriving by train from Liverpool.

They disembarked from the liner *Mauretania* which had sailed from New York on 27 February. She cruised at 25 knots, without escorts, and changed her course every seven minutes "to prevent U-boats getting a head on us". Observed Master Sergeant Horn: "You don't know how good North America looks till you see 'er a-slippin' over the horizon."

Their aircraft, P-47 Thunderbolt fighter-bombers — of 509 Squadron, 510 Squadron, and 511 Squadron of the U.S.A.A.F. — will begin arriving next week.

Thursday 9 March
More Anti-Aircraft Squadrons to guard Tarrant Rushton.

In view of its growing use and importance, the protection of Tarrant Rushton Aerodrome has been reinforced, with the

"GEORGIA PEACH": OOPH-GIRL ANN SHERIDAN GRACING LIEUTENANT CURRY POWELL'S P-47 THUNDERBOLT OF 510 SQUADRON OF THE 405TH FIGHTER BOMBER GROUP WHEN ADVANCE LANDING GROUND CHRISTCHURCH BECAME STATION 416 OF THE 9TH UNITED STATES ARMY AIR FORCE IN MARCH 1944

AIRBORNE THUNDERBOLT: 2Z-M "TOUCH OF TEXAS" FLOWN BY LIEUTENANT CHARLES MOHRLE FROM CHRISTCHURCH AERODROME BETWEEN MARCH AND JULY 1944

arrival today of the main body of 2733 Anti-Aircraft Squadron of the R.A.F. Regiment from North Weald, Essex. Their advance party arrived in Dorset on 2 March.

The first arrivals of another unit, 2819 Anti-Aircraft Squadron from Marston Moor, Yorkshire, are due on Saturday, with their main body to follow on Monday.

Sunday 12 March
Tragedy mars Warmwell's welcome for the Yanks.

15.00 hours. Tragedy has brought an abrupt end to a flying display put on by four R.A.F. Typhoons of 263 Squadron to welcome the 474th Fighter Group of the United States Army Air Force on their arrival at the former Battle of Britain aerodrome at Warmwell. One of the R.A.F. fighters spun out of control from a low roll and crashed half a mile west of the airfield. The pilot of Typhoon HHS MN129, Pilot Officer Graham Smith, was killed.

Monday 13 March
R.A.F. Warmwell is now American Station 454.

The Americans have designated Warmwell Aerodrome as Station 454. The 474th Fighter Group of the United States Army Air Force are flying the strangest shape in the sky, the distinctive 400 mile per hour Lockheed P-38J Lightning fighter. This has a fearsome reputation with the Luftwaffe who dub the aircraft "the fork-tailed devil".

Tuesday 14 March
Hurn changes hands as the Albemarles leave.

R.A.F. Hurn has been transferred to No. 11 Group, Air Defence of Great Britain — as Fighter Command is now called — and its three squadrons of Albemarle troop and glider transports have left for Oxfordshire. 295 Squadron

and 570 Squadron have flown to Harwell and 296 Squadron has been redeployed to Brize Norton. Last month they flew supply drops from Hurn to Resistance forces in occupied France.

Group Captain W. E. Surplice is Hurn's station commander.

Friday 17 March
Canadian Typhoons and Hurricanes fly into Hurn.

143 Wing of 83 Group of the 2nd British Tactical Air Force flew into R.A.F. Hurn today. They are Canadian, comprising the Typhoons of 438 and 440 (Royal Canadian Air Force) Squadrons, and are to be joined by Hurricanes of 439 (Royal Canadian Air Force) Squadron. Escorted by the Hurricanes, the rocket-firing Typhoons will cross the Channel on offensive operations, to dive-bomb targets in northern France.

Monday 20 March
Mines exercise kills 29 Americans in Sherborne Park.

The 294th Engineer Combat Battalion of the United States Army lost 29 men today in an exercise at Sherborne. A live minefield had been laid in a training exercise in Sherborne Park which has an extensive American Camp on the ridge half a mile north-west of Haydon.

On completion of the practices for the morning, at noon, the mines were gathered and stacked on a truck. This then slipped backwards. It activated one of the mines and the truck-load burst apart in a colossal explosion which ripped through "C" Company. There were no survivors.

The dead, in order of rank, are named as Sergeant Donald J. Walsh; T/5s Francis X. Gallagher, Warren F. Rapp, and Lawrence C. Sharatta; Privates First Class Francis J. Murphy and Martin A. Norton; Privates Charles W. Brinkofski, Robert M. Bucella, Edward D. Chiarieri, Anthony Cutrone, John P. Deevy, John W. Gadek, Robert Gladen, Jr, George E. Gundy, Harry B. Hanschka, Joseph B. Henning, Leonard B. Kerr, Stephen E. Kosiorwski, Roger E. Kroeger, Leo A. Lyon, John J. McHugh, Thomas S. Nicol, Lucien P. Pessoz, Conrad Propp, Robert L. Ready, Anthony T. Russo, Fred C. Tracey, Andrew Ter Waarbeek, and Joseph J. Zanelli.

The accident happened 500 yards south-south-east of Sherborne Castle, in the field to the south of the public footpath running from The Slopes to Haydon Lodge, at Ordnance Survey grid reference ST 650 159. "It was the loudest explosion I've ever

CHRISTCHURCH THUNDERBOLTS: 2Z-M "TOUCH OF TEXAS" IN THE FOREGROUND, WITH LIEUTENANT CHARLES MOHRLE AT THE CONTROLS, AND 2Z-P BEHIND. "2Z" SIGNIFIES 510 SQUADRON OF THE 405TH FIGHTER BOMBER GROUP OF THE U.S.A.A.F. WHICH ARRIVED AT CHRISTCHURCH AERODROME IN MARCH 1944

BURTON CLIFF: THE 150-FEET OBSTACLE AT BURTON BRADSTOCK BEING DRAPED WITH ROPE-LADDERS AS ROCKETS FIRE GRAPNELS INTO THE GRASSLAND ON THE SUMMIT. TROOPS COWER AT THE TOP OF THE BEACH IN THIS SUCCESSFUL SCAM PROJECT OF SPRING 1944. THE FIRST WAVE OF ASSAULT LANDING CRAFT COMPRISE LCA858, LCA668, LCA850 AND LCA851

heard," said ex-Foster's schoolboy Tod Frost, working for Arthur Jennings of Horsecastles Farm who has expanded his operations under the emergency agricultural arrangements to include 80 acres of Sherborne Park. Jennings and his workers, including Frost who has just left school, were threshing a rick beside the private road in front of Sherborne Castle.

"It was a tremendous explosion. One of the vehicles disintegrated and several others were damaged. I was on the corn-rick pitching sheaves on to the threshing machine and the Land Army girl who was bond-cutting on the machine itself was hurled by the blast in a heap on top of me, a

predicament I would have enjoyed under different circumstances. She was most fortunate not to have been impaled on a pitchfork."

The threshing machine — "a huge contraption" — lurched against the rick and then righted itself: "Had the rick been lower, the machine would have toppled over completely."

For a while the farm workers thought that they might have been witnessing realistic war-games. Manoeuvres and explosions are not unknown, though not previously from this particular spot, but it soon became clear that this was not intentional. "Our worst fears were confirmed," Tod Frost continued, "after the ambulances returned to the camp. Open lorries passed along the

STAR SHELLS: LIGHTING UP LYME BAY AT NIGHT, WITH THE CONCRETE DRAGON'S TEETH OF ABBOTSBURY'S ANTI-INVASION DEFENCES SILHOUETTED AGAINST THE SEA. THE ILLUMINATIONS WERE FIRED FROM 2-POUNDER POM-POMS IN THIS SCAM PROJECT OF SPRING 1944

road directly beneath us. We could see rows of mutilated bodies covered by their comrades, as best they could, with ground sheets. It was nevertheless an appalling sight."

A spokesman for the United States Forces, speaking from an office at Priory House, Greenhill, confirmed that this has been the largest single loss of American servicemen since their arrival in England. The story has ended the day impounded by the Regional Censor at Bristol and will not be released for some time, no doubt with the vague "somewhere in the West Country" location, or even its transfer to "a south-eastern county".

Footnote: Further "locational sensitivity", as it was called in an American document, followed from the fact that the spot came within the confines of United States Army Hospital 229th Camp Unit, operating under the auspices of the International Red Cross, in and around Haydon Park. Therefore the presence of ammunition, let alone its deployment in an exercise, was a contravention of the Geneva Convention.

Because of that the Germans were blamed. The story was allowed to gain credence that two "enemy agents" — named as Kurt Henlein and Ernst Buchner — had infiltrated the camp and placed a string of mines on an Army physical training course. The two agents would be executed by the British military at Salisbury in May 1944. The tale was hardly credible. Smuggling one landmine into a restricted area would seem possible but hardly the acquisition and placement of a lorry-load. It would also seem something of a coincidence that the victims were all members of an Engineer company whose specialist tasks included mine-laying.

Tuesday 21 March
Tyneham radar foils E-boat incursion.

An attempt last night by the German 9th Schnellboot Flotilla to carry out a raid in Weymouth Bay was foiled last night by the R.A.F. radar apparatus at Brandy Bay, Tyneham, which its counterpart on Portland Bill was able to correlate the movements of the enemy vessels.

As a result, the gun laying by coastal batteries of the Royal Artillery, from Swanage in the east and to the west from Upton Fort, Osmington, converged with commendable precision in the sea off St Alban's Head. It was so accurate that S84 collided with S139 as the attack was abandoned in disarray.

Tuesday 21 March
Friendly dog-fight at Hurn ends with death crash.

Hurricanes of 439 (Royal Canadian Air Force) Squadron, flying since January from Wellingore, Lincolnshire, today returned to their home skies above R.A.F. Hurn, where they were originally formed. Unfortunately, two American Thunderbolts were unable to resist the temptation of joining in their dog-fights, over the Avon valley and the New Forest.

As Hurricane LD972 levelled off from a manoeuvre it was hit by one of the Thunderbolts. The metal airframe of the American fighter sliced off the end of the Hurricane's wood and canvas starboard wing. Norval E. Pollock was able to pull the Hurricane out of an initial spin but he then lost all control and spiralled to his death, in meadows near Sopley, two miles east of Hurn.

Wednesday 22 March
Nine die as Hurn Halifax crashes on Moordown.

The seven-man crew of Halifax JP137 and two civilians were killed at 00.35 hours this morning when the bomber crashed in open ground below Meadow Court flats on the eastern side of Wimborne Road in the Bournemouth suburb of Moordown. It had lifted off from R.A.F. Hurn, a mile and a half to the north-east, three minutes earlier.

Either the heavily laden four-engined Halifax failed to gain enough height to clear the Bournemouth plateau, from a runway height of 33 feet above sea level to a townscape at 120 feet plus elevation of buildings, or the pilot gathered insufficient speed and the aircraft stalled. Sergeant Dennis Evans was taking it on an outward flight, from 1658 Conversion Unit, to deliver the Halifax to an R.A.F. base in North Africa. It was fully tanked with fuel and carried a cargo of ammunition and medical supplies.

As it lost height, the aeroplane clipped debris from the tops of Willis's builders' merchants, in a converted Victorian chapel, and the nearby former tram depot, on the east side of Wimborne Road. Then it bounced off the roof of a house in Malvern Road, causing the aircraft to ricochet above the home of Mr and Mrs Claw and family before diving into the ground beside the garages to Meadow Court. Both wings were ripped off and the corner of the main building was hit, killing Mrs D. Bennett in flat number 9.

The fuselage and tail rolled over on to the back wash-houses, behind two pairs of Victorian cottages, next to the flats. Percy Chislett was killed in the centre cottage, at 1027 Wimborne Road, but his wife and teenage son were able to escape from an inferno of exploding ammunition by scrambling out of the front bedroom window.

Sergeant Evans, aged 20, was from Middlesex. His navigator, 37-year-old Henry Roberts, was from Cheltenham. The other crewmen were Flying Officer Stanley Appleton (30) from Wembley; flight engineer Stanley Gent (22) from Portslade; Sergeant George Alexander, whose age is not given, from Bedford; and Sergeant Reginald McGregor (21) from New Westminster in British Columbia. The seventh man has not been identified.

Thursday 23 March
Blandford A.A. gunners go to London.

The remainder of the American 184th Auxiliary Anti-Aircraft Artillery Battalion is on the move from Blandford Camp to London to supplement the capital's air defences. Its "A" Battery left for Essex in January. It is feared that the Germans will bombard London with flying bombs.

Friday 24 March
Top brass watch Tarrant Rushton mass take-off.

The Halifax tug-planes of 298 Squadron at R.A.F. Tarrant Rushton today put on a showpiece take-off for the benefit of visiting top brass. Air Marshal Sir Douglas Evill had flown in earlier in the day with Air Commodore Francis Masson Bladin.

They watched as four Halifax aircraft, each towing a Hamilcar glider, prepared for a synchronised take-off. All four were airborne within 100 seconds.

Saturday 25 March
Seaplane saves 12 from glider sinking off Swanage.

A Walrus amphibian biplane of 276 Squadron successfully searched today for the glider of an airborne forces unit that came down in the sea six miles south of Swanage.

The twelve men aboard were rescued and the Walrus then taxied on the surface for 30 minutes to bring them into Swanage Bay. Here the soldiers were transferred to a launch.

MILITARY POLICEMAN: STAFF SERGEANT DANIEL EWTON, FROM CHICAGO, DID HIS BEST TO CONTROL WEYMOUTH'S GIS FOR A YEAR, BEFORE THEY WENT TO NORMANDY

Saturday 25 March
Mosquitoes fly into Hurn to defend the night skies.

Mosquito Mark XVII night-fighters have flown into R.A.F. Hurn from R.A.F. Valley in Anglesey. They are with 125 (Newfoundland) Squadron and will be controlled by Starlight, as Sopley radar is codenamed, in defensive interceptions over central southern England.

During March
Pluto is laid across Poole Bay.

Pluto, the acronym of Pipe Line Under The Ocean, has been laid by the *Tweedledum* — a great drum with cone-shaped ends — pulled by H.M.S. *Conundrum* and a tug across twelve miles of Poole Bay to the Isle of Wight. This experiment by the Petroleum Warfare Department seeks to prove the feasibility of laying an underwater pipeline from a pumping station at Shanklin, on the Isle of Wight, across the English Channel to the proposed invasion beaches on the coast of Normandy.

During March
'Scam' projects tested in Dorset.

Boffins are trying out their Scam Projects on the Dorset coast. A floating airfield, codenamed Lily, has been tested in Studland Bay by a Royal Navy Swordfish biplane carrying a bomb load and using rockets to enable an exceedingly short take-off.

"Scam" is the fun side of the secret war, experimenting publicly with projects of deception, this can be seen as applicable in seaborne attacks against the strongly fortified coast of north-eastern France — rather than the soft sands of Normandy.

For the Army there is a floating pier, the Swiss Roll, which has carried heavily loaded Bedford lorries across choppy waters in Weymouth Harbour. More practical are the rockets being used to fire grapnels attached to rope ladders for commandos to scale the 150-feet cliffs between Bridport and Burton Bradstock.

During March
Swanage Great War V.C. passes on his experience

Chief Petty Officer Ernest Pitcher of Swanage, who won the Victoria Cross in 1917 for staying at his gun in the classic action between an armed merchantman, a Q-boat, and a submarine, is back in uniform in this war at the age of 57. He rejoined in 1939 and is now training naval gunnery ratings.

Footnote: Ernest Pitcher died at Gosport in 1946. He is buried at Swanage, in the cemetery on the northern side of the railway, west of Northbrook Road.

Tuesday 4 April
Warmwell airman saves drowning child.

Corporal Jerry Liroff, an off-duty American serviceman from the 474th Fighter Group at Warmwell Aerodrome, dived fully clothed into the sea off Plymouth today to rescue a drowning child.

Friday 7 April
Hurn Mosquitoes on the sidelines for Window's private view.

Mosquito night-fighters of 125 (Newfoundland) Squadron from R.A.F. Hurn have been flanking, at a wide distance, the 25 Lancaster and Stirling bombers involved in Exercise Eric. The bombers flew a Good Friday circuit from Brighton inland to Stockbridge on the Hampshire Downs and then flew seawards across the New Forest to Lymington.

Here, taking advantage of the coastal blind-spot on German radar screens that is created by the Isle of Wight, they dropped strips of metalled paper, codenamed Window, which creates deceptive radar images.

The object of this exercise in the "radar hole" over the Solent is to practice the dropping of Window in a pattern that would suggest to a radar operator that a convoy is approaching steadily at about seven knots. There will have to be a long series of orbits that gradually overlap and which edge towards the enemy coast for a period of five hours. Precision flying will be required to create an illusion of ships rather than aircraft, and the paper will have to be dropped in bundles, to simulate objects of the required size.

Footnote: Over 100 aircraft would take part in the actual deception, in the early hours of 6 June, including two squadrons of Lancasters. One was 617 Squadron of Dambuster fame. The feint was intended to make the enemy think that the D-Day landings were taking place in the area of Boulogne (Operation Glimmer) and Cap d'Antifer (Operation Taxable) though the Germans went one better than this and thought the main invasion was happening much further east in the Pas de Calais.

Small naval craft, reflector balloons, and Moonshine electronic devices were also deployed. To complete the elaborate diversion, Stirlings of No. 3 Group Bomber Command dropped dummy parachutists, and acoustic machines that emitted the sounds of mock-battle.

Tuesday 11 April
Christchurch Thunderbolts visit France.

Fifty-six P-47 Thunderbolts of the 405th Fighter Bomber Group of the United States Army Air force today took off from Christchurch Advance Landing Ground. They assembled into their fighting formation at 20,000 feet over the English Channel and went on their first day trip to France.

The low-risk sweep of north-western France was intended to familiarise the pilots of 509, 510, and 511 Squadrons with the general geography and location of potential targets in the forthcoming offensive war. All the Thunderbolts returned safely.

Friday 14 April
Air-Sea Rescue Squadron drafted to Warmwell.

Another R.A.F. squadron has returned to Warmwell Aerodrome, which is the base for 48 P-38J Lightnings of the American 474th Fighter Group.

The Spitfires of 275 (Air-Sea Rescue) Squadron are specially adapted to drop dinghies, for pick-ups in the English Channel beyond the reach of the launches from Lyme Regis, Weymouth, Portland, or Poole. A Walrus seaplane will carry out the actual rescues. The squadron also deploys a two-engined Anson for carrying out searches and general reconnaissance patrols.

Sunday 16 April
British Force G makes way for American Force O.

Though expected to gather in Portland and Weymouth for Operation Overlord, British invasion Force G (for Gold) has been relocated eastwards to the harbours and inlets of the Solent and Southampton Water. Instead, in a case of musical chairs being played out on a grand scale, the Dorset ports are being re-allocated to United States Force O (for Omaha). As a consequence their target beaches have also been transposed, with the Americans to land on what is now designated Omaha Beach and the British troops to take the next sector to the east, codenamed Gold Beach.

Captain J. J. McGlynn of the United States Navy today takes up his post as Commanding Officer United States Navy Advanced Amphibious Base Portland and Weymouth. This includes the three hards at Portland and H.M.S. Grasshopper, the Royal Navy shore-base at Weymouth, plus ancillary facilities.

The Advanced Amphibious Base will be responsible for the embarkation of V Corps of the First United States Army which comprises the 1st U.S. Infantry Division, 2nd U.S. Infantry Division, 2nd U.S. Armored Division, and two Ranger battalions. Their departure will be in the hands of the 14th Major Port of the United States Transportation Corps.

Sunday 16 April
Headquarters of America's 'Fighting Firsts' moves to Langton House, Blandford.

The "Fighting Firsts" or "Big Red One", as America's famous First Infantry Division is known from its badge, has moved its Divisional Headquarters from Devon to Langton House, in parkland at Langton Long Blandford. The Commanding General, Major-General Clarence R. Huebner, has at his command 34,142 men and 3,306 vehicles.

Monday 17 April
80,000 American soldiers have moved into Dorset.

It is estimated that a total of 80,000 American soldiers are now billeted in Dorset, from the chalets of Freshwater holiday camp on the coast at Burton Bradstock to Nissen huts in hazel coppices on Cranborne Chase.

SEASIDE SERENADE: WITH THIS EVOCATIVE PHOTOGRAPH OF A PILLBOX BELOW BURTON CLIFF HAVING ITS STORY TOLD IN THE CONTEMPORARY CAPTION FROM APRIL 1944. "IN 1940 THE VILLAGE BEACH WAS GUARDED AGAINST INVASION, FIRST BY LOCAL DEFENCE VOLUNTEERS, THEN BY HOME GUARDS. TODAY, WITH THE TABLES TURNED, U.S. TROOPS CAN SPEND THEIR LEISURE HOURS ON IT. SITTING ON A CONCRETE BLOCKHOUSE, BEHIND WHICH BRITAIN'S AMATEUR ILL-ARMED SOLDIERS WERE PREPARED TO SELL THEIR LIVES DEARLY, CORPORAL BERT MARKOWITZ, 30-46, 23RD STREET, ASTORIA, BORRUGH OF QUEEN'S N.Y.C., PLAYS HIS VIOLIN. MARKOWITZ, A STUDENT AT THE UNIVERSITY OF MIAMI, PLAYED WITH THE N.B.C. AS STUDIO MUSICIAN. LISTENING TO HIM IS T/5 G. R. MILLER, 4106 VERMONT AVE., LOUISVILLE, KENTUCKY"

GENERATION GAP: BRIDGED BY COCOA, IN N.A.A.F.I. CUPS, PROVIDED BY CORPORAL DAVID W. ROBERTS, FROM IOWA, WHO LEANS OUT OF HIS HOLIDAY CAMP BILLET AT FRESHWATER, BURTON BRADSTOCK. BETTY "FRECKLES" MACKAY, A LONDON EVACUEE FROM THE BLITZ, IS ACCOMPANIED BY LOCAL BOY CHRIS KERLEY

CHESIL BEACH: EYES TOWARDS FRANCE IN APRIL 1944, FROM BURTON BEACH, AS AMERICAN GIS PREPARE TO TAKE THE WAR BACK ACROSS THE CHANNEL

GUN BELT: BEACH-FOUND, ACCORDING TO THE ORIGINAL CAPTION, THOUGH THAT SOUNDS CONTRIVED. THE SOLDIERS AROUND THE IRON SEAT THAT CIRCLES THE SYCAMORE TREE, ON THE TRIANGLE OF VILLAGE GREEN IN BURTON BRADSTOCK VILLAGE, ARE JOHN L. LAWSON OF PORT JERVIS, NEW YORK; ROBERT S. HASTINGS OF AZUSA, CALIFORNIA; LEO H. PEARSON OF SPRINGVILLE, NEW YORK; AND CORPORAL ROLAND HENRY OF HOLLAND, PENNSYLVANIA

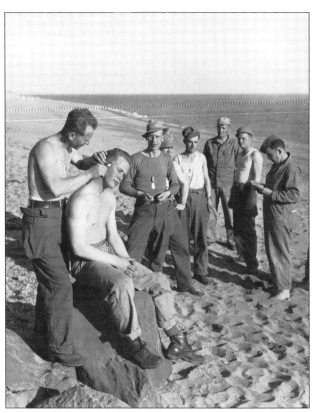

HAIRCUT TIME: ABOVE THE EARS, IN APRIL 1944 AT A LATE AFTERNOON OPEN-AIR HAIR SALON ON A BOULDER IN THE SHINGLE AT FRESHWATER, BURTON BRADSTOCK. THE AMERICANS OCCUPIED THE NEARLY HOLIDAY CAMP

GAS STATION: VILLAGE BOY MANS A. E. CHENEY'S PUMPS AT RED HOUSE GARAGE, BURTON BRADSTOCK, AS ANOTHER CLEANS THE WINDSCREEN OF AN AMERICAN JEEP, IN APRIL 1944. BEHIND THE THATCHED COTTAGE IS THE VILLAGE PLAYING FIELD WITH THE CHURCH TOWER IN THE DISTANCE. THE PRESENCE OF AN "HEADQUARTERS" VEHICLE SHOWS THE IMPORTANCE OF THIS PHOTOGRAPHIC SESSION

VILLAGE CANTEEN: GUNNER WEIGHTMAN OF THE BRITISH ARMY, AN OLD HABITUE, HANDS ROUND HOME-MADE CAKES IN APRIL 1944, AT BURTON BRADSTOCK, TO CORPORAL JAMES FLOWER OF WALPOLE, MASSACHUSETTS, PRIVATE FIRST-CLASS ROY ST JEAN OF SPRINGFIELD, MASS., AND CORPORAL ALLAN DECKER OF CHICAGO

RECTORY TEA: ON THE LAWN BEHIND ST MARY'S PARISH CHURCH AT BURTON BRADSTOCK, IN APRIL 1944. THE HOSTS ARE REV AND MRS ARTHUR DITTMER AND THEIR WHITE-PAWED TABBY CAT. THEIR UNITED STATES ARMY GUESTS ARE LIEUTENANT S. M. WEITZNER OF RIDGEWOOD, NEW YORK, AND MAJOR E. M. BEEBE OF BURLINGTON, VERMONT. THE LATTER WAS THE MANAGER OF THE TELEPHONE COMPANY IN BURLINGTON. THE DETAIL IN THESE CAPTIONS MAKES IT CLEAR THAT THEY WERE INTENDED FOR A TRANS-ATLANTIC AUDIENCE

TASTING TEA: "BRITAIN'S TRADITIONAL SOCIAL MEAL" AS THE CAPTION HAD IT IN APRIL 1944, BEING POURED BY THE VILLAGE SCHOOLMASTER'S WIFE AT BURTON BRADSTOCK. SERGEANT HAROLD D. KREGAR, FROM CHEYENNE WELLS, COLORADO, WON THE LEGION OF MERIT IN ICELAND

ASKING DIRECTIONS: "THE WAY TO THE VILLAGE CANTEEN", ACCORDING TO THE ORIGINAL CAPTION, WITH PRIVATE FIRST-CLASS ROY ST JEAN OF SPRINGFIELD, MASSACHUSETTS, CHATTING TO PETTY OFFICER PODGER "LATELY INVALIDED OUT OF THE ROYAL NAVY" WHO WAS BORN IN BURTON BRADSTOCK AND SERVED IN BOTH WORLD WARS

LUCKY HORSESHOE: BEING PRESENTED BY BLACKSMITH BENJAMIN BURTON TO THE COMMANDING OFFICER OF THE AMERICAN UNIT, IN THE SMITHY AT BURTON BRADSTOCK. THE OFFICER HAS A STICKING-PLASTER OVER A RECENT WOUND TO HIS FOREHEAD. APRIL 1944 WAS A TIME OF MUCH TRAINING AND FAMILIARISATION WITH LIVE EXPLOSIVES

MAKING FRIENDS: THIS WAS A GENERAL THEME IN THIS SET OF PROPAGANDA PHOTOGRAPHS, WITH AN AMERICAN ARM ON THE BOY'S SHOULDER AND BURTON BRADSTOCK BLACKSMITH BENJAMIN BURTON SHOWING THE HORSE'S HOOF. "U.S. TROOPS ARE DISCOVERING THAT THE BRITISHER IS NOT AS STAND-OFFISH AS HE IS SAID TO BE," THE CONTEMPORARY CAPTION READS

COMMON CULTURE: THE PROPAGANDA BEHIND THIS SUPERB SERIES OF PHOTOGRAPHS WAS EVERY BIT AS GOOD AS THE PHOTOGRAPH — FOR HERE THE SUBTLE INFERENCE IS THAT WITH A DATE BEFORE 1783, BRITAIN AND THE UNITED STATES SHARE A COMMON HISTORY. THE RECTOR OF BURTON BRADSTOCK, REV ARTHUR DITTMER, POINTS OUT AN INSCRIPTION ON ONE OF HIS TABLE-TOMBS, TO MAJOR E. M. BEEBE OF BURLINGTON, VERMONT, AND LIEUTENANT S. M. WEITZNER OF RIDGEWOOD, NEW YORK

DELIBERATE DISINFORMATION: THE LOCATION OF THESE PHOTOGRAPHS REMAINED A NATIONAL SECRET UNTIL THEY WERE FIRST SEEN BY THE PRESENT AUTHOR. THIS SCENE, IN THE DOVE INN AT SOUTHOVER, BURTON BRADSTOCK, HAS A PROMINENT POSTER FOR BREWERS H. AND G. SIMONDS LIMITED OF READING. THERE IS ALSO A SIMONDS CALENDAR, DATING THE SERIES TO APRIL 1944. THOUGH THE COMPANY ALSO HAD A DEPOT IN BLANDFORD, THE PROMINENCE OF THE POSTER AND THE PROJECTING NAIL HOLDING IT IN PLACE ARE UNLIKELY TO BE COINCIDENTAL; EVERY EFFORT WAS BEING MADE TO SUGGEST THAT THE INVASION WOULD COME FROM FURTHER EAST. AS FOR THE SETTING, THE GI OFFENSIVE BEGAN WITH ENGLISH PUBLIC HOUSES. THEIR PINT WAS BEER — DARKER BUT LESS POTENT THAN THE ROUGH CIDER OF THE LOCALS

Monday 17 April

Canadian soldiers occupy Bournemouth.

Bournemouth has been occupied by a succession of units that form the 3rd Canadian Division. Currently the town's hotels are taken over by the 8th Canadian Brigade which comprises the Queen's Own Rifles of Canada, Le Regiment de la Chaudiere, and the North Shore Regiment from New Brunswick. Brigade headquarters is the Lynden Hall Hydro in Boscombe.

Monday 17 April

Two killed as Halifax crashes at Tarrant Rushton.

Two Halifax tug-planes of 644 Squadron are tasked tonight for an operation over France but the shock for the squadron came earlier in the day when a routine take-off went wrong.

Halifax E for Easy stalled, and flopped on to the end of the runway, killing the pilot and the rear gunner. It had a glider in tow but its crewmen were unhurt.

Tuesday 18 April

The King watches Exercise Smash at Studland.

The 1st Battalion of the Dorsetshire Regiment returned to its native heath to take part in a series of mock-invasion assaults on the sands of Studland Bay. Unlike normal manoeuvres, Exercise Smash has been

distinguished by the widespread use of live ammunition, from small-arms fire to bombs and rockets. It has been studied intently, as a piece of military theatre, by high ranking officers and a succession of visiting war-lords.

Their row of field glasses has lined the slit of a massive concrete bunker, Fort Henry observation post, which looks northwards across the bay and beach from Redend Point, beside the grounds of Studland Manor.

Users of the binoculars have included His Majesty King George VI, Prime Minister Winston Churchill, General Dwight D. Eisenhower (Supreme Commander Allied Expeditionary Force), General Sir Bernard Montgomery (effectively, for the assault, commander-in-chief Allied land forces, commanding the British 21st Army Group), General Omar Bradley (commanding the First United States Army), and Lieutenant-General Miles Dempsey (commanding the Second British Army).

FORT HENRY: V.I.P. OBSERVATION BLOCKHOUSE ON REDEND POINT, STUDLAND, WITH THE RECESSED SLIT BEING 80 FEET LONG, IN CONCRETE WALLS ALMOST THREE FEET THICK

FROM BEHIND: THE BACK OF FORT HENRY, TOWARDS STUDLAND MANOR, SEEN FROM AND BLOCKING THE FIELD OF FIRE FROM A 1940-BUILT GUN BATTERY

MONTY'S VISIT: GENERAL SIR BERNARD MONTGOMERY, OVERALL LAND-FORCE COMMANDER OF ALLIED ARMIES IN WESTERN EUROPE, LOOKING AT HOME IN HIS ROYAL TANK CORPS BERET ON AN INSPECTION OF BOVINGTON CAMP, 19 APRIL 1944

The King's visit today was especially loud, being arranged to coincide with a demonstration of aerial carpet and pattern bombing. The royal train, also bringing Churchill and Montgomery, arrived in Swanage. Police then toured the town and villages to warn people to open all their windows — to minimise blast damage — before the air and ground of the Isle of Purbeck began to vibrate to the concussive thud of Studland's war.

Afterwards the King and the generals are dining in Swanage at the Hotel Grosvenor.

Wednesday 19 April
Montgomery inspects units at Bovington Camp.

The Driving and Maintenance Wing of the Armoured Fighting Vehicles School at Bovington Camp was inspected today by General Sir Bernard Montgomery, the overall land-force commander of Allied armies in western Europe. He came to Wool in his own train, the *Rapier*.

Wednesday 19 April
Bournemouth coast guns in action.

Royal Artillery coast batteries at Hengistbury Head, Mudeford, and the Needles opened up last night on E-boats of the German 5th Schnellboot Flotilla as they laid magnetic mines across the eastern approaches to Poole Bay and the Solent.

S64 and *S133*, belonging to the 8th Schnellboot Flotilla, were damaged in a separate engagement when a Hunt-class destroyer, H.M.S. *Whitshead* caught up with them in foul weather.

Saturday 22 April
Eisenhower and Leigh-Mallory at Tarrant Rushton.

General Dwight D. Eisenhower, the Supreme Commander of British and Allied Forces in western Europe, today flew into R.A.F. Tarrant Rushton to see the readiness of the British 6th Air Landing Brigade and its associated 6th Airborne Division.

He was accompanied by Air Chief Marshal Sir Trafford Leigh-Mallory, Commander-in-Chief of the Allied Expeditionary Air Force, and by Air Vice Marshal Leslie Hollinghurst. They addressed air crews in the station briefing room. Tarrant Rushton houses a total of 700 men of 198 Squadron, 644 Squadron, and "C" Squadron of the Glider Pilot Regiment.

PROJECT LILY: ROCKET-ASSISTED TAKE-OFF FOR A FAIREY SWORDFISH, LOADED TO 9,000 POUNDS, FROM A FLOATING AIRSTRIP IN STUDLAND BAY

Saturday 22 April

Warmwell's Lightnings sweep Brittany.

The full operational strength of 48 Lightnings of the 474th Fighter Group of the United States Army Air Force, from Warmwell Aerodrome, today crossed the Channel for a three-hour sweep across Brittany in their first combat air patrol. All the planes returned safely.

V.I.P. VISITORS: INCLUDING GENERAL BERNARD MONTGOMERY AND ACTING ADMIRAL LOUIS MOUNTBATTEN (CENTRE) ON STUDLAND BEACH FOR EXERCISE SMASH, IN APRIL 1944

Saturday 22 April

York transport flies from Hurn to Cairo.

Avro York transport MW103, in wartime military camouflage but manned by a civilian British Overseas Airways Corporation crew, has taken off from R.A.F. Hurn. The York is based on the Lancaster's wing configuration and power-plant but has been rebuilt with a wider box-shaped fuselage and different tail assembly.

MW103 is destined to make the inaugural flight on a service to Morocco and along the southern Mediterranean to Cairo. Most Yorks, however, will be used as VIP transports and flying conference rooms.

Monday 24 April

Two killed in Bournemouth fire-bombing.

Incendiary and phosphorus bombs fell at around 02.17 hours this morning and damaged a total of 156 properties in and around the Charminster suburb of Bournemouth. The fire-bombs landed in Stour Road, Avon Road, Gresham Road, Strouden Road, Beatty Road, Portland Road, Charminster Road, West Way, Malvern Road, Shelbourne Road, and Holdenhurst Road.

Two people are dead and seven injured.

Monday 24 April

Three die in Poole incendiary attack.

Houses were damaged last night in an incendiary attack on the northern parts of Poole and at Broadstone. Three people were killed, including fire-watcher Arthur Martin, aged 59. Many fires were started but almost all were swiftly brought under control, leaving only 13 people homeless.

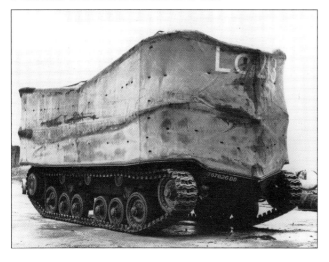

SKIRT DOWN: VALENTINE DD (DUPLEX DRIVE) AMPHIBIOUS TANK (top), SEVERAL OF WHICH SANK IN EXERCISES (below) IN POOLE BAY AND MORE IN ACTION ON D-DAY

Footnote: B. T. Condon recalled the night for me, in 1987: "I was home on leave from the R.A.F. When the sirens sounded I decided to go down to the A.R.P. Wardens' Post in the annexe of the Broadstone Hotel to see if I could be of any help to my former A.R.P. colleagues. My way took me past Willis the builders' merchants shop at the side of which was the lorry entrance to their paint store behind it. There I saw Mr Bryant, one of Willis's lorry drivers who lived nearby, and he asked me for my help in reeling out a small hosepipe to fight a fire which had started in the paint store.

"Imagine our dismay when we found that we could get no water through the tap, presumably because the Fire Service were using all the mains supply elsewhere. Some of the bombs dropped on that occasion were fiendish Ibsens [Incendiary Bomb Separating Explosive Nose]. These were designed with a delayed action fuse on an explosive device which separated from the fire-bomb on impact and exploded shortly afterwards with the object of maiming anyone fighting the fire caused by the incendiary."

Monday 24 April
Hurn Mosquitoes claim three Ju.88 bombers.

Eight Mosquitoes of 125 (Newfoundland) Squadron from R.A.F. Hurn last night intercepted a formation of Junkers Ju.88 bombers. All the night-fighters returned safely to the station, with claims that they had shot down three of the bombers, and that two others were damaged.

Tuesday 25 April
American A.A. gunners arrive at Gillingham.

The 554th Anti-Aircraft Artillery Battalion of the United States Army has taken up positions near Gillingham. Its headquarters is at Sandley House, between the town and Buckhorn Weston, standing above the tunnel which carries the Waterloo-Exeter railway line beneath its grounds. The low hill now bristles with guns.

Wednesday 26 April
Moving targets constructed on Kimmeridge cliffs.

Training for the Sherman tanks of the American 2nd Armored Division has become more sophisticated with the construction of a series of moving targets that are winched along narrow-gauge railway tracks.

The rails and winching wires are protected by stout embankments. Targets spring up behind them and can be made to move and stop like vehicles. Shells harmlessly overshoot the clifftop and fall in the sea.

This range has been created near Swalland Farm, on the Smedmore Estate east of Kimmeridge, and extends in six zig-zag sections from a point west of Clavell's Hard to midway between Rope Lake Head and Swyre Head. The main tank gunnery ranges are on the other side of Kimmeridge Bay, extended to Lulworth, having been massively expanded by the inclusion of Tyneham parish and other lands on 19 December 1943.

Friday 28 April
638 Americans massacred off Portland.

At around 02.50 hours a convoy of eight American tank landing ships [LSTs], sailing as Convoy T-4 in a circuit of Lyme Bay as part of the big Exercise Tiger practice landings at Slapton Sands, Devon, were intercepted by E-boats in the English Channel.

Motor torpedo boats of the 5th and 9th Schnellboot Flotillas ran amok amongst the Americans south-west of Portland Bill. A total of 441 United States soldiers have been killed or drowned, together with 197 seamen, with the sinking of *LST507* and *LST531*. What is described as a "handful" of Royal Artillery Bofors gunners have also been killed and an unknown number of men are injured. Twelve tanks have been lost and a third ship, *LST289*, has been damaged by a torpedo and is limping westwards towards Dartmouth. *LST511* is damaged by gunfire but has escaped the other way, into Weymouth Bay.

The coastal gun batteries at Blacknor Fort, Portland, prepared to open fire, but the American commander ordered them not to do so, in view of the number of his men who were in the water.

The only protection for the LSTs was a single Flower class corvette, H.M.S. *Azalea* of 925 tons and just two

Driving off: Humber armoured car F195705 drives into Weymouth Bay, with "40 MPH" being its stated speed limit

A Daimler: scout car F47943 "Razzle" heading straight towards Belvidere and Victoria Terrace, where Weymouth's 1940 anti-invasion defences run along the top of the beach

Dragon entry: F118445, a Humber scout car, carrying the Wyvern emblem of the 43rd (Wessex) Division. It is heading towards Weymouth's Jubilee Clock Tower (centre, with Gloucester Row to the left and Royal Crescent to the right)

Splash down: F195704, a Humber armoured car, stirs the calm water off Weymouth Sands as it drops from the landing craft

APPARENTLY SWIMMING: A HUMBER SCOUT CAR PLUNGES INTO FOUR FEET OF WEYMOUTH BAY

WADING EXERCISE: STUART TANKS PASS IN FIVE FEET OF WATER (NOTE THE "V" DEPTH INDICATOR ON THE STERN EXHAUST FLUE), OFF WEYMOUTH ESPLANADE

NEARLY UNDER: A STUART TANK DRIVING THROUGH MORE THAN SIX FEET OF WATER, WITH ITS GUN AND COCKPIT AND NOT MUCH ELSE ABOVE SEA LEVEL, ACROSS WEYMOUTH SANDS (WITH ANTI-INVASION DEFENCES VISIBLE IN THE BACKGROUND)

ORDEAL OVER: THE TIMEKEEPER'S RAISED FLAG SIGNIFIES THAT THE REQUIRED SIX MINUTES IMMERSION HAS BEEN ACHIEVED IN THE WEYMOUTH EXERCISE

HOBART'S FUNNIES: "IROQUOIS" FAILS TO CLIMB A
STUDLAND SAND-DUNE, SO AN "AVRE" DEVISED BY
MAJOR-GENERAL PERCY HOBART OF THE 79TH
ARMOURED DIVISION LAYS IT A CARPET FROM A GIANT
BOBBIN AND THE CHURCHILL TANK THEN SURMOUNTS
THE OBSTACLE THANKS TO HOBART'S UNDER-LAY

INFANTRY LANDINGS: LCIs (LANDING CRAFT INFANTRY) COMING ASHORE ON SLAPTON SANDS, DEVON, IN EXERCISE TIGER

guns, and the closest other Allied warship at sea at the time was 15 miles away. This was the 1918-built destroyer H.M.S. *Saladin* which would be followed to the scene by a modern destroyer, H.M.S. *Onslow*, built in 1941.

H.M.S. *Scimitar*, a 1918-built destroyer of 905 tons, had been assigned to join H.M.S. *Azalea* in escorting Convoy T-4 but she was withdrawn yesterday morning to Plymouth Naval Base, for repairs to slight damage to her bows arising from a collision with a LCI [Landing Craft Infantry], which occurred the previous night in Tor Bay.

Eastwards, the six MTBs of the 63rd Motor Torpedo Boat Flotilla had just returned to Portland Harbour from patrols into enemy-occupied French water that had extended over three consecutive nights. Leading Telegraphist Nigel Cresswell, the 20-year-old senior wireless operator in *MTB701*, heard tonight that the 63rd's services had been offered as replacement escorts for Convoy T-4, but this was apparently rejected by a senior American officer.

Their crews were sleeping when the alarm bells rang in Portland Naval Base at about 03.00 hours and the men of two of the 63rd Flotilla's MTBs were woken and ordered to put to sea. They included Leading Telegraphist Nigel Cresswell and Telegraphist Ken Leigh who switched on both their wireless telegraphy sets: "There was a fair amount of W/T traffic but it was all in code; a code that Coastal Forces boats are not issued with."

After an hour or so, *MTB701* was stood down, but only for a couple of hours. She warmed up her engines again at dawn and slipped from the jetty at 06.45, passing the harbour gate at 07.00, and proceeded at 21 knots on

various courses into Lyme Bay. In half an hour, *MTB701* was nosing her way amongst floating bodies, her navigator reported, and had brought four or five on board for identification.

This evening the 63rd MTB Flotilla resumed its usual patrol "on the other side" — across the Channel — and will return to Portland tomorrow morning.

Footnote: The dead would be stacked in piles on Castletown Pier in Portland Naval Dockyard. Offshore, teams of Navy divers worked for days to recover the identity discs from the other bodies, to account for all the missing and give Allied Naval Headquarters the welcome news that none had been fished out alive from the sea by the Germans and taken prisoner. Confirmation of their demise was accompanied by immense feelings of relief. "This cloud's silver lining," as it was put in a secret memorandum, "is that the invasion plans remain safe and secure."

The D-Day secret could have been compromised as 20 United States officers with the security classification "BIGOT" had to be accounted for, because they knew when and where the invasion of Europe would take place, and its American codename sector beaches, Utah and Omaha. General Dwight D. Eisenhower, the Supreme Commander Allied Expeditionary Force, had given strict instructions that no Bigot-classified personnel should go on any operation before D-Day, in case they were captured by the Germans.

The result was a cover-up that created the folklore of Slapton Sands. E-boats were credited with an audacious attack on massed Allied invasion craft, plus 30 Allied warships up to the size of a cruiser, off

THE SURVIVORS: LSTs (LANDING SHIP TANKS) THAT DID MAKE LANDFALL ON SLAPTON SANDS AFTER THEIR AMERICAN SISTER SHIPS WERE SUNK IN LYME BAY ON 28 APRIL 1944

the mid-Devon coast. That did not break the Eisenhower edict.

Had the true location been admitted, 70 kilometres to the east in the open water of Lyme Bay — in reality the English Channel — 25 kilometres off Portland, then not only had Eisenhower been defied but the question would have been asked as to why such a risky exercise had been mounted. Not only was there a lack of sufficient escort vessels but the manoeuvring of the LSTs was a simulation that could have revealed the route and battle-plan of D Minus One and D-Day itself. A disaster was nearly a calamity.

As for the horrendous detail, Leading Telegraphist Cresswell, living in retirement at Wimborne in 1999, was still haunted by the memory: "On a bright, sunny late spring morning I saw us approach what looked like an outdoor swimming pool, but there were hundreds of bodies in the water and they were all dead. I was not quite 21 and had seen the odd dead body, but nothing to what we saw before us. It had a profound effect on us young men and I will never forget it, ever. I remember examining two or three bodies that had been brought on board. Their Army denim uniforms had the button crimped to the material so that the buttons could not be removed. I remember two of the dog-tags had 'Rome City, New York'.

"Their life-jackets were different from ours, with two circular rings sewn together with a small cylinder of gas at one end. When depressed the life-jacket would inflate. We were ordered by another MTB to return the bodies to the water and in a letter to me, Able Seaman Torpedoman Wood said that we were supposed to puncture the life-jackets, as we had seen too much. I do distinctly remember seeing a very few bodies in the water wearing British Army khaki battledress with the square red badges of Royal Artillerymen.

Returning to Portland on the morning of 29 April, Nigel Cresswell walked through the dockyard to see his current girlfriend, Wren Torpedo Mechanic Doreen Smedley. He was told that the Wrens were not about: "Looking into the Torpedo Workshop from a distance of

a few yards I saw lots of shrouded bodies. I was quickly ushered away."

Immediately after the disaster, the Allied High Command initiated a total blackout of the event, and dispersed the survivors to various military hospitals along the South Coast. Medical staff were briefed not to inquire into the circumstances of their injuries. The penalty for breaking this injunction would be courts martial.

Sunday 30 April
R.A.F. Hamworthy closes.

The short direct connection between military flying-boats has ended at Poole with the closure of R.A.F. Hamworthy. Service flying-boats can, however, still be refuelled and oiled in Poole Harbour, by B.O.A.C. staff.

COSTLY VICTORY: MORE THAN 600 AMERICANS HAD BEEN MASSACRED BY E-BOATS OFF PORTLAND AS THEY TOOK PART IN EXERCISE TIGER, WHICH CONCLUDED WITH THE CAPTURE OF SLAPTON SANDS ON 30 APRIL 1944

Sunday 30 April

Thunderbolt crashes at Highcliffe School.

19.05 hours. Police confirm an aircraft has crashed near the Globe Inn, Lymington Road, Highcliffe. Christchurch A.R.P. have had a report of a parachute descending south-east of Hoburne House,

19.20. Damage reported to two houses in Woodland Way.

19.25. Report of damage to Highcliffe School and the A.R.P. store there, as well as water-mains fractured. A rescue party is being sent from Sandhills depot.

19.35. The aircraft crashed in the playground at Highcliffe School. It was a P-47 Thunderbolt of the 405th Fighter Bomber Group of the United States Army Air Force and had been preparing to land at Christchurch Advance Landing Ground. Its remains lie in a crater and pieces of metal and other debris cover the trees on the other side of the road.

19.40 It has been confirmed that the American pilot landed in the nearby recreation ground and is unhurt.

Footnote: Les White of Glenville road, Walkford, Christchurch, recalled chatting with the "Snowdrops" (U.S. Military Police) at their road block between Humphreys Bridge and S.R.D.E. (later Plesseys) as the Thunderbolts were landing. "Several were down when we noticed that one was circling at about 3,000 feet and as we watched we saw that the port wing was so badly damaged that it was visibly flapping. A coloured soldier came across the airfield on a bike and told the 'Snowdrops' that the pilot had decided to head out to sea and use his parachute.

"As we watched he baled out and the aircraft, now without any control, was caught by the stiff sea breeze and turned back inland. As my friend and I pedalled our bikes back towards Highcliffe we heard the thud of the crash and arrived on the scene to see the remains of the Thunderbolt lying in a shallow crater in the school yard."

During April

No. 83 Group has six rocket squadrons at Hurn.

Rocket-firing Hawker Typhoons of 181 Squadron, 182 Squadron and 247 Squadron, which form 124 Wing, are now based at R.A.F. Hurn. They bring to six the number of offensive squadrons at the airfield that comprise No. 83 Group of the 2nd British Tactical Air Force.

They are flying regular ground-attack missions across Brittany and Normandy. The rockets have their own propellant and fire clear of the aircraft without recoil. Eight are carried by each aircraft.

KOHIMA CAPTURED: ON 13 MAY 1944, BY THE 2ND BATTALION, THE DORSETSHIRE REGIMENT, AFTER LOSING 75 MEN IN A THREE WEEK BATTLE. THE JAPANESE WERE OUSTED FROM A HILL STATION AT 5,000 FEET ON A RIDGE IN CENTRAL BURMA. ONLY THE CHIMNEY IS STILL STANDING OF THE DISTRICT COMMISSIONER'S BUNGALOW. THE TENNIS COURT (ABOVE, TO THE RIGHT) WAS THE SCENE OF BITTER HAND-TO-HAND FIGHTING

SILENCE SIGN: "CIVILIANS ARE FORBIDDEN TO LOITER OR TALK WITH TROOPS." ITS LOCATION, ON THE A35 ROAD INTO DORCHESTER, BESIDE AN AMERICAN ARMY CAMP ON THE EDGE OF WOODLAND AT STINSFORD, IS GIVEN AWAY BY THE NOTICE ABOVE. THIS GIVES THE DORCHESTER 765 TELEPHONE NUMBER OF THE NATIONAL FIRE SERVICE AND THE POSITION "D.3". THE BADGE ABOVE THE SERGEANT'S SHOULDER FLASHES IS THAT OF AN ARMY FILM AND PHOTOGRAPHIC UNIT. HE IS NOT ONLY ONE OF OUR CONTEMPORARY PHOTOGRAPHERS BUT PROBABLY TOOK THIS AS A SELF-PORTRAIT, HAVING SET-UP THE TRIPOD MOUNTED CAMERA WITH A TIMED RELEASE

During April
Americans bring death to Dorset roads.

The increase that the United States Army has brought to traffic on Dorset's roads is reflected in this month's accident fatalities, which have risen to seven, from only two in April 1943. Colonel Frederick R. Lafferty, the Provost Marshal of 7-Base Section of the U.S. Army, is to instigate five Military Police Patrol Groups to control traffic flow at major junctions.

During April
Unexploded phosphorus bomb at Holton Heath.

A five kilogram German bomb packed with phosphorus has failed to explode inside the Royal Naval Cordite Factory at Holton Heath. The contents have been steamed out and the case put on display as a trophy.

Monday 1 May
Second Mosquito squadron comes to Hurn.

604 (County of Middlesex) Squadron arrived today at R.A.F. Hurn. They are the second Mosquito squadron at the station and are led by Wing Commander Gerald Maxwell.

Friday 5 May
Hurn Mosquitoes claim two kills.

Directed by Starlight, as the R.A.F.'s radar station at Sopley is known, the Mosquitoes of 125 Squadron and 604 Squadron were airborne last night. The Hurn-based night-fighters were successful in making a number of interceptions of Luftwaffe raiders.

125 Squadron claimed a Junkers Ju.88 bomber destroyed and a Messerschmitt Me.410 damaged. Their comrades in 604 Squadron reported a Dornier Do.217 shot down and a Junkers Ju.88 damaged.

Sunday 7 May
Warmwell loses two Lightnings in France.

Two American Lightnings from Warmwell Aerodrome, escorting United States B-26 Marauders into France, have been shot down. Lieutenant Merkle and Lieutenant Thacker are missing. The returning planes claimed one probable kill, a Focke-Wulf FW.190, which is little consolation. The station mood is grim.

Footnote: Lieutenant Merkle had been killed but Lieutenant Thacker would surprise his colleagues by escaping into Spain and making it back to Warmwell in June.

Saturday 13 May
2nd Dorsets lose 75 men to recapture a piece of Burma.

Having cost 75 Dorset lives in fierce fighting against the Japanese that has dragged on for three weeks, the 2nd Battalion of the Dorsetshire Regiment today achieved its costly objective and ousted the enemy from Kohima Ridge. Here a second-class hill station stood at 5,000 feet in the highlands of central Burma.

For the Japanese it is a major strategic disaster but for the West Country infantrymen it has been a visit to hell.

HOLES BAY: THE POOLE BACKWATER FILLING WITH ASSAULT LANDING CRAFT PRODUCED IN BOLSON AND SON'S SHIPYARD, AT THE RATE OF ONE A DAY IN THE SPRING OF 1944

SHORT SUNDERLAND: MILITARY FLYING-BOATS LEAVE POOLE HARBOUR TO MAKE MORE ROOM FOR LANDING CRAFT

POOLE BUILT: ROCKET-FIRING LANDING CRAFT, RCL (B) 640 UNDER CONSTRUCTION AT BOLSON AND SON'S YARD, EARLY IN 1944

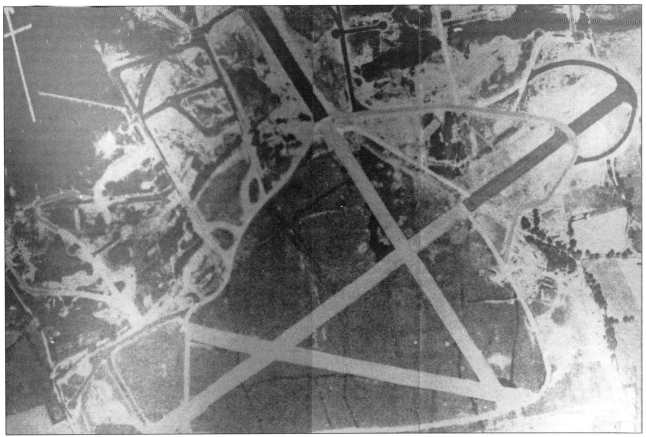

MASSIVELY EXPANDED: SHOWING THE HUGE EXTENSIONS ALONG THE ENTIRE NORTHERN SIDE OF HURN AERODROME, TO DOUBLE ITS CAPACITY FOR D-DAY RELATED ACTIVITY

Many of the Dorset dead had been left where they fell since battle commenced on 27 April.

The padre held a service on the tennis court near where "C" Company had sustained the greatest losses in the initial attack. The men were joined by Richard Sharp of the B.B.C.:

"We are still on the six hills in the centre of Kohima. We've mopped up nearly all the Japs on them, and we've taken the famous tennis court. A half-smashed bunker on one of the hills was giving us a good deal of trouble; but we took it at one [13.00 hours] today, and I've seen the hill myself. It's covered with dead Japs. I counted up to 40 of them and then stopped. Our men have been sprinkling them with quicklime — a necessary precaution in this weather.

"The men who took it came from a battalion of a West Country regiment. They've been plugging away at that tennis court for 16 days and they'd become personal enemies of the Japs there, who used to taunt them at dusk, calling across the tennis court, 'Have you stood-to yet?'

Today they're on top and they walked on their toes, laughing, among the bulges in the earth of dug-out roofs; their muscles limber, ready to swivel this way or that in an instant.

"There was a company commander [Captain Clive Chettle], a robust man with a square, black jaw covered with stubble. The skin between his battle-dress trousers and his tunic was bloody, and he swayed as he stood with his legs straddled. But his brain was working at full speed,

and he laughed and shouted to his men as they went eagerly from fox-hole to fox-hole with hand grenade and pole charges — that's 25 pounds of explosive at the end of a six-foot bamboo."

Saturday 13 May
Eisenhower meets the 1st Dorsets.

The Supreme Commander Allied Forces, General Dwight D. Eisenhower, today visited the 231st Infantry Brigade, who are training in the New Forest at Cadlands Camp, Fawley. Representatives of the 1st Battalion of the Dorsetshire Regiment were among those whose confidence he gained.

TRAILER PARK: RUNNING ALONG THE HEDGEROW, WITH THEIR TRACKED TOWING VEHICLES TO THE RIGHT, BETWEEN DORCHESTER AND WEYMOUTH IN MAY 1944. EACH SAYS "U.S.A."

HORSA GLIDERS: MANUFACTURED AT CHRISTCHURCH BY AIRSPEED LIMITED, AND SEEN AT HURN AERODROME WITH ALBEMARLE TUG-PLANES BESIDE THEM ON THE GRASS. THE ABSENCE OF D-DAY STRIPES SHOWS THAT THE PHOTOGRAPH PRE-DATES THE AIRBORNE INVASION, AND MUST HAVE BEEN TAKEN ON AN EXERCISE IN THE SPRING OF 1944. SOUTH-WEST IS AT THE TOP, WITH THIS STRIP OF RUNWAY BEING THE NORTH-EASTERN EXTENSION TO THE AERODROME. ITS INNER TAXI-WAY CURVES ACROSS AT THE TOP OF THE PICTURE

AIRSPEED KIT: HORSA MARK B GLIDER, CONSTRUCTED AT CHRISTCHURCH AND LAID OUT FOR INSPECTION AT TARRANT RUSHTON AERODROME BY 87 SQUADRON PERSONNEL ON 25 MAY 1944

Monday 15 May
Junkers Ju.88 shot down off Portland.

While on routine defensive patrol at midnight, a Beaufighter Mark VI night-fighter of 68 Squadron, from R.A.F. Fairwood Common in the Gower peninsula. made visual contact with a high-flying bandit over the English Channel. The interception, at 25,000 feet, was brought about by radar control, from Hope Cove in the hills above Salcombe, Devon. A single German reconnaissance aircraft was suspected — looking down on a Channel full of vessels as a big American fleet gathered off Portland.

The sighting was brought to a conclusion at 00.43 hours this morning. Beaufighter pilot Flying Officer Gilbert Wild and his observer, Flying Officer Frederick Baker, detail the kill of the Junkers Ju.188 in their combat report:

"Bandit had been gently waving during the chase. On closing in to 800 feet bandit was identified as a Ju.188 by the oval-shaped nose, long pointed wings and tapering tail-plane with single fin. From 25 yards range a two second burst of cannon fire was given and strikes were seen on the fuselage and port engine. We then got into the enemy aircraft's slipstream and dropped to port and below.

GLIDER TAKE-OFF: A TROOP CARRYING HORSA (RIGHT) BEING TOWED INTO THE AIR BY A TWIN-ENGINE ALBEMARLE TUG-PLANE

TETRARCH TANK: BEING LOADED INTO THE BELLY OF A HAMILCAR GLIDER

"On coming out with a slow starboard turn, we noticed that the bandit was turning slowly to port and falling. We closed in to 150 yards and gave a long burst, from dead astern, of about four seconds. Strikes were then seen on fuselage and starboard engine, which burst into a bright orange flame, spreading along the fuselage. Bandit then fell away vertically below fighter's port wing with flames growing larger and brighter.

"We then did a hard port turn and dived after bandit but by the time we got round the enemy aircraft fell into hazy cloud about 10,000 feet below, well ablaze. The time was then 00.43 and position some 35 miles south-south-west of Portland. As soon as bandit went down we gave 'Murder' over the R.T. and understood that a fix was taken by Hope Cove at Z 0560.

"In view of the continuous succession of strikes and the size of the fire which was spreading throughout the aircraft and the fact that it appeared obviously out of control when it fell away, we claim one Ju.188 destroyed. No window [radar-confusing foil] was seen, enemy aircraft was interrogated [asked to Identify Friend or Foe] three times on A.I. [Airborne Interception] set and gave no response. No return fire was experienced. No exhaust flames were seen."

The Beaufighter had taken off from Fairwood Common at 22.22 last night and returned at 01.30 this morning. Its four cannon, mounted in the fuselage, had used a total of 787 rounds of 20-millimetre ammunition, principally heavy explosive incendiaries. There had been

stoppages. The six smaller wing-mounted Brownings were not used.

Footnote: This kill was confirmed on 17 May 1944 when wreckage was found by the Royal Navy. The combat report was sent to Rodney Legg on 22 December 1991 by Beaufighter observer F. F. Baker, from retirement at Holme-next-Sea, Hunstanton, Norfolk.

Monday 15 May
Zeals Mosquito shoots down Dornier.

A German raider which penetrated Dorset air space in the early hours this morning was tracked by radar along a northerly course, inland from Lyme Bay, apparently towards Bristol. It was engaged by a Mosquito night-fighter of 488 (New Zealand) Squadron from R.A.F. Zeals, to the north-west of Mere, Wiltshire, which was flown by Flying Officer Ray Jeffs, pilot, and Flying Officer Ted Spedding, the navigator.

Their target, a Dornier 217K, was illuminated by Yeovil's searchlights as it crossed into Somerset. The Mosquito proceeded to rake it with fire. The Dornier's

ROYAL INSPECTION: REPRESENTATIVE AIRCRAFT OF THE BRITISH 6TH AIRBORNE DIVISION AT NETHERAVON, WILTSHIRE, FOR KING GEORGE VI AND QUEEN ELIZABETH

ROYAL WATCHERS: TETRARCH TANK T5309 EMERGES FROM THE BELLY OF HAMILCAR GLIDER, AT NETHERAVON, FOR THE BENEFIT OF KING GEORGE VI AND QUEEN ELIZABETH

ORDNANCE DEPOT: STORES AT THE FOOT OF AN ESCARPMENT NEAR WEYMOUTH, WITH UNITED STATES ENGINEERS LAYING A TEMPORARY ROAD OF WOOD AND WIRE, IN MAY 1944

LANDING REHEARSAL: A MOBILE CRANE TRANSFERS STORES FROM AN AMPHIBIOUS VEHICLE (RIGHT) TO A REGULAR TRUCK, IN AN AMERICAN ARMY EXERCISE NEAR WEYMOUTH THAT SIMULATED BEACH-HEAD CONDITIONS, IN MAY 1944

starboard engine was blazing as it lost control and crashed into the countryside at West Camel.

The pilot, Johannes Domschke (20), died from his wounds, but the three crewmen parachuted into captivity. They are observer Emil Chmillewski (21), wireless operator Waldemar Jungke (22), and gunner Otto Schott.

Footnote: Opened in May 1942, Zeals Aerodrome lay on a 550-feet plateau a mile north-east of Dorset, which is Dorset's most northerly parish, between the villages of Zeals and Stourton. It closed in January 1946.

Monday 15 May
Four hurt by Purewell bomb.

Four casualties were rescued from Purewell Hill House, Christchurch, after it had been hit at 02.22 hours by a German bomb.

Another fell at West View, Stanpit, at almost the same time. It damaged houses over a wide area. Bombs also dropped behind the OK Garage, Somerford, and at Woolhayes, Highcliffe. The latter failed to explode.

HAMILCAR 770: PREPARING FOR D-DAY, ON THE GROUND AT TARRANT RUSHTON AERODROME

ALMOST READY: HALIFAX TUG-PLANE WITH ENGINES GOING AND A HORSA GLIDER (BEHIND) ABOUT TO TAKE-OFF FROM R.A.F. TARRANT RUSHTON

AIRBORNE FORCES: HALIFAX TUG-PLANE AND A HORSA GLIDER LIFT-OFF FROM TARRANT RUSHTON AERODROME

THE CLIFF: BEING THE ESCARPMENT IMMEDIATELY NORTH OF TARRANT RUSHTON AERODROME, WITH THE AIRFIELD ROAD HAVING BEEN RE-ROUTED ACROSS IT. GOING "OVER THE EDGE" ARE A HALIFAX TUG-PLANE (LEFT) AND HAMILCAR GLIDER, HEADING FOR TARRANT MONKTON

COMING BACK: HAVING BEEN TOWED TO 8,000 FEET, THE REQUIRED HEIGHT FOR MANOEUVRING, A HAMILCAR GLIDER RETURNS TO TARRANT RUSHTON AERODROME

DORSET HAMILCAR: WITH INVASION STRIPES (RIGHT) BEING TOWED BY A HALIFAX TUG-PLANE, ABOVE CRICHEL ESTATE WOODLAND WITH BADBURY RINGS JUST VISIBLE ("A" AT BOTTOM RIGHT)

BLANDFORD CAMP: BELOW THE HALIFAX-HAMILCAR COMBINATION FROM R.A.F. TARRANT RUSHTON, WITH D-DAY STRIPES, IN A VIEW LOOKING NORTH-WEST TOWARDS A DISTANT DUNCLIFFE HILL WITH TELEGRAPH CLUMP BETWEEN THE AIRCRAFT AND WELL BOTTOM PLANTATION BESIDE THE CLOSEST CLUSTER OF HUTS (BOTTOM RIGHT)

Thursday 18 May

Mass glider exercises at Tarrant Rushton.

11.04 hours. Twelve Halifax-Hamilcar combinations of 208 Squadron, plus a further dozen of the same type of tug-planes and gliders from 644 Squadron, have lined up beside the main runway at R.A.F. Tarrant Rushton for a mass take-off.

19.00 hours. This morning's exercise is now to be repeated at Tarrant Rushton Aerodrome, this time with 18 Halifax-Hamilcar combinations, from 298 Squadron and 644 Squadron, in order to give the pilots experience of mass take-offs and landings at dusk.

Similar large-scale practices will also take place on 22 May and 29 May.

Sunday 21 May

American pilot killed at Cheselbourne.

An American pilot from Warmwell Aerodrome, Lieutenant Kimball, was killed when his Lightning fighter crashed near Cheselbourne.

Sunday 21 May

Acoustic mine defused in Lyme Bay.

Lieutenant-Commander Bryant and Petty Officer Clark of the Royal Navy have successfully defused one of the new type of acoustic pressure mines that the Germans recently laid in Lyme Bay.

They were dropped from Schnellboote *S136*, *S138*, and *S140*, on the night of 18 May. Conventional mines have also been sown by Schnellboote *S130*, *S144*, *S145*, *S146*, *S150*, and *S168*. The E-boats withdrew to the French coast on the appearance of three Royal Navy destroyers, accompanied by three motor gun-boats, from Portland Harbour.

Monday 22 May
Another Warmwell Lightning lost in France.

Lieutenant Usas, an American Lightning pilot from Warmwell Aerodrome, was killed in France whilst on a mission to dive-bomb a strategic target.

Tuesday 23 May
Two Junkers fall to Hurn's Mosquitoes.

Both night-fighter squadrons based at R.A.F. Hurn were operational over Southampton and Portsmouth last night.

604 Squadron failed to find the German bombers but nine Mosquitoes from 125 Squadron came upon them at 00.15 hours. Their first claim was a Junkers Ju.88 that was shot down at 00.20. It was followed by another Ju.88 damaged at 00.40. A third Junkers was then engaged and seen to be crashing to the ground at 00.46.

Thursday 25 May
Wellington crashes at Christchurch.

13.00 hours. An R.A.F. Wellington bomber has crashed near Christchurch Aerodrome, to the north of the railway line.

Saturday 27 May
More fire-bombs dropped on Bournemouth.

Incendiary bombs have been dropped by an enemy aircraft in the vicinity of the Roxy Cinema in Holdenhurst Road, Bournemouth.

Footnote: This relatively trivial incident would prove to be the town's last bombing. Bournemouth's wartime casualties now totalled 219 dead and 507 injured from a total of 2,272 explosive and incendiary devices of all types. Seventy-five properties were destroyed by direct hits and a further 171 were left so badly damaged that they had to be demolished. Another 13,345 required repairs; some were virtually rebuilt but the vast majority in each raid were patched-up with new glass and replacement slates. Half of the death and destruction were contributed by just one raid — at Sunday lunchtime, on 23 May 1943.

Sunday 28 May
Weymouth air-raid damages 400 houses.

At 01.00 hours the air-raid sirens warbled at Weymouth but two minutes earlier the bombs had started to drop and they were to damage 400 houses. About 100 of them have been rendered uninhabitable. Fire has also damaged Weymouth Hospital and the Christian Science Church. Three Civil Defence volunteers and a junior Auxiliary Territorial Service commander have been killed and 13 of the injured have been detained in hospital.

Patients from Weymouth and District Hospital, hit by a bomb and with another lying unexploded beneath it, have

FIELDING "ARMOR": AN INCREDIBLE MASS OF AMERICAN TANKS GATHERED AROUND DORCHESTER, FOR TRANSIT VIA PORTLAND TO THE BATTLE OF NORMANDY

LAST BOMBS: THE STREET SCENE IN MELCOMBE AVENUE AFTER WEYMOUTH'S FINAL HEAVY AIR-RIAD, ON 28 MAY 1944

been evacuated by Colonel Knoblock and the Medical Corps of the United States Army, to the Emergency Hospital established in Weymouth College.

Footnote: The hospital bomb had buried itself 28 feet into the ground and could not be reached and deactivated for several days.

HOSPITAL BOMB: DEACTIVATED AND RAISED, FROM 28 FEET BELOW GROUND ADJOINING WEYMOUTH AND DISTRICT HOSPITAL, HAVING FAILED TO EXPLODE WHEN DROPPED ON 28 MAY 1944

Sunday 28 May
German mine-layers driven off.

An attempt last night by the German 5th Schnellboot Flotilla to lay mines off the Dorset coast was seen off by a vigorous inter-service response. Beaufighters from R.A.F. Holmsley South in the New Forest aided the coast defence batteries of the Royal Artillery, from Poole Bay across to the Isle of Wight, and Royal Navy destroyers from Portland and Portsmouth.

The fleeing German boats used their speed to escape but took home some damage.

Tuesday 30 May
Mass glider moonlit take-off at Tarrant Rushton.

Tonight a mass take-off of Halifax-Hamilcar combinations at Tarrant Rushton Aerodrome is to test the station's expertise at mounting an airborne operation in moonlight.

During May
Paddle-steamers lay hundreds of British mines.

Requisitioned paddle-steamers have joined the mine-layer H.M.S. *Plover* in laying 1,200 mines in

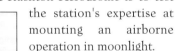
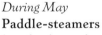

MORNING AFTER: THE SEVERITY OF THE DESTRUCTION VISITED UPON MELCOMBE AVENUE, WEYMOUTH, ON THE NIGHT OF 28 MAY 1944

BEHIND WIRE: AMERICAN GIs, FILING INTO A TENT FOR THEIR TOP-SECRET D-DAY BRIEFING AT A WOODLAND CAMP NEAR DORCHESTER ON 30 MAY 1944

FINAL BRIEFING: LIEUTENANT CHANDLER OF CLEVEDON, OHIO (top right), TELLING HIS MEN WHAT THEY ARE TO DO ACROSS THE CHANNEL, IN A WOODLAND AMERICAN CAMP NEAR DORCHESTER, ON 30 MAY 1944

SIGNAL CORPS: MEN OF AN ASSAULT UNIT JOIN "QUEUE UF" (right) TO WAIT FOR ORDERS TO FILE ON BOARD UNITED STATES LANDING SHIP 374 AT THE SPECIALLY CONSTRUCTED CASTLETOWN HARDS, PORTLAND, ON 30 MAY 1944

D-DAY BRIEFING: FOR MEMBERS OF AN AMERICAN ENGINEER UNIT AT DORCHESTER ON 30 MAY 1944. FOREGROUND (LEFT TO RIGHT) ARE PRIVATE ALBERT V. OTTOLINO OF BILLINGS, MONTANA; PRIVATE FIRST-CLASS HOWARD D. KRAUT OF BRUSH, COLORADO; AND PRIVATE J. H. JAMES OF WOODVILLE, TEXAS

POLO CHARGES: BEING PREPARED IN A WOOD NEAR DORCHESTER, FOR USE AGAINST PILLBOXES ON THE NORMANDY BEACH-HEADS, ON 1 JUNE 1944

WAR FOOTING: IN FIELDS BETWEEN DORCHESTER AND WEYMOUTH THE UNITED STATES 2ND ARMORED DIVISION CAST ASIDE THEIR TRAINING ROUNDS ON 1 JUNE 1944, TO LOAD LIVE AMMUNITION FOR THE IMMINENT CHANNEL CROSSING

MAP READING: THOUGH NOT OF DORSET BUT NORMANDY, FOR THE CREW OF A SHERMAN TANK OF THE UNITED STATES 2ND ARMORED DIVISION, PARKED NEAR DORCHESTER AT THE BEGINNING OF JUNE 1944

AMERICAN GRAFFITI: PLUS A FEW R.A.F. CONTRIBUTIONS, ON A BEECH TREE IN KNIGHTON HEATH WOOD, BESIDE WARMWELL AERODROME, MOSTLY DATING FROM 1944

defensive barriers to protect the concentration of invasion craft in Dorset and Hampshire estuaries from incursions by German E-boats.

The Auxiliary Paddle Minesweepers *Medway Queen*, *Ryde*, *Whippingham*, and *Sandown*, and the 10th, 51st, and 52nd Mine-Laying Flotillas have been carrying out the task under the watchful eyes of an assortment of escort vessels. These have been provided by the 9th, 13th, 14th, 21st, and 64th Motor Torpedo Boat Flotillas.

Footnote: These minefields were to claim the richest haul of Axis shipping in the English Channel of the whole war; 102 enemy vessels would be accounted for.

During May
700 Americans invade Charborough Park.

A United States mechanised supply unit of 700 men with 100 heavy six-wheeled vehicles has camped in Charborough Park and dug slit trenches for protection in the event of air attack. The only accident so far has been caused by a red stag that was nibbling grass and pushed its head into the sides both of a tent and a sleeping Yank.

The Americans have swiftly developed a taste for young peafowl — not unlike turkey, when roasted — and those from the Wild West are adept at throwing knives into the trunks of the cedar trees. Admiral Drax's staff have noticed that the Americans will drive everywhere, even for distances of only a few yards, and there is hardly a lawn or patch of grass that isn't being worn bare.

Saturday 3 June
'Most damaged' bomber makes it to Hurn.

Halifax Mark II bomber LV792, carrying the squadron code NP of 158 Squadron and identification letter E for Easy, took off last night from R.A.F. Lissett, near Driffield, in Yorkshire. Serving with No. 4 Group, Bomber Command, it was tasked to attack railway marshalling yards at Trappes, five miles from Versailles, to disrupt German reinforcements bound for Normandy in the aftermath of the impending invasion of Europe.

En route home, at Evreux to the north-west of Paris, it was attacked by a German night-fighter with "Nacht Musik" — an upward firing cannon — which hit the port inner engine of the four-engined Halifax and which was set on fire and had to be feathered. The port wheel was damaged. The wireless operator, Sergeant Len Dwan, was wounded as his position was struck, with a hole three feet long being blown out of the side of the aircraft.

The same shell shattered the radio in the cockpit, and holed the Perspex over the pilot's head, causing "a tremendous draught of air through the plane". It also disabled the magnetic compass. Another large hole was blown through the starboard wing, inboard of the engine, and through the main petrol tank.

The bomb doors were blown away and the bomb bay set on fire. From the underside of the fuselage both the H2S airborne radar scanner and the DR compass were completely blown away. The air bomber, Flying Officer Eric Tansley, surveyed the damage around him: "The fire in the bomb bay was hydraulic fluid burning, so the flaps fell half down, and later the undercarriage control could only be lowered by the emergency release. All radio and electrics and hydraulics were out of commission."

The flight engineer, Sergeant Len Cotterell, and the mid-gunner, Sergeant Len Leheup, baled out, mistakenly thinking the pilot had given the order to abandon the aircraft. Later the badly injured wireless operator baled out. The rear gunner, Sergeant Dave Arundel, was

jammed in his turret and could do nothing until he hacked his way out with his axe. He then went forward to see the situation: "When he saw us he went back, got his parachute and two fire extinguishers, and tackled the blaze. The flames were leaping high and he soon used up the two extinguishers. Then he beat out the fire with his feet and hands."

The pilot, Flying Officer Doug Bancroft of the Royal Australian Air Force, was unaware that the P4 compass had a piece of shrapnel in it and was stuck on the course being flown at the time of the attack.

Flying Officer Tansley resumes his account: "Some time later the navigator asked the pilot what course he was flying and Doug replied, 'Oh, about north.' I looked ahead of the cockpit and saw the moon dead ahead. Something registered with me and I said to Doug, an Australian, that we never have the moon in the north. His mental view of the sky was that in the southern hemisphere. Then he looked around for the Pole Star, by which time we were apprehensive about how far we had flown in a south-westerly direction, and whether we would still reach England on a northerly course."

Though problematic, that new line proved to be their salvation, as it would keep them clear of the higher cliffs of Dorset to the west and the Isle of Wight to the east.

SUPPLY CRAFT: MATERIAL BECAME ALMOST AS IMPORTANT AS MEN, AND LAUNCHES WERE CONSTANTLY SPEEDING FROM THE SHORE TO SHIPS AT ANCHOR IN PORTLAND HARBOUR, ALL THROUGH THE LAST WEEK OF MAY AND THE FIRST DAYS OF JUNE 1944

FOND FAREWELL: LANDLADY ELIZABETH COMBEN (CENTRE) SAYING GOODBYE TO THE UNITED STATES NAVY OUTSIDE THE COVE HOUSE HOTEL, PORTLAND, ON 3 JUNE 1944. ONE OF THE MEN, JOHNNY DUNPHY (FAR LEFT, STANDING) WOULD KEEP IN TOUCH WITH HER FOR THE REST OF HIS LIFE

HURN LANDING: FOR THE WAR'S "MOST DAMAGED BOMBER" WHICH MIRACULOUSLY SURVIVED, THOUGH WITH ONLY SOME OF HER CREW, ON 3 JUNE 1944

Between these obstacles is a low plateau at the 120-feet contour, rising to 200 feet with in-depth hazards such as rooftops, steeples, and chimneys, which was enough of a barrier.

"These coastal cliffs were only just cleared and the landing was made inland, fortunately as it was by complete chance, on Hurn Aerodrome behind the town of Bournemouth. The bomb bay was still burning. As we came to rest it was the sight of an R.A.F. ambulance that made us realise that by a miracle we had happened to land on an airfield."

This combination of low cliffs and an operational base with full-length runways, only four miles inland, occurs in only a handful of locations along the South Coast. The Air Ministry is preparing a press report — omitting such locational details — to the effect that this is the most damaged plane to return to England. The four returnees are being rewarded with immediate Distinguished Flying Crosses (for Bancroft and Tansley, plus the navigator, who is Flying Officer Alwyn Fripp of the Royal Australian Air Force) and a Distinguished Flying Medal (for Arundel).

LV792 is being declared "Category B/FB" — which is a complete write off.

Footnote: Doug Bancroft removed the instrument panel as a souvenir and presented it to the R.A.A.F. Museum in Canberra, where it is now on display. The pilot went on to have other flying misadventures, including the crash of a Dakota in post-war India, where his heroism earned him the George Medal.

AMERICAN DUKWS: LINED-UP ALONG THE CHESIL BEACH ON 3 JUNE 1944, WATING THEIR TURN TO GO INTO LANDING SHIPS ON THE CASTLETOWN HARDS

LIGHTNING FIGHTER: AMERICAN CROSS-CHANNEL ATTACK AIRCRAFT WERE BASED AT WARMWELL AERODROME DURING THE SUMMER OF 1944

The wireless operator was never heard of again, but Len Cotterell met up with the French Resistance and went on several operations with them, before reaching Allied invasion forces in Normandy.

Ken Leheup, though he landed at the opposite end of the same field as Cotterell, found a very different fate. He stumbled on a German arms dump in a wood and the Gestapo threatened to kill him for refusing to name the farmer who had given him food and clothes. He gradually recovered in peacetime, and enjoyed a long retirement in west Dorset, at Broadwindsor, where he died in 1999.

Contemporary news management, as happens so often in wartime, went somewhat awry. "Seldom can an aircraft have remained in the sky after having been so badly damaged," the report went, but either envelopes or wires were crossed. For it is Pilot Officer Bancroft of Pennant Hills, Sydney, who is the hero for the London Daily Telegraph. Flying Officer Tansley — then from St Albans and later Upper Brailes, near Banbury, Oxfordshire — had his story published on the other side of the world, in the Sydney Sun.

Sunday 4 June
Montgomery — 'The time has come'.

Message to all ranks of 21st Army Group from its Commander-in-Chief, General Sir Bernard Montgomery: "The time has come to deal the enemy a terrific blow in Western Europe. To us is given the honour of striking a blow for freedom which will live in history."

Sunday 4 June
Invasion postponed for 24 hours.

21.00 hours. Wind speeds in the English Channel are predicted for the morning to be west-north-west Force Five [19 to 24 miles per hour], termed a "fresh breeze" on the Beaufort Wind Scale, with consequent mid-Channel waves six feet in height.

Hearing this, and that the wind should then back to west-south-west and slacken to Force Three [8 to 12 miles per hour] or Four [13 to 18 miles per hour], General Dwight D. Eisenhower and Admiral Sir Bertram Ramsay and their chiefs of staff have had to reconsider the plans for tomorrow's invasion of Europe.

Meeting in the library of Southwick Park, near Portsmouth, they have postponed Operation Overlord for 24 hours. The lesser winds forecast for Tuesday amount to only a gentle or moderate breeze.

Sunday 4 June
French battleship in difficulty off Bournemouth.

22.00 hours. The D-Day postponed signal has been sent to anchorages and aerodromes across southern England. Some slower vessels were already at sea, such as the old French battleship *Courbet* which was being

21 ARMY GROUP

PERSONAL MESSAGE
FROM THE C-in-C

To be read out to all Troops

1. The time has come to deal the enemy a terrific blow in Western Europe.

The blow will be struck by the combined sea, land, and air forces of the Allies—together constituting one great Allied team, under the supreme command of General Eisenhower.

2. On the eve of this great adventure I send my best wishes to every soldier in the Allied team.

To us is given the honour of striking a blow for freedom which will live in history; and in the better days that lie ahead men will speak with pride of our doings. We have a great and a righteous cause.

Let us pray that " The Lord Mighty in Battle " will go forth with our armies, and that His special providence will aid us in the struggle.

3. I want every soldier to know that I have complete confidence in the successful outcome of the operations that we are now about to begin.

With stout hearts, and with enthusiasm for the contest, let us go forward to victory.

4. And, as we enter the battle, let us recall the words of a famous soldier spoken many years ago :—

> " *He either fears his fate too much,*
> *Or his deserts are small.*
> *Who dare not put it to the touch,*
> *To win or lose it all.*"

5. Good luck to each one of you. And good hunting on the mainland of Europe.

B. L. Montgomery

COMMANDER'S MESSAGE: FROM GENERAL BERNARD MONTGOMERY, COMMANDER-IN-CHIEF ALLIED LAND FORCES. IT IS ADDRESSED TO "ALL TROOPS" IN 21 ARMY GROUP, WHICH COMPRISES THE FIRST UNITED STATES ARMY, THE FIRST CANADIAN ARMY, THE SECOND BRITISH ARMY, AIRBORNE FORCES, CONTINENTAL CONTINGENTS, AND HEADQUARTERS STAFF

Codename Phoenix: one of the 146 concrete caissons, of varying height and weighing between 1,500 and 6,000 tons, that will be towed across to Normandy to arrive on the top of tide on D+3, if weather conditions are suitable. They will be sunk on the offshore sands to form two huge prefabricated harbours, each the size of that at Dover. These are codenamed Mulberries and will be protected by Gooseberry blockships

Weather map: 4 June 1944, at 21.00 hours. The "Most Secret" meteorological chart of the North Atlantic which promises a respite of 24 hours between vigorous depressions and their associated south-westerly winds. It is "chancy" and below "minimum requirements," explained the senior Overlord meteorologist, Group Captain J. N. Stagg, "but it does represent something of a lull on Tuesday". The Supreme Allied Commander, General Eisenhower, eventually made up his mind that Tuesday 6 June would be D-Day, saying "I am quite positive we must give the order ... I don't like it, but there it is. I don't see how we can do anything else."

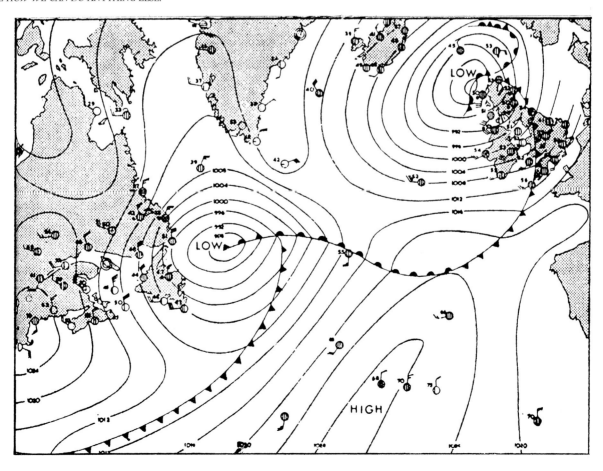

REFRESHMENT POST: COFFEE AND DOUGHNUTS *"FROM THE FOLKS BACK HOME THROUGH THE AMERICAN RED CROSS"* FOR GIs OF FORCE O FOR OMAHA AS THEY PASS THROUGH GREENHILL AT THE NORTHERN END OF THE ESPLANADE, WEYMOUTH, ON 4 JUNE 1944

LAMBETH WALK: ASSAULT TROOPS OF FORCE O FOR OMAHA ON CUSTOM HOUSE QUAY, WEYMOUTH, ON 4 JUNE 1944. IT IS MOCK RELAXATION ON THE EVE OF WHAT THEY KNOW IS GOING TO BE THE LONGEST (OR SHORTEST) DAY OF THEIR LIVES

"STATIC TROOPS": NEGRO LABOUR, TO USE THE CONTEMPORARY NOMENCLATURE, WITH AN ALL-BLACK UNIT LOADING STORES INTO ASSAULT LANDING CRAFT MOORED BESIDE WEYMOUTH QUAY, ON 3 JUNE 1944. THE INFANTRY WOULD GO ABOARD THE FOLLOWING DAY

PORTLAND EMBARKATION: A FULLY-LOADED DUKW ENTERING THE GAPING JAWS OF AMERICAN LANDING SHIP 376 ON A PURPOSELY CONSTRUCTED JETTY CLOSE TO THE NAVAL OIL TANKS AT CASTLETOWN

FRENETIC ACTIVITY: PREPARING ASSAULT LANDING CRAFT MOORED BESIDE WEYMOUTH QUAY ON 3 JUNE 1944, SOUTH-WEST OF THE RITZ THEATRE (BURNT DOWN IN THE 1950S AND REPLACED BY THE PAVILION). WEYMOUTH'S LANDING STAGE STATION IS TO THE RIGHT

DORSET'S AMERICANS: RED FIGURE EMBLEM OF THE UNITED STATES 1ST INFANTRY DIVISION (left), THE "FIGHTING FIRSTS" WHO WILL SAIL FOR OMAHA BEACH FROM WEYMOUTH AND PORTLAND, ON D-DAY. THEY ARE TO BE REINFORCED ON D-DAY PLUS 1 BY THE 2ND UNITED STATES INFANTRY DIVISION, WHOSE SLOGAN IS "SECOND TO NONE". THEIR EMBLEM IS A SHIELD WITH A FIVE-POINTED STAR THAT FEATURES AN INDIAN HEAD (right)

TRANSPORTATION EMBLEM: SEEN EVERYWHERE AROUND WEYMOUTH AND PORTLAND, AND QUITE COMMON AT POOLE AS WELL, BEING THAT OF THE 14TH MAJOR PORT OF THE UNITED STATES ARMY TRANSPORTATION CORPS.

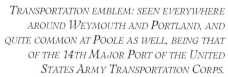

GI SINGING: PRIOR TO LOADING ON THE U.S.S. HENRICO, BOUND FOR NORMANDY, AT WEYMOUTH HARBOUR ON 4 JUNE 1944

ATTENTIVE AUDIENCE: AMERICAN INFANTRY, WITH BLACKENED FACES AND CAMOUFLAGED HELMETS, LEARNING THE LESSONS OF THEIR LAST EXERCISE INTO DORCHESTER'S COUNTRYSIDE PRIOR TO D-DAY

ASSAULT UNIT: AMERICANS TRAMPING AS TO WAR, ALONG THE PROMENADE, PASSING THE WESTMINSTER BANK AND DOROTHY RESTAURANT, TOWARDS EMBARKATION FOR OMAHA BEACH FROM WEYMOUTH HARBOUR, 4 JUNE 1944

ASSAULT CRAFT: LANDING CRAFT ASSAULT BEING BROUGHT INTO POSITION FOR LOADING ON THE MORNING OF 4 JUNE 1944. LCA421 AND LCA626 ARE IN THE FOREGROUND WITH LCA622 (CENTRE) AND LCA550 (RIGHT) MIDSTREAM IN WEYMOUTH HARBOUR. THERE IS A FIFTH LCA ON THE OTHER SIDE, TO THE LEFT OF THE PLEASURE-STEAMER OFFICES OF "COSENS & CO LTD"

D-DAY DRIVERS: FIRST LIEUTENANT ROBERT T. ELDIN (LEFT) OF LOS ANGELES AND FIRST LIEUTENANT STANLEY WHITE FROM NEW JERSEY, AT THE CONTROLS OF AN ASSAULT LANDING CRAFT OPPOSITE COSENS'S STEAMER OFFICE IN WEYMOUTH HARBOUR, ON 4 JUNE 1944

POINTING FINGER: ONE AMERICAN SOLDIER HAS SPOTTED THE CAMERA, BREAKING THE MONOTONY OF THE LONG WAIT BESIDE PORTLAND HARBOUR ON D-DAY MINUS ONE

"BATTLE BOUND": THE MESSAGE ON THE BONNET OF ONE OF THE VEHICLES OF THE AMERICAN ARMY WAITING AT CASTLETOWN, PORTLAND, FOR THE SIGNAL TO CROSS THE ENGLISH CHANNEL

NIGHTMARE VOYAGE: ASSAULT TROOPS BEING PACKED ABOARD A LANDING CRAFT IN WEYMOUTH HARBOUR, ON 4 JUNE 1944, WITH THE PROSPECT OF WASTING THE FOLLOWING DAY WAITING FOR THE WEATHER

towed south of the Needles and made heavy going off Bournemouth. Filled with concrete, she is a "Gooseberry" Blockship and is to be sunk off the coast of Normandy. Meanwhile, with considerable difficulty, her tug has brought her into the lee of Durlston Head, Swanage, where she has dropped her 7-tonne anchor.

As the engines and boilers have been stripped the great vessel has no power with which to weigh anchor tomorrow evening. It will therefore have to stay on the seabed. The cable will be slipped when she is due to be towed to her final resting place.

Monday 5 June
The invasion — it's on again!

04.00 hours. The Supreme Commander Allied Forces Western Europe, General Dwight D. Eisenhower, has given the order that the invasion of Europe is to take place tomorrow. It should have gone ahead today but has been postponed because of the heavy seas.

A lull is expected in the winds tomorrow but they are forecast to gather strength again in the evening.

This would rule out Wednesday, the 7th being the last day of the present favourable tidal cycle, and it is therefore imperative that unless the entire operation is stood-down it must begin at midnight.

FINAL YARDS: AN ENGINEER COMPANY APPROACHING AMERICAN LANDING SHIPS 374 (LEFT) AND 376 ON THE PURPOSE-BUILT HARDS BETWEEN THE OIL TANKS AND CASTLETOWN, PORTLAND, ON 4 JUNE 1944

ON TRACK: LINES OF TRACKED VEHICLES AND THEIR TRAILERS ENTERING THE GAPING JAWS OF AMERICAN LANDING SHIPS ON THE SPECIALLY BUILT ADDITIONAL HARD AT CASTLETOWN, PORTLAND, ON 4 JUNE 1944

Monday 5 June
American conference aboard 'Ancon' at Portland.

There has been a dawn meeting aboard the United States Ship *Ancon* in Portland Harbour. She is the Command Post (Advanced) of Admiral John L. Hall and will be the headquarters craft off Omaha Beach for Leonard T. "Gee" Gerow who is in command of V Corps of the First United States Army. U.S.S. *Chase* will stand by as Command Post (Alternative).

Major-General Clarence R. Huebner, whose 1st Infantry Division is to land on Omaha Beach, has been joined by General Omar Bradley and Admiral Alan G. Kirk, in overall command of the naval invasion force.

Their consensus is that the operation should not be further postponed. "It will be disastrous to have troops cooped up on board for another two weeks," one of them said. Their message to General Eisenhower, which is being relayed by Admiral Kirk, is that the invasion must take place tomorrow.

Monday 5 June
Americans forewarned of a 'chaotic' Omaha Beach.

14.00 hours. Brigadier-General Norman D. Cota of the 29th Infantry Division has called a meeting of his staff in the wardroom of the United States Ship *Charles Carroll*, at anchor in Portland Harbour.

He warned his men: "This is different from any other exercises that you've had so far. The little discrepancies that we tried to correct on Slapton Sands are going to be magnified and are going to give way to incidents that you might at first view as chaotic.

"You're going to find confusion. The landing craft aren't going in on schedule and people are going to be landed in the wrong places. Some won't be landed at all.

"We must improvise, carry on, and not lose our heads."

Monday 5 June
Three Warmwell pilots killed on the Seine.

A cross-Channel cloud-base near to ground level forced the Lightnings of the American 474th Fighter Group from Warmwell Aerodrome into the trees as they approached their target bridge over the River Seine.

REVERSING IN: SO THEY COULD DRIVE OUT FORWARDS, WITH THIS BEING THE NINTH OF THE TWELVE VEHICLES TO BE PACKED ABOARD UNITED STATES LANDING SHIP 195 AT CASTLETOWN, PORTLAND, ON 4 JUNE 1944

U.S.S. HENRICO: GENERAL INFANTRYMEN OF THE UNITED STATES ARMY ABOARD A TROOPSHIP IN PORTLAND HARBOUR, ON 4 JUNE 1944

ANTI-AIRCRAFT GUNNERS: STEWARDS MATES JONES AND FURRELL BROWNING, FROM DALLAS, KEEP WATCH FOR THE LUFTWAFFE, ALONG A 5-INCH BARREL ON THE U.S.S. HENRICO IN WEYMOUTH HARBOUR, ON 5 JUNE 1944

D-DAY STRIPES: THE LAST WALK ACROSS TARRANT RUSHTON AERODROME, TOWARDS HORSA GLIDERS, BEFORE FLYING TO WAR ON THE NIGHT OF 5 JUNE 1944

CENSORED MESSAGE: "THE CHANNEL STOPPED YOU BUT, NOT US. REMEMBER COVENTRY, PLYMOUTH, BRISTOL, LONDON. NOW IT'S OUR TURN. YOU'VE HAD YOUR TIME YOU GERMAN ..." THE ORIGINAL LAST WORD WAS RUBBED OUT ON THE SIDE OF THE HORSA GLIDER AT TARRANT RUSHTON AERODROME, FOR THE BENEFIT OF THE PHOTOGRAPHER AND EVENTUAL READERS. INSTEAD THE MEN WERE ALLOWED TO HAVE "SWINHUNDS"

PEGASUS TAKE-OFF: MASSED TUG-PLANES AND GLIDERS IN POSITION AT TARRANT RUSHTON AERODROME ON THE MORNING OF 5 JUNE 1944. THE FIRST HALIFAX WILL LIFT OFF AT 22.56 HOURS WITH ITS GLIDER-BORNE TROOPS BEING TASKED TO TAKE AND HOLD THE BRIDGES ON THE RIVER ORNE AND THE CAEN CANAL BUT TO BREAK THOSE ACROSS THE RIVER DIVES. THE AIRCRAFT ARE ON THE ENE-WSW RUNWAY, FACING EAST-NORTH-EAST, WITH BADBURY RINGS BEING THE WOODED HILL ON THE SKYLINE. A SOUTH-WESTERLY WIND WAS STILL BLOWING BUT A LULL WAS FORECAST, CORRECTLY

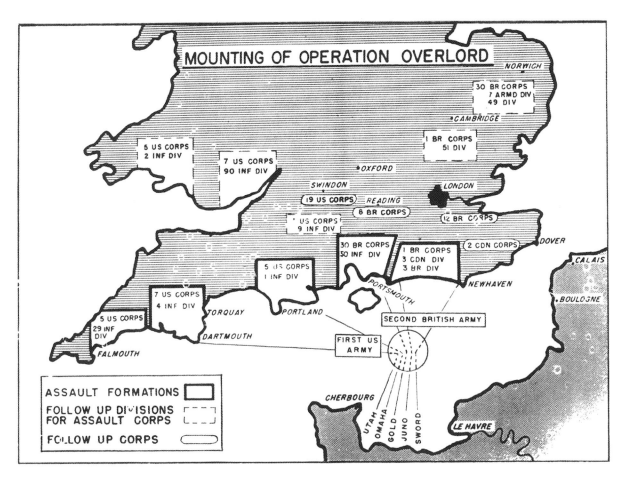

Dorset's D-Day: centre point on the assault map, as the springboard for the American First Infantry Division to attack Omaha Beach. Their comrades in the Second Infantry Division are the back-up troops, waiting in South Wales

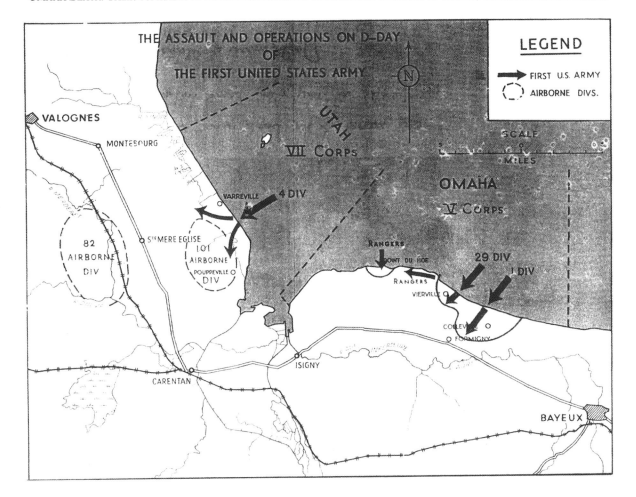

GLIDER DROP: HORSAS FROM TARRANT RUSHTON ON THE GROUND IN NORMANDY, 6 JUNE 1944

Major Bedford, Lieutenant Coddington, and Lieutenant Temple were killed and several of the surviving pilots brought back tree boughs in their tail-frames.

Monday 5 June

Hurn joins attacks on German radar stations.

Group Captain Denys Gillam, commanding 20 Sector at R.A.F. Thorney Island, together with 22 Sector, under Group Captain Davoud at R.A.F. Hurn, have been responsible for pre-D-Day attacks by the Allied Expeditionary Air Force on German radar stations across the English Channel.

Sir Trafford Leigh-Mallory, commanding the A.E.A.F., reported: "These radar targets were heavily defended by flak, and low-level attacks upon them demanded great skill and daring. Losses among senior and more experienced pilots are heavy."

By the night of 5 June, fewer than ten of the 47 German radars were still able to transmit, and some of these have been deliberately preserved from Allied attack in order that they should relay bogus signals indicating an offensive in the area towards the Pas-de-Calais.

Monday 5 June

Hurn Wing Commander plucked from sea and back in air.

Dr Reginald V. Jones, the chief of scientific intelligence at the Air Ministry, flew over the Solent today and realised the invasion was "on" as the armada that had been in

MIDWAY ACROSS: A FRACTION OF THE ALLIED SEA ARMADA, WITH EACH VESSEL PROTECTED FROM AIR ATTACK BY A BARRAGE BALLOON, AT DAWN ON 6 JUNE 1944

Spithead two days ago is no longer there.

He then flew westwards to R.A.F. Hurn: "I was silently wishing them good luck when we had a head-on encounter with a whole wing of American Thunderbolts." These had just taken-off from Christchurch Aerodrome. "It was like standing in a butt whilst a covey of enormous grouse is driven past you on all sides. What was more, the Thunderbolts with their big radial engines were climbing, and so none of their pilots could see us."

Having managed to land at Hurn they heard that the Norwegian Wing Commander had been taking part in the cross-Channel attacks on German radar stations: "He had been shot down earlier in the day, picked up out of the sea by one of the Air-Sea Rescue launches, and had already flown another sortie."

Twenty-eight Typhoons delivered 96 rockets, each of 60 pounds, and seven tons of bombs on German coastal radar stations. They had to take care to keep that at Fecamp intact so that it could report spoof activity aimed at convincing the enemy that the main thrust of the Allied invasion is further up-Channel, east of the Seine.

Five squadrons of Typhoons and Mosquitoes are now operating from R.A.F. Hurn, as are P-61 Black Widow night-fighters of the 9th United States Army Air Force and B-26 Marauders of the American 97th Bombardment Group.

Monday 5 June
Battleship 'Rodney' in Weymouth Bay.

Weymouth Bay has seen its largest gathering of big warships since the Reserve Fleet was dispersed in 1939. The danger of air attack then prevented anything larger than a destroyer operating from Portland Harbour.

Naval Operation Neptune has now brought five American and two British cruisers to the central Dorset coast, plus the strange cut-short silhouette of the 34,000-ton battleship H.M.S. *Rodney*. The terrific destructive force of her broadsides is to be used tomorrow in French coastal bombardment. She is preparing to deploy her full armament of nine 16-inch, twelve 6-inch, and six 4.7-inch guns, against batteries at Le Havre.

The great armada of smaller craft is to sail east up the English Channel, passing Bournemouth Bay, to gathering point Z for Zebra in a huge circle 40 miles

south-east of the Isle of Wight. It will then turn due south for the assault crossing.

Monday 5 June
Gliders ready at Tarrant Rushton.

Painted with invasion-day stripes, trains of Horsa troop-carrying gliders are being prepared for take-off at R.A.F. Tarrant Rushton. The men are part of the British 6th Airborne Division and will drop to the east of the Normandy beachheads — at Benouville, Merville, Ranville, Varaville, Bures, and Troarn — to take and hold the bridges on the River Orne and to break those across the River Dives. In all, 39 aircraft are taking part, from Tarrant Rushton Aerodrome.

The first three twin-engined Albemarle transports to leave, towing Horsa gliders carrying a unit of the Oxfordshire and Buckinghamshire Light Infantry, are tasked to take-out a German coastal battery near Merville.

The next take-offs involve six four-engined Halifax-Horsa combinations that are to carry out a surprise inland attack. This is Operation Coup de Main. The Horsa gliders will carry 171 troops, also from the Oxfordshire and Buckinghamshire Light Infantry, under orders to capture, intact, a bridge across the Caen Canal and an adjacent swing-bridge over the River Orne to the north of Caen. They will take-off shortly before midnight and the gliders are to be released five miles short of their target, to glide down into the meadows, at about 01.30 hours on Tuesday. Having released the gliders, these Halifax tow-craft will then become bombers — going on to attack a powder factory to the south-east of Caen — in order to create a diversion.

Thirty Halifax-Horsa combinations are detailed to carry out Operation Tonga. The Horsa gliders will be released at point LZ-N, to the east of the Caen Canal, to drop the 3rd and 5th Parachute Brigades, beginning about half-an-hour after Operation Coup de Main.

Once the infantry and paras have secured the immediate dropping zones the two Halifax squadrons

OMAHA BEACH: OFFSHORE, INSHORE AND ON THE SHORE. ASSAULT LANDING CRAFT PLOUGH TOWARDS NORMANDY, ON 6 JUNE 1944 PASSING THE FLAGSHIP OF FORCE O, UNITED STATES SHIP AUGUSTA. GIs WADE ASHORE BETWEEN BURSTS OF WITHERING ENEMY FIRE. MANY ARE HIT. ONE WOUNDED INFANTRYMAN IS COMFORTED BY A COMRADE WHO REMOVES HIS BANDOLEER. A THIRD SOLDIER TURNS HIS ANGUISH TOWARDS THE CAMERAMAN

from Tarrant Rushton will return to Normandy, at about 21.00 hours on Tuesday, in Operation Mallard. This will be a convoy of 30 Halifax-Hamilcar combinations, with these larger gliders carrying the British 6th Air Landing Brigade. They will be bringing the 6th Airborne Division's heavier equipment, including Tetrarch tanks, Bren-gun carriers, 25-pounder field guns, scout guns, and Bailey bridge pontoons.

These gliders are to be released over point LZ-N, and 18 containers with ammunition and food are to be dropped by parachute, at point DZ.

Monday 5 June
Gliders lift-off from Tarrant Rushton for 'Pegasus Bridge'.

22.56 hours. The first Halifax has roared along the central runway at Tarrant Rushton Aerodrome and lifted off, towing a Horsa glider of the British 6th Airborne Division towards France. There are 36 Halifax tug-planes and their gliders to be cleared at one minute intervals. Their divisional commander is 47-year-old Brigadier Richard Gale.

Into the sky has gone the 1st Platoon of "D" Company of the 2nd Battalion, the Oxfordshire and Buckinghamshire Light Infantry, in Operation Coup de Main. They are commanded by Major John Howard.

BEACH AND UNDERWATER OBSTACLES (Küstenvorfeldsperre)

⊗	Holzpfähle seewärts geneigt mit eine T-Mine	Wooden stake slanting seawards with one T-Mine
◿	Hemmbalken seewärts geneigt mit Stahlmessern	Ramp slanting seawards with steel knives
◿	Hemmbalken mit Mine	Ramp with mine
✳	Tschechenigel auf Pfähle oder Betonsockel gesetzt	Hedgehog on stakes or on concrete base
⫼	Belgische Rollböcke, in weichem Boden auf Pfähle gesetzt, mit or ohne Mine	Element C (on soft ground supported by stakes) with or without mine
△	Beton Tetraeder (O.T.) mit Stahlstachel	Concrete tetrahedra with steel stakes
△	Tetraeder mit Mine	Tetrahedra with mine
◿	Betonhemmbalken (O.T.) Stahlmessern	Concrete ramp with steel knives
◿	Betonhemmbalken mit Mine	Concrete ramp with mine
⚓	chwimmende Balkenmine	Floating raft with mine

WARNING SIGNS: GERMAN MILITARY SYMBOLS, ON A SHEET ISSUED TO AMERICAN GIS LANDING ON OMAHA BEACH, SO THEY CAN INTERPRET THE MARKINGS ON ANY CAPTURED CHARTS. IN THEORY THESE "BEACH AND UNDERWATER OBSTACLBES" SHOULD HAVE BEEN ELIMINATED BY AERIAL AND NAVAL BOMBARDMENT. IN FACT, HOWEVER, MOST REMAIN INTACT. THIS DOCUMENT WAS PRODUCED BY THE MILITARY INTELLIGENCE RESEARCH SECTION OF THE UNITED STATES ARMY

He arrived with his men at Tarrant Rushton on 26 May and they have been confined to camp, awaiting the codeword to "Go" which arrived at 09.00 hours on Sunday 4 June. To everyone's disappointment this was cancelled because of the windy weather.

This morning Major Howard received the order again and it became another day of loading and re-checking the contents of their six gliders, leading up to a fat-less evening meal to calm the men's stomachs. Faces are blackened and all have clambered aboard — for a promised gap in the German flak at Cabourg — with everyone's faith in the renowned abilities of the Glider Pilot Regiment.

Howard's "D" Company will be cast-off at 5,000 feet to land near Benouville, west of the pair of bridges over the Caen Canal (codenamed "Ham"), and the River Orne (codenamed "Jam").

Footnote: The Orne canal bridge would henceforth be known as Pegasus Bridge, from the mythical flying beast that provided the airborne emblem. Operation Coup de Main proceeded so smoothly that four of the six gliders landed only yards from their target spot. They were the first Allied soldiers to arrive in France on D-Day and had opened the Second Front in the European theatre of war. Both bridges were secured intact.

"Ham and Jam, Ham and Jam," Lance-Corporal Edward Tappenden radioed from a captured pillbox, just 15 minutes after the attack on Pegasus Bridge. It confirmed that D-Day's first battle had been successfully concluded. They had also liberated the first building in France, namely the Café du Tramway, owned by the Gondrée family, on the other side of the canal in Ranville.

Operation Tonga, involving the other 30 Halifax-Horsa combinations, encountered more problems. Five of the aircraft failed to release their gliders within the landing zone and Halifax K288 went down with its port wing blazing.

A total of 670 Horsa gliders for the Airborne Divisions were constructed at the Airspeed factory beside Christchurch Aerodrome.

Tuesday 6 June
Invasion Day — the sky fills.

00.15 hours. Sergeant Victor Swatridge of Dorset Police was patrolling the Victoria Park, Dorchester, with the intention of meeting his beat constable there at 00.30 hours. From the darkness of the black-out, without a glimmer of light from any house or premises, he was looking out at a clear starlit night with perfect visibility. He was about to witness the greatest mass movement of aircraft that has ever taken place:

"Suddenly I became aware of the heavy drone of aircraft coming from inland. As it drew nearer, the sky lit up. Thousands of coloured lights had burst forth and the whole atmosphere exploded into activity.

"It was an amazing transformation as hundreds of bombers, towing gliders with their masses of human and vehicle cargo, flew overhead and across the English Channel. This huge armada was a continuous procession for more than two hours. It was clearly evident that the invasion of Europe had commenced.

"I was excited but the civilian population remained quietly sleeping in their beds. People are immune to the noise of aircraft overhead, though had they been enemy planes the whole place would have been alive with activity, as sirens wailed and awoke them from their slumber.

"Invasion Day has been very secretively guarded. Everyone was warned that it would be treasonable to give the slightest indication to the enemy that it was about to take place, and the civil population kept their part of the bargain. Police were warned to expect heavy counter bombing, so we have been bracing ourselves for frightening reprisals, but to our amazement no enemy air action has occurred."

Tuesday 6 June
Weymouth wakes up to sound of the air armada.

Twenty-two-year-old Weymouth teacher Miss Barbara Baker writes in her diary: "Early this morning was awakened by the throbbing of low-flying aircraft. Looked out of the window and saw the sky full of bombers towing gliders. Presume airborne troops are being dropped behind enemy lines in France. Heard later that all ships anchored in Weymouth Bay had sailed across the Channel to land troops in Normandy. The long awaited invasion has begun."

This first day back at school after the Whitsun holiday is already on its way into history.

Tuesday 6 June
D-Day: Navy Operation Neptune.

The sea forces being deployed today are an armada without equal in history. On a broad front along the central English Channel, from Devon to Sussex, the invasion of Normandy has seen a total of 6,488 vessels acting under Admiralty orders in naval Operation Neptune. The main launching points have been from Plymouth to Torquay for Force U for Utah; Weymouth and Portland for Force O for Omaha; Poole to Portsmouth via the Solent for Force G for Gold; Poole to Portsmouth via Spithead for Force J for Juno; and Chichester to Newhaven for Force S for Sword.

The maritime deployment is as follows: 138 warships carrying out bombardments; 221 destroyers and other escort vessels; 287 minesweepers; 491 miscellaneous light craft; 441 auxiliaries; 2,463 landing ships and craft; 5 landing support vessels; 1,656 additional landing craft, barges, trawlers and "Rhinos" as ship to shore ferries and to assist damaged assault vessels; and 786 merchant vessels in a myriad of other support roles.

Tuesday 6 June
'Fishpond' reveals the Dorset armada.

The armada off Dorset of V Corps of the First United States Army, on their way from Weymouth and Portland to Omaha Beach, was such a concentration of steel that it showed on the Fishpond airborne radar set in Roland Hammersley's Lancaster of No. 5 Group, Bomber Command. This was taking part in Air Operation Mallard.

Hammersley's first report of the blips put the pilot, Ron Walker, on alert for an enemy fighter force. Instead they saw to their astonishment that it had been activated by flotillas of landing craft heading towards Normandy. What Roland does not realise is that his brother, Walter, is down there on the water.

Roland Hammersley was born at Swanage and lives at Bovington. He is a gunner with 57 Squadron. Their Lancaster bombers took off this morning, at 01.30 hours, from R.A.F. East Kirkby, Lincolnshire, on a mission to attack German coastal gun batteries at La Pernelle.

Tuesday 6 June
Dorset's Americans get the bloodiest beach.

H-hour for Dorset's Americans in Army Operation Overlord, when they were to begin the assault on Omaha Beach, was set for 06.45 hours this morning. In the event, 06.34 was the moment the first troops touched the sands of Normandy, but that was about all that went ahead of schedule for V Corps of the First United States Army, with 34,000 troops and 3,300 vehicles due to be delivered there today.

They attacked on a broad front — ten miles wide — with two regimental combat teams, one each from the 29th Infantry Division and the 1st Infantry Division, supplemented by Ranger Battalions. The 29th Division is tasked to capture Vierville-sur-Mer as its initial target. The 1st Division is to secure Colleville-sur-Mer, about three miles to the east. The landing area for Force O for Omaha extends from the Pointe du Hoc to Colleville, to the north-west of Bayeux, which is famous for an historic invasion tapestry depicting the Norman assault on the other side of the Channel, in 1066. The main assault has been coming ashore along five miles of sandy beach between Vierville in the west and Colleville in the east with St-Laurent being the village half a mile inshore at the centre.

It was almost a disaster from the start. Heavy seas and numerous underwater obstacles have caused considerable losses to the leading wave of Americans in landing craft and DD [Duplex-Drive] amphibious tanks. The latter went down the ramps into the water about 6,000 feet out and all but two sank with their crews, 'going down like stones'. Resistance was strong from the start. Murderous fire began to take its inevitable toll. It was obvious that aerial bombardment had been inadequate — impaired by poor visibility — and mostly fell some distance inland. Naval bombardment was also largely ineffective, due to the topography of the ground, and went over the top of its targets.

Worse was soon to follow. It is now known that German coastal forces were recently augmented by the 352nd Infanterie Division. This field formation happened to be holding a stand-to exercise and was manning the defences as the Americans waded ashore. They therefore ran into an enemy division that was ready for action and were consequently pinned to the beaches. Likewise the Ranger Battalions on the western flank met with stiff resistance.

V Corps has therefore received the bloodiest reception of the day, with between 2,500 and 3,000 casualties, and for several hours it has seemed that they might well be thrown back into the sea. Extreme sacrifice and gallantry — at the price of 1,000 dead — had by nightfall saved the situation and secured a beachhead a mile in depth, between Vierville and Colleville. This foothold was established after follow-up regimental teams arrived, with the reinforcements enabling the storming of the enemy batteries. Forward elements are now two miles inland and have been pushing towards higher ground in the vicinity of Formigny.

The novelist Ernest Hemingway has arrived from Portland, as a war correspondent, with the assault forces aboard the troopship *Dorothea L. Dix*.

Major Stanley Bach, a liaison officer from Brigadier-General Norman D. Cota's 29th Division who was

DEEP WATER: OMAHA BEACH AT DAWN ON 6 JUNE 1944 AS WEYMOUTH'S AMERICANS OF THE FIRST INFANTRY DIVISION, INITIALLY UP TO THEIR SHOULDERS IN THE SEA AS THEY LEAP FROM AN ASSAULT LANDING CRAFT. THEY ARE PART OF THE FIRST WAVE OF INVADERS, APPROACHING A SECTION OF OMAHA BEACH AND A LINE OF LOW HILLS THAT ARE HELD BY DETERMINED GERMAN DEFENDERS

RELATIVE CONSOLIDATION: BY MID-AFTERNOON ON 6 JUNE 1944, OMAHA BEACH COULD RECEIVE ITS FIRST REINFORCEMENTS, PILING OUT OF AN ASSAULT LANDING CRAFT AS NORMANDY'S WORST LANDING ZONE IS TURNED FROM A KILLING FIELD INTO A BEACH-HEAD. ALREADY ASHORE ARE DUKWS AND HALF-TRUCKS, WITH THE LATTER TOWING 57-MM ANTI-TANK GUNS. LINES OF GIS MARCH TOWARDS THE SMOKE, WHERE THE FRONT-LINE OF GERMAN BUNKERS AND BATTERIES HAVE NOW BEEN BATTERED INTO SUBMISSION

OMAHA BEACH: ON THE EVENING OF 6 JUNE 1944 WRECKAGE OF AMERICAN VEHICLES (top) WITH BARRAGE BALLOONS ABOVE A SHERMAN TANK KNOCKED-OUT BESIDE THE SAND DUNES. FROM HERE THE GERMAN DEFENDERS, OF THE 352ND INFANTERIE DIVISION (centre) WERE PINNING DOWN THE AMERICAN FIRST INFANTRY DIVISION. IN THE FOREGROUND IS A STICK-GRENADE AND A RUSSIAN-MADE 7.62-MM MACHINE-GUN. ONE OF THE GI DEATHS AT THE FIRST HURDLE (right) LIES BESIDE A WOODEN STAKE, ABOVE A WATERPROOF TELLER MINE

attached to the 1st Division assault troops in their sector of the beach, scrawled these potted descriptions of the day on a couple of old envelopes, which were his only available paper:

"11.30. Mortar, rifle, 88-mm, and machine-gun fire so heavy on beach, it's either get to ridge in back of beach or be killed.

"Noon. Beach high tide, bodies floating. Many dead Americans on beach at high-water mark.

"12.15. Heavy mortar and 88-mm fire started on beach from east end to west end — series of five shells in spots. Direct hit on Sherman tank, men out like rats — those alive.

"12.30. LCT [Landing Craft Tanks] hit two mines, came on in — hit third, disintegrated and rear end sank. At burst of shell two Navy men went flying through the air into water and never came up.

"14.40. More mortar fire and more men hit. LCVP [Landing Craft Vehicles and Personnel] unload five loads of men, they lie down on beach, mortar fire kills five of them, rest up and run to fox-holes we left a couple of hours ago.

"16.50. Established CP [Command Post] and saw first time the 1st Division friends who were quiet, fighting men — gave me heart.

"17.00. Prisoners began to come up road — a sorry looking bunch in comparison with our well-fed and equipped men.

"Duck. I've seen movies, assault training demonstrations and actual battle but nothing can approach the scenes on the beach from 11.30 to 14.00 hours -men being killed like flies from unseen gun positions. Navy can't hit 'em, Air cover can't see 'em — so Infantry had to dig 'em out."

Footnote: The Americans could indeed have lost the beach if the German High Command had not held back its reserve units, thinking that the Normandy assaults were a feint, and that the main invasion force would land between the Seine and Calais. Though Operation Overlord fielded a total of 39 divisions the Germans wildly exaggerated its strength and believed that between 75 and 85 divisions had been assembled for the Allied Second Front. This miscalculation, encouraged by Allied deception and disinformation which had already caused them to reinforce Norway, had Hitler and the High Command holding back their forces from Normandy. They continued to prepare for non-existent second assaults.

Tuesday 6 June

1st Dorsets among the first Britons ashore in France.

The moment *LCH317* touched the beach to the northeast of the village of Les Roquettes, at 07.30 hours this morning, the 1st Battalion of the Dorsetshire Regiment had arrived in France with the British 50th Infantry Division.. LCH [Landing Craft Headquarters] is a converted LSI [Landing Ship Infantry] modified to act as headquarters ship for officers commanding the sector assault.

They and their men sustained heavy casualties but made reasonable progress, helped by a sustained naval bombardment from the cruiser H.M.S. *Emerald*, supported by the destroyers H.M.S. *Cottesmore*, *Grenville*, *Jervis*, *Ulysses*, *Undine*, and *Urania*, with the Polish destroyer *Krakowiak*. Four fighter-bomber squadrons also made their contribution.

"A" Company of the 1st Dorsets is led by Major A. A. E. Jones and "B" Company by Major P. Chilton. They have landed on the east flank of Jig (Green) sector of the G for Gold Beach bridgehead and with the Hampshires — who arrived 1,000 yards to the east — can claim to be the first British troops to land in Normandy from the sea. Captain C. R. Whittington, the Unit Landing Officer, wore a rainbow-coloured battle bowler. He was soon wounded but continued to organise the clearing of corridors up the beach. Major Jones was withdrawn wounded and Major Chilton led both companies in crossing the minefields.

Pluto tested: initially being laid across Poole Bay, in March 1944, before becoming a "Pipeline Under The Ocean" to supply petroleum to a beached tanker on the sands of Normandy after D-Day

Pluto working: petrol from the Isle of Wight coming ashore in Normandy, having been laid from Shanklin by H.M.S. Conundrum in June 1944

"C" Company (led by Major R. M. Nicholl) and "D" Company (led by Major W. N. Hayes) helped the Hampshires take Asnelles-sur-Mer. They proceeded together to attack strongly defended high ground at Point 54. Here "C" Company had most of the fighting though the enemy eventually abandoned its four 155-mm guns and by 18.00 the 1st Dorsets had found and occupied convenient dugouts for Battalion Headquarters. This is on the hillside north of Ryes. Meanwhile, "B" Company moved into the village of Ryes, which was captured by the Devons.

The Dorsets have now achieved all the day's objectives. It has, however, been at a heavy cost — with three officers killed; 30 other ranks killed; 11 officers wounded; and 84 other ranks wounded.

Tuesday 6 June
Hurn Typhoons notch up 88 sorties.

Rocket-firing Typhoons of 83 Group of the 2nd British Tactical Air Force have flown 88 cross-Channel sorties from R.A.F. Hurn today in Air Operation Mallard. They have been sweeping across the Normandy beachheads all day and have been making ground-support attacks on enemy positions and the railway lines along which their reinforcements would arrive.

Tuesday 6 June
Warmwell missions over Cherbourg peninsula.

Today and for the foreseeable future the American Lightnings of the 474th Fighter Group from Warmwell Aerodrome will dive-bomb strategic targets in the Cherbourg peninsula and provide cover for Allied cross-Channel reinforcements and supply convoys.

Footnote: These sorties would continue until 15 June. The Americans lost two pilots on these combat air patrols. They were Lieutenant Doty and Lieutenant Robert Hanson. Coincidentally, there was a second Robert Hanson flying with the 474th, who survived to organise its veterans association.

Tuesday 6 June
H.M.S. 'Lyme Regis' clears Monty's passage.

The minesweeper H.M.S. *Lyme Regis*, paid for and adopted by the west Dorset town in 1941-42, is clearing a safe channel into S for Sword Beach at the eastern extremity of the Normandy bridgehead. She is buoying it with French tricolour pennants.

The swept waterway is being prepared for the passage into France of General Sir Bernard Montgomery and his Advance Headquarters staff of 21st Army Group.

Wednesday 7 June
Hurn Typhoons fly 138 Normandy sorties.

The air war has intensified as the front lines widen in Normandy. Typhoons of 83 Group of the 2nd British Tactical Air Force have been taking off and landing all day at R.A.F. Hurn.

They have logged 138 sorties in support of the Second British Army on the coast to the north of Caen. There are many Canadian flyers operating from Hurn and their special interest is with the central beachhead — the J for Juno sector — where the 3rd Canadian Infantry Division and the 2nd Canadian Armoured Brigade went ashore at Courseulles.

Thursday 8 June
Surviving rocket-firing craft limp into Poole.

The first of the returnee vessels from the Normandy landings are a group of LCRs [Landing Craft Rockets]. These American rocket-firing landing craft, which have limped into Poole Harbour, are peppered with shell-holes after their onslaught against the enemy beaches.

Saturday 10 June
Hurn Typhoons manage a record 154 Normandy sorties.

The Typhoons of 83 Group of the 2nd British Tactical Air Force have had a record day. They went on 154 sorties today from R.A.F. Hurn.

DESTROYER LOST: H.M.S. BOADICEA, SUNK OFF PORTLAND ON 13 JUNE 1944 WHILE ESCORTING THE NORMANDY CONVOYS

Pilot Officer Grey of 181 Squadron can boast that he has become the first fighter pilot from Hurn to stand upon liberated Europe. He found himself in difficulties and brought his Typhoon down on a newly-made temporary airstrip. Here the problem was sorted out and he was able to return home with the story.

Monday 12 June

Marshal of the Royal Air Force visits Tarrant Rushton.

Viscount Trenchard, the Marshal of the Royal Air Force made an informal visit today to R.A.F. Tarrant Rushton to address the aircrew of 298 Squadron and 644 Squadron. As part of the follow-up to D-Day, over the past 48 hours, they have been taking part in Operation Rob Roy. Their Halifax tug-planes released Hamilcar gliders to deliver jeeps, field-guns, and ammunition and fuel to Allied forces in Normandy.

Lord Trenchard met his men in a succession of small groups, in their respective crew rooms, and also members of the Glider Pilot Regiment in the briefing room. He congratulated them on their perseverance and performance which had now been brought to perfection after months of repetitive training.

Tuesday 13 June

H.M.S. 'Boadicea' is sunk off Portland.

A 1,350-ton Royal Navy destroyer, H.M.S. *Boadicea* which was launched in 1930, has been sunk off Portland with the loss of almost all her crew. She was a mile or so ahead of convoy EBC8, steaming up-Channel at 6 knots, and was herself zig-zagging at 9 knots when what was thought to be an Allied aircraft approached at 04.45 hours this morning. R.A.F. Beaufighters had been seen in the area.

Instead, descending towards her port side, it turned out to be a Junkers Ju.188 bomber, and was in the process of releasing two aerial torpedoes. The second hit *Boadicea's* forward magazine and the resultant explosion instantaneously destroyed the front half of the ship. The stern half was immediately inundated and sank in a couple of minutes.

There were only a dozen survivors, picked-up by the destroyer H.M.S. *Vanquisher*, and taken to Portland.

Tuesday 13 June

More ships lost by both sides.

The past three days have seen other sinkings off the Dorset coast. Having evacuated from Cherbourg, the German 2nd Schnellboot Flotilla has regrouped in Ostend, from where it is concentrating on cross-Channel supply convoys.

As one of these, S-NS 08, assembled in Poole Bay it was spotted by a German reconnaissance plane. The Schnellboote intercepted it in mid-Channel. The engagement resulted in *S177* sinking the *Brackenfield*, a 657-ton steamer, and the *Ashanti*, 534 tons. *S178* claimed the *Dungrange*, 621 tons.

Then a Norwegian destroyer, the *Stord*, sailed to the aid of the convoy, with units of the Royal Navy. The Schnellboote were too fast for them, outpacing the Allied response, and escaped to Boulogne.

Despite their hit-and-run tactics, the E-boats have been less successful in avoiding the Royal Air Force, though they are not easy targets. Beaufighters of 143 Squadron and 236 Squadron, operating from the New Forest, claim to have damaged or sunk three Schnellboote and one Raumboot mine-layer, plus a Minensuchboot minesweeper. Two of the fighters failed to return. One was brought down by anti-aircraft fire and the other has been credited to a Messerschmitt Me.163 Komet fighter.

Footnote: John Pitfield tells me that a Komet could not have potted the Beaufighter as these rocket-propelled planes had a short range and were only operational from German airfields. He says that it must have been a mistaken identification of one of the other remarkable new aircraft which the Germans deployed as the war drew to a close. These were the Messerschmitt 262 and the Arado 234C — with the former being most likely — which had top speeds of 541 m.p.h. and 530 m.p.h. respectively. The poor Beaufighter could only do 320 m.p.h.

Tuesday 13 June

500-lb bomb removed from Highcliffe.

11.50 hours. A 500-lb bomb that fell at Woolhayes, Highcliffe, on 13 May has been removed by a bomb disposal squad.

Wednesday 14 June

Bomber Command soups up the Channel defences.

Bomber Command has supplied some four-engine aircraft to No. 19 Group, Coastal Command, who are now hard-pressed to keep the English Channel reasonably safe for the succession of convoys that are supplying the Normandy forces. Half a million tons of food, munitions, and medicines is awaiting shipment, as well as manpower and vehicles.

Footnote: By the end of June, No. 19 Group had sunk 14 German U-boats in the Channel. Three of them were in the Dorset sector between Start Point and the Isle of Wight.

Thursday 15 June

Portland divers carry out underwater welding.

To the surprise of American Engineer James Spearman and the rest of the unit in *LST1000*, major seam repairs to its bottom have been carried out underwater, in Portland Harbour. The tank landing ship had to turn back for England after cracking across the middle in heavy seas.

She is carrying a Bailey bridge-building outfit, plus pontoons, and trucks.

Footnote: LST1000 was by no means the only casualty of the storm. Unfavourable weather during the first five days after D-Day meant that only 38 per cent of the planned tonnage of stores was actually brought ashore in the American sectors.

Friday 16 June

U-boat sinks H.M.S. 'Blackwood' off Portland.

Last night the 3rd Escort Group of the Royal Navy, steaming at 12 knots off Portland, lost the frigate H.M.S. *Blackwood* to a torpedo from *U764*.

The mast instantly disappeared and the bridge folded backwards, in a tremendous explosion of yellow smoke, at 19.11 hours. The collapse of the superstructure left the bows and stern raised virtually out of the water.

R.A.F. Air Sea Rescue launches *HSL2696* and *HSL2697* were joined by the frigate H.M.S. *Essington* as the crew abandoned ship. By about 21.00 hours all were taken off. Of the survivors about 35 are wounded.

The wreck remained afloat almost until dawn. Radar contact with it was lost at 04.10 hours this morning.

Friday 16 June

An American bombs Warmwell.

As an engine cut-out on his Lightning fighter over Warmwell Aerodrome, American pilot Lieutenant Cumbie of 430 Squadron of the U.S.A.A.F. followed standard procedure and jettisoned his bombs. These — contrary to correct practice — turned out to be armed. He scored a direct hit on the field's transformer station.

The pilot returned safely to the airfield, to congratulations from its R.A.F. contingent: "Jerry's been trying to hit that for years!"

Sunday 18 June

Supply ship sunk off Dorset.

A supply ship, the 1,764-ton *Albert C. Field*, has been sunk by German aircraft off Dorset. She was heading from south Wales to the Normandy beaches. Her owners are the Upper Lakes and St Lawrence Transportation Company.

Wednesday 21 June

War interrupts Warmwell's dress parade.

The American pilots of the 474th Fighter Group of the United States Army Air Force dressed for inspection by General Kincaid, at Warmwell Aerodrome, and were due to receive medals. Instead they received an unexpected order to scramble and found themselves back over France.

Two of the Lightnings were lost. Lieutenant Vinson was killed but the pilot of the other aircraft, Captain Larson, parachuted to safety and has lived to receive his citation.

Tuesday 22 June

Airborne rescue turns into a boat trip.

Lieutenant Dumar of 509 Squadron of the 405th Fighter Bomber Group of the United States

Army Air Force, flying a Thunderbolt from Christchurch Aerodrome, had three lucky escapes today off the enemy coast.

His engine seized over the German side of the English Channel, 30 miles from Cherbourg, and he parachuted into the sea.

He was located and picked-up by Walrus amphibian of the Air-Sea Rescue service. Then the Walrus found itself in difficulties as choppy conditions prevented it from lifting off.

The crew decided that their only alternative was to taxi through the waves and make for home on the surface. The Walrus was a sitting duck for the 40-mile slog back into home waters but fortunately no one from the Luftwaffe happened along.

Friday 23 June

Hurn Mosquitoes claim six Ju.88s over Normandy.

The night prowl of the Hurn Mosquitoes took in the Normandy beachheads last night and the pilots returned with claims of six kills. They had intercepted a formation of six Junkers Ju.88 bombers.

Squadron-Leader Petrie claimed two and Flying Officer Grey three, for 125 Squadron, and Flight-Lieutenant Sandemann claimed one for 604 Squadron. The gale which has raged across the Channel for three days finally eased last night.

Friday 23 June

U.S. 3rd Armored Division embarked from Portland.

The 3rd Armored Division of the United States Army is now arriving on Omaha White Beach, near Isigny, for the tank actions that will decide the Battle of Normandy. The landing ships had been kept in Portland Harbour for the past four days by a violent gale. Others have crossed from Southampton Water.

The arrivals include the 32nd and 33rd Armored Regiments, supported by the 486th Armored Anti-Aircraft Battalion and the 23rd Armored Engineer Battalion. Headquarters staff and the division's artillery, comprising the 54th, 67th, and 391st Armored Field Artillery Battalions, are following tomorrow. The 36th Armored Infantry Regiment will then embark, for arrival on Sunday, to complete the current wave of reinforcements.

Saturday 24 June

Bridport officer killed in Normandy.

Lieutenant-Colonel J. W. Atherton, from Bridport, was killed today in Normandy. He was blown up by a shell whilst fighting off a counter-attack by German tanks. Until recently, Colonel Atherton was serving with the 5th Battalion of the Dorsetshire Regiment.

Sunday 25 June

Two U-boats sunk off Portland.

In the past 24 hours, two German U-boats have been destroyed between Portland Bill and Start Point by patrol ships of the Royal Navy's invasion-landing escort groups that have been shadowing the constant shuttle-service

PEGASUS BRIDGE: THE PRIME TARGET OVER THE CAEN CANAL, CAPTURED BY AIRBORNE FORCES FROM TARRANT RUSHTON (NOTE THEIR GLIDERS BEHIND THE TREES)

AIRBORNE COMMANDER: MAJOR JOHN HOWARD, WHOSE TROOPS SEIZED PEGASUS BRIDGE ON D-DAY

between the Channel ports and Normandy.

Last night the frigates H.M.S. *Affleck* and H.M.S. *Balfour* accounted for *U1191*. Today it has been the turn of H.M.S. *Bickerton* to sink *U269*. The frigate then left her group to pick-up survivors and take them into port.

Meanwhile, another frigate, H.M.S. *Goodson*, was hit in the stern by an acoustic torpedo from *U984*. Though crippled, she is still floating, and has been towed from mid-Channel to the coaling pier in Portland Harbour. There are many casualties and it is obvious that the damage is irreparable.

Sunday 25 June

Portland Task Force bombards Cherbourg.

Commanded by Rear Admiral Deyo, a formidable Allied Task Force departed from Portland at 04.30 hours this morning, to bombard German gun emplacements that defend the port of Cherbourg. Its capture is seen as vital to the next stage of the Battle of Normandy.

Split into two bombardment groups, the fleet comprises three battleships — United States Ships *Texas*, *Arkansas*, and *Nevada* — and four cruisers. These are the U.S.S. *Tuscaloosa* and U.S.S. *Quincy*, with H.M.S. *Glasgow* and H.M.S. *Enterprise*. They are protected by nine destroyer escorts.

Two hundred rounds have been pounded into German batteries to the east and the west of the port but some of the return fire was accurate. *Glasgow* was hit twice. There were injuries on the bridge of the *Enterprise* from shell fragments. She has headed to Portsmouth for repairs.

The other ships had returned to Portland by 19.30 this evening. A bomb disposal team has been called to Admiral Deyo's flagship, U.S.S. *Texas*. They are removing an unexploded 240-mm shell that penetrated the warrant officers' bunk-bay.

Meanwhile, taking advantage of the bombardment, advance units of General Joe Collins's VII Corps of the United States Army broke into Cherbourg, capturing two of its main forts and reaching the arsenal.

Monday 26 June

St Alban's Head battle sends Germans packing.

Last night there was a short but fierce naval engagement off St Alban's Head which resulted in German

Schnellboote *S130* and *S168* departing for Dieppe , and *S145* sustaining damage and being forced to flee for repairs to the nearest bastion that the enemy still holds. This is the occupied Channel Island of Alderney.

Monday 26 June
Change-over of Typhoons at Hurn.

With the gathering momentum of the siege of Cherbourg, following the capture of its Maupertus airfield on Friday, the Typhoons of 124 Wing and 143 Wing from R.A.F. Hurn are now stationed in Normandy.

They comprise No. 83 Group of the 2nd British Tactical Air Force and are being replaced at Hurn by arrivals from 123 Wing and 136 Wing, also flying rocket-firing Typhoons.

These, together with 146 Wing which is also coming to Hurn, comprise No. 84 Group of the 2nd British Tactical Air Force.

Thursday 29 June
Sixteen killed as Thunderbolts crash on Mudeford.

Foxwood Avenue at Mudeford, Christchurch, was devastated today by three American P-47 Thunderbolt fighter-bombers in two separate mishaps on take-off from Christchurch Advance Landing Ground. In the first, at 06.45 hours, the pilot survived and no one was hurt on the ground.

Then at 14.00 hours the same pilot tried again to lift off in another Thunderbolt. Once more he failed to gain proper height and this time overshot the runway and crashed into a bungalow. His fuel tanks and bombs exploded, with the blast bringing down yet another Thunderbolt, Scarab 2, that was also coming off the runway. All three planes belonged to the 509th Squadron of the 405th Fighter Bomber Group of the United States Army Air Force.

As rescue workers pulled the wounded out of the debris, another bomb exploded, killing a fireman and wounding others. Sixteen are dead and 18 injured.

The mortally wounded pilot, 22-year-old Lieutenant Vincent R James, was comforted by nurse Irene Stevenson and died in her arms in Boscombe Hospital.

Footnote: Mrs Stevenson would become a local councillor and Mayor of Christchurch. Lieutenant James, who was unmarried, is buried at the American Cemetery in Cambridge. The 405th Fighter Bomber Group, based at Christchurch, had lost a total of 15 pilots during June 1944.

Thursday 29 June
Hurn Mosquitoes show the Yanks how to do it in the dark.

The Mosquito pilots of 125 Squadron at R.A.F. Hurn are inducting the twelve crewmen of six P-61 Black Widow night-fighters of the 71st Fighter Wing of the 9th United States Army Air Force in how to carry out blind radar-guided interceptions.

The Black Widows flew in today from R.A.F. Charmy Down, on the hills north of Bath, and will carry out operational night interception flights.

Friday 30 June
Three more Warmwell pilots killed over France.

For the past week the Lightning fighters of the 474th Fighter Group of the U.S.A.A.F., operating from Warmwell Aerodrome, have been crossing the Channel to continue causing chaos on the railway system across northern France. These sorties have claimed the lives of three more pilots — Lieutenant Gee, Lieutenant Heuermann, and Lieutenant Danish.

Many of the attacks were on targets of opportunity. "You guys can just go over and hit anything that moves," they had been told.

Saturday 1 July
Wessex Division forces the Odon bridgehead.

Infantry of the 43rd (Wessex) Division have been fighting alongside the 15th (Scottish) Division since 28 June to force through the advance on the Odon bridgehead, against fierce Panzer counter-attacks.

Sunday 2 July
Another Thunderbolt crashes at Christchurch.

Today, at 17.00 hours, an American P-47 Thunderbolt landed short of Christchurch Aerodrome and came down in a perimeter field. It bounced on to the adjacent Lymington road and fell to rest upside down. There was no fire and the pilot escaped.

Monday 3 July
Twelve Tarrant Rushton aircraft in S.O.E. operation.

Twelve aircraft from R.A.F. Tarrant Rushton are tonight tasked to fly over occupied France for the Special Operations Executive. Men and materials will be dropped to the Resistance. Four Halifax aircraft are being provided by 298 Squadron and four from 644 Squadron.

Additionally the station has on stand-by the four aircraft that have been used on a regular basis for such operations. These are two Stirlings from 299 Squadron and two from 196 Squadron.

Wednesday 5 July
Christchurch Yanks give a Brit a Thunderbolt.

The Yanks lent a Brit a plane for the day, sent him out on a combat sortie over enemy occupied France, and then had kittens when he failed to return. Lieutenant Harris of the Royal Navy's Fleet Air Arm, a glider tug-pilot seconded to Airspeed Limited at Christchurch which makes Horsa troop-carriers, had talked 511 Squadron of the 405th Fighter Bomber Group of the United Army Air Force into loaning him a Thunderbolt.

He joined Blue Flight which today lifted off from Station 416, the Advance Landing Ground that is Christchurch Aerodrome, and crossed the English Channel. They beat up the railway system southwards across Brittany to Nantes.

The pilots of 511 Squadron returned to Christchurch for a de-briefing on their targets of opportunity and the bombing of a tunnel. Their fears grew as their British friend failed to join them — the concern was not just for him but that a court martial would result from the unauthorised loan and loss of the aircraft. Several hours later the panic turned to relief as Lieutenant Harris came home. He had overstayed his flying time in Brittany and had to force-land on an Allied-held beach in Normandy. Soldiers found him enough petrol to take-off for a nearby captured airfield where he was refuelled for the return flight to Christchurch.

Thursday 6 July
Christchurch Thunderbolts trap train in tunnel.

A train driver at Lisieux in German-occupied France, on the eastern side of the Allied front-line, today took refuge in a tunnel as United States Army Air Force fighter-bombers attacked. His train was safe but their bombs left it trapped.

Thunderbolts of the 405th Fighter Bomber Group, which had flown across the Channel from Christchurch, scored direct hits at each end of the tunnel.

Improved weather is enabling concentrated air support to be provided for our troops. Lancasters and Halifaxes of Bomber Command are being prepared for air attacks on German tanks and strong-points north of Caen, and against rocket-related structures in the Pas de Calais.

Thursday 6 July
Warmwell's two-all air battle over Brittany.

Clear weather saw Warmwell's American P-38 Lightning fighter-bombers streaking across north-west France once

Upside down: this American P-47 Thunderbolt landed short of Christchurch Aerodrome, on the Lymington road, on 2 July 1944. There was no fire or damage to buildings and the pilot was able to walk away from the wreckage

again but today they met with a flight of more than 20 Focke-Wulf FW190s.

Though they were able to claim two definite kills the Americans returned across the Channel without Lieutenants Rubal and Jacobs.

Footnote: In another bombing run over France, against the rail network, Lieutenant Moore was killed when his plane hit a bridge.

Sunday 9 July
Pigeon post from Normandy to Hurn in seven hours.

Pigeons supplied from Bournemouth lofts have been arriving today at R.A.F. Hurn some seven hours after being released from the battle-grounds in Normandy.

They are helping the front-line troops to keep contact with their air support units. In fact they are doing more than that and are proving themselves as an air support unit.

Monday 10 July
Hurn's 604 Squadron claims its 100th kill.

The Mosquito night-fighters of 604 Squadron at R.A.F. Hurn have claimed their one hundredth kill.

Last night, Wing Commander Gerald Maxwell shot down a Junkers Ju.88 and claimed a Dornier Do.217 as a probable kill, which took the claims total to its century.

Tuesday 11 July
Thunderbolts leave Christchurch for Normandy.

The noise, excitement and danger from bomb-laden crash-landings have ended for the people of Christchurch as the Thunderbolts of the 405th Fighter Bomber Group take off from Station 416 for the last time. They are heading for Airstrip 8, at Picauville in the Allied-liberated Cherbourg peninsula.

They have left Christchurch Aerodrome to the aeroplane and glider makers Airspeed Limited, and an American flag to the Priory church, as a memento of the United States Army Air Force. Their thousand-strong contingent will also leave a certain silence on the ground as the public houses and Bournemouth's places of entertainment clear up after the goodbyes of their liveliest clientele of all time.

Friday 14 July
Hurn Mosquitoes change-over.

The Mosquito night-fighters of 604 Squadron left R.A.F. Hurn yesterday and were replaced today by Mark VI Mosquitoes flown in by the Canadians of 418 (City of Edmonton) Squadron.

They will work with 125 Squadron in Anti-Diver sorties against incoming Doodlebug flying-bombs. The aim is to intercept and shoot down these V1 weapons over the sea eastwards of the Isle of Wight.

INFANTRY FOXHOLES: SERGEANT TURNER WITH PRIVATE MARTIN, PRIVATE TORRINGTON (A CANADIAN "DORSET") AND PRIVATE SMITH, PLUS LANCE-CORPORAL WILTSHIRE, FIRING A THREE-INCH MORTAR NEAR HOTTOT, AS THE 1ST BATTALION OF THE DORSETSHIRE REGIMENT MEETS RESISTANCE IN THE BOCAGE ON 11 JULY 1944

TYPICAL NORMANDY: THE 1ST BATTALION OF THE DORSETSHIRE REGIMENT, ADVANCING ACROSS THE BOCAGE ON 11 JULY 1944. INFANTRY AND ANTI-TANK GUNS ARE MAKING PROGRESS ALONG A TRACK THAT HAS BEEN SMASHED THROUGH THE HEDGEROWS BY ALLIED TANKS

Tuesday 18 July
Warmwell Americans claim ten FW190s.

The 474th Fighter Group from Warmwell Aerodrome have routed a formation of 25 Focke-Wulf FW190s over north-west France. They claimed ten, for the loss of three Lightnings.

Two of the Americans baled out but the third, Lieutenant Goodrich, died in his plane.

Thursday 20 July
84 Group Typhoons leave Hurn for France.

The three Wings of 84 Group of the 2nd British Tactical Air Force, flying Typhoons, today lifted off from R.A.F. Hurn for the last time. They crossed the Channel en mass and are re-grouping in France.

Sunday 23 July
Mosquito crashes at Poole.

A Mosquito fighter-bomber of 418 (City of Edmonton) Squadron, on a low-level daylight flight over Poole, has crashed 200 yards west of Alder Road Drill Hall. It appears to have been pulling out of a roll when a wing struck a building in Mossley Avenue.

There was only slight damage to the house but the aircraft exploded shortly after hitting the ground. Pilot Officer Bowhay and Pilot Officer Naylor, of the Royal Canadian Air Force, were killed.

Thursday 27 July
Warmwell pilot killed over Tours.

Lieutenant Patton, flying a Lightning from Warmwell Aerodrome on a reconnaissance mission over Tours, was killed in an attack by a number of Messerschmitt Me.109s.

During July
Hurn Mosquitoes bomb the V-3.

Mosquitoes of 418 (City of Edmonton) Squadron and 125 (Newfoundland) Squadron from R.A.F. Hurn flew together today in a bombing raid against the massive concrete emplacement of the German H.D.P. secret weapon project at Mimoyecques, near Calais. The Hochdruckpumpe [High Pressure Pump] is known to British scientific intelligence as the V-3 and is presumed to be a long-range artillery piece.

Footnote: Its intended function was not discovered until the site was overrun by the Second Canadian Corps in the last week of September 1944. Fifty smooth-bore barrels of 15 centimetres diameter, 127 metres in length, were pointing towards London. They had been designed to fire finned projectiles, each weighing 300 pounds, at the rate of ten per minute.

The technical achievement was a muzzle departure velocity of 5,000 feet per second. This was reached by boosting the firing charges with further propellants in side ports along the barrels.

There had, however, been a major glitch in the physics. Above speeds of 3,300 feet per second the shells toppled erratically. Even with more time and less bombing, their development was flawed, and they would have fallen well short of the capital.

During July
American Liberator crashes on Furzey Island.

An American Liberator bomber has crashed in Poole Harbour, hitting Furzey Island, with the loss of all its crew.

During July
Wounded American pilots rest at Shaftesbury.

The American Red Cross are using Coombe House, near Shaftesbury, as a Recuperation Centre for wounded and exhausted U.S.A.A.F. bomber crews.

Footnote: In 1945 the Institute of the Blessed Virgin Mary acquired the building. It became St Mary's Convent. The house stands in its own wooded valley, a short distance across the county boundary, in the Wiltshire parish of Donhead St Mary.

CAPTURED PANZER: BEING UNLOADED FOR BRITISH EVALUATION ON THE LULWORTH RANGES IN SUMMER 1944. IT IS A KPFW III, MOUNTING A SHORT 50-MM GUN

Tuesday 1 August
Mosquito night-fighters quit Hurn.

The Mosquitoes of R.A.F. Hurn were leaving today. Both 125 Squadron and 418 Squadron are being redeployed at Middle Wallop, on the Hampshire Downs, though from there they can still venture into the night skies over Dorset, in the unlikely event of German raiders coming this far west.

Thursday 3 August
U.S.A.A.F. takes over R.A.F. Hurn.

The B-26 Marauders of 596 Squadron, 597 Squadron and 598 Squadron of the 97th Bombardment Group of the 9th United States Army Air Force have taken over Hurn Aerodrome from the Royal Air Force.

Thursday 3 August
Another Warmwell pilot dies in France.

Lieutenant Chamberlain, flying an American Lightning fighter from Warmwell Aerodrome on a combat air patrol over France, has been killed by enemy action.

Friday 4 August
Sea-shell lands in Christchurch.

A shell fell this afternoon in the garden of 36 Seafield Road, Christchurch. Fortunately it failed to explode. It had been fired from the sea, during gunnery practice, by an unknown Allied vessel.

Saturday 5 August
Warmwell's Americans move to French base.

The 474th Fighter Group of the United States Army Air Force flew their final patrols from Warmwell Aerodrome today. All flights ended on an airstrip in Normandy.

This advance base on the other side of the Channel has been used for the past five days for refuelling and is now the Group's temporary home for the next stage of the war in Europe. It was still business as usual and two Messerschmitt Bf.109s were claimed as kills on their moving day.

Saturday 12 August
H.M.S. 'Rodney' bombards Alderney.

At 07.30 hours the battleship H.M.S. *Rodney* steamed gracefully from Portland Harbour, escorted by the destroyers H.M.S. *Jervis* and H.M.S. *Faulkner*, on a course that took them southwards into the English Channel.

She was heading for the Channel Islands, where the battleship opened fire with her huge forward turrets. The 16-inch guns pounded four German gun emplacements on the occupied island of Alderney. A total of 75 rounds were fired, hitting three of the batteries, in a bombardment that extended from 14.12 hours until 16.44.

The ships then made their way safely back to Portland, returning at 22.12 hours.

Monday 14 August

Hurn Yanks blow-up German ammo train.

B-26 Marauders of the American 97th Bombardment Group, flying from Hurn Aerodrome, have returned from a spectacular raid on the railway marshalling yards at Corbeil to the south of Paris.

They caught an ammunition train in the sidings. It was destined for the front-line troops of the Wehrmacht's First Army.

Friday 18 August

R.A.F. returns to Hurn for Air-Sea Rescue.

Three Walrus amphibians and six Air-Sea Rescue Spitfires of 277 Squadron have transferred from Warmwell Aerodrome to Hurn.

The American B-26 Marauders of the 97th Bombardment Group of the U.S.A.A.F. are due to leave Hurn, for France, on Sunday.

Footnote: 277 Squadron went back to Hurn on 29 August.

Sunday 27 August

Hurn Typhoons kill 78 British sailors.

A month after flying out of R.A.F. Hurn, to become part of the new front-line in Normandy, at Airstrip B3 just south of Caen, rocket-firing Typhoons of 266 (Rhodesia) Squadron have carried out their most distressing action. They were formed in the Great War and have as their motto "Hlabezulu: the stabber of the skies". Their instructions in Normandy were to fly with Wing Commander Johnny Baldwin in search of German E-boats which are currently playing havoc with Allied shipping.

On the water, four Royal Navy minesweepers of the depleted 1st Minesweeper Flotilla were sailing from the Mulberry Harbour at Arromanches to continue sweeping an enemy minefield off Cap d'Antifer. They had been clearing it since Wednesday and were returning daily up to and including yesterday.

Then, today, came a fateful change of orders. Commander T. Chick and Lieutenant H. Brownhill reviewed progress and decided the operation needed an extra day. They amended the orders and minesweepers H.M.S. *Britomart*, H.M.S. *Hussar*, H.M.S. *Salamander*, and H.M.S. *Jason* put to sea. They were joined by two armed Royal Navy trawlers, H.M.T. *Colsay* and H.M.T. *Lord Ashfield*.

The day proceeded routinely enough. The flotilla had arrived on station to clear mines. In the air, a total of 16 Typhoons, escorted by 12 Spitfire fighters — to watch their tails for the Luftwaffe — were heading towards them. At 13.15 hours, lookouts from the flotilla reported aircraft circling, and correctly identified them as Typhoons of the Royal Air Force.

Wing Commander Baldwin looked at his prospective targets. They seemed the right sort of shape and size but he puzzled over other details and in particular their dispersal pattern. There were disconcerting inconsistencies. So he radioed a Royal Navy liaison officer to check the situation.

"Are you quite sure they can't be ours?" Baldwin asked.

"Why, are you frightened?" came the reply. "We've no ships in the area today."

The Typhoons swung downwards and outwards, far into the Channel, and then turned into low-level attacking sweep at maximum speed.

"Christ, they're attacking us!" was the cry of disbelief on H.M.S. *Jason* as cannon-fire raked the vessel and rockets ripped apart the superstructure. "Hit the deck," shouted the captain, Commander Trevor Crick, who tried to get wireless operator Peter Wright to make contact with the aircraft before they turned to deliver more of the same. Wright's brother, Ted, was also in the crew. Peter was unable to send the message before the devastating second-strike. Crick ordered his gunners to refrain from returning fire and indeed none of the vessels responded with a single shot.

For the survivors it would be the longest eleven minutes of their lives. The Typhoons left minesweepers *Britomart*, *Hussar*, and *Jason* sinking. *Salamander*, though still on the water, was a floating wreck. The two trawlers sustained damaging hits, but would be able to rescue many of their comrades, aided by an R.A.F. Air-Sea Rescue launch which headed for the scene.

By nightfall it was clear there has been a debacle of disastrous proportions. A total of 78 officers and men have been killed, or are presumed to be dead, and 140 are wounded. The 1st Minesweeper Flotilla has virtually been annihilated.

Footnote: Commander Trevor Crick [1902-97] would recall the utter horror for the rest of his life. "The fury and ferocity of concerted attacks by a number of Typhoon aircraft armed with rockets and cannon is an ordeal that has to be endured to be truly appreciated."

Two days later the post mortem had been held and concluded. Naval command headquarters was held to account, in not telling the Royal Air Force about its last minute change of plans, and then denying them. But of the three officers who were court martialed the senior two were acquitted and the guilty junior received only token punishment, for what in most circumstances would have been only a minor lapse.

Apparently, the amended orders had not been correctly annotated, which prevented them reaching the right people on time. Friendly fire and its casualties always seen inexcusable in hindsight but we now realise it is an inescapable accompaniment to all wars. Whether it gets admitted, however, is often entirely another matter.

Monday 28 August

Wessex troops are first across the Seine.

Eight separate battalion attacks were launched today by the 43rd (Wessex) Division to put the first British troops across the River Seine. Among them were the 5th Battalion of the Dorsetshire Regiment.

Footnote: Lieutenant-General Brian Horrocks, the commander of 30th Corps, described it as "an epic operation". The logistical support behind the Allied advance had become stupendous and was more than sufficient in everything except petrol. The Allies now had two million men and half a million vehicles in France. In tanks their numerical advantage over the Germans was twenty to one.

During August
German Panzers to be tested at Lulworth.

Advanced examples of German armour — including Tiger and Panther tanks of Panzer Lehr and other divisions of the retreating Panzer Group West — are being shipped to England for evaluation on the gunnery ranges of the Armoured Fighting Vehicles School at Lulworth Camp.

In excess of 650 German tanks and thousands of other vehicles were destroyed during the annihilation of German forces caught in the Falaise-Mortain pocket. This bottlenecked salient of the enemy front-line was finally closed, in the area of Chambois, after limited escapes on 20 August. Often the Germans had immobilised themselves in bumper to bumper traffic congestion which provided Allied pilots with their easier pickings of the war. The wreckage was on such a colossal scale that in places it brought the Allied advance to a halt.

Total German losses are now in the order of 1,500 tanks and 3,500 guns, destroyed or captured, in the Battle of Normandy, plus tens of thousands of other vehicles from armoured car to horse and cart. The Wehrmacht has also lost nearly half a million men. The dead and wounded are estimated to exceed 240,000 and the number of Germans taken prisoner by the Allies has reached 210,000.

Footnote: The strategy was for the Americans to break-out from the west of Normandy and pivot round to the Seine, whilst the British and Canadians pinned down German armour east of Caen. It was devised by General Sir Bernard Montgomery. His promotion, to Field-Marshal, would be confirmed by King George VI on 1 September 1944.

During August
Poole blast kills three servicemen.

Three naval ratings were killed and six injured when ammunition detonated itself in one of the landing craft at H.M.S. Turtle. This is the Royal Navy's shore-base at Poole. The vessel was destroyed and nearby buildings were damaged.

During August
Dorset war poet killed in Italy.

Welshman Dylan Thomas, who joined the British Army in 1940, is not the only contemporary poet of that name.

Lieutenant Robert Dalzell Dillon Thomas, who went through school at Sherborne from 1931 to 1941 — his father teaches at Sherborne School — progressed to Oxford and joined the Grenadier Guards in 1942.

He had been keeping a notebook of the Italian campaign which claimed his life this month, at the age of 22. This was his song to "Dorset, Dear Dorset":

The spring has come to Dorset,
The larches don their green
And brightly shines the undergrowth
With starry celandine.
The hedges flaunt new-budded leaves
And withies tipped with red
No longer does the primrose fear
To rise from grassy bed.

(Chorus) *There is no land so dear to me*
come sunshine wind or rain;
And that is where I mean to be
If I come home again.
Dorset, dear Dorset,
I've left my heart in Dorset,
And I'll live and die in Dorset
When I come home again.

It's summertime in Dorset,
The woods are white with may,
Tall foxgloves guard the upland slopes
And buttercups gleam in the hay,
Dog-roses blush down every lane
And the wild thyme scents the hills,
And willow herb and meadow sweet
Dance by the wayside rills.

'Tis autumn now in Dorset
A glory of russet and gold,
Softly the leaves come drifting down
As the nights grow crisp and cold.
There are chestnuts strewn on the woodland paths
Fresh from their prickly shells,
And mushrooms spawn on the windswept down
And the berries are ripe in the dells.

'Tis wintertime in Dorset,
The fields are bleak and bare
And the cold sun sinks in a crimson haze
For there's frost in the evening air.
The milk is frozen in the pail
And there's ice in the ruts on the path,
And every yard is stacked with logs
For piling on the hearth.

Sunday 17 September
Tarrant Rushton Hamilcars join Arnhem airlift.

Nearly a hundred gliders, towed by their Halifax tug-planes, left R.A.F. Tarrant Rushton this morning to join the armada of 300 Allied aircraft that are to land behind enemy lines in the Netherlands. Operation Market

"UP YOURS": DEFIANT DEFEAT FROM THE BRITISH SOLDIER WHO DID NOT PUT HIS HANDS ON HIS HEAD AFTER THE ARNHEM DEBACLE, FOR THE BENEFIT OF A WEHRMACHT PHOTOGRAPHER, ON OR AFTER 17 SEPTEMBER 1944

according to Lieutenant-General Walter Bedell Smith, Chief of Staff at S.H.A.E.F. [Supreme Headquarters Allied Expeditionary Force]. General Eisenhower, the Supreme Commander, admitted in 1966 that "I not only approved Market Garden, I insisted on it". He had been so optimistic on the course of the war, on 5 September 1944, that he went as far as to declare "the defeat of the German armies is now complete".

For the German reaction to this, see the entry for 14 November 1944, and that for Boxing Day.

Garden is in the air and the Tarrant Rushton planes are towing the British 1st Airborne Division towards the farthest dropping zone, around Oosterbeek, four miles west of the great bridge over the Neder Rijn — the Lower Rhine — at Arnhem.

Footnote: This was the bridge too far. The Arnhem landings were a display of euphoric Allied over-confidence in the face of a mass of information that should have caused more than momentary reconsideration. Aerial photographs showed German tanks only a short distance from the drop-zone. The Dutch Resistance had reported "battered Panzer divisions" arriving in Holland to refit.

Crucially, there was an Enigma-coded radio intercept released from Bletchley Park just two days before Operation Market Garden was launched, giving the precise locations of these units. The intelligence statement was the Wehrmacht's Army Group B, under Field-Marshal Walther Model — veteran of the great tank battles in Ukraine — had moved its headquarters to the Tafelberg Hotel in Oosterbeek. This should have caused considerable alarm on two counts. Firstly, the hotel lay between the drop-zone and its target — the Arnhem bridge over the Lower Rhine — and secondly they were no ordinary enemy troops. These were known to be the 2nd S.S. Panzer Corps which comprised the crack 9th and 10th S.S. Panzer Divisions.

The information was available to those planning Market Garden, but Field-Marshal Sir Bernard Montgomery "simply waved my objections airily aside"

Friday 22 September
Ottawa Conference VIPs fly into Poole.

British VIPs returning from the Ottawa Conference have flown back into Poole Harbour aboard a B.O.A.C. Boeing Clipper.

The party includes the Chief of the Imperial General Staff, Sir Alan Brooke; the First Sea Lord, Admiral Sir Andrew Cunningham; and the Chief of Air Staff, Sir Charles Portal.

Saturday 23 September
Tarrant Rushton day-drops to S.A.S. troops in France.

Over the past two days, Halifax aircraft from R.A.F. Tarrant Rushton successfully undertook their first daylight operations over France, in supply dropping missions to units of the Special Air Service operating behind enemy lines. The principal night-time air lifts during the month were for Operation Market Garden, carried out by 298 Squadron and 644 Squadron, for three nights running from the 17th to the 19th. The station had been sealed for the duration of the Arnhem flights.

Earlier in the month they had carried out missions for the Special Operations Executive and made S.A.S. sorties over France, Belgium and Holland.

Friday 29 September
Dorsetmen enter the Reich.

Men of the 1st Battalion of the Dorsetshire Regiment today formed the first infantry patrol to cross into Germany. They are disappointed, however, to have been forestalled from claiming the honour of being the first unit of the British Army to enter the Reich. That has been snatched from them by the Sherwood Rangers in Sherman tanks.

The Dorsets are operating as support troops for the Guards Armoured Division in its breakout from the De Groote bridgehead. Trophies from the cross-border patrol include a German state flag and a black flag of the S.S. This evening, at the invitation of their supporting field battery, the Commanding Officer of the Dorsets and his second in command fired token shells into Germany. One was painted with a message: "A present for Adolf Schickelgruber."

During September
Mudeford mine kills two Sappers.

Two members of a Royal Engineers mine-clearance team have been blown-up while trying to remove a device from the beach at Avon Run, Mudeford. They were endeavouring to make safe the entrance to Christchurch Harbour.

During September.
Hurn's flying bomb tally.

Mosquito Mark VI night-fighters of 418 Squadron, which operated from R.A.F. Hurn between 14 July and 1 August,

and also from R.A.F. Holmsley South and R.A.F. Middle Wallop, have claimed a total of 80 scores in their interceptions of V1 flying-bombs. These, at the western end of their arc of fire, have largely been shot down over the sea. The method of scoring encouraged this, with a flying-bomb put into the sea counting as one enemy aircraft destroyed, while one claimed over land was rated as only being equal to half an aircraft.

Newspaper reports of these interceptions include eye-witness accounts of fighters flying level with missiles and then flicking them with a wing-tip to tip them into the countryside. Flight-Lieutenant G. L. Bonham D.F.C., from Christchurch, New Zealand, flying a Tempest, destroyed four flying-bombs in one patrol. He tipped three of them out of control by this method of "formating and flipping" as pilots call the wing-tip technique.

Wednesday 4 October
Dorset troops see the V2s go up.

The 1st Battalion of the Dorsetshire Regiment, holding what they call "The Island" at Bemmel, which is almost surrounded by Germans and linked only by a precarious corridor with the main Allied advance, have seen several V2 rockets rise towards London. They are being fired from the enemy-occupied Hook of Holland.

They are being launched skywards from positions to the east, north-east, and south-east of "The Island". The missiles go straight up to a height of about ten kilometres and then tilt into a 45 degree trajectory. The first to land on London hit Chiswick on 8 September and another fell the same evening at Epping.

FAG BREAK: AT VALKENSWAARD, SOUTH OF EINDHOVEN WHICH WAS SEIZED BY THE GUARDS ARMOURED DIVISION ON 17 SEPTEMBER 1944 AND OCCUPIED THE FOLLOWING DAY BY THE 43RD (WESSEX) DIVISION. VALKENSWAARD LIES SEVEN MILES INTO HOLLAND ON THE ROAD TOWARDS EINDHOVEN AND THE AIRBORNE LANDINGS BETWEEN THERE AND ARNHEM WHICH BEGAN AT 13.00 HOURS ON 18 SEPTEMBER 1944. THIS TRUCK, BELONGING TO THE 1ST BATTALION, THE DORSETSHIRE REGIMENT, CARRIES THE WYVERN BADGE OF THE 43RD DIVISION ON THE NEARSIDE WING. A WHITE "56", IN A DULL RED SQUARE ON THE OFFSIDE WING, INDICATES THEIR BATTALION CODE. THE FIVE-POINTED STAR IN THE WHITE CIRCLE IS THE UNIVERSAL MARKING FOR ALLIED VEHICLES IN NORTH-WESTERN EUROPE

Footnote: None of the German vengeance weapons caused damage in Dorset though the western strays fell into countryside around the New Forest. The closest V1 flying-bomb to land beside a building was that which hit Boldre churchyard. The Daily Telegraph saw the shape of things to come: "V2 indicates the kind of weapons with which the Third World War will be fought if there is one."

Saturday 14 October
Twelve drown in landing craft on Chesil Beach.

An American tank landing craft, *LCT (A) 2454*, was washed up on the Chesil Beach at Wyke Regis last night in mountainous seas. The state of the water prevented both the Weymouth Lifeboat and a dockyard tug from Portland Harbour in their attempts to come round Portland Bill to its aid.

Ten of the landing craft's British crew were drowned despite the desperate efforts of members of Fortuneswell Lifesaving Company who had run along the pebble bank from Portland. They succeeded in firing a rocket-line into the stricken vessel. Two sailors were then rescued by

Coastguard Treadwell as a tremendous wave swept most of the crew and everything else that was moveable into the sea.

Rockets fired more lines into the craft but these fouled as she shifted across the swirling pebbles. Captain Pennington Legh and Coastguard Treadwell were swept away, never to be seen again, as they struggled to free the lines. The four surviving rescuers continued to risk their lives and saved two more of the sailors.

Cyril Brown, wearing a lifebelt, battled through the waves to get the line to the crewmen, and then had to be hauled ashore himself and was taken to hospital. The line broke before the last crewman could be brought ashore and this time it was Albert Oldfield, without any safety line of his own, who managed to wade out to throw another line into the landing craft. The fourth man leapt from the vessel and was pulled from the water.

Footnote: The four surviving rescuers were awarded Lloyd's silver medal for lifesaving but one, V. F. Stephens of Wyke Regis, died in a car crash before he could receive it at a civic reception in Weymouth Guildhall. Cyril Brown, of Portland, was also presented with the Stanhope Medal, for the bravest deed of 1944.

Wednesday 18 October
Hurn Aerodrome is R.A.F. Hurn once again.

Formal control of Hurn Aerodrome was today resumed by the Royal Air Force on its transfer from the United States Army Air Force.

NAVAL AERODROME: CHARLTON HORETHORNE ROYAL NAVAL AIR STATION, A WARTIME SATELLITE AIRFIELD FOR THE FLEET AIR ARM BASE AT YEOVILTON, WAS SERVICED VIA SHERBORNE. DESPITE THE CLOUD, 72 AEROPLANES – MOSTLY LIGHT TRAINERS – ARE VISIBLE IN THIS PHOTOGRAPH TAKEN ON THE MORNING OF 3 OCTOBER 1944. DISPERSAL BLAST-BAYS CAN BE SEEN AROUND THE NORTHERN PERIMETER, AND BLISTER HANGARS TO THE EAST AND SOUTH, TOWARDS SIGWELLS FARM (BETWEEN THE ROAD AND THE ENDS OF THE GRASS RUNWAYS)

Sunday 22 October

Celebrations as Fighter Command is revived.

There will be celebrations tonight at R.A.F. Hurn and R.A.F. Warmwell, along with every fighter aerodrome in the land, following the message to all units from Air Marshal Sir Roderic Hill, Commander-in-Chief Air Defence of Great Britain. That title has now been dropped and Fighter Command is being revived as the name for the elements of the Royal Air Force tasked to defend the United Kingdom.

As Fighter Command, though still under the command of Sir Roderic Hill, it reverts to Air Ministry control. Officially, the change has been made in recognition of the fact that Air Defence Great Britain has now become a chiefly offensive operation, but reasons of sentiment undoubtedly influenced the decision. The clumsy replacement title was never popular with the pilots and ground crew of fighter squadrons.

Sir Roderick admits as much in his message: "To us, as heirs, Fighter Command is something more than a glorious name. I take this opportunity of paying my tribute to the illustrious past."

Monday 30 October

Poole bullets highlight a problem.

A Poole refuse disposal stoker, working at the town's Incinerator, literally had a close shave — a superficial face wound — when a cartridge clip exploded in his furnace. This has highlighted a serious danger and the public is asked to be more thoughtful with the disposal of explosives. Not that dustmen are going to lower their guard. Deadly objects are now lying around all over the country. Inevitably some of the smaller and less noticeable kinds will find their way into the dustbin.

During October

Coupon Controller approves Christchurch cassocks.

The vicar of Christchurch Priory, Canon W. H. Gay, writes in his monthly parish newsletter about allegations of having breached rationing restrictions:

"As some have questioned the legality of my appeal for clothing coupons to refit the choir with cassocks, may I state that the 143 coupons I have received will be sent to the Controller at Bournemouth who will issue the needed permission to the tailor. I notice that most of the coupons have come from spinsters, widows and bachelors."

Wednesday 1 November

Closure of R.A.F. Hurn.

R.A.F. Hurn has ceased to exist. At 00.00 hours today control passed from the Air Ministry to the Ministry of Civil Aviation. The military station has become a civilian airfield.

Wednesday 1 November

Poole craft attack Walcheren to free Antwerp.

Twenty-five Poole landing craft, manned by naval crews from the town's H.M.S. Turtle shore-base, have landed commandos on Walcheren Island. This German-held strongpoint blocked the approaches to the Belgian port of Antwerp. Nine of the craft, designated as the Support Squadron Eastern Flank, have been sunk. A further nine are immobilised.

Footnote: It took the British commandos and Canadian ground forces three days to capture the island. The channel to Antwerp would be opened to Allied supply ships on 28 November 1944.

Dorchester hero: Captain Lionel Queripel was awarded a posthumous Victoria Cross

Arnhem V.C.: for Shirburnian John Grayburn who held what became immortalised as "The Bridge Too Far"

LAST CARD: FOR WHAT WOULD BE THE FINAL CHRISTMAS OF THE WAR, FROM DISPATCH RIDER ARTHUR LEGG, WITH 6 BASE SIGNAL SECTION FROM CAIRO TO TRIPOLI AND THEN ACROSS ITALY. THE AIR-GRAPH WAS SENT TO HIS BROTHER TED, THE AUTHOR'S FATHER, WHO WITH WIFE GLADYS AND SON BARRIE WERE LIVING AT 21 EASTER ROAD, MOORDOWN, BOURNEMOUTH

Saturday 11 November
Dorsetmen are first gunners into Germany.

The 94th Field Regiment of the Royal Artillery, who were mainly recruited from Bournemouth and Dorset in 1939, have become the first field gun force to cross the German frontier. They are supporting the Anglo-American offensive in the Geilenkirchen sector.

Tuesday 14 November
4th Dorsets were the heroes in Arnhem escapes.

It became known today that it was largely due to the matchless heroism of 250 men of the 4th Battalion of the Dorsetshire Regiment — part of the 43rd (Wessex) Division — that 2,400 of the original 10,075 airborne troops succeeded in withdrawing from the Arnhem bridgehead on the night of 25 September.

Few, however, of the Dorsets escaped — and some of those had to swim for their lives, under fire as they crossed the Neder Rijn, to do so.

In the salient of the British advance, "The Island" at Bemmel, three battalions of the Dorsetshire Regiment — the 1st, 4th and 5th — found themselves fighting in adjacent fields for the same "thumb print" on the map. This was the first time that events had brought them together. Other Dorsets were able to give covering fire to men of the 4th Battalion as they rescued survivors of the 1st Airborne Division and the Polish Parachute Brigade with a shuttle service of assault boats across the Neder Rijn [Lower Rhine].

By dawn on 26 September, at 06.00 hours, the intensity of enemy fire made further rescue crossings impossible.

Sunday 3 December
Home Guard stands down.

With the movement of the war into and across Europe throughout the second half of this year there have been inevitable consequences on this side of the Channel. One of them is that from today the Home Guard is stood down.

Monday 25 December
802 Americans from Piddlehinton drown in the Channel.

The back-up troops for the clearance of the Germans from the Bretagne peninsula — the vanguard of the United States 66th Infantry Division — left Piddlehinton Camp just before Christmas. Eighty acres of huts housed a total of 5,000 American infantrymen but has been left a winter wasteland as, to their dismay, the young men found that instead of celebrating the festivities they were going to war. They arrived in Dorset on 26 November and have now sailed, for Cherbourg, with their ultimate objective being to clear the enemy out of the U-boat pens at Brest.

There has, however, been an attack on the Allied convoy in the English Channel. The casualty has been the 11,500-ton Belgian liner *Leopoldville*, acting as a troopship, which left Southampton Docks at 09.00 hours on Christmas Eve. Her complement was 2,237 members of the 262nd Regiment and 264th Regiment of the 66th Infantry Division. Cards and the odd mouth-whistle, wetted by a pint of beer apiece, were about the only seasonal spirit. Likewise aboard the *Cheshire*, with more troops, and their Canadian escort destroyers H.M.C.S. *Brilliant* and H.M.C.S. *Anthony*. Off Spithead, at 11.00 hours, they rendezvoused with another destroyer, H.M.C.S. *Holtern*, and the Free French frigate *Croix de Lorraine*.

They went on to a war footing at 14.00 hours, on passing Piccadilly Circus, as the point in the English Channel that is codenamed "PC" is generally known. Then, with the white cliffs of St Catherine's Point and the Isle of Wight behind them, almost out of sight, the convoy was ordered to increase speed and weave in a zig-zag pattern to lessen the chances of an encounter with a German submarine.

One was detected, or at least suspected, after a 'ping' on *Brilliant*'s asdic screen. She raised a warning flag as the convoy ploughed into heavier seas. The combat watch, in an intensely cold wind, continued until 14.30 and was then relaxed. "Bunk duty" was the next order aboard the *Leopoldville* as the men attempted to recover from disrupted sleep amid bouts of sea-sickness. The crump of depth-charges disturbed them at 15.20 as the destroyers reacted to their second U-boat alert. Nothing appeared to have been hit.

By 17.45 the convoy charted a course that brought it 5.5 miles north-east of the Allied-occupied port of Cherbourg, where lights proclaimed a confidence that wartime blackouts were now beyond their time. "The place seems to be having a party!" someone remarked laconically; which indeed it was, this first Christmas of liberation.

Then came the fatal torpedo, into the stern of the *Leopoldville*, on the starboard side. This was facing the open sea. The liner would take a couple of hours to sink, though when she did so the process was fast, within ten minutes of the pressure of the water bursting the bulkheads. Meanwhile, lifeboats were lowered, and H.M.C.S. *Brilliant* led a rescue operation that should have won medals, but the help expected from partying Cherbourg never arrived.

A total of 802 Americans are drowned, killed, or missing, presumed dead. Survival time in the icy waters was minutes rather than hours.

Footnote: When they woke to the reality on Christmas Day, the military commanders in Cherbourg passed the buck back to the *Brilliant* and blamed the escort vessels, for the rescue debacle. The wreck of the *Leopoldville* has been surveyed by divers Penny and Mike Rowley. It lies on its port side and the highest point is under 38 metres of water. The hull, superstructure, and bridge are remarkably intact. Poignantly, its bows point south towards Cherbourg, and the visible damage is restricted to the impact hole caused by the torpedo and a crumpled stern behind it.

The loss, claimed by *U486*, would be overshadowed by another disaster over this final wartime Christmas. To the east, at the other extremity of the front-line, the Germans had broken through the snowy forests of the Ardennes in their last great counter-offensive of the war. Their story became a legend of book and screen, remembered as the Battle of the Bulge, whereas the tragedy of the *Leopoldville* is hardly known.

Tuesday 26 December
Blandford sees the cost of the Ardennes.

The news today is that General George Patton has at last been able to lead the tanks of the 3rd United States Army in the relief of Bastogne. The tide of the great German counter-offensive in the snowy forests of Luxembourg and southern Belgium — the Battle of the Ardennes — has been turned.

It has, however, been an achievement of American grit. The staunch determination of the American soldier since 16 December has prevented the Germans from coming back across the River Meuse.

Casualties are streaming into Dorset. Up to 500 wounded Americans have been flown into R.A.F. Tarrant Rushton by Dakota transports in a single night, en route for the 22nd General Hospital at Blandford Camp.

Emergency supplies of penicillin have been requisitioned from British Drug Houses Limited. "Control of it is so tight," says director R. R. Bennett, "that if I needed some for a dying brother I could not obtain it from my own firm but would have to apply through a government department."

Footnote: The Ardennes reserves for the Germans were to be worse; estimated losses of 120,000 with 600 tanks and assault guns, plus dozens of aircraft. There was nothing in reserve for another counter-attack.

Friday 29 December
American freighter sinks in Worbarrow Bay.

The *Black Hawk*, a United States steam-freighter, has sunk in Worbarrow Bay after being hit by a torpedo from a German U-boat.

During December
Posthumous V.C. for Dorchester's Arnhem hero.

Captain Lionel Ernest Queripel of Dorchester has been posthumously awarded the Victoria Cross for his gallantry in the battle following the airborne landings at Arnhem. Born in 1920, he was fighting with the 10th Battalion, the Parachute Regiment.

The citation reads: "At Arnhem on 19 September 1944 Captain Queripel was acting as company commander of a composite company composed of men of three parachute battalions.

"At 14.00 hours on that day his company were advancing along a main road which runs on an embankment towards Arnhem. The advance was conducted under continuous machine-gun fire, which at one period became so heavy that the company became split up on either side of the road and suffered considerable loss. Captain Queripel at once proceeded to reorganise his forces, crossing and recrossing the road whilst doing so under extremely heavy and accurate fire. During this period he carried a wounded sergeant to the Regimental Aid Post under fire and was himself wounded in the face.

"Having reorganised his force, Captain Queripel personally led a party of men against a strong-point holding up the advance. This strong-point consisted of a captured British anti-tank gun and two machine-guns. Despite the extremely heavy fire directed at him, Captain Queripel succeeded in killing the crews of the machine-guns and recapturing the anti-tank gun. As a result of this the advance was able to continue.

"Later in the same day Captain Queripel found himself cut off with a small party of men and took up a

WAR BADGES: AMONG THOSE TAKEN BY CREWMEN OF THE WEYMOUTH LIFEBOAT, FROM MEMBERS OF THE LUFTWAFFE, THE GERMAN DEEP SEAS FLEET, A COASTAL E-BOAT SAILOR, AND A U-BOAT SUBMARINER

position in a ditch. By this time he had received further wounds in both arms. Regardless of his wounds and the very heavy mortar fire, he continued to inspire his men to resist with hand grenades, pistols, and the few remaining rifles. On at least one occasion he picked-up and threw back at the enemy a stick-grenade which had landed in the ditch.

"As, however, the enemy pressure increased, Captain Queripel decided that it was impossible to hold the position longer and ordered his men to withdraw. Despite their protests, he insisted on remaining behind to cover their withdrawal with his automatic pistol and a few remaining hand grenades. This is the last occasion on which he was seen.

"During the whole of a period of nine hours of confused and bitter fighting Captain Queripel displayed the highest standard of gallantry under most difficult and trying circumstances. His courage, leadership, and devotion to duty were an inspiration to all."

During December
Shirburnian's posthumous V.C. for the bridge too far.

Lieutenant John Grayburn, a platoon commander with the 2nd Battalion, the Parachute Regiment, has been posthumously gazetted with the Victoria Cross, for three days of gallant fighting between 17-20 September 1944. He went to Sherborne School.

His orders upon landing close to the bridge over the Lower Rhine at Arnhem were to seize it and hold it.

After the north end of the bridge had been captured, Grayburn was ordered to take his platoon and seize and hold the southern end. This they kept attempting to carry out until casualties made further attempts futile: "He directed the withdrawal from the bridge personally and was himself the last man to come off the embankment into comparative cover."

Then, the citation continues, he occupied a house that stood in an almost indefensible position, and managed to hold off sustained attacks by infantry, mortars, tanks, and self-propelled guns: "He constantly exposed himself

to the enemy's fire while moving among and encouraging his platoon and seemed completely oblivious to danger."

Fire finally drove them from the building, on 19 September, and John Grayburn then led a fighting patrol back to the bridge to prevent the Germans from laying demolition charges. Despite being wounded in the back he continued to defend an untenable position.

In full view of a German tank he personally directed his men back to safety but stayed on the front-line, wounded and hungry and without having eaten for days, and was killed on the night of 20 September. The citation concludes: "There is no doubt that, had it not been for this officer's inspiring bravery, the Arnhem bridge could never have been held for this time."

During December
Henstridge airmen fight the Japs.

Two Seafire squadrons from Henstridge Royal Naval Air Station, H.M.S. Dipper, on the Somerset border at Stalbridge, are flying from the aircraft-carrier H.M.S. *Indefatigable* in offensive operations against Japanese forces in the Pacific theatre.

887 (Fleet Air Arm) Squadron and 894 (Fleet Air Arm) Squadron comprise No. 24 Royal Navy Fighter Wing. The Seafire is the marine version of the Spitfire. At Henstridge a key element of flight training are landings on a dummy deck, represented by a rectangle of concrete in the grey tarmac of the central runway, with the grass on either side representing the sea. Arrestor wires add authenticity to the experience.

Footnote: On 1 April 1945, H.M.S. *Indefatigable* became the first British aircraft-carrier to be hit by a Japanese Kamikaze plane. "Divine wind" is the translation of the suicide-bombing unit's name. Among the British pilots of 887 Squadron was Sub-Lieutenant R. Lygo. He would retire as Admiral Sir Raymond Lygo.

1945

During January

Warmwell joyrider takes a Spitfire to Cheselbourne.

Sergeant Victor Swatridge of Dorchester Police was called by telephone at 02.45 hours by the constable on the Broadmayne beat and told that a Spitfire had been stolen at 02.00 from R.A.F. Warmwell. As there was a blizzard at the time he thought this a little unlikely but the Observer Corps post at Poundbury Camp confirmed they had heard an aeroplane overhead at about 02.30. The missing plane was said to have flown west from the aerodrome and the Observers reported the unmistakable sound of a Rolls-Royce Merlin engine. They reported it disappearing about six or seven miles to the north-east.

Moonlight followed the snow and Swatridge went with another officer on to the Dorset Downs around Cheselbourne in the centre of the county:

"At about 05.00, on approaching Cheselbourne Water, to our amazement we saw a lighted hurricane lamp in the drive to a cottage. Naked lights were regarded as somewhat treasonable and very much frowned upon, as Black-out regulations were strictly enforceable. Even the headlamps of cars were only allowed narrow slotted beams.

I immediately investigated the reason for this breach and a woman, on answering my call at the cottage, stated that she had heard a plane overhead about two hours previously which appeared to have landed nearby. She went on to say, that she had been expecting her husband home on leave from France, and that it was the sort of stupid thing he would do — come by any means possible. She had placed the lighted lamp as a guide to him. Amazing as it seemed, we trudged on and clambered on to a high bank overlooking an unploughed cornfield where to our utter surprise we came upon tyre marks. On following them we found the missing fighter with its nose embedded in the hedge and bank at the other end of the field, on Eastfield Field, a quarter of a mile north-east of Cheselbourne church.

Climbing on to the wing we found the cockpit lights burning but the 'bird' had flown. There was no trace of blood inside and we found footmarks in the snow made by the culprit, when walking away from the scene, but they quickly became extinct owing to the drifting snow. I returned to the divisional station, after leaving a constable to guard the plane and a search party was sent out in daylight. A Canadian airman on the ground staff was arrested, having celebrated too liberally the previous night, and in a rash moment embarked on this venturesome journey. There was only slight damage to the aircraft; the man was concussed and later dealt with by the authorities. So the escapade resolved itself."

During January

Tarrant Rushton flies S.O.E. sorties over Norway.

Halifax aircraft from R.A.F. Tarrant Rushton have been taking part in Norwegian operations for the Special Operations Executive. These will continue through February.

Tuesday 6 February

Cargo ship sunk off Dorset.

Claimed by German submarine *U1017*, a cargo ship was torpedoed today off the Dorset coast and has been identified as the *Everleigh*. This 5,222-ton vessel was steaming down Channel, having left for New York.

Tuesday 20 February

Christchurch hears of a record 4,000 feet Bailey Bridge.

The Experimental Bridging Establishment of the Royal Engineers, based beside the River Stour at Barrack Road, Christchurch, has heard that the longest of their Bailey Bridges yet constructed is now open for traffic across the River Meuse at Gennep, Netherlands. Its total span is more than 4,000 feet.

Designed by Donald Coleman Bailey, in 1939, the first prototype prefabricated steel bridge was put across the Stour at Christchurch on 1 May 1941. It spanned 70 feet. The operation took 36 minutes from commencement to the first lorry reaching the other side.

The new record-breaking bridge across the Meuse has taken ten days to erect, being delayed by the fact that its approaches were under two feet of water, and complicated by the height and speed of the river.

It will enable 21 Army Group to intensify its relentless pressure against German forces behind the breached Siegfried Line in the second phase of the Battle of the Rhineland. The defenders of Goch, at the confluence of the River Niers with the Meuse, surrendered yesterday to the Canadian 15th and 51st Divisions. South of Gennep, progress of the 52nd Division has been held up at Afferden, by the floods.

Sunday 25 February

2nd Dorsets cross the Irrawaddy.

The 2nd Battalion of the Dorsetshire Regiment today saw the "flyin' fishes play" as they crossed the Irrawaddy. Now, in Rudyard Kipling's words, the British Army is "On the road to Mandalay."

This has influenced the Dorsets' current battle cry, parodying *The Green Eye of the Yellow God* by J. Milton Hayes: "There's a dirty white pagoda to the east of Payadu."

Monday 12 March

Burton Bradstock pensioners save crashed pilot.

A Martinet from the Armament Practice Camp at Warmwell Aerodrome today developed engine problems over the Chesil Beach Bombing Range. The pilot crash-landed at Burton Mere, on the coast between Swyre and Burton Bradstock, but found himself trapped in the wreckage.

Two heroes ignored the flames which were about to engulf the aircraft and succeeded in freeing the pilot's feet. They were Miss Harriet Evelyn Bendy, aged 68, and Levi Rogers, aged 65. Both live in Burton Bradstock. As they pulled the shocked airman to safety his aeroplane became an inferno.

Monday 19 March
Christchurch Aerodrome goes to Transport Command.

R.A.F. Christchurch was today transferred from No. 11 Group, Fighter Command, to 46 Group, Transport Command. It is to be a satellite airfield to the major transport base on the western side of the New Forest at Ibsley, between Ringwood and Fordingbridge.

In the past nine months, Christchurch Aerodrome has been used as a diversionary airfield when intended destinations were closed by fog or other bad weather. Incoming flights from across the Channel have brought Allied wounded and German prisoners.

Aircraft types visiting Christchurch have included the Boston, Liberator, Stirling, and Douglas C-47 Dakota.

Tuesday 20 March
2nd Dorsets help take Mandalay.

Having left 27 dead along the road to Mandalay, the 2nd Battalion of the Dorsetshire Regiment have arrived at their objective and are mopping up opposition as the Japanese withdraw.

General Sir Oliver Leese, Commander-in-Chief Allied Land Forces South-East Asia, visited the men this afternoon and told them they would have to make the next 400 miles to Rangoon before the monsoon broke — though this time, he promised, they would not have to walk all the way.

Hearing the news of the capture of the ancient Burmese capital, Winston Churchill remarked: "Thank God they've at last got to a place I can pronounce!"

Wednesday 21 March
6th Airborne Division leaves Tarrant Rushton.

The British 6th Airborne Division, with its 60 Halifax tug-planes and their Hamilcar and Horsa gliders, is today leaving Tarrant Rushton Aerodrome for its new location, R.A.F. Woodbridge.

This Suffolk airfield is closer to the division's next objectives on the far side of the Rhine.

Footnote: These landings, codenamed Operation Varsity, began at 09.45 hours on 24 March and continued for three hours. The 6th Airborne Division took Hamminkein and the bridges over the River Issel. Fifty-

OPERATION VARSITY: THE LAST AIRBORNE LANDINGS OF THE WAR, ACROSS THE RHINE, REQUIRED THE RELOCATION OF THE BRITISH 6TH AIRBORNE DIVISION. THEY LEFT TARRANT RUSHTON AERODROME ON 21 MARCH 1945 AND WERE REASSEMBLED AT R.A.F. WOODBRIDGE, SUFFOLK, FOR TAKE-OFF AT 09.54 HOURS ON 24 MARCH (THEY ARE SEEN AT WOODBRIDGE)

Wehrmacht surrenders: the signature of General Hans Kinzel on behalf of the German Army, witnessed by Field-Marshal Sir Bernard Montgomery, at 18.30 hours on 4 May 1945

Wehrmacht surrenders: the signature of General Hans Kinzel on behalf of the German Army, witnessed by Field-Marshal Sir Bernard Montgomery, at 18.30 hours on 4 May 1945

two of the ex-Tarrant Rushton gliders landed successfully.

During March
Duchess of Kent visits Blandford.

H.R.H. the Duchess of Kent has visited the 22nd General Hospital of the United States Army, which now works with the 125th, 131st and 140th General Hospitals in a major medical complex across the former Anson-Craddock Lines at Blandford Camp.

It received 17,000 patients of the long-term type, many of whom are needing complicated surgery. The commander is Lieutenant-Colonel Leonard D. Heaton.

During March
Poles sink U-boat in Poole Bay.

Polish pilots have claimed a U-boat in the Channel. It was sunk in the south-east extremity of Poole Bay, towards the Isle of Wight.

Monday 9 April
Warmwell ceases to be an operational airfield.

152 Squadron, which has been operating from R.A.F. Warmwell since the dark days of 1940, has been withdrawn and the station is now retained only for training, by the Central Gunnery School.

Tuesday 17 April
Puddletown lad dies forcing the Argenta Gap.

Trooper James Legg from Puddletown, aged 21, has been killed in action in Italy. Serving with the Queen's Bays, he drove the first tank to force its way through the enemy's main defensive line, in the Argenta Gap.

Thursday 26 April
B.O.A.C. Lancastrian flies from Hurn to Sydney.

The first Lancastrian of British Overseas Airways Corporation's new civilian fleet has landed in Australia at the end of a proving flight that lasted 53 hours. Airliner

G-AGLF carried the military markings of the R.A.F.'s South-East Asia theatre but was on a pathfinding flight to determine the feasibility of a peacetime service.

After flying out of Britain, from R.A.F. Hurn, on Monday, the Lancastrian touched down en route at Lydda in Palestine, Karachi in India, Ratmalana in Ceylon, and Learmonth in Western Australia.

The pre-war flying-boat service from Southampton Water used to take nine days, but though so much faster the Lancastrian has restricted room, for bunks and seats for only six passengers. The Empire flying-boat used to carry 24 passengers.

Friday 4 May
Dorsets hear there is no longer a war in northern Europe.

Cipher clerks to the units of Dorsetshire Regiment in Germany received the following message at 20.30 hours today: "SECRET . all offensive ops will cease from receipt of this signal . orders will be given to all tps to cease fire 08.00 hrs tomorrow saturday 5 may. full terms of local surrender arranged today for 21 ARMY GP front follow . emphasise these provision apply solely to 21 ARMY GP fronts and are for the moment excl of DUNKIRK . ack."

In other words, it's over. The times are stated in British Double Summer Time and result from the Instrument of Surrender which was signed by General-Admiral Hans George von Friedeburg, the emissary of Grand Admiral Karl Dönitz who is exercising command in Schleswig-

Submarine Surrenders: U1023 approaching Weymouth Harbour on 10 May 1945

Holstein in place of Hitler — who has shot himself — and General Hans Kinzel, as Chief of Staff to Field-Marshal Ernst von Busch.

Their unconditional surrender of all enemy forces in northern Germany was signed at 18.30 hours today in the Tactical Headquarters of Field-Marshal Sir Bernard Montgomery on Lüneburg Heath.

Tuesday 8 May
V.E. Day.

15.00 hours. The war in Europe is officially at an end. Street parties, bonfires, and church services will mark Victory in Europe Day this evening.

Wednesday 9 May
Dorset gunners to occupy the Channel Islands.

The officers commanding the German garrison in the Channel Islands today surrendered aboard the destroyer H.M.S. *Bulldog*. The islands, which in normal times have their main English port at Weymouth, were passed by during the Battle of Normandy to avoid unnecessary Allied and civilian casualties.

The War Office contingency plan, prepared for the present eventuality, is for the Channel Islands to be occupied, garrisoned, and then demilitarised by the 522nd (Dorset) Coast Regiment of the Royal Artillery. This unit

will cease to exist as such and be reformed for the purpose, as the 618th (Dorset) Garrison Regiment, Royal Artillery.

Thursday 10 May
Tarrant Rushton Halifaxes land in Oslo.

Halifax aircraft from R.A.F. Tarrant Rushton have spent the past 48 hours ferrying the British 1st Airborne Division to take over Oslo Gardemoen airfield in Norway. Phase III of Operation Doomsday will be completed tomorrow and Phase IV, their re-supply, is scheduled for a week later. Transport duties are now the Order of the Day.

Thursday 10 May
U-boats surface and surrender at Portland.

The first U-boat to give itself up in British home waters, under the unconditional surrender terms, has been *U249* which sailed on the surface into Weymouth Bay this morning. The vessel flew the German naval ensign at half-mast with a Union flag above after Oberleutnant Kock sent a signal to the Royal Navy that he wished to surrender.

The frigates H.M.S. *Amethyst* and H.M.S. *Magpie* escorted the U-boat. She was followed this afternoon by *U825* which came into Portland Harbour. It is also understood that *U1023* has joined them in Weymouth as the surrender of Grand Admiral Karl Dönitz's fleet gathers pace.

MEMORIAL DAY: THE MEN OF THE 22ND GENERAL HOSPITAL OF THE UNITED STATES ARMY PAY TRIBUTE TO THE DEAD OF THE SECOND WORLD WAR, AND THEIR LATE PRESIDENT FRANKLIN DELANO ROOSEVELT, ON 30 MAY 1945

Saturday 12 May
Dorsets in first Victory Parade.

The 5th Battalion of the Dorsetshire Regiment marched past Lieutenant-General Brian Horrocks, the commander of the 30th Corps, at Bremerhaven today. This has been the first Victory Parade to be held in Germany.

Wednesday 16 May
Isle of Wight villagers send their prize to Portland.

Villagers at Freshwater in the Isle of Wight were amazed when a German U-boat surfaced offshore in the bay and requested someone to take its surrender.

Freshwater has a parish councillor or two but it has no mayor or anyone of the standing that a German officer might respect. Anyway it has no port facilities apart from a beach and the inhabitants considered they were in line for a rollicking from the Royal Navy.

So *U776* was asked to surrender somewhere else and it departed for Portland Harbour. Someone in the Isle of Wight has turned down a splendid opportunity. Think of how he might have answered that inevitable question: "Grand-dad, what did you do in the war?"

Wednesday 30 May
Roosevelt Park opened at Blandford.

Roosevelt Park inside the confines of Blandford Camp is the first overseas memorial to the late President of the United States of America. It was declared open today by Colonel J. Fourrier of the

COLOUR PARTY: FIRING THE SHOTS TO OPEN ROOSEVELT PARK AT BLANDFORD CAMP ON 30 MAY 1945

United States Army and a colour party fired ceremonial rounds.

The park is dedicated "to the everlasting memory of our fellow soldiers, at home and abroad, who gave their lives in this war, so that we who live may share in the future of a free and better world".

It has been provided through voluntary contributions of members of the Army Medical Department. The landscaping was designed by a patient at the General Hospital, Private George H. Stuber.

Colonel Fourrier handed the park over to Colonel T. Topham of the Royal Engineers who received it on behalf of the British Army. A six-feet high monument is under construction to enshrine the ideals behind the park permanently in stone.

During June
Gunnery School leaves as Warmwell closes.

Dorset's only Battle of Britain aerodrome, at R.A.F. Warmwell, effectively closes this month with the departure of the Central Gunnery School to Sutton Bridge, Lincolnshire.

Footnote: Official closure would follow in November 1945.

During June
Sherborne School's 242 death toll.

The roll of honour published in *The Shirburnian* school magazine, during the course of the war, has now accounted for 242 lives. It compares with a death toll of 218 in the Great War, but Sherborne School was then much smaller.

The most distinguished of the old Boys in the present conflict was the brilliant mathematician Alan Turing who broke the German military's Enigma cipher codes. The bravest was Lieutenant John H. Grayburn of Abbey

House who was posthumously awarded the Victoria Cross for persistent gallantry devoted to the impossible task of holding the bridge at Arnhem. John's was among the first Victoria Crosses to be won for the Parachute Regiment and the only one by a Shirburnian in this war.

Thursday 5 July
Churchill confident as the nation goes to the polls.

General Election day. All the pundits agree about the result. Wilson "Jack" Broadbent, the political correspondent of the Daily Mail, has told its million and a half readers that the Prime Minister "can be certain of victory at the polls on Thursday, barring accidents". He "will have a working majority; he may have a substantial majority" as "there is no general swing against his Government" and "his personal stock stands as high as it ever did". Broadbent concludes: "It is true, of course, even to the ordinary observer that the Labour Party campaign in this election has been ineptly handled, and completely lacking in inspiration."

The Manchester Guardian concurs: "There is no reason to be other than frank about these matters. The chances of Labour sweeping the country and obtaining a clear majority over all other parties are pretty remote."

Mr Churchill told electors yesterday: "We are going to win. I feel it in my bones that you are going to send me back to power with a great majority. The eyes of the world will be on us tomorrow. If we go down, then all the ninepins of Europe will go down with us. France and Belgium will go forward, not to decent Labour or Socialism, but to a vile form of Communism."

Ballot boxes will be sealed tonight and their counting delayed for nearly three weeks, to enable the practicalities of retrieving and sorting votes from overseas forces, particularly those fighting the Japanese in South-East Asia.

Sunday 15 July
Flying Fortress crash-lands at Christchurch.

American aircrew being brought to Bournemouth for a period of recuperation had a lucky escape today at Christchurch Aerodrome.

Flying Fortress 866, carrying men of the 306th

Typhoon mishap: MN311 overshot the rather short runway at Christchurch Aerodrome on 25 July 1945. The pilot stepped out unharmed and jumped down on to the Lymington road

WOMEN FIREMEN: AS FEMALE FIRE-FIGHTERS WERE KNOWN, WITH THOSE OF NATIONAL FIRE SERVICE DIVISION 16-C SEEN MARCHING THROUGH BOURNEMOUTH GARDENS IN A VICTORY PARADE, 1945

Bombardment Group from Thurleigh, Bedfordshire, overshot the western boundary of the notoriously short airfield when landing into a light wind. It plunged into scrubland. The near-side port engine was ripped out but the aircraft came to a halt without catching fire. No one was hurt.

Thursday 26 July
Churchill's Government is thrown out.

Declaration day. The nation is stunned that contrary to the pundits not only has Winston Churchill's Conservative Party failed to retain power but had a crushing defeat inflicted upon it in the General Election which took place on 5 July. Instead it has been a Labour landslide. The state of the parties tonight is Labour, 393; Conservative, 198; and the Liberals eclipsed with just 12 members of Parliament.

Individual results tell the same story. There are no less than 26 Labour members enjoying majorities of over 20,000 votes, with the greatest of these enormous majorities being Emanuel Shinwell's 32,257 at Seaham, which is Ramsay MacDonald's old seat. Only true-blue Bournemouth is in the same league, for the Conservatives, having returned Sir Leonard Lyle with a surplus of 20,312 votes.

U.S.S. MISSOURI: THE AMERICAN BATTLESHIP IS SEEN AT SOUTHAMPTON BUT ALSO VISITED PORTLAND HARBOUR IN 1945

GOING HOME: THE TROOPSHIP QUEEN ELIZABETH *PREPARING TO SAIL DOWN* SOUTHAMPTON WATER *IN* AUGUST *1945, LOADED WITH* AMERICAN GIS *AND GIVEN A FLYPAST SALUTE BY A FIGHTER FORMATION (TOP LEFT)*

Pre-war memories are blamed for the scale of the Socialist success which has also surprised correspondents from across the world in its rejection of the country's acknowledged saviour. To them, and no doubt to him, it is an unwarranted dismissal.

Even in Dorset it has been a close-run thing for the Conservatives. The Parliamentary constituency of East Dorset returned Lieutenant-Colonel Mervyn Wheatley with 26,561 votes against 25,095 to his Labour opponent, Lieutenant-Commander Cyril Fletcher-Cooke, with Liberal candidate Colonel Mander having the remaining 8,975. Out of 80,816 voters on the electoral registers there was a poll of 60,629, which included 8,352 votes from men and women in the armed services. That is 75 per cent participation.

Counting had been delayed to await the arrival of ballot papers from overseas soldiers, sailors and airmen.

Footnote: Clement Attlee became Prime Minister on 27 July 1945 with Ernest Bevin as Foreign Secretary, Sir Stafford Cripps at the Board of Trade, and Dr Hugh Dalton as Chancellor of the Exchequer.

Winston Churchill would return to power in October 1951 and completed his "unfinished business" of finally removing rationing in time for the coronation of Queen Elizabeth II, and his reward of a knighthood in 1953.

Wednesday 15 August
Henstridge pilots celebrate V.J. Day.

It is Victory over Japan Day. Nowhere in Dorset have the celebrations been more heart-felt than in Stalbridge and in particular the Wrens' Quarters on the Dorset side of H.M.S. Dipper, the Royal Naval Air Station at Henstridge which straddles the county boundary with

THOUSAND SUNS: THE PENULTIMATE MESSAGE TO THE RISING SUN *NATION, PHOTOGRAPHED FROM LONE BOMBER* ENOLA GAY *AS SHE HEADED SOUTHWARDS AND SEAWARDS FROM THE PORT TOWN OF WESTERN* JAPAN, *ON 6* AUGUST *1945*

DUMMY DECK: THE RECTANGLE OF CONCRETE ALONG THE RUNWAY AT THE CENTRE OF THIS PHOTOGRAPH OF HENSTRIDGE NAVAL AIR STATION. IT WAS USED TO TRAIN FLEET AIR ARM PILOTS IN LANDING TECHNIQUES FOR OPERATING FROM AIRCRAFT-CARRIERS

Saturday 4 August warned: "Your city will be obliterated unless your Government surrenders."

That was ignored, apart from the cutting of useless firebreaks, and it was Hiroshima's misfortune to be the one of four potential targets that was basking in sunshine on the morning of Monday 6 August. The blow — with a flash "like a thousand suns" — was delivered by a single bomb called Little Boy, which was carried by a lone United States Army Air Force Boeing B-29 Superfortress piloted by Paul Tibbets Junior and named *Enola Gay*, for his mother. Then Nagasaki was threatened with its "rain of ruin the like of which has never been seen on Earth" which was wrought by the Fat Man dropped by another B-29 Superfortress, *Bock's Car*, on Thursday 9 August. The third atomic bomb, standing-by and apparently destined for Tokyo, did not have to be delivered.

Japan began the surrender process at the weekend.

Somerset. Here a bonfire has been kept burning all night, despite a soaking at 05.00 hours when the rain intensified. It was lit a few minutes after midnight when the station Tannoy roused everyone from sleep: "Attention everybody. Attention. Japan has surrendered!"

The party began and is still carrying on in the Red Lion and the Swan at Stalbridge and in the Fountain Inn and Virginia Ash at Henstridge. This, to the end, was an operational airfield. For Henstridge and its staff and families, V.E. Day had been only half the story, with young New Zealand pilots and others still under training for a war that continued to be a going concern.

What was becoming "the forgotten war" would be ended by the atomic bombs. Leaflets dropped on Hiroshima on

Tuesday 21 August
'Our man in Berlin' — Lindsay is dead.

Sir Ronald Lindsay, of Stepleton House near Blandford, died today. The retired diplomat was born in 1877. He rose through the ranks at the Foreign Office to become an Under-Secretary in 1920 and progressed to the highest postings in the service — being Ambassador to Berlin [1926-28] and Washington [1930-39]. When he bowed out the war, as they say, was an extension of diplomacy by other means.

His home, the classical Stepleton House and its park where Peter Beckford wrote the classic book on fox-hunting, has passed to Sir Ronald's nephew, Lord Crawford.

Wednesday 22 August

U.S. Ambassador unveils Portland memorial.

Portland's memorial to the Americans who passed through Castletown and the hards and dockyard en route to D-Day and the fierce fighting on Omaha Beach was unveiled today in the rain by the United States Ambassador to London, Gil Winant.

He was welcomed by the chairman of Portland Urban District Council, A. N. Tattersall, after driving along the newly re-named Victory Road.

The stone is in Victoria Gardens where the Stars and Stripes flies beside the Union Flag.

Footnote: "Fine, fine, perfectly fine," was Gil Winant's famous remark of the war, which he kept repeating over the trans-Atlantic telephone when President Roosevelt told him of the Japanese attack on Pearl Harbor which brought America into the war. By now, however, he was engulfed in personal problems and would shoot himself in 1947, after his return to the United States.

He is said to have set his heart on Winston Churchill's daughter, Sarah Churchill, but she was unable to reciprocate his love.

Friday 31 August

Canford School counts 139 dead.

Canford School's roll of war dead has closed at a total of 139 lives at the end of its first war. As the school was founded in 1923, it happened that all Old Canfordians were of an age to serve, and indeed nearly a thousand of them held commissions.

During August

Penicillin works wonders at Shaftesbury.

The apparently miraculous cures brought about at Shaftesbury Military Hospital, Guy's Marsh, with M&B tablets have now been upstaged by the use of penicillin. This has reversed impossible infections which previously would have certainly killed even the strongest soldiers. It has taken years to bring the drug into commercial production; in 1942 the entire world supply was needed to treat a single case of meningitis.

Remarkable surgery is also taking place. Strabismus is being corrected by an easing of the muscles around the eyeball. Major John Charnley has carried out a pioneering hip-replacement operation at Shaftesbury which

NAVAL COLOURS: PRESENTED BY THE UNITED STATES NAVY TO ST JOHN'S CHURCH, FORTUNESWELL, PORTLAND, IN A POST-WAR SERVICE

was as much a feat of carpentry as an exercise of the surgeon's craft.

Footnote: Post-war, Guy's Marsh became a Borstal, and is now a Young Offender Institution.

UNVEILING CEREMONY: PAYING TRIBUTE TO THE AMERICANS IN DORSET, AT VICTORIA GARDENS, PORTLAND, ON 22 AUGUST 1945

During August

British military back in Blandford Camp.

The British Army has returned to Blandford Camp — which saw out the war as a major American General Hospital — with the arrival of the 1st and 2nd Searchlight Regiments, Royal Artillery, in the huts of the Craddock and Benbow Lines. These units will train conscripts who have been called-up to serve their national service with the Royal Artillery.

Tuesday 18 September

First Jap prisoners arrive home in Poole Harbour.

The first B.O.A.C. flying-boat to bring repatriated prisoners-of-war home to Britain from Japan has touched down in Poole Harbour, amid sensational press interest in the men's stories of degrading and inhuman treatment.

They were given a civic welcome at a reception on Poole Quay. Many thousands are on their way home by air and sea.

Tuesday 18 September

Skymaster drops into Hurn from New York.

An ex-military C-54 Skymaster of Pan American Airways has landed at Hurn Aerodrome from La Guardia Airport,

New York, in a proving flight that took 17 hours. The airliner, carrying nine crew and ten staff as observers, stopped off en route at Gander in Newfoundland and Rineanna in Eire.

This was the first time a four-engined land-plane — as distinct from a flying-boat — has crossed the Atlantic on a civilian flight.

Former Halifax bombers, in conversions known as Haltons, are currently operating from Hurn on the B.O.A.C. route to Lagos via the other West African colonies.

Wednesday 19 September

'Lord Haw-Haw' remembered at Farnham.

The Fascist hireling and traitor William Joyce smiled in the dock at the Old Bailey today as the black-capped judge told him: "You will be hanged by the neck until you are dead." He gave the Nazi salute to people at the back of the court.

The voice of Radio Berlin, for its wartime broadcasts to England, he had been captured near the Danish frontier, by British troops in the last week of May. He was identified and brought to London where he was charged with treason, on the grounds that although Irish-born he

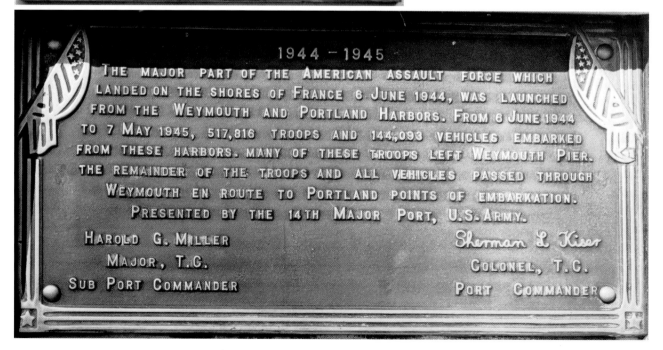

PORTLAND PLAQUE: THE ORIGINAL WORDING OF AUGUST 1945 RECORDS THE PIVOTAL PART PLAYED BY PORTLAND HARBO(U)R IN THE INVASION OF EUROPE. LATER VERSIONS WERE RE-WORDED TO ACKNOWLEDGE WEYMOUTH'S CONTRIBUTION

AMENDED VERSION: WEYMOUTH GIVEN DUE CREDIT FOR ITS PART IN THE CONFLICT, IN THE REVISED WORDING OF THE MEMORIAL PLAQUE FROM ITS AMERICAN PORT COMMANDERS

had put himself under His Majesty's protection by obtaining a United Kingdom passport.

"Lord Haw-Haw" is remembered in Dorset for his pre-war cottage sojourn at Farnham, as the guest of Captain George Pitt-Rivers.

Thursday 3 October
Christchurch colonel fires a V2.

Colonel Raby, the Director of the Signals Research and Development Establishment at Christchurch Aerodrome and Steamer Point, Highcliffe, today test-fired a German V2 rocket which he had reconstructed from captured parts. It has been flown northwards, along the coast from Cuxhaven, near Bremerhaven, into the North Sea off Denmark.

This has been a secret test, codenamed Operation Backfire, and tomorrow another rocket will be fired. Raby's establishment is working on the programme for British guided weapons.

Footnote: A third V2 was fired by the British team on 15 October 1945; this time the world's press would be invited and bill it as "the first Allied test-firing of a V2 rocket".

During October
Blandford hospital staff leave on the 'Queen Mary'.

The 22nd General Hospital of the United States Army has finally pulled out of Blandford Camp.

The last of its staff are now sailing back across the Atlantic, from Southampton, aboard the liner Queen Mary.

During October
Arnhem Major remembered in Bournemouth.

Major Richard Harris of the Dorsetshire Regiment, among those killed at Arnhem, has been commemorated by his parents and family with a memorial in St Peter's churchyard at Bournemouth.

Sunday 25 November
Five Poole flying-boats exit for Argentina.

Argentina, a Sandringham-2 flying-boat, lifted off from Poole Harbour today for Buenos Aires. The Sandringham-2 is a Mark V Sunderland powered by American Pratt and Whitney Twin Wasp engines and fitted out for 45 passengers. She and *Uruguay*, another Sandringham-2, has been sold to Dodero, the Argentine airline.

Dodero has also purchased three Sandringham-3 flying-boats. These have more spacious accommodation for their 21 passengers and are intended for longer flights. They are the *Brazil*, *Inglaterra*, and *Paraguay*.

Each is being delivered across the Atlantic by a British Overseas Airways Corporation crew with Argentinians aboard as observers. The flight time is estimated at 36 hours.

Monday 31 December
Home Guard is disbanded.

New Year's Eve has seen the last rites for the Home Guard which has been finally and formally disbanded by the War Office.

Its last County Commander, General Henry Jackson, paid a glowing tribute to his men: "The spirit of comradeship and service which was brought to life by service to the Dorset Home Guard must never be allowed to die."

During December
Japan's PoWs still in Hell at Shaftesbury.

The pitiful casualties of this war, beyond the help of surgery and drugs, are the psychologically distressed ex-prisoners of the Japanese who have been brought home from the Far East to recover at Shaftesbury Military Hospital, Guy's Marsh. Many are also emaciated but it is the mental damage that will take longer to correct. They suffer horrific memories when they are awake and lapse into agonising nightmares in sleep.

Such dehumanised wrecks become even more pathetic as they regain their physical strength without a comparative recovery from mental anguish. They are men returned from Hell.

Their ordeal is worse in its way than the more clear-cut cases on life's edge with tuberculosis. These three wards would once have been one-way nursing towards death but here expectations and hope have been transformed as a result of the introduction of the wonder-drug Streptomycin.

During December
Plaque at Portland commemorates D-Day logistics.

The 14th Major Port of the Transportation Corps of the United States Army has presented a bronze plaque to Portland Royal Naval dockyard commemorating the logistics of the invasion of Europe:

"1944-1945. The major part of the American assault force which landed on the shores of France 6 June 1944, was launched from the Weymouth and Portland Harbors. From 6 June 1944 to 7 May 1945, 517,816 troops and 144,093 vehicles embarked from the harbors. Many of these troops left Weymouth Pier. The remainder of the troops and all vehicles passed through Weymouth en route to Portland points of embarkation.

"Presented by the 14th Major Port, U.S. Army. Harold G. Miller, Major, T.C. [Transportation Corps] Sub Port Commander. Sherman L. Kiser, Colonel, T.C. Port Commander."

LANDSLIDE VICTORY: ATTLEE STEALS CHURCHILL'S V-SIGN TO WIN THE 1945 GENERAL ELECTION

Post-war echoes

During February 1946
War's upheavals bring Uplands School to Parkstone.

Uplands School, which was founded in 1903 at St Leonards-on-Sea, Sussex, is on the move to Parkstone. It has come via Monmouthshire, where it was evacuated when invasion threatened in 1940, and it had been hoped to return to Sussex in 1944 but the flying-bombs caused these plans to be abandoned.

Instead it is coming to Parkstone, to the buildings of a sister church school for girls, Sandecotes, which was itself closed in 1940 when the buildings were requisitioned by the military.

Monday 4 March 1946
Flying-boat 'Hailsham' crashes beside Brownsea Island

Having travelled uneventfully for a week from the other side of the world, the British Overseas Corporation flying-boat *Hailsham* encountered fog on its homecoming to Poole Harbour. It attempted to land in Poole Harbour but veered off the main water-runway and ran into a sandbank on the northern shore of Brownsea Island.

The nose and floats embedded firmly and the cabin was soon awash with the rising tide. For the five crew and 16 passengers, however, it was a lucky escape as they were all rescued unhurt by an Air Ministry Fire Tender.

Footnote: Hailsham would be floated free and towed to the slipway at Hamworthy. Meanwhile, however, she had been inundated by several tides, causing her to be written-off for scrap.

Monday 1 July 1946
2nd Dorsets mount Tokyo's 'Buck House' guard.

The 2nd Battalion of the Dorsetshire Regiment has been hastily consigned to Tokyo in Operation Primus; named for its "Primus in India" motto. The warriors from Burma are relieving the New Zealanders on ceremonial duties in the Japanese capital. The Americans are its army of occupation on the streets but Dominion and British soldiery share some of the static duties.

Dorset sentries are preparing for what they call "No. 1, Buck House Guard" at the Imperial Palace of Emperor Hirohito. Rosters assume that the battalion's 800 men will be able to maintain 200 sentries at posts around the city.

Footnote: Sharing the Imperial Guard with the Americans was hardly to Buckingham Palace standards.

IGNOMINIOUS RETURN: THE FLYING-BOAT HAILSHAM ON ITS ARRIVAL FROM SINGAPORE, 4 MARCH 1946, A LITTLE TOO CLOSE TO BROWNSEA ISLAND. IN RETROSPECT, CHRISTOPHER RAVEN POINTS OUT, THIS COULD BE CAPTIONED "END OF EMPIRE"

Lieutenant-Colonel Geoffrey White recalled the experience in *Straight on for Tokyo*:

"It is not easy when your companion on the post allows himself a more relaxed form of stand-at-ease, and it is most disconcerting to have a doughnut offered you at the end of a bayonet."

Saturday 17 August 1946
Bournemouth Pier back in business.

A wooden gangway, twelve feet wide, has been constructed from the entrance to Bournemouth Pier and runs parallel to the remains of the structure to its "island" at the far end. Work has been progressing on this restoration project since the end of May and it was completed in the middle of the week.

This enabled the Red Funnel steamer *Princess Elizabeth* to come alongside the landing stage, on the sheltered eastern side, at 11.00 hours today. The Mayor, Councillor R. H. Old, welcomed her arrival, following which he led 600 passengers as they boarded her for the first post-war pleasure steamer trip out of Bournemouth. She cast-off at 14.00, with Swanage as the destination.

Work will begin later this month on the reconstruction of the gap in the centre of the pier, which was cut in 1940 to prevent it being utilised by German invaders.

Footnote: The missing section was bridged on 29 April 1947 and other fixtures replaced by November that year. Buildings at the end were not rebuilt until April 1950. Meanwhile Boscombe Pier languished in its sad wartime state for another decade, reconstructed in 1958-60.

Saturday 7 September 1946
Mine explodes at Southbourne.

Despite all the efforts to remove anti-invasion defences along Britain's prime holiday coast, at least one mine escaped detection and disposal. It was washed out of the cliffs by recent heavy seas but then disappeared beneath the sands before a Naval squad could deal with it.

Today its location is no longer a mystery as it has exploded on its own accord, bringing down a substantial section of cliff-face and blowing out windows in the Southbourne Hotel. Fortunately no one has been hurt.

Monday 4 August 1947
3,200 mines cleared from a mile of Ringstead Bay.

Major A. B. Hartley of Southern Command announced yesterday that the 16th and 17th Bomb Disposal squads of the Royal Engineers had so far disposed of 9,000 anti-invasion mines along the coast eastwards from Weymouth. This includes a total of 3,200 mines from a mile of shingle beach and clayey cliffs at Ringstead Bay.

The operations have so far cost the lives of three officers and 22 other ranks. One officer has been blinded. Ringstead Bay is now open to the public, with the exception of an area on the side towards White Nothe headland.

In the course of a weekend only one of the 25 mines holding up the issuing of a clearance certificate was exploded. It had been detonated by a high-pressure water jet. The remaining 24 may take months to clear.

Unstable cliffs, coast erosion, and dynamic sea action have combined to make this minefield very difficult from its theoretical layout as originally charted. Rough seas continue to confound the clearance efforts.

The principal disposal method is to gouge the beach with a powerful jet of water — delivering 1,400 gallons a minute — which is pumped from the sea. This water goes initially into clifftop tanks. Then four V-Eight motors boost the water to the nozzle by means of two pairs of pumps operating in tandem.

This jet nozzle is fitted in an armoured shield, looking much like a gun barel, mounted on a Bren carrier. Two operators watch their quarry from over the top, through periscopes, as an ambulance and corpse-crew stand-by on the cliffs.

The casualty rate works out at 348 mines blown for each operator killed. That is the overall figure for every method of clearance, including the dangerous detector scanning, and Lieutenant Ralph Ruby, from Wareham, points out that Ringstead "has been a safe beach".

The great jet bowls great lumps of mud away into the sea. Often it then does the work of detonation but some obdurate explosives prove insensitive to distrurbance and require an actual charge to set them off.

Tubular steel carries the sea intake pipe, with the structure being intended to keep it clear of the surf. Seaweed is another problem, and men in diving frog-suits used to have to go down and clear the inlet, but current practice is to haul it ashore for cleaning.

Lieutenant Ruby and Lieutenant Rex King and their small datachment are assisted by German prisoners of war. They are also on call to examine and clear any suspicious object found on other Dorset beaches, and frequently have to respond to requests for expert attentions: "Sometimes for old saucepans."

More dangerous objects, such as bombs and shells, are removed for disposal if it is practical to lift them. "We take them to Punfield Cove, which is tucked below Worbarrow Tout on the Lulworth Gunnery Ranges," said Lieutenant Ruby. "That is well shielded by rocky cliffs on the landward side and being in the middle of the ranges it doesn't have windows or residents within a couple of miles."

During December 1947
Government accepts Purbeck 'broken' pledge.

In its Command White Paper number 7278, the Attlee Government has conceded that in the case of some

MINE CLEARANCE: THE WASHING-OUT AND EXPLODING OF JUST ONE OR TWO OF THE 3,000 MINES THAT WERE CLEARED FROM RINGSTEAD BAY IN 1947

wartime training areas, "particularly Stamford [Lincolnshire] and the Purbeck tank gunnery ranges, that pledges were given, or understood to be given" that land would be returned after the cessation of hostilities. Such promises will not be an issue at any public enquiry.

The Government goes on to say that "if an area in respect of which a pledge was given were surrendered and a new area taken up, one result would be the eviction of residents in the new one for the benefit of those originally displaced".

Wednesday 17 March 1948

Tyneham villagers ask to go home.

J. Scott Henderson K.C., representing the villagers from Tyneham who were evicted in December 1943 for the expansion of tank firing ranges, has told a two-day public enquiry in Wareham that "it should be made free to them". Brendan Bracken M.P., the wartime Minister of Information, supported the Hands off Purbeck campaign. He had written: "I think it is disgraceful that the Isle of Purbeck should not be freely available for the many who love it for its beauty and peace."

Sir Cecil Oakes, the chairman, said that the Government freely accepted that pledges for its return had been given and said there was no need for the point to be proved.

For the War Department, Brigadier Nigel William Duncan, the Commander of the Royal Armoured Corps Centre, explained that the first tanks in Great War only required a range of 300 yards, whereas from 1942 onwards American machines were firing upwards of 2,400 yards. Heavier fire-power had become the norm. There could be no diminishing of the range area, which now extended along seven miles of coast from Lulworth Cove to Kimmeridge Bay, with the sea as an overshoot area.

Footnote: War Minister John Strachey duly upheld "the national interest" and decided that the Army could keep the land.

During December 1948

Worbarrow is the 'Happy minefield'.

Lieutenant Ralph Ruby, in command of the Royal Engineers Bomb Disposal squad clearing the final wartime minefields in the Isle of Purbeck, rounds off our diary by looking back at the making safe of Worbarrow Bay, inside the Army's Lulworth and East Holme Ranges. Worbarrow, Kimmeridge and Swanage were the last three minefields to be cleared in Dorset since, in conjunction with Ringstead Bay, they were initially classified as "too dangerous to clear".

All four fields were affected by sea action, soil erosion, and land-slippage but in all these respects Worbarrow did not suffer as much as the others. Worbarrow was a comparatively small minefield and on relatively flat ground which allowed easy "sweeping".

The main problem with Worbarrow was that being in a restricted area not open to the public, no one saw fit to maintain its perimeter wires which were in many cases missing, rusted away or displaced. To complicate matters the minefield was in a ricochet area for tank training and hence peppered with shrapnel. Much of this was buried in the earth.

When the boundaries of the minefield could not be determined a generous allowance had to be made and cordoned off. This area was mainly on the landward side, covered with vegetation such as brambles that had to be burnt off and with a plethora of embedded shrapnel to make the operators' work one of continuous exploration with a trowel.

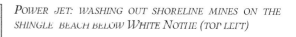

Despite this Worbarrow was a "happy" minefield since it was out of bounds to the public and the Sappers could enjoy a little sunbathing in their break periods. Even the military from Bovington and Lulworth strayed into this area since it mainly served as a safety curtain for the firing ranges though this in turn raised interruptions with our work since it had to be co-ordinated with tank training exercises.

Another snag at Worbarrow was that some mines had clearly been claimed by the sea and no one could determine the number. The minefield charts were also misleading and capable of more than one interpretation. The B-type C-mines employed were invariably laid in a grid pattern and zeroed on some clearly distinguishable object or objects.

Most "reference points" for the mines were no longer extant and every Sapper knew from experience that most minefield charts were, at best, mere approximations. In some cases the charts were first marked out on a map and then laid down not according to the chart but with variations to allow for local conditions. Thus according to the chart the soldier was expected to put a mine here, but on finding a slab of bedrock he laid it as near as he could, which was liable to be many feet away at any point of the compass. Conversely, sometimes the mines were laid and then a chart drawn up, again frequently with little regard to accuracy or, in some cases, even numbers.

Most minefields were not laid out by Sappers, who knew about such things, but in a time of panic by any

Army unit nearest to hand, including the Home Guard and Canadian troops.

The Worbarrow clearance was also interrupted because the team had to be withdrawn to sweep a large area of heathland at Creech and free it of small arms ammunition left over from Army training. This was to enable the digging and removal of ball clay, which was being used in the cosmetics industry and exported to America, so the task was given priority.

Whilst the Sappers would normally have looked on such a job as non-dangerous and a light relief, they soon hated it because they found themselves chivvied to get on with it. They were often treated inconsiderately. Lieutenant Ruby received one complaint that a Sapper who was rather deaf due to war service had committed the unpardonable sin of not addressing his superior as "Sir". Ruby accordingly informed the person that the Sapper was deaf and could only accept orders from his Corporal. He stated that he would withdraw the Sapper, if necessary, and also any other Sapper who gave offence, but under no circumstances would a replacement be provided.

When the squad returned to Worbarrow, there was little trouble, apart from a few mines which were lost to the sea and never accounted for. Its clearance did not end their contact with the area as they returned to the ghost village of Tyneham and the former fishing hamlet to detonate defused bombs and carry out trepanning operations, steaming out unexploded bombs.

A pillbox had been strategically placed during the war, on a piece of raised ground covering the live beaches separated by the headland of Worbarrow Tout that juts into the sea and creates a unique setting. They would place a bomb on the beach nearest to Swanage, in Pondfield Cove, and fire it from the safety of the pillbox.

Pillboxes were classified as strong enough to withstand a near miss from a "modest" bomb (such as 50-kilograms) and Lieutenant Rex King and Ralph Ruby decided it would be quite safe to explode their first 50-kg bomb some 50 feet from the safety of the pillbox: "This indeed proved to be the case. Unfortunately the pillbox had accumulated the dust of ages and a pile of loose sand was promptly whipped into a dust devil by the blast which swept through the firing slots. We both emerged more like chimney sweeps than Sapper officers."

One prize bomb they detonated at Worbarrow was a cross-Channel armour-piercing shell which was transported down to them from Dover, where no one could dispose of it locally: "I inspected the shell with Lieutenant King and we both came to the conclusion that due to the thickness of armour-piercing skin it would need a massive charge to explode it. Since the shell clearly had the kick of a mule and was no respector of pillboxes it was decided to explode it electrically from a considerable distance away.

"Rex kept admiring the driving band on the shell which consisted of a massive ring of copper. He felt that the copper band could easily be removed and that it would be a nice keepsake. Well, I left Rex working on the copper band whilst I prepared the charges, selected a safe-firing hide, and appointed lookouts at strategic points. All were at a considerable distance from the scene of action. One lookout was placed about half a mile away at the top of a hill on the Swanage side of Worbarrow. A really massive charge was put on the shell and the former detonated with one hell of a bang. Rex and I duly trotted off to admire the new crater and couldn't believe our eyes - to look down at this unexploded six-feet monster which was now glowing deep red with anger and could have gone off at any second."

It seemed an age before the shell had cooled down sufficiently for the second attempt: "This just about exhausted our store of explosives since we packed it with TNT, gelignite and amatol, all in good measure. The resulting bang was unbelievable and immediately followed by a noise that I can only describe as similar to that of an express train disappearing into the distance which, in this case, was Swanage. The lookout on the hill came down as white as a ghost and swore that a chunk of white hot metal as big as a saucer had streaked past him head high and at a mere arm's length. If the lookout's words were an exaggeration then the look on his face and the buckling of his knees clearly indicated otherwise. This Sapper was a relative newcomer to Bomb Disposal and as one can't have Sappers wandering around looking like ghosts and knocking at the knees, it was dutifully explained to him that everyone in B.D. had to have an 'initiation'. He could therefore look on this as his personal initiation which would warrant the customary free pint at the next pub call."

During September 1953
Crichel Down becomes a cause célèbre.

Lieutenant-Commander Toby Marten of Crichel House has lost patience with the attitude of civil servants over the proposed derequisition of the Crichel Down Bombing Range on his family's Cranborne Chase estate. "I intend, with local support, to demand an enquiry into this business, which I am sure will expose many unpalatable facts," he warned Christopher Gilbert Eastwood, the Permanent Commissioner of Crown Lands, after 18 months of fraught and stalemated negotiations.

He walked into the village Post Office at Witchampton to send the following telegram to Sir Thomas Dugdale, the Minister of Agriculture: "URGENT AND PERSONAL STOP CRICHEL DOWN PROTEST COMMITTEE HAS BEEN FORMED TO PRESS FOR ENQUIRY INTO DISPOSAL OF THIS LAND STOP RESOLUTION HAS BEEN PASSED TO REQUEST ENQUIRY FORTHWITH WHICH WILL REFLECT ADVERSELY ON YOUR ADMINISTRATION STOP FURTHER REQUEST DISPOSAL OF LAND BE STOPPED UNTIL ENQUIRY COMPLETED STOP"

Fifty people attended a public meeting, chaired by neighbouring landowner Ronald Farquharson, at which Commander Marten said that a year earlier he would never have believed such a situation could have arisen in England. In effect he had been told: "Provided you put up a lot of buildings and find your own tenant I, as Minister, will sell this land to you."

He told how Sir Thomas had turned himself into a Commissioner of Crown Lands, and formed a commitment between himself as Minister and himself as Commissioner, to sell himself the land and vice-versa. Then, as Minister, he declares: "You can't have the land."

This, he went on, was a "Crazy Gang performance" which was liable to become, literally, a folly, built up brick by brick, as "an ever-present reminder, a permanent memorial to the extravagance and bad faith of the State".

Tuesday 20 July 1954

Sir Thomas Dugdale falls on his sword.

Agriculture Minister Sir Thomas Dugdale today cancelled the party to celebrate his 57th birthday and was at 15.40 hours seated on the Treasury bench in the House of Commons between Prime Minister Sir Winston Churchill and George Nugent M.P., Sir Thomas's Parliamentary Secretary. They listened grimly as Sir Thomas opened the historic Parliamentary debate on the debacle surrounding a Dorset field - now known across the nation as the Crichel Down scandal - saying there had been inaccuracies and deficiencies in the information on which he had made his decision. To an extent he had been mislead, though not "wilfully", by civil servants who had already suffered the punishment of public censure and reprimand.

"Who were they?" came a shout from his own Conservative benches. Sir Thomas said that Christopher Eastwood, the Permanent Commissioner of Crown Lands, was being recommended for a transfer to another post. Three of the other four officers involved had already moved to other work. He declined to name them or say what had happened to the fifth.

All organisations involved in the Crichel Down negotiations would be investigated in an independent public review of the administration of Crown Lands. Agricultural land that had been acquired compulsorily by the War Office as a training ground might be passed to the Air Ministry for use as a bombing range or for another military purpose but it could not be transferred to another agency for management as agricultural land: "This will mean that such a transfer as took place at Crichel Down from the Air Ministry will not happen in the future."

Disposals of such lands would begin "with the desire that, where circumstance show that the land can properly be offered to a former owner or his successor who can establish his claim, this will be done at a price assessed by the district valuer as being the current market price".

There were cries of dismay from the Conservative benches as Sir Thomas said that these undertakings covered the circumstances of the Crichel Down case, but did not necessarily apply to Crichel Down itself, as they could not be made retrospective. However, the Government would treat the Dorset land as a special case, though the existence of a tenancy currently made it impractical to sell the land to the three successors of the former owners, unless they agreed amongst themselves that one of them should be the sole purchaser of all the land.

Then, 47 minutes into his typewritten speech, Sir Thomas reached last three lines and read the final sentence in a flat voice. A stunned House of Commons realised that he was falling on his sword: "Having now had this opportunity of rendering account to Parliament of the actions which I thought fit to take, I have, as the Minister responsible during this period, tendered my resignation to the Prime Minister, who is submitting it to the Queen."

Friday 13 May 1955

Five Swanage boys blown up by a mine.

One of the mines that was missed by post-war clearance teams was discovered today by a group of 20 boys from Forres Preparatory School at Swanage. It had been noted by Lieutenant Ralph Ruby and Lieutenant Rex King that "a discrepancy of 58 mines exists" but this was ignored and the beach declared safe. This oversight has had tragic consequences.

Five boys were killed as they prodded a rusty steel cylinder in a rock pool at the northern end of the beach. One of the victims was totally blown to pieces with only one of his shoes being recovered — which has been identified by "a brass school number, 29, punched into the sole". Two boys were wounded.

Footnote: The survivors, including Robert Key who would become Tory spokesman on landmines for the Major Government, returned to class and had to endure weeks of explosions as the Royal Engineers returned to complete the task of clearing "the forgotten minefield".

Index

The Daily Sketch

No. 11,307 ★★   WEDNESDAY, AUGUST 15, 1945   A KEMSLEY NEWSPAPER   ONE PENNY

RADAR SECRETS PAGE 5

Peace has once again come to the world. Let us Thank God for this great deliverance and His mercy. Long live the King—Mr. Attlee

JAPAN SURRENDERS

World Told At Midnight
VJ-DAYS TO-DAY AND TO-MORROW

JAPAN has accepted the Allies' surrender terms—unconditional capitulation—it was announced simultaneously in London, Washington, Moscow and Chungking at midnight.

The London announcement was broadcast by Mr. C. R. Attlee and President Truman's statement was made to Pressmen 1,347 days after the Japanese attacked the American fleet at Pearl Harbour.

In Britain and America to-day and to-morrow will be celebrated as VJ-Day holidays.

Emperor Hirohito Will Tell Japan

And while the whole of the United Nations will be celebrating the "Cease Fire," Emperor Hirohito will be reading the Imperial announcement of Japan's capitulation.

The King was told that Japan had surrendered before the Premier's broadcast. An announcement of a National Thanksgiving Service will be made to-day.

The service will probably be held at St. Paul's Cathedral on Sunday, and will be attended by the King and Queen.

President Truman announced that General MacArthur has been appointed Supreme Allied Commander to receive the Japanese surrender, and Britain, Russia and China will be represented by high-ranking officers.

Arrangements had been made for the formal signing of the surrender terms at the earliest possible moment. In the meantime the Allied armed forces have been ordered to suspend offensive action.

President Truman disclosed that the Japanese Emperor will order all military, naval and air authorities and the Japanese forces wherever located to cease active operations and surrender their arms.

Turn to Back Page, Col. 1

Mr. Attlee

PREMIER TELLS BRITAIN

MR. ATTLEE, broadcasting at midnight, said:

Japan has to-day surrendered. The last of our enemies is laid low. Here is the text of the Japanese reply to the Allied Command:

With reference to the announcement of August 10, regarding the acceptance of the provisions of the Potsdam Declaration and the reply of the Governments of the United States, Great Britain, the Soviet Union and China sent by Secretary of State Byrnes on the date of August 11, the Japanese Government has the honour to reply to the Governments of the four Powers as follows:

1.—His Majesty the Emperor has issued an Imperial rescript regarding Japan's acceptance of the provisions of the Potsdam Declaration.

2.—His Majesty the Emperor is prepared to authorise and insure the signatures by his Government and the Imperial headquarters of the necessary terms for carrying out the provisions of the Potsdam Declaration.

3.—His Majesty is also prepared to issue this communication to all military, naval and air authorities to issue to all forces under their control, wherever located, to cease active resistance and to surrender arms.

(Signed) TOJO.

The Tide Turned

Let us recall that on December 7, 1941, Japan, whose onslaught China had already resisted for over four years, fell upon the U.S.A. and upon ourselves, who were so oppressed in our death struggles with Germany and Italy.

Taking full advantage of surprise and treachery, the Japanese forces quickly overran the territories of ourselves and our Allies in the Far East, and at one time it appeared as though these invaders would reach the mainland of Australia and advance into India.

But the tide turned.

With ever increasing speed the mighty forces of the United States and the British Commonwealth and Empire and other Allies were brought to bear. Japanese resistance has now everywhere been broken.

Turn to Back Page, Col. 2

General MacArthur. See "MacArthur—The Man On The Spot."—Page 2.

CABINET PLANS OUT TO-DAY

The Prime Minister, Mr. Attlee, drove to Buckingham Palace to see the King last night. It is understood he submitted the draft of the Speech to be made at the State opening of Parliament to-day.

By 'Daily Sketch' Political Correspondent

WHEN the King reads his Speech to both Lords and Commons to-day it will contain the main legislative proposals to be placed before them by the Government.

Afterwards the Commons will go to St. Margaret's, Westminster, for a thanksgiving service. Members of the Upper House will go to Westminster Abbey.

Congratulation Address

On return from the services the Government will move in each House addresses of congratulation to the King.

It is not yet known if there will be a Conservative amendment to the address putting forward their views on the Government's proposals.

The Commons debate will open on Thursday and continue on Friday of this week and Monday and Tuesday of next week. On the Wednesday and Thursday the Commons will debate the ratification of the United Nations Charter and will adjourn on Friday, August 24, until October 9.

THE BRIDGE OF TEARS

TOKYO'S Niji Bashi, the bridge in front of the Imperial Palace where the people gather in times of crisis, became the bridge of tears yesterday.

A report broadcast to its bureau in the Far East by the Japanese News Agency, describing in colourful language the scene of the "hon. Jap." crowd bowed and weeping in defeat, broke off without explaining what the Imperial decision was.

"On August 14, 1945, the Imperial decision was granted," the Japanese report said.

"Honoured with the Imperial edict in the sublime palace grounds, the loyal people are bowed to the very ground in front of the Niji Bashi. Tears flow unchecked.

"Alas, in their shame how can the people raise their heads?

"With the words 'Forgive us, O Emperor, our efforts are not enough' heads bow lower and lower as the tears run unchecked.

"Ever since December 8, 1941, when we received the Imperial Rescript (the declaration of war), causing his Majesty deep anxiety . . ."

It was at this point that the agency broke off the report.

Extra Leave for Forces— Piccadilly Celebrates

HERE is victory news for the fighters given out in the following joint statement by the Admiralty, War Office and Air Ministry this morning:

"All personnel of Royal Navy, Army and Royal Air Force now on leave from Home Commands, other than personnel on embarkation or drafting leave, may add an additional 48 hours to their leave."

This does not apply to those on leave from Commands overseas, personnel on sick leave, and those on embarkation or drafting leave.

Piccadilly provided the only scene of jubilation in the West End last night when the midnight news came through that war was over.

"It's finished—it's official," excited young Canadian Air Force men shouted, as if they hardly believed themselves.

Americans, Australians, New Zealanders and our own Tommies all joined hands and sang "Auld Lang Syne."

But the East End also celebrated, and late workers in the City taking the air on rooftops saw the red glow of bonfires in the eastern sky, perhaps not without a thought of less happy vigils when the sky of the capital had been reddened with the glare of bomb fires.

The Queen Mary Leads

Ships in Southampton dock greeted the news with hooting sirens, the Queen Mary leading them with repeated V signals in Morse on her deep-noted fog signal. Ships played their searchlights over the town and fired Very lights.

A victory "snowstorm'" of ticker-tape and tons of torn paper blotted out New York's streets within a few minutes of the surrender announcement.

Ships sounded victory blasts on their sirens in New York Harbour. Motor-cars moved through the streets with their horns screaming.

In Washington, President Truman appeared in front of the White House with his wife in response to clamorous shouts from the crowd "We want Truman."

The President declared through a microphone: "This is a great day. This is the day we have been waiting for since Pearl Harbour."

TIMELY WORDS OF FAITH

Finally brethren. . . . Be perfect . . . be of one mind, live in peace.

2 Corinthians, 13, 11.